The European Union, the World Bank and the Policymaking of Aid

Based on the experience of the author, an IPE scholar and former trade policy consultant at the World Bank (WB), the book offers an in-depth exploration of the EU–WB relations, conceptualized as hybrid delegation.

Coupling cross-time analyses of their interaction in the regions of the Middle East and North Africa, Europe and Central Asia and Sub-Saharan Africa with an original investigation on the coordination among the EU member states at the Executive Board of the International Bank for Reconstruction and Development over the 'voice and participation reform' of 2008–2010, the book advances an innovative theoretical framework to assess the EU–WB joint institutional and field policy performances. Augmented PA models of delegation, role theory and performance analyses are engaged, and selectively recombined, to investigate the nature, evolution and impact of the interactions of the two organizations, both in their everyday and constituent politics. Hybrid delegation-in-motion is reconstructed, against the background of post-Washington Consensus and post-Lisbon EU, to unveil the changing division of labour between the two largest development multilaterals of the new global context.

The book will be of interest to scholars, students and practitioners in European Politics, Development, International Relations, International Political Economy and Global Economic Governance.

Eugenia Baroncelli is Associate Professor of Political Science at the University of Bologna, Department of Political and Social Sciences, where she teaches IPE, IR and Global Development courses at both undergraduate and graduate levels. Between 2001 and 2006 she has worked at the World Bank as a consultant on trade, tariff and IPR policies for the Research Department – Trade Group, as well as for the MENA, SASIA and Africa regions. In her research she has focused on the international political economy of trade, democracy and security, as well as on the political economy of development. Among other things, she has investigated the peace dividend from SAFTA trade preferences between India and Pakistan, the role of neo-Gramscian IPE applied to development studies, and Susan Strange's contribution to IPE studies. Her work on the World Bank and on the EU–World Bank relations includes journal articles and chapters in edited books.

The European Union, the World Bank and the Policymaking of Aid

Cooperation among Developers

Eugenia Baroncelli

Routledge
Taylor & Francis Group
LONDON AND NEW YORK

First published 2019
by Routledge
2 Park Square, Milton Park, Abingdon, Oxon OX14 4RN

and by Routledge
605 Third Avenue, New York, NY 10017

First issued in paperback 2021

Routledge is an imprint of the Taylor & Francis Group, an informa business

Publisher's Note
The publisher has gone to great lengths to ensure the quality of this reprint but points out that some imperfections in the original copies may be apparent.

British Library Cataloguing-in-Publication Data
A catalogue record for this book is available from the British Library

Library of Congress Cataloging-in-Publication Data
Names: Baroncelli, Eugenia, author.
Title: The European Union, the World Bank and the policymaking of aid cooperation among developers / Eugenia Baroncelli.
Description: Abingdon, Oxon ; New York, NY : Routledge, 2019. | Includes bibliographical references and index.
Identifiers: LCCN 2018015395 | ISBN 9781409410584 (hardback) | ISBN 9781315558493 (e-book)
Subjects: LCSH: World Bank—European Union countries. | European Union. | Economic assistance—Political aspects. | Economic development—Political aspects. | International economic relations.
Classification: LCC HG3881.5.W57 B368 2019 | DDC 332.1/532—dc23
LC record available at https://lccn.loc.gov/2018015395

ISBN 13: 978-1-03-209392-5 (pbk)
ISBN 13: 978-1-4094-1058-4 (hbk)

Typeset in Times New Roman
by Apex CoVantage, LLC

Contents

Figures

Tables

Acknowledgements

The research conducted for this book has benefitted from support and insight from a variety of actors, both individuals and institutions. I however bear full responsibility for the ideas that are advanced in the chapters below. Any errors or inconsistencies are mine.

I am indebted to Knud-Erik Jorgensen who has provided me with invaluable insight in the concept phases of the research, and for sharing his ideas on EU's roles and performance in International Organizations. I also wish to thank Sonia Lucarelli, for her insight on the relevance of others' perceptions on the making of the EU's own identity. Emilia Galiano has patiently read the first draft of this effort, and Gabriele Liotta has provided research support for the drafting of Chapter 3: I am grateful to both for their valuable support. Finally, my heartfelt gratitude goes to the many World Bank EDs, VPs, economists and specialists, to the EU officers from the Commission (DG DEVCO-EuropeAid, EEAS) and the EU Parliament, who have given me their time and ideas, to help me in this inquiry about EU–World Bank relations.

Support to the empirical portion of this research has come from the ECRP-ESF 2009–2013 Eurocores Program, in the context of a Project on the Performance of the EU in International Organization, and from the Italian Ministry of University and Research, in the context of a Project on the External Image of the EU-Survey II.

1 Researching the EU–WB cooperation

Inter-organizational relations and the making of multilateral development

1.1 Introduction

The European Union (EU) and the IBRD (International Bank for Reconstruction and Development, hereinafter World Bank) are currently the two major multilateral actors in development policy. In addition to being a key player in the world trade system and the largest provider of foreign direct investment (FDI),[1] the EU and its member states (MS) are collectively the most generous donor worldwide, supplying Euros 75.5 bn, or almost 60% of total development assistance (European Commission–DG DEVCO 2017a).[2] In turn, the World Bank is the major multilateral development bank, and the sole with a global vocation, having provided more than USD 500 bn loans since its creation (World Bank 2017a). The EU-cum-MS tops the donors' list, accounting for approximately 60% of the World Bank's contributed resources.[3] In recent years, both organizations have made tangible progress to increase transparency on their relations. Yet, surprisingly little is known about why EU's aid allocation through the World Bank ('channeling') takes place, and to what effect, for citizens in donor and lending states.

The EU and the World Bank have navigated multiple challenges since their inception: the EEC-EC-EU enlargement rounds and deepening phases, the World Bank's adjustments to the post-colonial developments since the 1950s, the post-debt crisis challenges in the early 1980s, to name a few. Between the 1990s and the 2000s, the EU and the World Bank have faced the tests posed by the double transitions in post-Communist regimes, and by the redefinition of the Washington Consensus, respectively. Across the turn of the millennium they have jointly engaged in the achievement of the Millennium Development Goals (MDGs), a task that has become particularly challenging after the global crisis in 2008, and the ensuing 'Great recession'. Reaffirmed with the EU 'Agenda for change' (2011) and the support to the launch of the 2030 Agenda and the Sustainable Development Goals in 2015, both organizations have focused on coupling the poverty eradication goal to that of reducing inequality (the World Bank's 'twin goals' of ending extreme poverty and boosting shared prosperity) through sustainable and inclusive practices across a range of new challenges.[4]

At specific junctures, the EU and the World Bank appear to have also influenced one another, in their normative and policy practices. Relative to the former, the template for the EU's 'Brussels Consensus' on development, agreed in 2005 and launched in 2006, does bear several similarities with the 'Comprehensive development framework' developed by the World Bank in the mid-1990s, and with its broader 'post-Washington Consensus' (Baroncelli 2018). With respect to the latter, there is evidence that the World Bank has influenced the recent EU's venturing the business of loan leveraging through (EU-led) trust funds – a business traditionally run by the World Bank. Influence at the policy level is also being played by the EU on the World Bank, which has furthered its role as a 'knowledge bank' in the new EU MS and broader Neighborhood. Redefinition of the 'division of labour' in development policymaking is certainly at play between the two multilaterals.[5] The extent to which these evolutions have responded to strategic behavior, by either organization, or to other non-consequential logics is specifically investigated in this book.

From the EU side, the normative and policy developments described above are evidence of a broader transformation that has taken place since the new millennium in the Union's aid policy, particularly advocated by the search for a more vocal role by the EU Commission (European Commission 2007). The existence, and strength, of an EU distinct actorness in aid policy has been the subject of specific analyses in EU studies (Holland 2002). To a large extent, these contributions have been mostly interested in the domestic determinants of the Union's identity in development policy. Yet, the EU's assumption of a more assertive role in aid policymaking in the 2000s has responded to several triggers, both internal and external to the organization (Carbone 2007). Still largely unexplored is the extent to – and the ways in which the change in EU's aid policy has been influenced by its relation with the World Bank, and by the redefinition of the World Bank's own mission over that period. Equally uncharted by the academic literature is the reverse dynamic, whereby the World Bank's programs and strategies have been impacted by EU policies in sectors and geographical contexts where the two organizations have cooperated during those same years.

Since the 2000s a lot more is known about the dynamics of states' delegation to International Organizations (IOs), much thanks to the seminal work of IR (International Relations) institutionalists. Resorting to transaction cost literature and, subsequently, Principal-Agent (PA) models, IR institutionalism has contributed to make sense of the puzzling endurance of IOs deviating from the mandates of their founding members. However, the anomaly of multilaterals which delegate to one another (to accomplish tasks that fall well within their original missions) has yet to be fully explained. Perhaps even more baffling is why IOs should fund one another without claiming formal principality rights in each other's main decision-making bodies, limiting themselves to express preferences in a piecemeal fashion, in *ad hoc* boards and across multiple funding facilities. Furthermore, given such piecemeal representation, how does the interaction between global governors influence their respective actions and policies? What is the role played by political decision makers (states and their representatives) and managements, respectively, and what are the logics that inform these processes?

To solve these puzzles and answer the above questions, the book conceptualizes the nature and effects of the multiple ties that exist between the EU and the World Bank in the promotion of multilateral development. To this aim, it builds an original eclectic framework, that encompasses both IR–IPE (International Political Economy) rationalist and reflectivist approaches to the study of IOs, and which includes insights from EU, political economy of development and business studies. Empirically, it unpacks the relations between the two governors, at both the political and organizational (management) levels, tracking their interactions since the late 1990s, against the broader changes that were taking place in multilateral development norms and practices across the turn of the millennium. Particularly, it looks at the EU's performance, at the World Bank's Board and, in the field, in selected joint and parallel programs. Engaging with implementation issues, the book unveils how different interactional dynamics between the two multilaterals have impacted on their performance on the ground. Providing specific inputs into the EU's making of its aid policy, the analysis also sheds light on how the changing 'division of labour' between the two organizations is likely to feedback on the broader making of development policies at the multilateral level.

The rest of this chapter is organized as follows: section 1.2 discusses the core questions that are addressed throughout the book, arguing about the need to shed light on the interactions between the two largest multilaterals in development policies, on grounds of both EU-specific and global development perspectives. Section 1.3 offers a synthetic overview of the different EU, IR and IPE contributions that have provided seminal inputs on the EU's role in international organizations. Section 1.4 discusses selected inputs from the rationalist and reflectivist literatures on the relations between states and IOs, particularly in aid policymaking. Reviewing their merits and limitations on the basis of IR seminal academic debates, the section provides fresh insights on their potential and pitfalls in the analysis of the relations among global governors. Building on the previous discussion, Section 1.5 makes a case for analytical eclecticism[6] as the best approach to study the interactions between the EU and the World Bank and, more broadly, the microfoundations of global governance processes. Section 1.6 concludes, outlining the goals and structure of the book.

1.2 Studying global governors through their interactions: the EU–WB case

While the role of the United States (US) at the World Bank has been under scrutiny for a while (Ascher 1992; Brown 1992; Woods 2003; Fleck and Kilby 2006), the EU's relations with the World Bank, and more specifically the EU's role at the Executive Board, have to a large extent been *terra incognita* in the academic debate on multilateral governance (Baroncelli 2011). The theoretical void may be justified by the fact that the EU institutions do not have voting rights in the World Bank's Board, and that, on the contrary, the US are to date the only World Bank shareholder which can singlehandedly mobilize its voting power to veto proposals of constitutional change (i.e. to block attempts at amending the Articles of Agreement). The shared character of the EU's competence in development policies, and, more broadly, the EU's peculiar nature (not a state, not a fully supranational organization), also concur to explain the dearth of scholarly interest in its role at the World Bank. Adding to the sheer magnitude of their joint support to development financing, there are in fact several reasons, of theoretical and practical relevance, to take a closer look at the role played by the European Union at the World Bank and with the World Bank in the making of development policies.

Both formal (even if piecemeal, through the EU's channeling via World Bank-managed trust funds) and informal (but regular, via the coordination of EU MS at the World Bank's Executive Board), the cooperation between the two global governors has grown to a level that makes it increasingly difficult to avoid considering its shape, determinants and implications. As said, the EU-cum-MS are collectively the main supplier of financial resources to the Washington-based IFI (International Financial Institution), via capital subscriptions by EU MS, on the one side, and via EU institutions and MS channeling to World Bank managed trust funds, on the other. The World Bank shares part of its membership with the EU (all the EU's MS sit in the World Bank's Executive Board), but neither organization has representatives in each other's executive bodies.

In official practice the EU and the Bank interact as two distinct multilateral agencies, cooperating with other actors (private donors, NGOs, civil society and different institutions in MS and at the transnational level) in a wide variety of programs and projects to alleviate poverty worldwide. Generally neglected by the academic literature, however, the interactions between the EU and the World Bank have in fact crucially influenced the evolution of the system of multilateral aid since the late 1990s. Disregarding such a relational dimension would substantially limit the opportunities to investigate the transformation of today's development policies and practices. It would also narrow down the analytical avenues that scholarly research may pursue to understand processes followed and outcomes achieved by each of the two governors.

Under the policy angle, then, a major incentive to look at EU–WB relations is provided by the evolution of their joint financial efforts and by the EU attempts at strengthening informal coordination at the World Bank's Executive Board. The resources devoted by the EU to multilateral development financing through the World Bank have remarkably increased in the new millennium: in 2005 the Commission channeled to the Washington-based institution an amount that was 50 times that supplied in 2000 (ADE 2008; Faini and Grilli 2004).[7] At the high institutional level, progress has also occurred since 2003, when an informal consultation group (the so-called Eurogroup) was set up by the Office of the Italian Executive Director (hereinafter ED) to coordinate the position of EU EDs at the

Board on matters of joint European interest. Along such an increased effort, however, as noted above, the EU has shown its readiness to build on its grant-making core activity and provide for its own trust funds, potentially entering the (once) World Bank's preserve business of blending facilities for loan-leveraging among potential donors.

To make sense of these apparently paradoxical developments (EU increased channeling, no formal voice, creation of own trust funds), the book explores how the different missions of the two organizations have either boosted or impaired their cooperation at different points in time. Global in reach and – in theory – a-political in its mandate, the World Bank has officially claimed for itself a neutral role in times and places of military, political and diplomatic tensions, always paying particular care to find a compromise among the heterogeneous preferences of its member states. Conversely, the EU has an explicitly principled nature, and has actively engaged in norm promotion through its cooperation with developing countries. How has such divergence in missions been reconciled by the two organizations when they have cooperated in fragile contexts? More generally, are partially divergent missions a positive element for successful cooperation, or should aid multilaterals converge on both ends and means?

The overtly political mission of the EU, a partially supranational organization composed by states, originally regional in scope, makes arguing about the (formal) WB presence in EU *fora* a matter of mostly taxonomical interest. The issue has however gained salience relative to the World Bank's membership in the EU's grant-leveraging facilities such as the WBIF (Western Balkans Investment Framework), launched in 2009. Conversely, the absence of an EU's official representation in the World Bank's Executive Board – notwithstanding the prominence of EU institutions among World Bank's donors – has been the subject of several speculations, and has gained momentum in policy circles, particularly after the establishment of an EU external legal standing, through the Lisbon Treaty of 2009. Specifically addressed in the book is why the most generous multilateral donor, and the main creditor to the World Bank, is still not a shareholder at its Board. Official statements indicate that the issue of the EU external representation in the Bretton Woods institutions has made its way to EU formal declarations (EC SEC (2010) 420, 34). In May 2011, the post-Lisbon upgrading of the Union to an 'enhanced observer' status in the United Nations General Assembly (UNGA) suggested that a similar evolution could take place also in the Washington-based IFIs. However, the EU's endorsement of such key role through its political rhetoric, was not reflected in Brussels' policy targets at the time (Grimm and Phillips 2006; Maxwell and Gavas 2010). In spite of academic think tanks, and Commission-based calls, the EU MS, through the Council (in its Foreign Affairs composition), deleted the question of a common representation of the EU in the two Washington-based IFIs from the list of priorities in the 2010 Spring Package.[8] The consequences of the Eurozone crisis first, and the expected impact of Brexit subsequently, have led the Juncker Commission to focus on internal priorities, driving attention further away from the issue. However, the migration emergency, as well as the conflict-related crises in the Middle East and North Africa (MENA) region (Iraq, Syria), amidst the broader challenges from Sub-Saharan and MENA fragile countries, indicate that a renewed attention to how the two governors coordinate their development efforts is both timely and prospectively relevant.[9]

Besides the gap between devoted resources and principality rights, the book investigates how informal coordination has served as a substitute for an enhanced role of the Union at the World Bank's Board so far. Concomitantly, it explores how cooperation between the EU and the Bank has proceeded on the ground, in partner countries, most notably considering the changes that have occurred in development policymaking since the launching of the MDGs in 2000, and in the post-Soviet enlargements.[10] Deepening the focus on the early EU motivations to channel through the World Bank Trust Funds, it analyzes the subsequent creation of EU blending facilities since 2007. Plausibly, they are a further indication that Brussels is trying to forge a more effective and pragmatically oriented role for the Union in multilateral aid. What has been the influence of the World Bank, and of the EU–World Bank relations, on Brussels' new venture? Given the parallel redefinition of the World Bank role, particularly as a strategic knowledge provider for some new EU MS, a further issue raised by the book concerns the welfare implications of the two organizations' incursions into each other's respective domains.

Mostly interested in the relations between states and IOs, only recently have IR and IPE begun to explore the ties that exist between IOs (Avant et al. 2010; Bierman and Koops 2017). In this vein, the analysis of the EU–World Bank relations offered here aims to contribute to the scholarly research on how global governors interact. Investigating their endogenous connection, through imperfectly overlapping membership, and their exogenous tie, through the trust fund track, the book conceptualizes the set of links that connect the EU to the World Bank as a hybrid encompassing different forms of delegation. Unpacking the mix of ties between the two organizations, the book looks at how its evolution has impacted on Brussels' redefinition of the EU's role in development policymaking, and, more broadly, on the wider process of aid delivery and politics at the multilateral level.

1.3 Researching the EU in international organizations: European studies and the political economy of the 'governance turn'

In spite of the vagaries of the ratification of the Constitutional Treaty, finally adopted in December 2009 as the Lisbon Treaty, the EU's role in international affairs has not ceased in these recent years to be the object of extensive research by the academic and policy communities.[11] Indeed, since the 1990s the number of contributions in EU studies investigating the Union's role in world politics has distinctly increased (Carlsnaes and Smith 1994; Hill 1996; Piening 1997; Bretherton and Vogler 1999).[12] Somehow parallel to the ups and downs of the EU's integration and enlargement trajectories, those studies have explored actorness, power (substantial and normative) and foreign policy (style and impact).

In trade policies, along with Japan and the United States, the EU was among the main proponents of a renewed impetus for the process of multilateral trade liberalization behind the launch of the Doha Round in 2001. Through the enlargement process, and the subsequent launching of the European Neighborhood Policy (ENP) the EU took a clear stance on associating social and economic actions to the political redefinition of its borders. Early after since the launch of the MDGs by the UN, within the framework of the Monterrey Consensus in 2002, the EU successfully engaged in an effort to scale up its collective (Commission and MS) provision of official development assistance (ODA) flows to the poorest partners. Partnerships with developing countries, notably the negotiation of the EPAs with African, Caribbean and Pacific partners, and the creation of the broader Strategic Partnership between the African Union (AU) and the EU witness the geographical breadth of the scope of the Union's action in development policy. Since Lisbon, the EU has its own legal standing, and a High Representative is now in charge of the external representation of the Union in EU matters, supported by the External Action Service (EEAS), which is tasked to ensure consistency between broad foreign policy and sectoral goals in the EU's external relations.

A key feature of these diverse policy avenues has been the emphasis officially put by the EU on their multilateral nature, or on their compatibility with a multilateral vision of each particular sector, whether institutional guidelines existed or not at the multilateral level. Brussels has repeatedly affirmed its preference for a multilateral approach to trade liberalization, and has claimed for enhanced coordination in the ongoing process of harmonization among donors. A number of contributions, both in academic and policy circles, have praised the evolution of an elaborated institutional structure, lamenting however the gap between the EU's sheer resource weight in the international system and its ability to act cohesively and purposively in many of these policy areas.

Research on foreign policy has long since explored the role of own beliefs in the decision-making of national leaders, while IR research on how perceptions form and evolve at the aggregate (national, multilateral) level has produced a consistent body of literature (Adler 1987; Goldstein 1993; Goldstein and Keohane 1993; Legro 1995, 2005; Wendt 1999). Other contributions have investigated the links between role theories and foreign policy analysis, a domain that had remained relatively unexplored for a long time (Harnisch et al. 2011). The debate on the role of the EU in international affairs has significantly benefited from these insights, with studies that examine the influence of collective ideas on the EU from national and multilateral sources (Elgström 2007; Lucarelli 2007; Lucarelli et al.. 2007), its foreign policy roles (Elgström and Smith 2006a), the relation between different role components (Bengtsson and Elgström 2011), and the dynamics between institutional and interactional factors to understand role change in European member and non-member states (Folz 2011).

Academic work on the EU's role in world affairs has been a product of its expanding foreign policy reach. On the other side, however, the diversification of research on the EU's external role owes much to a major scholarly change, which has been developing since the 1990s. During that decade, major disturbances in the global economy triggered visible intellectual (though not unanimously foundational) shifts, within the IR and IPE literatures, that were to have substantial influence on the study of the EU's role in international affairs. Most notably, the earlier emphasis on regimes and interdependence (Krasner 1982; Keohane 1984) was being gradually integrated by the theme of governance in a globalized world (Rosenau and Czempiel 1992; Nye and Donhaue 2000). Policy failures, such as the World Trade Organization (WTO) debacle in Seattle (1999), combined with mounting criticisms against the poor results of International Monetary Fund (IMF) emergency rescue packages, during the Asian crisis in the late 1990s, first, and in the Russian (1998) and Argentinian (2001) crises, thereafter. Those developments, added to the adverse effects of several structural adjustment programs (SAPs) that had been sponsored by the World Bank since the late 1980s, fiascoes in multilateral trade liberalization, and the catastrophic results of IMF packages, brought steam to the intellectual reassessment of global aid and financial architectures. A momentous redefinition also ensued in mainstream political economy literature on the roles that the two Bretton Woods institutions were to play in the new context (Eichengreen 1999; Rodrik 1997; Stiglitz 2002a).

Following the drive on 'effective multilateralism' (European Commission 2003b; Biscop 2004), a new avenue of inquiry emerged in EU studies as well, mostly interested in the influence of the Union in multilateral *fora* (Eide 2004; Elgström and Smith 2006a). In addition to studies on the Union and the United Nations (UN) (Laatikainen and Smith 2006a), research started to focus on the EU relations with, respectively, the WTO and the IMF. In the first case, exclusive competence in trade policy, the creation of a new multilateral institution in 1994 and the inclusion of new matters in the trade envelope stimulated research on the EU trade policymaking (Meunier and Nicolaidïs 1999; Young 2000 and 2007; Dür and Zimmermann 2007; Poletti 2012). In the second case, the increased relevance of the Union in monetary affairs, after the launch of the Euro in 1999, generated interest on the coexistence of MS memberships and a single currency at the IMF (McNamara and Meunier 2002; Bini Smaghi 2004, 2006). Subsequent research has expanded the focus on the effectiveness of the EU's action in a number of other international institutions (Pisani-Ferry 2005; Jørgensen 2009), also deepening the investigation on specific aspects of its performance (Jørgensen et al. 2011a).

Illuminating on inside-out dynamics, EU studies have mostly focused on institutional-ideational processes, two themes that had not been addressed in the earlier economic analyses of IFIs, primarily interested in the political-economy side of the shortcomings of the World Bank and IMF's programs in that period. As a result, the former have at times downplayed the influence of sector-specific dynamics (aid policies entailing diffuse costs and concentrated benefits, to recipients that are outside the donors' jurisdiction; effects of (usually high) implementation costs on aid effectiveness), while the latter have steered away from the complexity of power dynamics inherent in the making of IFIs policies. More generally, unit-level approaches, centering either on EU- (or World Bank-) specific variables have neglected the role that their interactions, within the broader international system, have played in shaping their behavior.

Speaking to the literature on the influence of international institutions on the EU (Costa and Jørgensen 2012), this book contends that outside-in dynamics have significantly influenced the redefinition of the EU's development policy across the turn of the millennium. Similarly, evidence has emerged about the reverse process, as shown by the effects of the EU's enlargement on the World Bank's redefinition of its mission in the EU Enlargement and Neighborhood countries. By incorporating the outside-in relational dimension, the investigation conducted here ascertains key causal mechanisms underlying the changes in the two organizations' respective missions and policies. Abstaining from strict causal inferences, this inquiry advances hypotheses on complex causal chains, which often operate through different logics (both rationalist and reflectivist) at several governance levels.[13]

The analysis is based on an original eclectic framework, built on a combination of seminal insights on the behavior of IOs from IR rational insitutionalism, constructivism, EU and aid policy studies. The book also touches on the need, often expressed by decision makers, practitioners and interested stakeholders, to assess the financial viability and welfare implications of policy outcomes stemming from the interaction of development multilaterals. In particular, to investigate the effectiveness of the EU's cooperation with the Bank, it engages inputs on performance analysis from the public policy and development literatures. The choice for analytic eclecticism needs however to be appropriately grounded. On the one side, discussed in the next section (1.4), the selection is based on the perceived shortcomings of other approaches in the rationalist and reflectivist camps, in explaining the micro-dynamics of global governance that pertain to the relations between IOs. On the other side, addressed in section 1.5, the preference for analytic eclecticism draws on the benefits that an original recombination of (inductively) selected insights from those different approaches brings to the understanding of complex interactions among multilaterals. While cautioning about the limits that are potentially associated with approaches that are at once inter-paradigmatic[14] and inter-disciplinary, the book makes a case for the overall advantages of carefully bounded eclecticism in advancing IR and IPE studies on global governance.

1.4 Rationalism, reflectivism and the study of multilateral aid policies

Determinants and implications of aid policies have long been analyzed by rational choice political economists under both motivational and effectiveness angles (McKinley and Little 1979; Maizels and Nissanke 1984; Trumbull and Wall 1994; Burnside and Dollar 2000; Easterly et al. 2004; Alesina and Dollar 2000; Rajan and Subramanian 2008). Some attention has also been devoted to study allocation choices between bilateral and multilateral aid (Balogh 1967; Rodrik 1996; Neumayer 2003; Andreopulos et al. 2011). In the same rationalist vein, the application by IR neo-institutionalists of the PA model to the relations between states and IOs has provided a first, convincing, refutation of the realist critique about an (allegedly) insurmountable endogeneity between states' interests and the interests and actions of the international organizations created by them (Mitchell 2009). In essence, the deviation of an IO's behavior from the preferences of its founding members is premised on the fact that the former operates through delegated bureaucrats, whose interests often diverge from those of the principals that have hired them in the first place (Keohane and Martin 2003). Seminal IR institutionalist studies drew on both economic and political science studies. Among the former, the transaction costs literature and business studies on contract making figured prominently (Coase 1937, 1960; Alchian and Demsetz 1972; Jensen and Meckling 1976; Fama 1980; Williamson 1975, 1985).[15] Among the latter, a privileged reference for IR institutionalism was the political science literature on Congressional delegation to specialized agencies within the US (McCubbins and Schwartz 1984; Kiewiet and McCubbins 1991; Epstein and O'Halloran 1999; Huber and Shipan 2002). Very succinctly, classic PA models focused on explicit (formal) contracts, whereby principals would delegate authority and resources to selected agents, in return for their solving technical problems, which would have otherwise required too much information-expertise on the side of their political principals, thus unnecessarily burdening their role in decision-making.

Seminal rationalist contributions in the EU literature have employed the PA model to study the relations between MS and EU institutions (Pollack 1997). Through a cross-policy perspective, Pollack has investigated the Commission's dual accountability to the member states (acting as a collective principal in the Council in treaty-based delegation), and to both the Council and the Parliament (when they appoint the Commission and when they delegate under the co-decision procedure, which is the case in development cooperation), concluding about the hybrid nature of the EU system (Pollack 2006). IR institutionalist scholars have resorted to PA models to study delegation from states to IOs, focusing on non-conformity through shirking and slacking by international bureaucrats in defiance of member states (Hawkins et al. 2006). On the relation between the Washington IFIs' management and member states, these studies have successfully explained, among others, the timing in the adoption of greener templates by the World Bank in the 1990s (Nielson and Tierney 2003, 2005), the consequences of modeling principals differently in US aid allocations to the IADB (Lyne et al. 2006), and the variation in the autonomy of IMF staff (Martin 2006).

These institutionalist analyses have offered parsimonious and compelling explanations of why states delegate to IOs, accounting for instances of weak performance directly linked to agency losses. They have however been criticized by contributions in the realist vein for having at times magnified the importance of bureaucratic shirking in the study of IOs' behavior, and for having neglected power relations and time consistency issues (Stone 2009). Additionally, their formal rigor and tight rationalist logic has at times clashed against the complexity of real world interactions in development policy. Relevant to the analysis conducted here on the relations between multilaterals, such distance between analytical abstraction and the practical concerns of everyday politics appears even wider, particularly because the EU and the World Bank, as many other global governors, are connected through multiple and highly differentiated accountability ties. Overall, IR institutionalism has successfully responded to these criticisms, with augmented models that incorporate a thicker portion of the many relations at play between states and IOs.

By disaggregating principals, refined applications of the PA template have looked at states' domestic constituencies (Milner 2006) in the allocation between bilateral and multilateral aid. Deepening the focus on principality problems, they have explored the composition effects of intra-principal politics, refining the identification and modeling of principals, and drawing inferences on whether delegation is likely to succeed or not (Lyne et al. 2009). However, while acknowledging the importance of third-parties – as external 'informants' (Lake and McCubbins 2006) –, early IR analyses of the states–IOs relations have not explicitly investigated the role that the latter could play in modifying the delegation relation. Also, IR contributions have focused primarily on the 'success/failure' of the delegation process from the principal's point of view, with little interest on the implementation outcomes ensuing from these changes. Conversely, offshoots from the literature on endogenous trade policies (Grossman and Helpman 1994) have relied on both endogenous foreign economic policymaking and PA models to investigate interactions among different actors in aid policies (Murshed 2004), exploring states' compliance to IOs' decisions through a political economy model of domestic constituencies (Dai 2005). Studies on donor–recipient relations (Azam and Laffont 2003; Torsvik 2005) have revised classic Principal-Agent frameworks (Murshed and Sen 1995), contending that recipient sovereignty and post-contractual opportunism could be studied more convincingly through strategic signaling games (Murshed 2009).[16] By design, political economy, IR and IPE rationalist studies assume that a strictly consequential logic informs the behavior of involved players. However, in most social interactions choices are rarely based on purely strategic motivations, and happen to be a mix between consequentiality and appropriateness concerns, with ideas (either strategic or not) playing crucial roles on numerous occasions.

IR studies in the constructivist–structuralist vein have explored the transformative potential of belief systems, looking at the influence of transnational ideas at the systemic level on both states and IOs (Risse-Kappen 1994, 1995). Constructivist research on perceptions has examined the sources and evolution of perceptions from actors external to IOs (see Lucarelli and Fioramonti 2010, on the EU). Specifically, IR constructivist analyses of international organizations have studied the evolution of IOs policymaking through the lens of their organizational culture (Florini 1996; Finnemore and Sikkink 1998; Barnett and Finnemore 2004; Chwieroth 2009) and policy norms (Park and Vetterlein 2010). Those studies have relevantly called attention to how ideas (and ideational changes) have influenced IOs on multiple grounds, exploring dynamics equally distant from neo-Gramscian and policy diffusion literatures. The emphasis on the importance of organizational culture has provided a powerful critique to the rationalist premise of IOs as passive-reactive agents in the hands of MS, with incursions into the role of norm entrepreneurs as drivers of change in increasingly autonomous IOs (Oestreich 2012). Fertilized through role theory applied to foreign policy analysis, these contributions suggest that agency components can successfully be incorporated in non-rationalist analyses of IOs' policymaking, thus expanding their analytical reach beyond that of mostly structural accounts of the role of shared norms or broader belief systems. At times, however, the primacy of ideational causation, and the exclusive reliance on single-variable explanatory frameworks, have weakened the analytical meaningfulness of some IR constructivist accounts of IOs' policy and organizational changes. These types of change have been lumped together with norm-specific change, inaccurately conflating two outcomes whose inherent complexity has been acknowledged by constructivist authors themselves (Park and Vetterlein 2010, 227–231).

The most sophisticated and persuasive among these studies tend to be more eclectic than strictly constructivist in their take, as shown by the pioneering study of Barnett and Finnemore (2004), which decenters both the realist-statist and liberal-institutional perspectives towards the hitherto neglected role of peculiar organizational cultures of groups of international bureaucrats. Similarly, the fertilization between rationalist models of public policy and sociological analyses of organizational behavior has led to innovative conceptualizations of leadership, pioneering analyses on the Commission's role in the making of EU's foreign aid policy (Carbone 2007). PA models have also been amended by IR–IPE and economic studies, to shorten the distance between theoretical abstraction and the complexity of real world interactions. Eclectic models have been built, based on PA and signaling frameworks, to incorporate the possibility of multiple interactions between principals, their agents and third parties. Also, largely relaxing the simplifying assumptions of purely reactive agents, contributions in the IR and economic institutionalist strands have allowed for the possibility of double moral hazard (by both agents and principals), and have begun to study the role of intermediate agents in longer delegation chains (Murshed and Sen 1995; Murshed 2004 and 2009; Hawkins and Jacoby 2006). Rationalist analyses in the realist vein have also relied on bargaining models, arguing that IOs' institutional designs are the outcome of strategic interactions through which powerful and weak states seek to balance their respective interests (Stone 2011).

While some of these studies have trespassed paradigm-specific boundaries, the majority of them has kept the realist, liberal and constructivist cores intact, both epistemologically and ontologically. In variable measures, however, all of them have blended insights from different approaches to the study of interactions in world politics. The variety of processes in which the EU and the World Bank are involved as major development players, the different sources of their authority, as well as the legitimacy claims to which they are subject from different constituencies, should guard against relying *a priori* on a single approach. As argued in the next section, analytic eclecticism, in turn, offers a convincing alternative to address the theoretical puzzles and practical issues that pertain to the study of their relations.

1.5 Advantages (and limitations) of an eclectic approach

While a growing number of studies in the social sciences appears to be informed by eclecticism, the intellectual potential of eclectic research as a distinct analytical choice has been recognized only recently.[17] Its structural acceptance of 'extensive endogeneity' (Sil and Katzenstein 2010), its acknowledging the 'ubiquity of complex interaction effects in the study of politics' (Hall 2003, 387) provides a compelling basis to analyze the microfoundational aspects of global governance that bear on the questions outlined in the previous sections. Relevant to the study of the relations between states and IOs, the datum acquires increased significance for the investigation of complex interactions between multiple – imperfectly overlapping – delegation chains, as those that characterize the relations between global governors. The empirical records discussed in the following chapters suggest that the EU–World Bank relations have been informed by mechanisms that transcend pure delegation, most notably bargaining and signaling, and by logics that are not strictly consequential-strategic, such as imitation and role change. Specific to the purpose of this book, analytic eclecticism has several advantages when applied to the study of interactions between international organizations.

First, while paradigm-contained priors are essential starting points in hypothesis formulation, their eclectic recombination increases the degrees of freedom to investigate complex processes and their outcomes, particularly when they occur at different governance levels. The research presented in this book has been largely informed by an inductively oriented multicausal approach.[18] Applied to the study of the EU–World Bank relations, analytic eclecticism has provided the possibility of arriving at mid-range causal accounts through the exploration of multiple factors and mechanisms. Cutting across different levels of analysis, the eclectic approach adopted here has allowed a more accurate identification of the explanatory power of domestic variables, on the one side, and of relational and systemic determinants, on the other.

Second, inductively oriented eclecticism has offered the most flexible, yet convincing, alternative for a comprehensive analysis of the interactions between global actors that operate according to both consequential and appropriateness logics. Where institutionalist models of delegation, or endogenous models of foreign policymaking appear weaker, it is role theory, and constructivist analyses of normative policy change, that hit the mark. The research challenge is to identify when and under which conditions.[19] Beyond the evaluation of paradigm-specific merits and shortcomings, however, the eclectically analytic approach that informs this book recombines selectively their insights to improve the understanding of the complex interactions between global development governors.

Third, an eclectic take seems the most promising choice to provide answers to key practical questions about problems of coordination and effectiveness in the evolving context of development policies. How best should large multilaterals that operate in the same issue area coordinate-cooperate to improve outcomes at the global level? How has the early 'division of labour' between a finance provider (EU) and a manager-implementing agency (WB) changed since the 1990s, and to what effect, for the different actors in the development community? Pragmatic engagement is a feature of most policy-oriented studies of EU and World Bank-centered studies. Conversely, theoretically informed analyses have been most often interested in process – rather than outcome-specific issues. None of the two strands has investigated the influence of the interactions between the two governors on their respective actions and policies, and, more broadly, on the making of development policies across the turn of the third millennium.

As outlined in Section 1.3, inter-paradigmatic dialogue has advanced research on the institutionalization of international cooperation. Early structural-modified institutionalism had looked at the role played by international regimes in the transformation of the structural insecurity stemming from anarchy (Keohane 1984), while constructivists focused on how regimes themselves are the expression of contingent social goals shared by states (Ruggie 1982). Liberal-institutionalist analyses based on PA models have responded to the realist critique of complete endogeneity of interests between states and IOs, thus explaining these latter's deviation from the mandates of their (most powerful) member states. Constructivist analyses have looked beyond delegation dynamics, shedding light on non-strategic logics, and have argued about the role of international bureaucrats as autonomous sources of IOs' norm and policy changes. Contributions in the two paradigms have thus explored the relations between an IO and its MS, and the influence that institutionalized cooperation/bureaucratic cultures could play at the international level, on the 'external environment' where both IOs and states operate. Often, the result has been a partition into spatially and logically self-contained relational segments. Heuristically insightful, these outcomes have at times reduced the study of global governors to bilateral ties (between IOs and member states, between IOs and the external environment).

Relevant from an epistemological standpoint, most IR studies on IOs have not specifically explored the relational sources and dynamics of those very changes in preferences, either on the principal or on the agent's side, that were to yield policy/institutional variation connected with changes in the delegation relation. More broadly, the early IR and IPE literatures on IOs in either the constructivist or institutionalist strand have not explicitly investigated the influence that the interactions between different IOs may have on their respective behavior.

Along the seminal path traced by Avant et al. (2010), this research looks at how interactions between two IOs (the EU and the World Bank) have influenced their behavioral changes at different levels (mission, polity, policy and program). Particularly, the book explores the role that the EU–World Bank relations since the late 1990s have played on the Union's redefinition of its development policy. As depicted in Figure 1.1, inter-organizational relations add a new horizontal flow, to the flows that typify the relations between an IO and its MS, on the one side, and the interactions between an IO and its external environment, on the other. This study explores the role of both principals and agents by looking at their relevant constituencies (within the EU and within the Bank), including in the analysis external 'significant others' ('stakeholders' in the parlance of organizational studies). Epistemologically, the sort of analytic eclecticism adopted here departs simultaneously from the domestically bounded approach mostly employed in comparative politics and public policy studies, on the one side, and from the 'state–IOs–system' triangulation that has informed most IR literature in the realist and (early) institutionalist veins, on the other. By taking into account the effects of imperfectly shared membership on both EU and World Bank's behavior, which explicitly cuts across the traditional levels of analysis adopted in paradigm-contained studies, the book also innovates on multi-level approaches to the study of global governance, exploring the implications of hybrid forms of delegation on the making of development policy and development finance by large multilaterals.

From a theoretical standpoint, engaging role theories to investigate the EU–World Bank relations opens potential avenues to research on the changes that have occurred in the EU foreign policy roles since the 'poverty turn' occurred in the 1990s, shedding light on a number of unexplored aspects of the EU's role in international affairs (Aggestam 2006; Elgström and Smith 2006a), against the wider context of institutionalized cooperation to development. The exclusive focus on

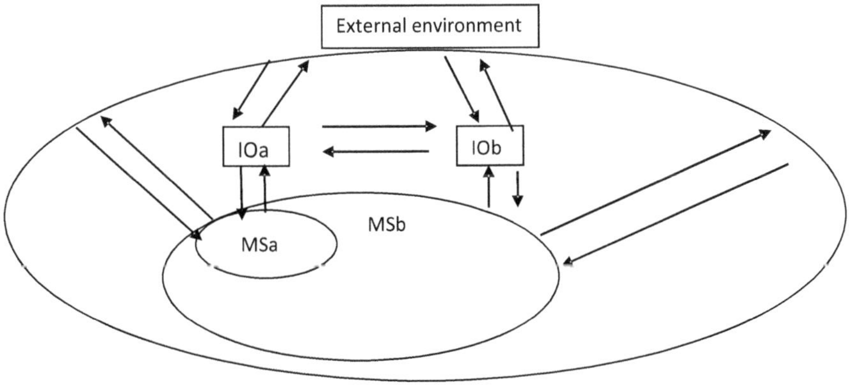

Figure 1.1 An eclectic take at studying IOs' actors, levels and processes

the EU's role at the World Bank, which bears the limitations common to case-study analyses in organizational performance (Mitchell 2009), allows in fact to control for changes that have occurred in the underlying 'structure of problems' in the past twenty years, observing their impact on the EU institutional praxis and policy achievements. Looked at from the angle of inter-organizational analyses (Laatikainen and Smith 2006b; Jørgensen 2009), the coordination of EU MS at the World Bank's Board provides an opportunity to investigate the external performance of the Union when acting though largely informal coordination mechanisms, adding to the literature on delegation theories and performance analyses (Gutner and Thompson 2010).

An additional benefit of the analysis presented in this book is that it tracks the roles, policies and performance of the Union at both decision-making and implementation levels, thus returning a richer picture of its relations with the Bank. Compared to previous analyses on the EU's foreign policy role, or on studies on IOs' institutional performance,[20] this research also explores the impact that the relation between the two multilaterals has produced in terms of joint outcomes, in selected field cases, in Chapters 7 through 9.

There are costs associated with increased complexity: endogenizing too much increases the toll on the explanatory power of any given approach. The strategy adopted here, and the one most commonly followed in analytic eclecticism, has been one of corroborating the hypothesized causal chains with robust empirical evidence and careful process tracing. In turn, such a choice has expanded the range of dynamics under investigation. In-depth analysis and increased accuracy in observation have been pursued, to compensate for potential losses in theoretical parsimony and analytical clarity. Neither the institutionalist nor the constructivist 'protective paradigmatic belts' may be invoked to substantiate the validity of the eclectic reconfiguration advanced here. However, staying on beaten paths (both approach-specific and paradigm-contained) would not have allowed to 'track the blind spots' (Sil and Katzenstein 2010) that have emerged so often in the course of this research

1.6 The book: aims and structure

The book primarily centers on what the EU does at the World Bank and with the World Bank, why it does it and, especially, how and how well it does it. Empirical references are by and large a recurrent feature of the volume, an ineludible task for a virtually untouched subject. The analysis that follows is nonetheless explicitly set to serve three main theoretical goals.

First, the book conceptualizes the EU–WB accountability ties as a hybrid between internal and external typologies, discussing its mixed features under both institutionalization and acceptance of mutual commitments (Chapter 2), the core criteria that shape PA relations according to the seminal institutionalist literature (Keohane 2003, 141–142). It fertilizes PA models with insights from implementation and business literatures, to endogenize the behavior of 'external stakeholders', 'would be principals' and 'significant others', in the explanation of inter-organizational dynamics. While the EU is the main subject of the analysis, the focus purposefully encompasses relational components, with prominence given to World Bank views, preferences and behavior, touching on the role of both multilaterals.

Second, the book investigates the changes in the EU's role in development policy, through the evolution of its relation with the World Bank over the course of two decades (1990–2010). It advances new hypotheses to understand key dynamics at work in the interaction between global governors with partially overlapping memberships, thus contributing to the literature on 'intersecting multilateralisms' (Laatikainen and Smith 2006b) and on inter-organizational relations (Bierman and Koops 2017). To this effect, it incorporates and critically reviews insights from the IR institutionalist and constructivist literatures. Chapter 3 discusses the evolution of the EU's approach to development policymaking, investigating the influence that external inputs were to have on the EU's redefinition of its own development policies. Relying on concepts advanced by role theory, Chapter 4 deepens the focus on the formation and change of the EU's role in development, by mirroring these processes through inputs from the World Bank and relevant stakeholders from the development community, most notably the OECD and anti-globalist NGOs. The EU's role in development policy has undergone core changes throughout the 1990s and 2000s. While the Union has certainly projected a more inclusive and participatory concept of development in the new millennium, through its 'Brussels Consensus' of 2006, compared to either its previous role and to the roles played by other major actors, it has also developed a more autonomous role in the day-to-day practice of development promotion. A relevant point that is made throughout the book is that these changes, while crucially supported by the Commission's entrepreneurship and mediated by MS, have been initiated through pressures from stakeholders that were external to the EU's context in strictly organizational terms. In particular, a number of these developments have been significantly influenced by the World Bank's adjustments to respond to inputs external even to its organizational milieu. Thus, both World Bank's choices and Brussels' receiving of those choices proved to be important elements in the process of the EU's role and policy change. Additionally, it is hypothesized that several of those major changes have roots that are ideational in nature, and may not be explained solely by resorting to dynamics of interest-based preference aggregation and correlated behavior taken up by proximate principals and proximate agents, the 'usual suspects' of PA-institutionalist analyses. The evidence indicates the importance of a deeper dialogue between the constructivist and institutionalist literatures on IOs, and the potential for identifying the conditions under which either approach is most effective to analyze IOs interactions across time and space.

Third, the book looks at both unit-specific and system-wide 'welfare effects' of those interactions, unpacking multilateral performance through an innovative framework, to analyze the EU's effectiveness at the World Bank and with the World Bank in the field. In chapters 5 and 6 the focus is moved closer to the dense set of micro-interactions entertained at several levels between the two organizations and the other key actors in the policy process. On the one side, these close-ups offer an opportunity to test the hypothesis of hybrid delegation advanced in Chapters 2 and 3, discussing the merits and limitations of the PA model. The book argues that, while remaining a key instrument to grasp intra-institutional dynamics under formalized delegation rules, its usefulness to interpret behavior and outcomes necessarily declines when employed to study hybrid delegation between multilaterals and its evolution across time. As discussed above, PA models appear weaker than constructivist frameworks, that are higher on the ladder of abstraction, in shedding light on the broad transformations in the official mission and roles of the Union and the Bank, even when changes in one organization appear closely connected – even if with lags – to changes occurring in the other, as shown in Chapter 2 through 4. Additionally, they lose much of their explanatory strength when applied to non-hierarchical, bargaining dynamics, that do constitute a sizeable portion of the broad set of the EU–WB relations in their day-to-day interactions. The analysis conducted here confirms, however, that key concepts from classic PA models retain explanatory cogency if applied to EU–WB relations when constituent politics (Löwi 1972) is at stake, precisely because their power is maximum when principals debate on the very delegation criteria upon which the interactional practice of their respective organizations is based. While the absence of an EU seat at the Bank may not hinder the achievement of an EU-friendly outcome (and perhaps even represent an advantage in tactical terms) if the matter at stake is non-foundational (sufficiently consensual, relatively low in salience, and shrewdly pushed by a proactive management), such an absence becomes a crucial impediment to advancing the 'EU cause' at the Board on matters of internal governance, as discussed about the World Bank 'voice and participation' reform in Chapter 5.

On the other side, through the micro-analysis on the EU's performance at the World Bank's Board and in the field, the book explicitly tackles effectiveness, of both institutional and implementation outcomes. Coupling data on EU MS behavior at the World Bank's Board with inputs on the EU's performance in World Bank-led projects and programs in the field, as well as in parallel missions, the book analyzes the contribution that the Union provides to advance the broader cause of poverty eradication through its cooperation with the Bank. Insights from the IR literature on IOs' performance are employed alongside concepts from implementation and business studies, and a framework is built, to conceptualize and investigate the EU's effectiveness at the World Bank's Board (Chapter 5 and 6) and with the World Bank in selected case studies in three regions (Europe and Central Asia (ECA), MENA and Sub-Saharan Africa (SSA), in Chapters 7, 8 and 9, respectively). Tributary to those multiple genealogies, the framework investigates performance by disaggregating it into several components, through the lens of effectiveness. As discussed in Chapters 5 and 6, the concept of effectiveness is employed as broadly informed by Susan Strange's ultimate IPE question, 'Cui bono?'

(Strange [1988] 1998, 121). Such a choice has necessarily required to relax the assumption of the EU and World Bank as 'unitary actors', to look beyond states and management's preferences and actions within the Bank and, respectively, the EU. Also, it has implied taking into account several other beneficiaries of the EU–World Bank cooperation (or absence of thereof) beyond a strictly bilateral inter-institutional set of relations, encompassing the role of third actors, such as NGOs, advocacy coalitions, and, most relevantly, citizens in partner countries.

It is important, however, that the reader be advised on what this book is not about. While making frequent reference to technical reports, a big chunk of the secondary literature on the topic of interest, this book is not intended as an exhaustive assessment on the performance of the EU development policy. Seminal studies of this kind have appeared on the matter, spurred by the post-Washington consensus and the drive towards increased transparency and aid effectiveness. Also, the EU–WB cooperation has been substantiated in numerous types of commitments through the years (channeling of funds by the Commission through the Bank, joint engagement in projects on the ground, parallel presence, participation of the Bank to EU-led facilities). Along such increased cooperation, a growing number of technical evaluations has ensued, commissioned by sources that are both internal and external to either organization (Pisani-Ferry 2005; ADE 2008). Highly informative, albeit endowed with substantial prescriptive components, those contributions on the EU–WB cooperation primarily offer assessments that are specific to each type of engagement. Most often, they concern specific actors (Commission, single MS) and instruments (such as the European Neighborhood Instrument (ENPI)- or Instruments for Pre-Accession Assistance (IPAs)), World Bank's units or programs (notably studies by the Operations Evaluation Department (OED), then Independent Evaluation Group (IEG)) and offer, by design, outputs that are in between technical and operational. Low in abstraction and rich in details, these studies respond to an explicit evaluation need expressed by policymakers and other stakeholders, but do not primarily claim to understand, let alone, explain why and how the outcomes they describe have come about.

This is precisely why the exercise in 'unpacking performance' (Jørgensen et al. 2011b) conducted in the second part of the book is not intended as an operational toolkit to measure the EU's performance at the Bank or quantify the effectiveness of cooperation between the two IOs in the field. Rather, the conceptualization of performance-as-effectiveness advanced here should be read within the broader theoretical hypotheses on hybrid delegation, against the background of the diachronic analysis on role changes. Finally, the usefulness of the performance analysis is less similar to that of a scorecard, and more akin to that of a torch, unveiling spots at different governance levels in the making of multilateral development policies. Under a prescriptive angle, the extent to which those sights, tracked back through in-depth case studies, earn either organization praise or shame, remains primarily an empirical matter. This does not however dispense us from deriving the necessary implications for future improvement, at both theoretical and policy levels, as discussed in Chapter 10, which concludes the book.

Notes

1 According to Eurostat (2017a), in 2015 the EU accounted for 15.5% of world exports, and for 14.5% of world imports, ranking second after the US on both lines. In that same year, the EU28 was the first provider of FDI outflows, with Euros 537.2 bn or 33% in total world outflows (Eurostat 2017b).

2 In 2016, the EU institutions ranked fourth, after the US, Germany and the UK, as providers of official development assistance (ODA), with USD 15.74 bn (Net ODA disbursement, OECD International Development Statistics 2017).

3 In 2008 the share of EU MS core resources in total Development Assistance Committee (DAC) resources contributed to the World Bank amounted to 60.62%, while non core resources (EU institutions and MS) accounted for a share of 66.08% (OECD 2010). Between 2002 and 2010, the European Commission channeled almost USD 5 bn to the World Bank Trust Fund System, thus becoming its third major contributor, after the US and the UK (Independent Evaluation Group (IEG) 2011, 16). Between 2010 and 2015, the EU still ranked third, albeit with a smaller contribution of Euros 2 bn – USD 2.28 bn (World Bank 2016).

4 The relevance of the 'Brussels Consensus' of 2006 and Agenda for change (2011) have been reaffirmed by the Union in its recent New Consensus on Development (European Union 2017). The New Consensus further endorses the Agenda 2030 to implement the Sustainable Development Goals (SDGs) and prioritizes EU partnerships with other players – including other multilaterals such as the World Bank (item 90, p.44) – to foster inclusive, sustainable development and to reduce inequality. Partnerships are strategically listed as a priority for EU actions (Section 3, pp. 37–47).

5 While different in their meaning (aid flows being a means to foster development goals), 'aid policies' and 'development policies' have been used often as synonyms in the early literatures on the topic. The seminal economic literature, on its part, has mostly focused on typologies of flows (grants, loans, investments) and on their effect on growth, and subsequently, on development outcomes, usually conditional on a series of other constraints. Currently, the term 'development policy' has certainly gained wider diffusion in the policy community. In the scholarly literature, the analytical focus has been generally widened to encompass a large set of nexuses among a plurality of referents (donor, recipient, third parties, resource flows, processes, outcomes). However, due to the ample chronological focus adopted in the book, and to the changes that have occurred in the different roles of the EU (political actor, donor) and the World Bank (financial institution, loan-cum-knowledge provider, relevant political influencer), the terms 'aid policies' and 'development policies' will be used interchangeably.

6 In the words of Sil and Katzenstein, eclectic is 'any approach that seeks to extricate, translate, and selectively integrate analytic elements – concepts, logics, mechanisms, and interpretations – of theories or narratives that have been developed within separate paradigms, but that address related aspects of substantive problems that have both scholarly and practical significance.' (Sil and Katzenstein 2010, 10).

7 In 2000, the Commission provided Euros 11 mn through the World Bank. In 2005, including funds provided to HIPC (Highly Indebted Poor Countries) the total amount channeled through the Bank amounted to Euros 579 mn (ADE 2008, Vol. 1, 6).

8 See European Commission (2010a, 34): 'Europe's voice in the International Financial Institutions should be strengthened through consolidated, less fragmented European representation, with the ultimate objective of a single European seat at the IMF and the

World Bank and EU coordination should be stepped up', as well as the Conclusions of the EU Council on the MDGs for the UN Plenary (EU Council 2010a).

9 While no explicit mention is made on compacting the representation of EU MS in international *fora* in the New Consensus on Development (2017), the whole set of goals and priorities contained in the document are attributed to 'the EU and its member states' no less than 82 times (Faure and Maxwell 2017, 2). A departure from the previous two-part Consensus of 2006, whereby a first set of objectives was listed for the EU and its MS, and a second set, in a separate part, as specific commitments for the Commission, the New Consensus lists a common set of ambitious objectives, to be achieved jointly by the EU and its MS.

10 The reference here is particularly to the impetus given by the Commission to financing for development, after the Monterrey Consensus in 2002 (Carbone 2007), as well as to the cooperation between the two organizations within the broader Paris-Accra Agenda on aid coordination and donor harmonization, discussed in Chapters 2 and 3.

11 Apparently, judging from the number of publications on the subject, the French and Dutch cold responses in the referenda of 2004 have intensified the debate on the ability of the Union to define common goals and strategies, and to act consistently according to a shared vision of its role in international affairs. The current debate on the ability of Euro-zone countries to pass the tests of the Eurocrisis, Brexit and migration emergency is yet another example of how research on the EU's role in the world does not respond counter-cyclically to the changing fortunes of cohesion among EU partners.

12 Seminal contributions had appeared earlier, however (Galtung 1973; Sjöstedt 1977).

13 On the difference between causal inferences and causal mechanisms see King et al. (1994, 85–87).

14 The term 'paradigm' is employed here as a synonym of 'research tradition' – also shortened as 'tradition' in the text, in the interpretation advanced by Laudan, who refers to '(1) a set of beliefs about what sorts of entities and processes make up the domain of inquiry; and (2) a set of epistemic and methodological norms about how the domain is to be investigated, how theories are to be tested, how data are to be collected, and the like' (Laudan 1996, 83). Alternatively, the same concept is indicated throughout the text with the term 'School'. Laudan's conceptualization of paradigms appears as a better alternative to describe the IR field-constitutive trifurcation into Realism, Liberalism and Constructivism, compared to Lakatos' concept of 'research program' (whereby research programs can coexist but are neither foundationally opposed to one another along structurally enduring cleavages, nor simultaneously engaged in producing converging interpretations). On this point see Sil and Katzenstein (2010, 6–7)

15 As noted by Jensen and Meckling (1976) and Fama (1980), however, incentive problems from the separation between firm owners and managers had been first considered by classic political economists in the early days of the discipline (Adam Smith) or, in the 1930s by studies in corporate governance (Berle and Means 1932).

16 The implications of sovereignty, particularly for aid recipients in PA models of multilateral aid, had already been debated by IR institutionalists (Gutner 2005; Nielson and Tierney 2005).

17 According to Sil and Katzenstein analytic eclecticism is identified (and distinguished from paradigm-driven research) by three 'markers', i.e. an 'Open-ended problem formulation encompassing complexity of phenomena, not intended to advance or fill gaps in paradigm-bound scholarship', a 'Middle-range causal account incorporating complex interactions among multiple mechanisms and logics drawn from more than one paradigm', and 'Findings and arguments that pragmatically engage both academic debates and the practical dilemmas of policymakers/practitioners' (2010, 19).

18 On the significance of multi-level causality for the study of international relations see the seminal Waltz (1959).

19 While not comprehensively evaluating competing theories from different paradigms, the research presented in this book does engage with a comparative assessment of selected inputs and models from the IR liberal and constructivist traditions. As such, it seeks to overcome problems of translatability between the often language-specific jargons of different strands within those two IR Schools.

20 In addition to Carbone (2007) and Nielson and Tierney (2003, 2005), also see Martin (2006), Martin and Woods (2005), Woods and Lombardi (2006), that mainly focus on decision-making outputs. Gutner and Thompson (2010) and Stone (2011) discuss the relation between mandate, policy process and policy outcomes.

2 Intersecting accountabilities

The beauty of difference and the challenge of coordination

2.1 The EU and the World Bank: mission and role in the global political economy

Originally created by six European countries through the Treaty of Rome in 1957, as a customs union with future goals in the creation of a common market and in the construction of a political Europe ('determined to lay the foundations of an ever closer union among the peoples of Europe'[1]), the EU has evolved to expand a composite mission of promoting 'peace, prosperity and freedom for its 495 million citizens — in a fairer, safer world' (EU 2008). At the end of the 2010s, with its 500 million-plus citizens, the EU28 has become the third most densely populated polity after China and India, respectively. In addition to pursuing 'the constant improvements of the living and working conditions of their peoples, recognizing that the removal of existing obstacles calls for concerted action in order to guarantee steady expansion, balanced trade and fair competition', and to contributing 'by means of a common commercial policy, to the progressive abolition of restrictions on international trade', the EU MS have devoted time and effort to strengthen the 'solidarity which binds Europe and the overseas countries' ensuring the 'development of their prosperity, in accordance with the principles of the Charter of the United Nations'.[2] Since the end of the Cold war the Union has completed three enlargement rounds, and has broadened cooperation with developing countries beyond the African, Caribbean and Pacific group of states (ACP).

By sheer size, the EU is a key player in the world trade system and the main source of foreign direct investment (FDI). The Union's trade policy is perhaps the most quoted example of a joint, long-lasting and successful case of external action, a template for integration in other areas, most notably monetary policy. Across time, other regional groupings have looked at the EU approach to trade liberalization to design alternative integration paths for their countries. With the creation of the Euro (provided for in the Maastricht Treaty (1992) and adopted in 1999), the EU MS have renounced sovereignty in monetary affairs, and have pooled resources to stabilize their economies and strengthen their role in the global monetary system.

Most relevantly, the EU-cum-MS are collectively the major donor in the global community. In 2010, their estimated joint effort accounted for more than 83.55 billion USD, with a share of 56.59% in total official development aid (ODA).[3] In 2016 the EU and its MS still topped the list, collectively supplying an estimated USD 97.43 billion, or 57.21% of total world ODA (OECD 2017). On their side, and notwithstanding the mild contractions recorded in 2010, 2013 and 2015, between 2000 and 2016, the EU institutions alone have provided on average 9.3% in total annual ODA, with a yearly average of 11.74 billion USD. In turn, EU DAC MS have stably kept the lead over that period (see Figure 2.1).

In 2007, the EU institutions were the third largest provider of official aid flows after the US and Germany (see Table 2.1). In 2011, Brussels ranked second, with USD 17.39 bn ODA after the US. In 2015, the EU institutions were the fourth largest provider of ODA with USD 13.67 bn, after the US, the UK and Germany. In 2016, EU institutions have been the fourth provider of global ODA, with 15.74 USD billion, after the US (USD 33.59 billion), Germany (USD 24.67 billion) and the UK (USD 18.03 billion) (OECD 2017).

As shown in Table 2.2, ODA/GNI (Gross National Income) shares vary across EU MS. Best performers such as the Netherlands, Sweden, Luxemburg and Denmark have long since surpassed the 0.7 ODA/GNI target agreed with the MDGs. Others, such as the UK and Germany have just reached it (0.7 in 2015, the former, expected 0.7 in 2016, the latter). However, other EU MS, such as Portugal and Italy, with 0.16 and 0.22 ODA/GNI shares in 2015 respectively, still lag seriously

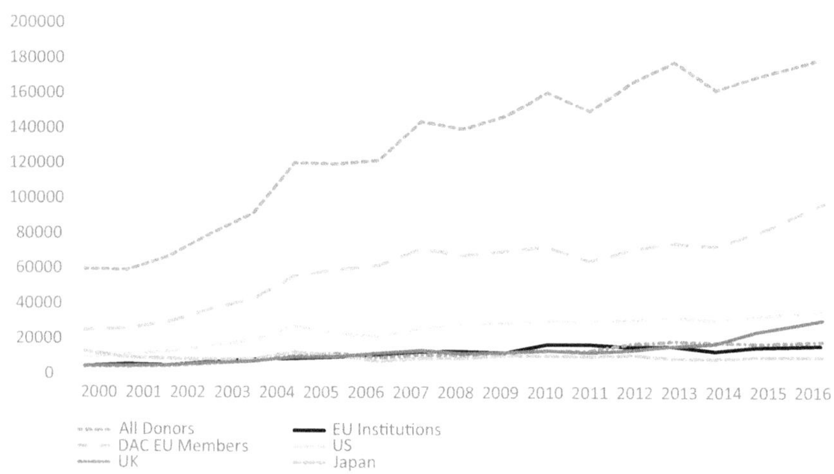

Figure 2.1 Trends in ODA provision, 2000–2016

Source: OECD IDS – QWIDS, ODA net disbursement, current prices, USD Million – Data as of June 2017. Data for 2016 preliminary

Table 2.1 Top 10 ODA donors, selected years

	2007			*2011*			*2015*	
1	US	21.79	1	US	30.97	1	US	30.99
2	Germany	12.29	2	EU Institutions	17.39	2	UK	18.54
3	EU Institutions	11.63	3	Germany	14.09	3	Germany	17.94
4	France	9.88	4	UK	13.83	4	EU Institutions	13.67
5	UK	9.85	5	France	13.00	5	Japan	9.20
6	Japan	7.70	6	Japan	11.09	6	France	9.04
7	Netherlands	6.22	7	Netherlands	6.34	7	Sweden	7.09
8	Spain	5.14	8	Sweden	5.60	8	Saudi Arabia	6.76
9	Sweden	4.34	9	Canada	5.46	9	Netherlands	5.73
10	Canada	4.08	10	Saudi Arabia	5.09	10	UAE	4.38

Source: OECD IDS (2017), ODA net disbursement, current prices, USD billion – Data as of June 2017

behind. Among the most generous contributors, and well within the top 10 aid providers by ODA/GNI since 2015, are the United Arab Emirates (second after Sweden with 1.18% of its GNI devoted to ODA). Comparing group performance, however, the average ODA/GNI ratio for the whole of EU DAC members has been steadily above the DAC average, improving from 0.38 in 2007 to 0.51 in 2016, vis-à-vis total DAC ODA/GNI shares ranging from 0.27 (2007) to 0.32 (2016). Overall, the EU and its MS are on top of aid provision on both absolute and relative grounds, and have remained leading forces in the universal attainment of the ODA/GNI 0.7 target endorsed in 2015 through the Sustainable Development Goals (SDGs).

Into the late 2000s the blue banner on the Bank's official website, 'IBRD and IDA: Working for a World Free of Poverty' eloquently displayed the mission of the major multilateral lending group in the world economy (World Bank 2008a).[4] In the 2010s the World Bank Group mission has explicitly been widened to attain two goals, 'end extreme poverty and promote shared prosperity'.[5] Since the Bank's inception, poverty reduction and the promotion of sustainable development in developing countries (middle-income, low income but creditworthy, and least developed, poorest countries) through different forms of lending (financial assistance) and technical services has been the business of a self-defined non-traditional bank. Founded in 1944 in the framework of the Bretton Woods Agreements, the original mission of the IBRD was to finance the European reconstruction after the end of the Second World War. Across time, the organization has redefined its mission multiple times. In the 1960s and 1970s came the promotion of growth and industrialization in newly independent, post-colonial countries. Subsequently, the Bank focused on supporting socio-economic development in countries hit by the debt crisis in the 1980s. Later on, it put a major effort in helping the transition from command to

Table 2.2 ODA/GNI, 2007–2016

	2007			*2011*			*2015*			*2016*	
1	Norway	0.95	1	Sweden	1.02	1	Sweden	1.40	1	Norway	1.11
2	Sweden	0.93	2	Luxembourg	0.97	2	UAE	1.18	2	Luxembourg	1.00
3	Luxembourg	0.92	3	Norway	0.96	3	Norway	1.05	3	UAE	1.12
4	Netherlands	0.81	4	Denmark	0.85	4	Luxembourg	0.95	4	Sweden	0.94
5	Denmark	0.81	5	Netherlands	0.75	5	Denmark	0.85	5	Turkey	0.79
6	Ireland	0.55	6	Liechtenstein	0.69	6	Netherlands	0.75	6	Denmark	0.75
7	Austria	0.50	7	United Kingdom	0.56	7	United Kingdom	0.70	7	Germany	0.70
8	Liechtenstein	0.44	8	Belgium	0.54	8	Finland	0.55	8	United Kingdom	0.70
9	Belgium	0.43	9	Finland	0.53	9	Germany	0.52	9	Netherlands	0.65
10	Finland	0.39	10	Ireland	0.51	10	Switzerland	0.51	10	Switzerland	0.54
11	France	0.38	11	France	0.46	11	Turkey	0.50	11	Belgium	0.49
12	Switzerland	0.37	12	Switzerland	0.46	12	Belgium	0.42	12	Finland	0.44
13	Spain	0.37	13	Germany	0.39	13	France	0.37	13	Austria	0.41
14	Germany	0.37	14	Australia	0.34	14	Austria	0.35	14	France	0.38
15	United Kingdom	0.36	15	Canada	0.32	15	Ireland	0.32	15	Spain	0.33
16	Australia	0.32	16	Portugal	0.31	16	Australia	0.29	16	Ireland	0.33
17	Canada	0.29	17	Spain	0.29	17	Canada	0.28	17	Canada	0.26
18	New Zealand	0.27	18	New Zealand	0.28	18	New Zealand	0.27	18	Italy	0.26
19	Iceland	0.27	19	Austria	0.27	19	Iceland	0.24	19	Australia	0.25
20	Portugal	0.22	20	Malta	0.25	20	Italy	0.22	20	New Zealand	0.25
21	Italy	0.19	21	UAE	0.21	21	Japan	0.20	21	Iceland	0.25
22	Japan	0.17	22	United States	0.20	22	Malta	0.17	22	Japan	0.20
23	Cyprus	0.17	23	Iceland	0.20	23	United States	0.17	23	Malta	0.20
24	Greece	0.16	24	Italy	0.20	24	Portugal	0.16	24	Estonia	0.19
25	United States	0.16	25	Japan	0.18	25	Estonia	0.15	25	Slovenia	0.18
26	Chinese Taipei	0.13	26	Turkey	0.16	26	Slovenia	0.15	26	United States	0.18
27	Slovenia	0.12	27	Cyprus	0.16	27	Korea	0.14	27	Portugal	0.17
28	Lithuania	0.11	28	Greece	0.15	28	Hungary	0.13	28	Czech Republic	0.14
29	Czech Republic	0.11	29	Slovenia	0.13	29	Greece	0.12	29	Lithuania	0.14
30	Poland	0.10	30	Lithuania	0.13	30	Lithuania	0.12	30	Korea	0.14

31	Slovak Republic	0.09	31	Czech Republic	0.12	31	Czech Republic	0.12	31	Greece	0.14
32	Turkey	0.09	32	Korea	0.12	32	Spain	0.12	32	Poland	0.13
33	Estonia	0.08	33	Estonia	0.11	33	Slovak Republic	0.10	33	Hungary	0.13
34	Hungary	0.08	34	Hungary	0.11	34	Poland	0.10	34	Slovak Republic	0.12
35	Korea	0.07	35	Chinese Taipei	0.09	35	Croatia	0.09	35	Romania	0.11
36	Israel	0.07	36	Bulgaria	0.09	36	Romania	0.09	36	Latvia	0.10
37	Latvia	0.06	37	Slovak Republic	0.09	37	Russia	0.09	37	Russia	0.08
38	Thailand	0.04	38	Romania	0.09	38	Cyprus	0.09	38	Croatia	0.07
39	EU Institutions	-	39	Israel	0.09	39	Bulgaria	0.09	39	Israel	0.07
40	Azerbaijan	-	40	Poland	0.08	40	Latvia	0.09	40	EU Institutions	-
41	Bulgaria	-	41	Latvia	0.07	41	Israel	0.07	41	Azerbaijan	-
42	Croatia	-	42	Russia	0.03	42	Chinese Taipei	0.05	42	Bulgaria	-
43	Kazakhstan	-	43	Thailand	0.01	43	Kazakhstan	0.02	43	Cyprus	-
44	Kuwait (KFAED)	-	44	EU Institutions	-	44	Azerbaijan	0.02	44	Kazakhstan	-
45	Malta	-	45	Azerbaijan	-	45	Thailand	0.02	45	Kuwait (KFAED)	-
46	Romania	-	46	Croatia	-	46	EU Institutions	-	46	Liechtenstein	-
47	Russia	-	47	Kazakhstan	-	47	Kuwait (KFAED)	-	47	Saudi Arabia	-
48	Saudi Arabia	-	48	Kuwait (KFAED)	-	48	Liechtenstein	-	48	Chinese Taipei	-
49	Timor-Leste	-	49	Saudi Arabia	-	49	Saudi Arabia	-	49	Thailand	-
50	UAE	-	50	Timor-Leste	-	50	Timor-Leste	-	50	Timor-Leste	-
51	Others	-	51	Others	-	51	Others	-	51	Others	-
	DAC countries, total	0.27			0.31			0.3			0.32
	DAC EU members, total	0.38			0.42			0.47			0.51

Source: OECD IDS (2017) Net disbursements as a share of GNI (last OECD revision June 2017. 2016 data is preliminary)

market economy in former communist countries, and providing preferential lending to Asian countries that were most severely hit by the crisis at the end of the 1990s. Parallel to the launching of the MDGs in 2000, the Bank has further pushed the envelope of poverty reduction, focusing its lending on projects that enhanced the sustainability of different socio-economic development trajectories.[6] The then President, Robert Zoellick clarified that the global mission of poverty reduction would be achieved by the Bank by prioritizing six strategic themes, that ranged from support to the poorest countries to get out of poverty and achieve sustainable growth (1), to help fragile and post-conflict states to meet the special challenges that they faced (2), to assistance with dedicated programs to the needs of middle-income countries (3), to the taking up by the Bank of an active role in the provision of global public goods (such as limiting the negative effects of climate change or controlling communicable diseases, or, again, dealing with international financial crises and promoting an open, multilateral trade system) (4), to the specific support of good governance, social services and private sector growth in the Arab World (5), and, finally, to pooling the best global knowledge to foster development (6) (Zoellick 2007). Since July 2017, Jim Yong Kim has been reappointed for another five year mandate as President of the World Bank Group, a position that he first took up in July 2012. True to his background (he is a medical doctor by training, with extensive experience in development), he has stepped up the Bank's envelope in global health, including emergency responses to address sudden outbursts of global pandemics (witnessed by the creation of a dedicated Pandemic Emergency Financing Facility or PEF, in cooperation with the WHO and Japan, operational since 2017). Under Kim's leadership, the Bank has also strengthened its engagement to address climate change and promote sustainable development, furthering its efforts to tackle the impact of conflicts and fragility in affected countries. At the end of 2016, a major step in that direction has been the launch of the Global Concessional Financing Facility (GCFF), to address refugee crises in middle income countries. Currently, the GCFF is regarded as a blueprint for action in low income countries too, and in broader concessional financing via the substantial – USD 75 bn – scaling up achieved in the International Development Association (IDA) 18th replenishment. The Bank has also reinforced its partnership with the UN (creating a Senior Vice-Presidency for the 2030 Development Agenda, United Nations Relations, and Partnerships (SVPMM)), eloquently claiming that its 2013 'twin goals' of poverty eradication and inequality reduction are in line with the 2015 SDGs (World Bank 2017b).

The World Bank has enjoyed a considerable reputation thanks to its ability to provide funds to its borrowing members and pay for its internal costs through lending and investments. The IBRD finances its activities by issuing bonds with triple-A ratings (grounded in repayment guarantees backed by member states) both to the public and private sector in more than a hundred countries, and has become 'the largest nonresident borrower in virtually all countries where its issues are sold' (Driscoll 1996, 2). In turn, these proceeds are lent to developing countries at preferential rates to finance development projects. Since the inception of its activity in 1946, the IBRD has provided its borrowers with loans for more than USD 500 bn, in return for USD 14 bn in capital by its shareholder governments (World Bank 2017a). Compared to the IMF, which manages a higher volume of resources, but mainly earns them from its members' quotas, the Bank obtains additional margins from its lending activities, independent from the contributions of MS.[7] In addition to risks, the Bank also 'pools' research resources (Woods 2006, 189), supplying knowledge and policy advice on development projects to client countries. Albeit hiring from top continental European Universities is growing, most of its staff is recruited from Ivy-league Anglo-Saxon Universities, with a majority of economists and a growing share of sectoral experts, in areas that range from infrastructural engineering (the core of the Bank's specialists in the early days) to anthropology and political science. More relevantly, the Bank combines a long-standing institutional memory and significant policy experience in client countries. Since the 1990s, the extent to which its current practices have improved from past learning has been the subject of constant debates. Certainly, its expertise in financing development projects is unique in width, depth and duration, compared to that of any other multilateral donor.

While different in their respective missions, and significant in their own merit, the Union and the Bank are the two major multilateral players in development finance. The gains generated by their cooperation in eradicating global poverty have been significant but their future potential should not be underestimated either, even discounting the role of emerging donors. Unpacking the web of their relations under core institutional, financial and geographical dimensions offers a basis to conceptualize their interactions and investigate their performance. The remainder of this chapter is organized as follows: Section 2.2 details the nature and scope of the EU–WB relations, under operational, geographical and institutional aspects. Section 2.3 compares the two institutions along four dimensions (actors, mission goals, internal decision making processes, core business), discussing their shared interests and policy complementarities. Section 2.4 delves into the formal basis of the accountability ties between the EU and the Bank: the Framework Agreement (FA, or Trust Funds and Co-Financing Framework Agreement). Section 2.5 in turn employs selected concepts from the institutionalist literature on delegation to analyze the different components of the relation between the two – imperfectly – overlapping multilaterals. Section 2.6 conceptualizes the EU–World Bank relations as a mix between external and internal accountabilities, advancing the hypothesis of the EU's hybrid delegation and role of 'would-be-principal' to the World Bank. Section 2.7 concludes, summarizing the key features of the EU–WB inter-institutional relations, to set the stage for the analysis of their evolution, in the broader context of the policy and role changes that have occurred across the turn of the millennium, addressed specifically in Chapters 3 and 4.

2.2 The EU and the World Bank: operational, geographical and institutional cooperation

If taken as a bloc, EU MS are – in principle – the largest shareholder of the WB, with their shares combined accounting for 27.53% in total IBRD shares (Aidflows 2017). In 2008 EU MS collectively accounted for more than 60% in total core funding channeled by DAC countries through the WBG (Table 2.3), Germany, the UK and Italy being the top-three providers in relative terms within the EU–DAC group (21.97%, 20.74% and 12.48%, respectively), followed by France, Spain, Sweden and the Netherlands. In 2017, Germany, France, the UK and Italy have been the top four shareholders to the IBRD among the group of EU DAC MS, with 4.35, 4.07 (UK and France), and 2.27% shares as a percentage of total subscriptions, respectively

Table 2.3 Contributions to the World Bank Group

Donor	*Core*	*% in total DAC*	*% in total EU DAC*	*Non-core*	*% in total DAC*	*% in total EU DAC*
Australia	146	1.71		214	7.99	12.10
Austria	122	1.43	2.36	23	0.86	1.30
Belgium	275	3.22	5.32	8	0.30	0.45
Canada	689	8.08		138	5.15	7.80
Denmark	183	2.15	3.54	2	0.07	0.11
EU Institutions				278	10.38	15.71
Finland	36	0.42	0.70	35	1.31	1.98
France	540	6.33	10.44		-	-
Germany	1136	13.32	21.97	15	0.56	0.85
Greece	80	0.94	1.55	0.3	0.01	0.02
Ireland	46	0.54	0.89	31	1.16	1.75
Italy	645	7.56	12.48	50	1.87	2.83
Japan	1251	14.67		0.3	0.01	0.02
Korea	79	0.93		2	0.07	0.11
Luxembourg	16	0.19	0.31	1	0.04	0.06
Netherlands	316	3.71	6.11	325	12.14	18.37
New Zealand	13	0.15		8	0.30	0.45
Norway	147	1.72		274	10.23	15.49
Portugal	41	0.48	0.79	1	0.04	0.06
Spain	342	4.01	6.62	210	7.84	11.87
Sweden	320	3.75	6.19	116	4.33	6.56
Switzerland	186	2.18		49	1.83	2.77
United Kingdom	1072	12.57	20.74	674	25.17	38.09
United States	848	9.94		223	8.33	12.60
Total DAC	8529	100.00		2677.6	100.00	
Total EU DAC	5170	60.62		1769.3	66.08	100.00
Non-core/total contributions				23,89		
Type of flow: gross disbursements in 2008 USD millions						

Source: OECD DAC Report on Multilateral Aid 2010

(Aidflows 2017, subscriptions as of 29.03.2017). In their capacity of shareholders, EU MS have an opportunity to influence the Bank's policies, even if only recently, and only on selected issues have they done so along EU-preferred lines.[8]

Operationally, cooperation between the Union and the Bank occurs through channeling (joint financing) and parallel financing. These instruments are also referred to as 'non-core' multilateral ODA, as opposed to 'core' ODA (the voluntary un-earmarked contributions supplied through the subscription and callable amounts of capital, provided and guaranteed by each shareholder to the Bank).[9] Channeling occurs mainly through a number of Trust Funds (multi- and, albeit largely reduced to date, single-donor ones), facilities in which resources are pooled with a focus on a specific theme, sector, region, or country of interest. In the joint financing scheme, the EU co-finances projects funded by a loan or a credit granted by the Bank, which also manages it in accordance with the terms of the FA, further examined below in section 2.4. The total project/program/fund cost is divided between the co-financing partners and all the contributions are pooled, so that the source of funding for a specific activity or type of expenditure within the project/program/fund cannot be identified. Parallel financing, on the contrary, takes place within a framework of integrated aid initiatives in which the EU provides funds directly to a recipient in the context of a project financed by the Bank. The project/program is broken down into clearly identifiable sub-projects which are each funded by the different co-financing partners (donors and banks/IFIs). Under parallel financing, and, more broadly, in partner/client countries where they lead separate programs, the EU and the Bank often work side by side. Bilateral development agencies of MS ('bilaterals') are also frequently involved, so that multiple loyalties are at play at both HQ and delegation/field levels.

As shown in Table 2.3, in 2008 the EU institutions prominently ranked among the top three donors by non-core channeling through the World Bank (accounted for by contributions to Trust Funds), with a share of 10.38% in total DAC non-core funds, after the UK (accounting for 25.17%) and the Netherlands (with a share of 12.14%), respectively.

Collectively, the EU MS have reduced their contributions to the WBG trust funds in the period between 2008 and 2009, with marked drops in resources channeled to single-donor trust funds recorded well after those years. However, their financial support to collective efforts – namely through multi-donor trust funds (MDTF) – has substantially increased in 2015, reaching a total of USD 1.56 bn in value for new contributions in that year.

Furthermore, the EU MS have provided stable support to IDA resources, with an average of USD 4.66 bn per year supplied over the period 2011–2016 (see Figure 2.3).

Between 2003 and 2016, the World Bank received from DG DEVCO–EuropeAid a total of Euros 2.9 bn (European Commission–DG DEVCO–EuropeAid 2016). The contribution by the EU institutions to World Bank managed MDTF, as reported by EuropeAid in 2016, and relative to the EU budget for a series of different periods – spanning from 2012 to 2020 – amounts to Euros 2.524 bn (*Idem*). Overall, according to the World Bank, between 2010 and 2015 the European Commission has

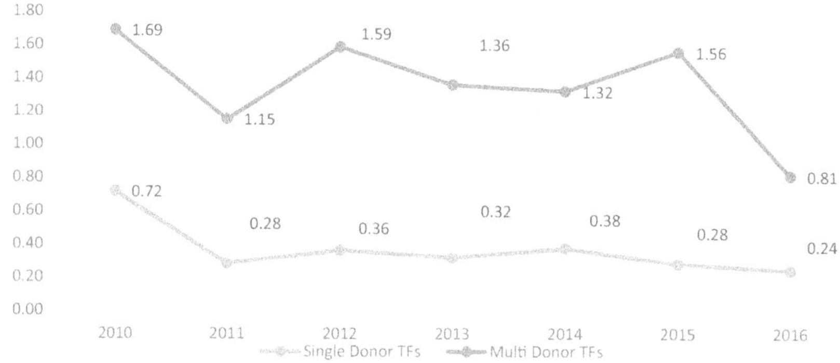

Figure 2.2 EU MS new contributions to Word Bank Group Trust Funds 2010–2016

Source: Aidflows database (2017). Data are expressed in USD bn and refer to new contributions per WB fiscal years. 2016 preliminary

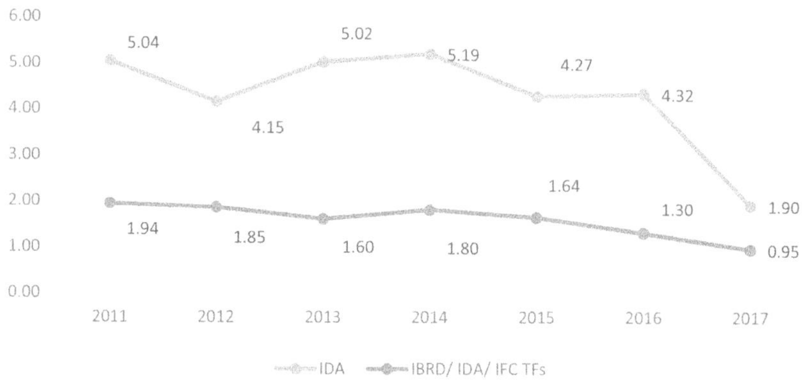

Figure 2.3 EU MS Paid-in Contributions to WBG TFs and IDA Budget, 2011–2016

Source: Aidflows database (2017). Data on contributions paid-in expressed in USD bn are referred to WB fiscal years

contributed over 2 billion Euros to the Group's Trust Fund System, thus becoming its third biggest contributor. The majority of EC contributions have financed projects in Africa (48%) and South Asia (26%) (World Bank 2016).

Flexible targeting to a wide number of sectors and countries is a first obvious benefit that the EU derives from channeling through the World Bank TF system.

Outsourcing the procedural supervision on disbursement is a second advantage. Pooling resources into WB TFs is motivated by the expected benefits from the WB's specific experience in areas where the EU has less knowledge and/or less deployed personnel, or where there is the need to rapidly mobilize large amounts of resources (as in post-crisis reconstruction in Timor-Leste or in the food crisis). Global convening power and expertise, as well as financial reliability have now become major incentives for the EU to channel resources to WB-managed Trust Funds that support the provision of global public goods. While PEF and GCFF are two recent examples, an early instance has been the EU channeling through the WB TF system in the context of the GFATM (Global Fund for Aids, Tuberculosis and Malaria), that has also facilitated the disbursement of large amounts of funds at a higher rate compared to EU direct interventions.[10]

Non-core funding entails potential benefits for donors that are also shareholders to the Bank, allowing them to exert a more immediate and visible influence on the Bank's programs, adding to the regular ways of the Board. From the World Bank's perspective, however, ramping up the funding for an increasing number of TFs may also weaken core policies agreed at the strategic level. In addition, non-core resources come with higher transaction costs for the Bank, generated by the negotiation and implementation of different donor-specific monitoring and reporting activities. The project/program/Fund has its own Board and is not bound to procedures other than its own.[11] Looked at from the partners' side, and compared to projects financed by lending through the regular Board path, non-core funding carries the benefit of additional resources, and, due to smaller TF Boards, potentially better coordinated and more targeted pooling. Among the downsides, however, projects financed through trust funds may not guarantee the level of visibility and transparency available through the Board track, entailing potentially less inclusive and less predictable processes.

As better detailed in sections 2.4 and 2.5, direct Commission contributions to the WB TFs have evolved in a context of growing support to aid allocations through the multilateral system and in the rethinking of development priorities which began with the Millennium Declaration (2000) and the MDGs. Other milestones followed: the Paris Declaration on Aid Effectiveness (2005), the European Consensus on Development (2005–2006), and the United Nations Millennium Review Summit (2005). To a large extent, the decision by the EU to provide funding to a specific TF is still taken at the HQ level on a case by case basis.[12] Evidence discussed throughout the book points however to steps that have been taken since the end of the 2000s by the Commission, to define a long-term comprehensive strategy to partner with the Bank along country, region and sector-specific issues.

The Bank has an Office for representation in Brussels, while the EU has its counterpart Office in Washington DC, via its delegation to the US, which also liaises with the two Bretton Woods institutions.[13] The EU Office in Washington has an observer status at the IMF, and its staff has regular contacts with political and technical Fund and Bank personnel, while the WB Office in Brussels equally has regular contacts with Cabinet members of the EU Commission on matters of mutual interest. Also, the Bank cooperates with EU institutions (mostly Commission Directorates-General (DGs)) in designing policy guidelines and training programs for senior management. Since 2008, the WB office in Brussels has undergone several major restructurings, which point to the increased relevance of the cooperation between the Union, as a collective entity, and the Bank. First, a position for a World Bank Special Representative to the European Union institutions, Belgium and Luxemburg has been created, also in charge of relations with other Brussels-based institutions, such as NATO. Second, since the closing of the Joint WB–Commission Office for South-East Europe Reconstruction in December 2008 (whose implications are anticipated below and further discussed in Chapter 7), the WB Special Representative also participates in the coordination of the activities of the Bank in the newly acceded member countries. The WB Brussels-based office has also expanded to incorporate a section in charge of managing the portion of the GFDRR (Global Facility for Disaster Reduction and Relief) devoted to the ACP partners. Among other locational advantages (Geneva and Brussels-based UN agencies for disaster relief), a substantial contribution worth of 65 mn Euros devoted by the EU to disaster relief in the ACP countries has been a major drive behind this organizational change. In 2012, the Europe 2020 Programmatic Trust Fund provided the European Commission with the Bank's technical assistance and analytical and policy work to achieve the goals of Europe 2020 (Poggi 2017).

The EU and the Bank partner on issues that are both sector-specific and global in reach (such as fighting major diseases), virtually worldwide. Three regions have, however, been the locus of their densest cooperation, under specifically negotiated soft law tools: Europe and Central Asia (ECA), Sub-Saharan Africa (SSA) and the Middle East and North Africa (MENA), as referred to in the World Bank organizational units with regional foci. Since the collapse of the USSR, the Bank has partially redefined its mission in the ECA region, and has become a key partner to the EU in supporting the political and economic transition in post-communist Central and Eastern Europe. The two organizations have been the main providers of technical and financial assistance to the Southern Balkans, where their collaboration is covered by a formal mandate provided by the Stability Pact for South East Europe. As detailed in Chapter 7, a World Bank–EC Joint Office for South East Europe Reconstruction was set up in Brussels from 1999 to 2008.[14] Along with the EU Eastern and Southward enlargements, and parallel to similar evolutions in the Africa region, the EU has set up the WBIF, its own facility to finance development in the Balkans. A transition took place within the Bank as well, as the new EU members were gradually moving out of their borrowing status. Their difficulties in absorbing EU structural funds, however, have pointed toward the enduring relevance of the World Bank as a key partner for the provision of technical assistance to implement post-accession provisions.[15]

While transition and security issues have been at the core of the Bank and EU agendas in the Balkans and Central Europe since the early 1990s, security challenges have accompanied their development efforts in a number of countries in Sub-Saharan Africa and the Middle East and North Africa regions. Conflict-torn states in these areas, as well as extreme poverty levels in SSA, have signaled the potential synergies of coordinating the provision of peace and development incentives.[16] Tackling poverty and insecurity has been a major challenge addressed since the launch of the UN MDGs. The relevance of partnerships among different actors, to support development strategies in fragile and conflict-affected countries has been further reaffirmed by the United Nations in its 2015 SDGs. The EU–WB cooperation in Sub-Saharan countries has significantly progressed in the past ten years, and the two multilaterals have since become the major players in development financing for Africa, jointly providing around half of total ODA flows to that region until recently. Since 2003 their cooperation through the Limelette Process has approached scaling up issues and coordination gaps (World Bank 2007b), and has expanded from earlier adjustment policies and budget support, to include broader strategic goals such as addressing state fragility through the promotion of good governance, and infrastructural development. Compared to efforts from other donors, results in terms of EU and World Bank deliveries have been highly positive. Relations between the two institutions have not been constantly smooth, however, and frictions have emerged on several issues. As discussed in Chapter 9, consistency problems have plagued the EU's approach to the SSA region at different levels, with Brussels' trade strategy representing one of the most critical tests. EU–WB frictions about respective roles and responsibilities in highly fragile countries, such as Zimbabwe and Ethiopia, have exposed the difficulties inherent in the approximation of the two IOs' respective accountability systems. Tension has arisen from differences in role conceptions and expectations with respect to Sub-Saharan Africa, as epitomized by the antagonistic reaction of the World Bank's management to the creation of the EU-AITF (Africa Infrastructure Trust Fund) in 2007. While time will tell in full what are the implications of these role conflicts, the EU's sponsorship provided to new, similar facilities in other regions (with notable progress in the Balkans and Neighborhood), suggests that dynamics of mutual learning, and a growing interpenetration of roles and responsibilities, are certainly underway.

The Southern Mediterranean and Middle Eastern countries are the third major geographical focus of joint EU–Bank efforts. Initiated in 2000 with the Luxemburg Process (a high-level policy dialogue, which also includes the European Investment Bank (EIB) and, with an advisory role, the IMF) the framework was formalized through a Strategic Partnership Agreement in 2004. On that occasion, the EC significantly scaled up its contribution to the MENA region (from less than USD 20 mn in 2003, to more than 120 mn in 2004). The Bank regularly provides technical assistance to the MENA partners, and supports policy reform to promote regulatory convergence within the EU Neighborhood Policy. Across the 2000s, the major recipients of EU support through the Bank's managed Trust Funds in the region have been the oPt (occupied Palestinian territories, West Bank-Gaza) and Iraq. The EU crucially cooperated with the Bank, to support West Bank and Gaza, with USD 65 million in 2004, and USD 120 mn to the Iraq Trust Fund (ITF), to which the Union has been the largest contributor (33% in total ITF).[17] Role and performance aspects of the EU–World Bank cooperation in the Maghreb and in the oPt are analyzed in Chapter 8. In spite of the Union's attempt to project itself as a normative power bloc, its difficulties in achieving geographical and sectoral consistency appear particularly acute in the Maghreb, where Brussels' credibility has been severely tested. However, the issue indicates a broader difficulty to engage with the most resource-rich middle-income countries in the region, which have often been able to set the tune of negotiations with each multilateral, at times playing them off one another. Progress has been achieved however on coordination over budget support in highly fragile countries, particularly the oPt: the two-decade-long learning process has exposed the weaknesses (and potential) of fine tuning between actors backed by radically different accountabilities, yet entrusted with increasingly overlapping mandates, to empower domestic actors in militarized contexts.

2.3 Institutional specificities, common interests and policy complementarities

> Let's not forget, we always say there is a difference between the World Bank and the European Commission. It is a good thing there are differences, or the world would be a sad place. . .but this difference stems principally from the different nature of our institutions. The World Bank is a bank and as such must comply with the imperatives of a bank, with all the rigor this entails. The European Commission is a political body, and so we are afforded a lot more flexibility in regards to intangible principles, so it is a little bit easier for us to take political stands and to express these in our actions than it is for a bank.
>
> Louis Michel, EU Commissioner for Development,
> Brussels, November 15 2006[18]

While sharing a number of goals and cooperating in several thematic and regional areas, the EU and the Bank are different in kind, and have peculiar missions and agendas on multiple counts. Structured along both supranational and intergovernmental features, the EU is a political-economic union, to which MS have delegated authority in different degrees in a variety of internal and external matters. In turn, the World Bank is the major multilateral organization in the business of lending for development. Composed by states, it operates through intergovernmental procedures, whereby – formally – majoritarian decision making occurs along an asymmetric, constituency-based voting system. The voting power of MS is allocated on the basis of a periodically revised framework that accounts, inter alia, for each member's contributed resources over the total of pooled resources (shares), as well as for the economic weight of each MS in the global system.[19]

A first key difference lies in the complex nature of the EU's mission, vis à vis the – relatively – thinner nature of the World Bank's – allegedly a-political – mission. While the World Bank pursues a set of diversified development-related goals, its core activities have traditionally revolved around the provision of loans and technical assistance to help client countries achieve their own development targets, short of political goals. On the contrary, the Union aims at goals that are explicitly political in nature. As a Senior Bank Official conveniently put it, 'while the EU can and should talk about preferred political systems in partner countries, the Bank cannot and should not. . .we are an economic institution, with primarily economic goals'.[20] Official goals however do not rule out that processes and tools embody political elements. Studies from different literatures have shown how politics was at the heart of the creation of the two Bretton Woods institutions, and persists in their everyday operations, from lending decisions to project-planning, implementation and evaluation.[21] What matters here is, however, the relative difference between the Bank and the Union. While the EU is formally called to attach political conditionalities to the concession of its grants, the Bank cannot condition its lending to the pursuit of explicitly political goals. In practice it has done so several times in the past, most blatantly during the Cold War years. Later on, the tensions inherent in its role as development-through-good governance-promoter have exposed the increasingly political nature of its decisions, even absent an attribution of formal competences to that end. Clashes between the Bank's supposedly neutral role and the political nuances involved in its projects and programs have not been the norm, however. Indeed, the Bank has often stuck to its original, technical and financial mandates, revealing the difficulty of coherently supporting simultaneous economic and political changes, as shown by the cases of Haiti and Rwanda, or by one of the most quoted 'success cases', Angola. There, lending has occurred despite high levels of corruption and well-known violations of basic human rights (Easterly 2007). The tension inherent in the World Bank's roles as an officially neutral lender, on the one side, versus a practically political development agent, on the other, has influenced its relations with the Union, at times causing frictions over the continuation of channeling under conditions of high political risk, a theme analyzed in the second part of this book. However contested, the World Bank's role as a financial intermediary is beyond doubt an evidence of its otherness with respect to the EU's role as an agent of political change through the concession of non-refundable grants.

A second difference pertains to the rules of internal governance of each organization. Intergovernmental criteria guide decision making at the WB Board, where, in spite of the official majority rule, decisions are usually reached by consensus among Executive Directors (EDs who represent the interests of their respective constituencies, formed by shareholder states, or of their state, in single-state constituencies). In turn, supranational criteria inform selected EU policies, with unanimity coexisting along qualified majority voting (QMV), in areas of exclusive EU external competence. While the relative stability of the EU supranational components from the push and pull of its MS varies across policies (and issues), the Union does in fact retain external unified powers in several development-related policy areas (such as trade, fisheries and agriculture).

A third element, strictly linked to the previous one, concerns the actors that operate under each institutional umbrella. True to its inter-governmental origins, the World Bank formally acknowledges as shareholders only states. Management and staff play a key role in the Bank's decision making – with varying degrees of relevance, as hypothesized in the delegation and constructivist literatures. Their weight on the adoption of specific programs and projects is formally subordinated to that of top-level decisions taken by the Boards (Governors and Executive Directors). The role of Civil Society Organizations and other non-state external players on the World Bank actions has grown significantly in the past 15 years, yet it had been close to nil until then. Differently, citizens and social groups formally enter the EU arena to debate the handling of domestic (EU) and external matters at several institutional levels, primarily through the European Parliament, but also via a number of other channels.

Table 2.4 The European Union and the World Bank: actors, goals, decision making processes and 'core business' activities in development policymaking

	Actors	*Mission goals*	*Internal decision making processes*	*'Core business' in development promotion*
EU	• Member states • EU institutions • EU citizens	• Composite (including explicit political goals) • Complex (internal-external reach)	• Mixed (Intergov-Supranational) • Unanimity, QM	• Financial assistance through grants (coordination with other EU policy areas) • Policy dialogue towards development aims
WB	• Member states	• Multiple, but formally a-political • Mainly external (even if internal organizational changes-adjustment)	• Inter-governmental • Consensus ('in the shadow of majority')	• Financial support to development through loans; • Knowledge provision (analytical, policy work); • Technical assistance

Fourth, along with knowledge and technical assistance, the Bank provides loans to finance projects in client countries, while the EU has traditionally focused on supplying financial assistance through its Commission-sponsored grants, in the broader context of Brussels' policies and dialogue with partner countries. The different streams of accountabilities arising between grant-recipients and donors, on the one side, and borrowers and lenders, on the other, have obvious implications on the triangular relations that occur among the two organizations and partner countries, as well as, ultimately, on the cooperation between the EU and the Bank.

The synthetic comparison presented above returns a static picture of two separate organizations. Reality-checks on the evolution of the EU–World Bank interaction via the role played by the EU MS at the Board is the subject of the next chapter, which approaches the topic of high-level informal cooperation adopting a dynamic perspective. Prior to that, however, the relations between the two organizations are investigated through the formal umbrella under which the EU's channeling through the WB TF system takes place, the major formal basis for the EU–WB cooperation, the Framework Agreement.

2.4 The Framework Agreement: institutional constraints, perceptions and practice

Signed first on November 1, 2001, to regulate the EU–WB financial cooperation, the Trust Funds and Cofinancing Framework Agreement was first revised in 2003. On March 20, 2009, a new FA was signed, to incorporate the changes that had occurred within the Bank (particularly the new Trust Fund Management Framework (TFMF) of 2007[22]) and the Union (namely its modified Financial Regulations and Implementing Rules of 2007, applicable to cooperation between the Commission and International organizations under joint management mode).

Responding to EU concerns expressed on the occasion of the 2006 discharge procedure by the EP Committee on Budget Control (Cocobu), EuropeAid addressed performance gaps in the channeling from the EC general budget through IOs[23] particularly highlighting problems of control, visibility and transparency on beneficiaries (EuropeAid 2010).[24] Following suit, the Commission made it a priority to define its own monitoring systems over the management of EU funds ('control'), building it on four main elements: compliance analysis, verification, reporting by the implementing organizations, and internal reporting (idem, 11–12).[25]

Lagging behind achievements on monitoring in EU–UN relations, where a common Terms of Reference had been agreed, the definition of shared verification terms in EU–WB relations has been a work-in-progress. Since the Cocobu complaint in 2006, the EU has openly appreciated the difficulty of singling out EC funds from resources provided by other donors to World Bank Trust Funds, by agreeing that verifications can be implemented only on the global budget. The Bank received Brussels' decision as a genuine understanding of the Bretton Woods IFIs' universal mission, and reciprocated by agreeing to receive on-the-spot checks and to provide timely information to EC officers and Auditors.[26] In turn, the Commission suggested further improvements for the EU–WB cooperation in monitoring common projects, within the context of its Multi Donor Monitoring (MDM) Missions. The Bank has made progress to meet the EU requests of more timely and transparent provision of information on how funds are spent and missions carried out in the field. Envisaged since 2000, verification missions have in practice substituted for vertical accountability ties, which would not have been appropriate given the absence of EU shareholding rights in the World Bank's Board.

Frictions have lingered, however, about respective boundaries and responsibilities. The Bank has lamented a 'scope creep', showing some uneasiness at the EU's insistence in requesting documentation from the Bank during verification missions, and in retaining it legally responsible for such provision, when in fact the Bank regarded implementing agencies in partner governments as the ultimately responsible agents for implementation.[27] Alleged impediments to full disclosure of information on cost of World Bank staff, on the side of the EU, and on privacy regulations on staff salaries, on the side of the World Bank, have complicated the matter further. Verification missions correspond in practice to a mix between the – legally not viable – audit (in fact a function already included in the 'Four pillars exercise', which entitles the Union to launch missions with the European Court of Auditors to improve its own understanding of the World Bank's system of accountability, not to perform audit per se), and result monitoring exercises, also performed through ROMs (Result Oriented Missions). Clearly leaning towards the latter, confidential inputs from Commission's sources suggested that a stronger focus on results be pursued, noting how excessive emphasis on access to information on salaries of WB personnel had diverted EU energies and time towards peripheral issues (Interview June 2011). Other voices from the Commission noted how, in spite of the quoted divergences, 'verification as an audit in disguise' provided evidence of efforts from both ends to strengthen cooperation through linguistic stratagems (ibid.).

Control by the Union on how its funds are spent when channeled through WB-managed trust funds has been also performed through reports, prepared by both World Bank and independent specialists. However, controversies have occurred over WB delays in submitting operational reports, as well as on their quality (Annual Consultation European Commission–World Bank Group 2010, 7). The Commission has responded by developing its own tools, such as Result Oriented Monitoring Programs, to assess the effectiveness of projects financed through its grants, be it through the Bank or other development agencies.[28] In turn, the Bank, the first IO to adopt a Results Measurement System in 2003, has since then enhanced its accountability system through multiple endeavors, such as the Open Data Initiative and Access to Information Policy,[29] and the Corporate Scorecard (IMF–WB Development Committee 2011). The emphasis on performance and results has encouraged a multitude of organizational innovations at the Bank since the Washington Consensus years. The establishment of the Quality Assurance Group (QAG) in 1996, the creation of the Integrity Department (INT) in 2001 (now Integrity Vice-Presidency (INT VP)), the many reforms of the IEG (OED until 2004), the said inauguration of the TFMF in 2007, and the reform of the Results Framework, are all cases in point.[30]

While the overall context of the EU–World Bank relations remained generally cooperative in the 2000s, particularly in light of their joint efforts in the Paris–Accra process on increasing aid effectiveness, joint monitoring exercises and verification missions have continued to be sensitive issues. Both impinge on aspects that are perceived as falling within the remit of organizational benchmarks which the WB has being autonomously setting and improving for a long while. Over time they have been the object of subsequent clarifications. The World Bank complained that the Terms of Reference of some of these EU verification missions ('checks' in official documents) reiterated procedural steps that pertained to compliance analysis already performed, and included requests of information from local WB offices that was already available from HQ in Washington. The Bank also noted how, at times, these missions doubled its own checks conducted through the INT VP on fraud and corruption issues in Bank-managed projects.[31]

While welcoming the EC initiative on joint monitoring, the Bank has also drawn attention on the 'difficulties of harmonizing the monitoring systems in use by the two institutions', recalling 'its legal obligations towards all donors', its 'own results framework and performance indicators' as well as confidentiality issues that would arise as EU monitoring missions are usually performed by external consulting firms (Annual Consultation European Commission–World Bank Group 2010, Operational Conclusions, 2–3). Progress in this area has involved the identification of focal points, the sharing of monitoring reports and dialogue on results, as well as the selection of a limited number of pilot projects to be monitored jointly under the MDM approach (idem, 3).

In turn, the EU's tightening on the Bank has gone beyond control issues. The Cocobu concerns expressed during the 2006 discharge procedure also touched on the 'visibility of EU funds when implementing external aid via other organisations' (European Commission 2008, 8). According to the EP Committee, 'the visibility, political guidance and possibility of control by the Commission of international trust funds (where the EU is a major donor) should be strengthened, without compromising the effectiveness of action in this field' (idem, 56). The EP also welcomed the possibility that an increase in the visibility of EU-financed actions through international trust funds occur for transfers from the EU budget above one billion Euros (ibid.). In turn, the Commission took up the matter and signed an action plan on visibility in 2006, working on joint guidelines with the UN and the World Bank, respectively. With respect to the latter, an Interpretive Letter was signed by the then RELEX Commissioner Ferrero-Waldner and the then WB President Wolfowitz, to clarify the scope of the visibility clauses in the 2001 and 2003 versions of the FA, and to ameliorate the course of actions for 'improving public understanding of the role of the Parties in cofinanced operations' (European Commission DG RELEX–World Bank Interpretative Letter on the visibility clause of the Framework Agreement 2006, 1). Two years after the first interpretive letter was signed, the World Bank raised concerns on its vague (too general) and confusing provisions, asking the Commission to work on a revised version. In the course of the May 2008 Annual Consultations, the Commission brought to the attention of World Bank representatives that WB disagreement on the Joint Visibility Guidelines (JVG) proposed by the EC (drafted along the template of a similar document agreed with the UN) would have caused problems with the EP, before whom then RELEX Commissioner Waldner was expected to report by September of that year on EC channeling to UN and WB Trust Funds, respectively. Eventually, both parties agreed on Joint Visibility Guidelines in May 2009, after the revised Framework Agreement was signed in March of that year.

On the one side, the 2009 FA clarified the direct obligation that, under the EU Manual (Communication and Visibility Manual for EU External Actions of April 2008), governments in partner countries had on communication and visibility activities in the field, thus shielding the World Bank from formal responsibility on the matter. On the other side, the Bank pledged to enhance the visibility of EC contributions in parallel co-financing, where the two organizations coordinated their actions but relied on different programs, managed by their respective agencies. Relative to EU visibility in World Bank administered Multi Donor Trust Funds, where the resources from Brussels are pooled with those provided by other donors, more detailed criteria have been spelled out, even if discretion and flexibility are assumed, to account for the multi-party nature of these financing instruments and the peculiar conditions that may apply in specific cases (EC–WBG Joint Visibility Guidelines 2009, 2–3). Early virtuous instances of cooperative actions in ensuring visibility to EC support have been the IRRF (International Reconstruction Fund Facility for Iraq), the Trust Fund for Aceh, and the Multi Donor Fund and the Java Reconstruction Trust fund in Indonesia.

Progress on EU visibility in EU–WB joint efforts is without doubt to be welcomed under multiple counts. As discussed in detail in Chapters 10 (MENA), 11 (Africa), and 12 (Conclusions), however, the debate on visibility should be considered against a broader background. Key elements that enter such a picture are the EU internal constraints (namely its inter-institutional and vertical accountability ties) as well as aid- and context-specific variables, such as the role of the Bank in multi-donor trust funds and the degree of fragility of partner countries. The latter has often spelled a preference for less, instead of more, visibility, also from the Commission's side.

Verification, along with transparency issues related to information on beneficiaries, and visibility of the EU's contribution to WB managed trust funds have continued to be among the most contentious issues between the EU (Commission and EP) and the World Bank management in recent years. In some cases, the institutional differences constraining cooperation have been overcome through practical solutions outside the scope of the Framework Agreement. Based on incremental learning, these adjustments have often led to higher accountability in channeling and better focused results.[32] Further progress has occurred via signing a new FA in 2014, later amended in 2016, to incorporate the new cost recovery policy and the new social and environmental safeguards adopted by the World Bank Group (FA 2016). In parallel, however, the EU has ventured a more independent course, developing in-house solutions to pool and deliver aid, via the launch of the Africa Infrastructure Trust Fund (EU-AITF) (Chapter 9). The Board of the WBIF, the blending facility set up by the EU for the Western Balkans along the lines of the EU-AITF, has later welcomed the World Bank among its associate partners, indicating that the interpenetration between the parallel sets of EU- and WB-led governance structures in fiduciary facilities is very much a two-way process. The evolution of these dynamics is tied to region – and policy specific – conditions, as discussed in Chapters 7 and 9. Its implications for the EU–WB relations, and, more generally for the interaction between large multilaterals, however, is worth considering further. The issue is taken up in the section below, which reconsiders the interplay between the different types of accountability flows discussed above, to conceptualize the EU–World Bank 'relevant' intersected space.

2.5 When multilaterals coordinate: the curse and the blessing of imperfect overlapping

The IR literature on delegation has mostly focused on the relation between an IO and its MS as proximate principals.[33] According to realists, endogeneity of interests between the two makes it particularly problematic to disentangle the influence of an IO's post-agreement behavior from the preferences, interests and actions of its members (Stone 2009). More plausibly, correlation between an IO's behavior and the interests of its members is a matter of degrees (Mitchell 2009). To address the matter, IR institutionalists have applied the PA framework to the analysis of delegation of authority to international institutions by sovereign states (Pollack 1997; Keohane and Martin 2003; Nielson and Tierney 2003 and 2005; Hawkins et al. 2006).[34]

Studying the interactions between separate IOs, in turn, widens the analytical focus to specific inter-organizational spaces, which are normally further partitioned, and whose components may operate simultaneously, often according to different logics. The EU and the World Bank's memberships overlap only in part. All EU MS are also shareholders to the Bank, where they represent their national interests, as mediated through the Bank's constituency system. Yet, within the EU, development cooperation is a shared competence, between Brussels and the MS. At the Board, then, the EU 'interacts' with the World Bank via its MS, which are in fact currently scattered across eight different constituencies (three of which are single-country). Absent EU's formal principality rights at the World Bank's Board, PA templates may appear a weak tool to study the relations between the two organizations. In practice, even if the EU is not a shareholder of the Bank, there are multiple mechanisms through which the former holds the latter accountable.

First, through the concerted behavior of its EDs in the Eurogroup, Brussels has an opportunity to exert informal principality rights at the Board.[35] The benefits of applying a PA framework to the analysis of the EU's role at the World Bank are obvious from a pro-EU policy perspective (Bini Smaghi 2004, 2006 on the EU at the IMF). In shared-competence matters such as development cooperation, or exclusive competence matters that are development-related, such as trade and agriculture, the Union, through either the Commission, the Parliament or, though more distantly, the European Court of Justice (ECJ), is a potential source of monitoring on its MS to ensure that their behavior at the Board is consistent with the EU general mandates (European Parliament, Council, Commission 2006). The relevance of coordinated action between EU institutions and MS, as well as their joint responsibility in carrying over the implementation of the SDGs along the Addis Ababa Action Agenda (AAAA), has been recently spelled out in the 2017 Consensus on Development. With respect to matters discussed at the Board that fall into the 'shared' area of development competencies,[36] and given that there is no formal standing for the Union at the Bank, the EDs, advisors and alternates from the 28 member countries should in principle behave as the EU's collective agent. In all those cases MS would be required 'to align their external obligations with the Community [now Union] framework' (Bini Smaghi 2006, 274).

Second, for the EU EDs, the duty to cooperate on EU-relevant items at the Board appears particularly significant in light of the volume of EU resources channeled to the Bank. Institutionalized since the 2011 FA, the participation of the EU institutions to the Bank's financing through the TF track has generated a second flow of accountabilities, in addition to the flow based on informal EDs coordination within the Eurogroup. Yet, the nature and implications of each set of accountabilities are substantially different from one another. While showing features that have been analyzed in the IR institutionalist literature on delegation, the two accountability strands do not exactly fit the assumptions of classic PA models.

Collective principality issues (Nielson and Tierney 2009) interact with problems of multiple principality at several levels, complicating the automatic transmission of a compact set of interests by a principal to 'its' agent.[37] The Bank operates on behalf of shareholding member states, which, while in principle deciding through majority voting at the Board, often have heterogeneous preferences and belong to different groupings, inside the Bank (via the constituency system), and in the world outside. The extent to which external groupings are reflected in the Bank's internal dynamics has varied across groups and time (Woods 2006; Woods and Lombardi 2006). In the past, the World Bank's programs have accommodated several intersecting agendas, with overlapping interests at times deviating from the observable 'borrower vs lender' cleavage. 'Western vs others', 'emerging markets vs industrialized countries' dichotomies, and other, sector and project-specific splits have added to the 'EU vs non-EU' cleavage under investigation here.

World Bank EDs are simultaneously agents of member states (through their accountability to the respective national Ministers in the Board of Governors) and, via the input they receive from respective Governors, principals to the Bank's management and staff.[38] Their appointment may depend either on constituency-specific selection criteria (for multi-state constituencies) or on the designation by relevant MS (which, in the case of the EU single-country constituencies has applied to the German, French and – ahead of Brexit – British ED posts). Thus, the World Bank's EDs are responsible for both guidance on the achievement of Bank-wide organizational goals and for the pursuit of their constituency and state's interests. These incentive systems further contribute to increase the tension inherent in the EDs' dual allegiance, under both accountability and effectiveness profiles. The physical and financial incentive structure that World Bank's EDs face while in service (they sit in World Bank's offices in DC Headquarters, and their salaries are paid by the World Bank) has spelt a low independence from top managers and staff inputs, which has implied a weakening in their supervisory role over the Bank's management (Woods 2001).

Such management capture syndrome may in principle be common to all the EDs, arguably varying by the number of MS, shares and voting power retained by each constituency. The behavior of the Union's EDs at the Board, however, also takes on the said EU-dimension, based on the shared nature of the competence on development policy in the EU Treaties. However, different from the IMF, where the EU has an observer status, and where EU MS must necessarily deal with the implications of a single currency, in the WB Board the absence of a formal EU representation is also matched by a low degree of uniformity in tools and goals between Brussels and EU MS.

Thus, while principality problems of development IOs have been addressed through refined applications of the delegation literature (Lyne et al. 2006), the EU–WB relations embody a complex mix of formal and informal, vertical and horizontal features, that cannot be entirely understood through the sole lens of PA templates. Bargaining over respective duties and prerogatives is, to a large extent, a daily business in inter-organizational relations. A major difference from doing so in a primarily hierarchical setting (as member states' representatives do with IO managements) is that, in the case of the EU–World Bank inter-organizational space, discussions between the two organizations often occur about the precise definition of those very ties, and about the context within which they occur. Relative to the TF track, the EU–World Bank relation has not originated from a vertical mandate, from sovereign states to a newly constituted intergovernmental agency, but from an – ongoing – negotiated deal between two separate international organizations.

The hybrid nature of delegation between the EU and the Bank in part stems from, and in turn is projected onto, their different missions, interests and incentive systems. The template of a shirking agent whose interests partly diverge from those of its principal, an assumption of PA models, cannot properly account for the EU–World Bank relation. Interest divergence is, in this case, a built-in feature. The goals of the two organizations overlap only in part, as a few institutionally codified interests have not coincided *ab origine* (the WB formally neutral vs the 'complex, and explicitly political mix' of EU goals). Further to the point, the a-political mandate of the World Bank has served as a credibility-enhancing mechanism for the continuation of EU's channeling in highly fragile contexts. Yet, the EU choice to channel through the WB TF system has generated the typical pathologies of delegation to highly independent agents (Majone 2001), as shown by the tensions about lending in weakly institutionalized contexts, investigated in Chapters 8 (MENA) and 9 (Sub-Saharan Africa).

Thus, the institutional accountability stemming from the (hierarchical) delegation of authority from states to high level bureaucrats in IOs that were created by the former, in the first place, should not be confused with accountability arising from a contract between a donor and an implementing organization – where the donor has neither played a foundational role nor enjoys a formal stance in the internal governance of the implementing agency (but may have fragmented voice rights in the boards of facilities run by that agency). The reference is to accountability ties originating from agreements with donors that are not subscribers to the Bank. They are usually allowed explicitly circumscribed monitoring rights, relative to the fulfillment of provisions that are agreement-specific. In the case of the EU–World Bank relations, the FA features a relatively wide range of mutual accountabilities, which are specified through ad hoc Administration Agreements (AAs). Relative to the TF track the relation between the EU and the Bank has an explicitly contractual, and therefore horizontal, nature (Williamson 1985). The latter technically 'shirks' only with respect to what is contained in each specific TF Administration Agreement, and the same applies to the former in its agreed duties, depending on how reciprocal rights and obligations have been negotiated within each set of contracts (FA and AA).[39] As a result, WB managed-TFs add 'a set of parallel accountabilities' to the 'Bank's mainstream accountabilities framework' (IEG 2011, 49).

The interaction between the Bank's mainstream (hierarchically delegated) accountabilities framework to its trust-funded (horizontally contracted) activities has admittedly influenced the organization's programs and specific results. Yet it has not been explored in its own merit beyond the level of policy reports or project/sector technical evaluations. As discussed above about the advantages and disadvatages of non-core ODA, donor-dedicated accountabilities, specific to different trust-fund types, require additional efforts to ensure results that are at once financially viable and development-effective. Compared to the vertical-delegating nature of the relation between the EU MS and World Bank's management, however, the horizontal-contractual component of either the FA and AAs has enhanced the potential for innovation from either side. Costs and benefits of contracting versus hierarchical delegation generally depend on delegated tasks and sectors ('market conditions' in the language of transaction costs literature), even if studies about contracting under anarchy have proven several drawbacks of that practice in security and development-related security issues (Singer 2003; Cooley 2010).

To the mixture of sector- and project-specific advantages and disadvantages of either strategy, one must add the impact of the multiple roles covered by the EU in its relations with the Bank. While being formally a contracting 'governor' (Avant, Finnemore and Sell 2010) under the FA and relevant AAs, the EU does not have an equally formalized position as a principal, not being a party to the Articles of Agreement. As discussed throughout the volume, however, the contractual accountability stream and the (indirect, mediated) hierarchical accountability-through MS stream have intersected at different junctures in the policy practice. Conflicting claims have emerged, as well as blames of poor legitimacy and effectiveness, particularly visible on the side of EU citizens and advocacies, but also symmetrically traceable in the World Bank's views on the Union's performance.

Terminological mix-ups on the role of the World Bank (trustee vs fiscal agent) and about each actor's preferred definition of monitoring, verification and accountability processes have unveiled differences between the two organizations' respective missions, structures and practices. Frictions have developed between WB local offices and EU delegations, as discussed in Chapters 7, 8 and 9. Quarrels have also originated from divergences between the two high managements on what should be intended as each organization's legitimate scope of action. At times definitional struggles have led to partial exit options, as in the case of the EU's launch of the AITF. Overall, these tensions have had an impact on the EU's and World Bank's own role conceptions and expectations as development providers. On the one side, EU–WB consultations on the multiple amendments of the Framework Agreement witness strengthened communication and better structured relations. On the other side, they reveal a stricter approach to inspecting respective behaviors on critical issues, and a heightened risk of disagreement about when and how to cooperate.

2.6 Conceptualizing hybrid delegation: the multiple accountabilities between the EU and the World Bank

From a theoretical standpoint, investigating the interaction between two multilaterals that partially intersect requires widening the focus beyond codified relations between formal shareholders and managements, to answer core questions such as 'Who is accountable to whom, how and to what effect?', and to define appropriate criteria to separate formal shareholders and legitimate stakeholders from other affected entities and people. Cosmopolitans, institutionalists and realists have elaborated a variety of frameworks to investigate accountability issues in the governance structures of an increasingly globalized world. In turn, conceptual variety has connected with development-substantive discussions. In the 'legitimacy vs effectiveness debate' on IOs' governance, privileging either the input or the output dimension of legitimacy (either the democratic side of representativeness or the pragmatic side of performance, respectively),[40] has led scholars to very different normative views on accountability.

Seminal institutionalist insights have drawn the line between internal and external accountability (Keohane 2003, 141–142). Applied to IOs, the former refers to principality identified in authorizing and funding sources that operate under a formal institutional umbrella (for our purpose, the intergovernmentally pacted deal among states, which creates, finances and provides legitimacy to a multilateral agent). In world politics, the remaining portion of relations, a much broader and thicker residual, is left to (potential claims of) external accountability, which is based on the claimed control and sanctioning rights by 'people' that are 'outside the acting entity', but are significantly affected by its actions.[41] Relevant for interacting IOs that have partially overlapping memberships, Keohane's concept of external accountability highlights the role of informal methods of control, based on power, influence and reputational mechanisms:

> To develop a theory of external accountability, it may be necessary to construct a theory of the duties that parties owe to one another in a poorly institutionalized but increasingly globalized world.
>
> (Keohane 2003, 142)

> . . .in the absence of a constitutional system, the ability to avoid being held externally accountable can be viewed as one dimension of power.
>
> (Ibid.)

World Bank MS provide both authorization and support to the organization,[42] with formal accountability due from bureaucracies (management and staff) to the national representatives (EDs, for the day-to-day practice, Governors, for the top-political decisions, twice a year), along a vertical chain of delegation. Brussels has no stance in the official delegation of authority to the Bank, which is based on the Articles of Agreement, negotiated by MS prior to the very creation of the European Community. Yet, the EU's role may approximate that of an informal shareholder, or, in Keohane's words, a 'would-be principal' (idem, 140). When meaningful and impactful, the coordination of the EU MS at the Board, through the Eurogroup, approximates a type of quintessentially internal control, if yet indirect, on the Bank's conformity to implementing mandates incorporating EU-specific interests. Coordination among EU EDs is, by definition, mediated and informal, which renders what is usually the agreed nature of formal PA relations subject to high context-specific uncertainty.

On the other side, the EU–WB relations in the TF track, formalized in the Framework Agreement and related AAs, return the picture of a principal (EU) authorizing its agent (WB) in the use of allocated funds (non-core resources), to precise ends and under specified conditions. In fact, in addition to the cleavage between formal and informal ties, a key element in Keohane's differentiation between internal and external accountability, the EU–World Bank relations possess other relevant characteristics, that make them peculiar under other respects.

The formalization of reciprocal rights and duties on the utilization of non-core ODA occurs on an essentially *ad hoc* basis, through a multitude of Administrative Agreements. Thus, the EU's legitimate claim to hold the Bank accountable on the matters regulated in the FA and AAs must pass through each TF Board, with monitoring and supervision actions concerted with other major donors to each specific fund (pluralistic accountability). Institutionalized control by the EU thus does not occur through the regular shareholders' rights to vote in the Board, but through the fragmented channels of the Trust fund system. In the latter, accountability between the EU and the Bank is formal but external: the two organizations are parties to an agreement (the FA), but neither has a formal stance in the other's representative bodies, the stream of reciprocal rights and duties being scattered across the many AAs. Additionally, and different from cases of 'foundational' delegation from MS to newly created IOs, which are essentially hierarchical, FA rights and duties have been negotiated and mutually agreed by the EU and the World Bank as two equal contracting parties.

Overall, as recapitulated in Table 2.5, these inter-institutional accountabilities approximate a hybrid, between formal and informal types, internal and external, vertical and horizontal, direct and mediated ties. This has not kept the Union (mostly upon pressure from the Commission and the EP on EU EDs, but also in management-to-management relations) from holding the Bank accountable as a whole (as opposed to instances of limited agency failure in specific trust fund management) on several occasions. In practice, as discussed in section 2.4, the EU has claimed special rights, due to the magnitude of its channeling to most World Bank multi-donor TFs, constantly bargaining over the shape and size of each organization's respective rights and duties. Since 2003, the EU has enhanced its informal influence at the World Bank's Board through the Eurogroup: while the unofficial nature of such influence limits its potential as an indicator of internal accountability, its impact in principled terms makes it more visible, and plausibly more strategic, compared to

Table 2.5 Hybrid delegation between the EU and the World Bank

Board	*Trust fund system*
Informal	Formal
Vertical (MS to IO)	Horizontal (IO to IO)
Internal (EU MS also MS to WB)	External (EU and WB as separate IOs)
Mediated (via coordination of EU MS)	Direct

the official monitoring exerted by Brussels in highly technical issues on the management of specific trust funds.

2.7 Conclusions

Detailing how the differences and overlaps in each organization's institutional design have impacted on the EU–WB relations, the chapter has conceptualized them through selected concepts from the institutionalist toolbox of contract and delegation models. More particularly, the EU–WB relations have been analyzed here focusing on the interaction between their two distinct delegation systems, which overlap primarily through partially shared membership at the high level, but also relate to each other through a parallel set of contractual, largely ad hoc accountabilities. While broadly regulated under a single Framework Agreement, they happen to be carried out often in non-routinized ways via the various Administrative TF agreements. The interplay of these multiple sets of loyalties approximates the case of the EU–World Bank relations to a mixture of hierarchical and horizontal features, pointing to a hybrid delegation scheme between two distinct, yet largely intermixed, multilaterals.

The institutional context of the EU–WB relations has been reconstructed in this chapter largely abstaining from diachronic considerations. Time should however be explicitly factored in, to make sense of the role played by policy and perceptual variables, discussed in Chapters 3 and 4, respectively. Institutional change has enjoyed a distinguished position in scholarly research on the EU, particularly considering the fluidity with which rules and mechanisms for external action have evolved through time (Nuttall 2005; Carbone 2008). In turn, the book argues that EU–World Bank relations, and the EU's performance at the World Bank, have also been influenced by policy changes occurring within the World Bank. In the next chapter, the evolution in the EU's approach to development policymaking is discussed, and connected to the broader transformation towards the post-Washington Consensus that had been taking place inside the Bank. The shifts in the two organizations' rule systems, the Lisbon treaty of 2009, on the one side, and the World Bank's 'voice and participation reform' of 2008–2010, are then investigated, and their implications discussed, for the EU's representation at the World Bank's Board, and for the EU–WB cooperation in promoting development across the world.

Notes

1 Preamble to the EEC Treaty (1957).
2 Ibid.
3 Net ODA Disbursement, OECD International Development Statistics (last revised June 2017, data for 2016 preliminary). Data on the EU includes contributions from EU non-DAC, non-OECD MS when these are reported in the OECD data, which may be different from Commission Data – which includes data reported from statistical agencies of EU MS.
4 IBRD, IDA (International Development Association), IFC (International Finance Corporation), MIGA (Multilateral International Guarantee Agency) and ICSID (International Centre for Settlement of Investment Disputes) constitute The World

Bank Group (WBG). Through the provision of loans, guarantees, risk management products and analytical and advisory services they share a common commitment to reduce poverty, increase shared prosperity and promote sustainable development. The IBRD lends to middle and low income-creditworthy countries, while IDA provides virtually interest-free loans and grants to the poorest countries.

5 In 2013, and in order to end extreme poverty, the then President Jim Yong Kim set for the WBG the goal of decreasing 'the percentage of people living with less than $1.90 a day to no more than 3 percent by 2030'. To promote shared prosperity, the WBG endorsed the goal of 'promoting income growth of the bottom 40 percent of the population in each country' (World Bank 2013).

6 See United Nations (2000). Since 2002, the Joint World Bank–IMF Ministerial Committee on Development has played a crucial monitoring function with respect to the UN MDGs. Starting in 2004, the IMF and World Bank have issued yearly Global Monitoring Reports on the progress being made in achieving the MDGs. While being a joint WB–IMF effort, the reports have been prepared with close cooperation from the UN, the WTO, the DAC at OECD and the EU Commission.

7 While under special conditions the IMF also borrows from official lenders, its operations are mainly financed through the quotas subscribed by MS.

8 Conceptualized below in this chapter, the Eurogroup's role and its influence on decision making at the WB Board is empirically investigated in Section 6 of Chapter 5, within the framework for performance analysis presented there.

9 See OECD (2010, 14) DAC Report on Multilateral Aid, on core and non-core channeling through multilaterals in general, and Woods (2006, 194) on core channeling through the World Bank.

10 ADE (2008, Vol. I, 31).

11 Most of the funded activities may be summarized in four main categories: debt relief, government budget funding; technical assistance (TA), training and capacity building, and, last, commodities, equipment and infrastructure (ADE 2008, Inventory Note, 47–48).

12 ADE (2008, Vol. I, 22).

13 The World Bank Brussels Office was created in 1996 to improve cooperation with the EU institutions.

14 World Bank Brussels Office (2007a), 'The World Bank in Brussels', prepared by the World Bank Office in Brussels, http://www.worldbank.org/eu. Additional information on the World Bank–EC Joint Office for South East Europe Reconstruction can be found at www.seerecon.org (Accessed February 2008).

15 In 1998, a Memorandum of Understanding (MoU) was signed between the Bank and the European Commission (EC), along with other IFIs to cover project co-financing in pre-accession countries. Since 2005 the MoU has been revised to incorporate Western Balkans and other parties such as the IFC and the Black Sea Trade and Development Bank (World Bank Office in Brussels, quot., p.3).

16 A notable exception to these geographical patterns is the tight cooperation between the EU and the Bank in addressing development, security and fragility issues in Afghanistan. Included in the South Asia regional unit of the World Bank, the country is outside the ACP group, but has been involved in multiple ad hoc development initiatives financed by the Union.

17 See 'The World Bank in Brussels', quot. p.4.

18 Press call. Paul Wolfowitz and EU Commissioner Louis Michel, Brussels, November 15, 2006, accessed at: http://web.worldbank.org/WBSITE/EXTERNAL/NEWS/0,,contentMDK:21131393~menuPK:64255981~pagePK:34370~piPK:34424~theSitePK:4607,00.html

19 See Chapter 3.

20 Author's interview with World Bank's high level official (Washington, 2008). In Article IV, section 5 of the World Bank Articles of Agreement, it is clarified that 'The Bank and its officers shall not interfere in the political affairs of any member; nor shall they

be influenced in their decisions by the political character of the member or members concerned. Only economic considerations shall be relevant to their decisions, and these considerations shall be weighted impartially in order to achieve the purposes stated in Article I'.

21 Seminal contributions on the origins and evolution of the World Bank are Mason and Asher (1973), as well as Kapur, Lewis and Webb (1997). The mainstream view has it that the US preferences prevailed, through the powerful influence of Harry Dexter White – who, albeit much less skilled than the UK representative Keynes, could count on a larger and better equipped delegation, and wield the unrivaled impact of the most powerful nation of that day. Political economy, economic history and IR studies have shown how the early design of the Bretton Woods institutions reflected a number of compromises, both within and between founding states (Woods 2006; Gavin 2004; Ikenberry 1992; Kindleberger 1977). Most ironically, even US left-wing idealists who genuinely believed in a virtuous engagement of all nations in the world economy, contributed to the creation of the Bank, which would later be retained as the domain of global managerialists (once defined 'business internationalists') (Murphy 2008). On the evolution of the relation between development aid and politics, for both multilateral and bilateral agencies, see Carothers and De Gramont (2013).

22 In addition to revising internal control and management processes, the TFMF aims primarily at 'bringing trust funds into the mainstream of Bank's business', i.e. to review and appraise trust-funded activities with the same quality assurance and risk reporting criteria employed in regular Bank lending activities.

23 EU–WB Operational Conclusions, 6th Annual Consultations (2008, 1). An updated list of annual consultations between the two organizations is available at: https://ec.europa.eu/europeaid/node/62749

24 Also see the letters from then Commissioner Waldner (Relex) at http://www.europarl.europa.eu/meetdocs/2004_2009/documents/dv/letter_ferrero_waldner/Letter_Ferrero_Waldneren.pdf and then Director Richelle (Aidco) at http://www.europarl.europa.eu/meetdocs/2004_2009/documents/dv/aidco_followup_note_to_cocobu/AIDCO_followup_Note_to_Cocobuen.pdf

25 Reporting from each organization and internal reporting have been substantially improved (the former through increased regularity, precision and specificity, the latter through a better matching of contracts in respective EU and WB information systems). Progress has occurred also on verification: 'In line with the EC [now EU] financing rules and procedures, the agreements with UN and WB provide for the Commission and the European Court of Auditors to carry out checks, including on the spot, in order to acquire an understanding of the organisation's system of accountability.' Seven out of a total 40 verification missions were carried out on WB-managed contributions in 2009, and nine out of 54 in 2010 (ibid. 12), with the majority being performed on UN missions, and a residual portion on other agencies' missions.

26 According to the 2009 FA: 'the purpose of such on the spot checks is to allow representatives from the European Union to be in a position to report to their own institution and to the European Parliament on the implementation of Projects and actions and whether value for money has been obtained' (Attachment 3 of the Framework Agreement, Agreement on the verification clause of the EU–World Bank Group Framework Agreement 1).

27 Interviews with EU and World Bank officers (May 2011). Similar concerns have emerged periodically in the Annual Consultations between the Commission and the Bank.

28 According to the updated Annual Consultations between the Commission and the World Bank, different from verification missions, aimed at supervising good financial practices, monitoring missions focus primarily on results based on the five DAC criteria to assess development assistance (relevance, effectiveness, efficiency, impact and sustainability), and are limited to projects above one million Euros (European Commission–World Bank Group 2009, 4–5).

29 Reversing the previous policy, according to which only documents within a positive list of items selected for disclosure would be accessible, the new policy is based on a negative list (mostly relating to personal information, internal deliberations, administrative matters and confidential information from partners or third parties).

30 Created under the presidency of McNamara in 1973, the Operations Evaluation Department (OED), Independent Evaluation Group (IEG) since 2004, was turned into a more independent unit during the 1990s. A major factor behind this change, under the presidency of Jim Wolfensohn, had been the content of the Whapenhans Report that had unveiled a serious deterioration in the share of satisfactorily rated projects. Since 1995, the OED/IEG has also been oversighted by CODE, a Committee on Development Effectiveness at the Executive Board. Overall, however, and in spite of these and other more recent institutional developments, a wide gap between the reformed IEG and its impact on the World Bank's performance has been lamented in the literature, see Weaver (2008).

31 Similar concerns have arisen with respect to overlap between (WB) INT investigations and (EU) ROM missions (European Commission–World Bank Group 2010, 11). Checks performed by its own INT World Bank department have been the object of contention in recent years. In 2007 the Volcker Report was released, an external evaluation commissioned by the World Bank after allegations of fraud and misconduct by some staff members, chaired by former Treasury Secretary Paul Volcker. In spite of the (forced) resignation of former INT VP Folsom in January 2008, it appeared that even conclusions reached in the Volcker Report included 'tainted testimonies' by interviewed staff, who were also targeted after it had been leaked to Folsom that they had provided negative feedbacks to the external evaluators. According to decisions by the World Bank Administrative Tribunal, the Bank was sanctioned to pay 2.5 million USD to staff for damages suffered between 2005 and 2008 under Folsom's Presidency of INT. See GAP–Government Accountability Project (2010) Bar Complaint and references therein.

32 See Chapter 7, on service contracts, and Chapter 8, on merging funds in cash transfer programs for Palestine.

33 Exceptions in the delegation literature on IFIs are Gilbert, Power and Vines (2000), Brett (2003) and Gutner (2005). These contributions have been however quoted critically in Nielson and Tierney (2005, 786), for having modeled borrowing governments in their implementation of development programs as agents on World Bank's mandates. In the opinion of Nielson and Tierney, this would amount to an unnecessary stretching of the meanings of principal and agent concepts: under rigorous PA frameworks, donor-recipient relations occur in the shadow of an explicit hierarchy, which, theoretically, implies the ability of the principal to alter the mandate granted to its agent (with the paradoxical outcome of a lending bank that could go as far as diminishing the sovereignty of a borrowing state). In world politics, and more so at transnational and global levels, the existence of hierarchies, markets and networks is very much a matter of contingency and degrees (Slaughter 2004). Research on the topic has further typologized relationships among 'governors' at the global level through four categories: delegation, contracting, networks and hierarchy (Avant, Finnemore and Sell 2010).

34 The seminal reference, related to delegation by parties in the US Congress, to committees-internally, and bureaucracies-externally, is Kiewiet and McCubbins (1991).

35 The Board's principality on the Bank's management and staff is of a collective nature, and the EU EDs have a duty to consult and coordinate with the other non EU EDs at the Board, to reach a decision (formally along majoritarian but, as seen above, practically consensual rules).

36 Typical cases are development cooperation in ACP countries, as well as other development-related policies, as trade or environmental ones, particularly in the light of the emphasis on coherence enshrined in the EU consensus of 2006.

37 Collective principality refers to situations where 'members. . .cannot act independently from one another but must first solve collective action problems before issuing authoritative directions to their agents. Members collectively hold only a single contract with

the agent, and no individual member of this group can alter the contract unilaterally' (Nielson and Tierney 2009, 4). Multiple principality, on the contrary, applies to cases where each member 'holds a discrete contract with the same agent' (ibid.) and is therefore entitled to alter the contract unilaterally. For the purpose of conceptualizing the EU–WB relations, both types of principality are relevant: collective when the EU MS are considered as agents of the EU, and the EU as a 'would-be' principal of the Bank; multiple relative to the EU contractual relation with the Bank, through the Framework Agreement. Neither the Bank nor the Union are exclusive to each other: even discounting the 'EU anomaly' and the significant collective financing of Commission-cum-MS, the Bank enlists a multiplicity of other donors that operate simultaneously at the Board and through the TF track. In turn, the Union chooses its preferred implementing agencies among a pool of potential candidates, according to their suitability for the project-program under scrutiny.

38 Such dual role of international civil servants accountable to their respective national governments was explicitly envisaged, though for different reasons, by both the US and UK founding plans, as detailed in Mason and Asher (1973, 34) and Keynes (1971–1989, vol.26).

39 More particularly, BETF, Bank-executed trust funds, are those for which the Bank has spending authority, while in RETF (Recipient-executed trust funds), the Bank passes it on to a third recipient party, retaining mainly an appraisal and supervising role (ADE 2008, Vol. II, Annex 6, Clarification note, 1). According to IEG, there were 180 IDA/IBRD trust fund programs, with many represented by a combination of activities, executed by recipients, third parties and World Bank (IEG 2011, 13). FIFs (Financial Intermediary Funds) regroup heterogeneous Trust Funds not covered by either BETF or RETF. Normally featuring complex financial schemes, FIFs are usually set up to finance global partnerships and programs, such as in the GFATM (Global Fund to Fight AIDS, Tuberculosis and Malaria, to which the European Commission has allocated 1.2 bn USD between 2001 and 2013, EU Rapid Press Release, 2010), or HIPC (Highly Indebted Poor Countries Initiative, to which the EC has been the 5th donor, with 1.6 billion Euros pledged between 2000 and 2008; see EuropeAid 2008b, 8). For FIFs' management the Bank generally provides specific administrative or financial services with a limited fiduciary or operational role (ADE 2008, Vol. II, Annex 6, 1).

40 The distinction is made by Scharpf (1999). Dahl differentiates between 'the ability of citizens to exercise democratic control over the decisions of the polity versus the capacity of the system to respond satisfactorily to the collective preferences of its citizens' (1994, 28).

41 Keohane offers separate elaborations on external accountability, depending on whether the analytical category applies to states or to non-state actors (transnational accountability), which includes IOs, regional organizations, NGOs, religious groups and multinational corporations. Specifically, he contends that 'multilateral organizations. . . are subject to accountability claims from almost everybody. . .but. . .they are in fact accountable, through internal processes, only to a few powerful states and the European Union' (2003, 145).

42 Even if, as noted above in Section 2.1 the Bank's ability to raise resources through its lending activity on international markets has left the organization wider autonomy margins, compared to other institutions that are solely, or primarily, funded through the contributions of member states.

3 Comprehensive and coherent

Change and stasis in the EU and the World Bank's policies across the turn of the new millennium

3.1 Introduction

While different on several counts, since the end of the 1990s the EU and the World Bank's missions have increasingly overlapped on numerous dimensions. This chapter first tracks the roots of two core mission and policy changes that have occurred in either organization. It examines the World Bank's 'poverty turn', focusing on the shift from structural adjustment programs (SAPs) to the adoption of the Comprehensive Development Framework (CDF) and Poverty Reduction Strategy Papers (PRSPs) at the end of the 1990s. It then investigates the EU transition from Lomé to Cotonou, leading the launch of the EU 'Brussels Consensus' of 2006. The chapter contends that the consensus that both multilaterals currently share on the need to address development by tackling poverty and governance issues through a comprehensive approach has emerged out of the same material and ideational triggers. In turn, these triggers had been articulated among large OECD donors after the critical events surrounding the debt crisis of the 1980s. The World Bank started to filter critical ideational inputs from its stakeholders after the 1990s, introducing relevant changes in its approach to development promotion. The deepening of the EU–WB interaction, in turn, allowed inter-organizational relations between the two global governors to activate learning dynamics that would have a non-trivial impact on the evolution of the EU's own approach to development assistance; this occurred in the new millennium through the launch of the EU Consensus on development of 2006. Change therefore took place inside both organizations, with respect to mission and policy goals.

Yet, the evidence from the EU Lisbon Treaty of 2009, and the World Bank's 'voice and participation reform' of 2008–2010, indicates that stasis is likely to remain the norm when it comes to upgrading the EU authority in development matters, on the one side, and to reduce the voting power of single EU MS at the World Bank's Board. In those two 'constituent policies' (Lowi 1972), resistance to institutional change, and the permanence of pre-existing higher order rules in both organizations, have most plausibly responded to strategic incentives, occurring along means-to-ends, often state-centered (as opposed to relational and inter-organizational) logics. Different from the transformation in non-constituent policies analyzed here (the 'poverty turn', from SAP-to CDF and PRSPs in the Bank, and the adoption of the Brussels Consensus by the EU, respectively), where reflectivist logics and inter-organizational exchanges played a substantial role, the failure to bring about 'constitutional' change' in the two organizations seems to be better appreciated by resorting to the rationalist toolbox provided by PA models of delegation.[1]

The chapter examines the EU–WB interactions to ascertain the relevance of inter-organizational relations and ideational dynamics in the study of changes in non-constituent politics by global governors operating in the same issue area.[2] It then qualifies the previous finding by investigating two attempts at reforming the governance of the two organizations, arguing that stasis in the institutional design of those multilaterals is better analyzed through rational-choice delegation models.

Sections 3.2 and 3.3 address the core dynamics behind mission and non-constituent policy changes in the World Bank shift to the 'poverty turn', and in the EU's road to the Brussels Consensus, respectively. In turn, sections 3.4 and 3.5 engage the evidence on the two efforts at institutional reform, namely the change in the EU's external representation post-Lisbon, and the World Bank's 2008–2010 'voice and participation reform'. Finally, the practical implications of such institutional stasis are taken up in section 3.6, which outlines the possible scenarios stemming from a redefinition of the EU's position at the World Bank's Board.

3.2 From structural adjustment to development policy lending, through revised investment lending: a demand-driven approach to the evolution of the World Bank's business model?

Initially, the World Bank had privileged project- over program-based lending, which was introduced, under the name of 'adjustment lending' in the 1980s, to help developing countries cope with the disequilibria in their balances of payments after the oil shock of 1979.[3] Usually, first-generation adjustment lending programs aimed at supporting a country's achievement of short term macroeconomic stability. During the debt crisis of the 1980s, a consensus had emerged inside the Bank that the way out of indebtedness, and towards improved growth, lay in limited lending (but quick disbursement), through structural adjustment loans (SALs) with attached detailed conditions (Mosley *et al.* 1991, 302–303). Coupled with pressures by the US Government to cover the arrears of the most indebted among its borrowers, the belief shared by the US, UK and Germany's conservative governments in the virtues of economic austerity had also played a key role in forging that consensus, further compacted at the Bank thanks to its executives' relative insulation from societal pressures. The standard template on which the Washington Consensus was based (Williamson 1990) also spared the

Bank from allegations of discriminatory treatment of its many borrowers via the application of different loan conditions (Woods 2006).[4]

Throughout that decade, utter environmental failures from projects financed also through World Bank programs (Wade 1997), and the dubious performance of several SALs in reducing macroeconomic volatility and improving prospects for growth (Mosley *et al.* 1991), alerted the WB leadership to soften the organization's austerity template, to remedy past failures and restore the Bank's deteriorating legitimacy. An increasingly shared awareness consolidated about the direction to reform SAPs, and more generally, on the need to redefine the Washington Consensus template: positive growth records and macroeconomic stability could not be achieved at the expense of the poor, nor should those goals be pursued by banking on the collateral depletion of environmental resources. The rise of democratic and left-wing moderate governments in key donor countries, the Clinton Administration in the US and the Blair Government in the UK, in itself a consequence of the way in which electorates in liberal-democratic systems had reacted to the socio-economic consequences of the supply-side policies of the 1980s, provided the ideational and practical foundations to that change.[5] Supposedly offering a new approach to political-economic management, a Third way between the straitjackets of both the conservative and radical ends, the new course had a profound influence on the making of development policy. Inclusion, participation, consultation and comprehensiveness were shared buzzwords in the World Bank 'poverty turn' (Murphy 2008, 91–94). Two key players in the process were James Wolfensohn and Joseph Stiglitz.[6] The former was a committed supporter of the Democratic Party who had been appointed President of the World Bank by the Clinton Administration in 1995: his genuine faith in the virtues of a comprehensive approach would prove crucial to the Bank's reform, influencing aid policies up to the present. Previously the chair of President Clinton's Council of Economic Advisors, the latter became Senior VP and subsequently Chief Economist of the World Bank in 1997, covering the post until 2000, and receiving the Nobel Prize for Economics in 2001. His intellectual leadership marked the return of institutional economics into development analysis and practice.

Stiglitz's work and ideas were instrumental in forging the intellectual bases for the post-Washington Consensus. While rejecting the purist versions of economic liberalism that had prevailed in the US during the years of Reagan's presidency, Stiglitz's reform proposals retained the foundational elements of the neo-classic economic approach to development. Yet, in Stiglitz's formulation, those seminal assumptions were combined with an emphasis on the role of institutions (including, notably, state-led ones), that were deemed necessary to correct the many market failures (particularly informational) plaguing most developing contexts. Far from leaving the matters to the invisible hands of the market, Stiglitz believed, governments in developing countries should explicitly prioritize social justice and democracy (Stiglitz 2002a, 248). Multilateral agencies, such as the IMF and the World Bank, ought to support governments in the endeavour, not least by giving borrowers a stronger voice in their boards (idem 224–229).

Wolfensohn, in turn, played a key role in providing the necessary policy and organizational frameworks to implement those ideas, through a reform of the Bank's programs. Second-generation adjustment lending programs in the 1990s increasingly incorporated references to policy selectivity and good governance promotion, as well as to poverty reduction and capacity building (Kapur et al. 1997, vol. 1, 51), under the aegis of the new 'poverty turn'. Based on the concept of comprehensiveness, the new CDF devised by the World Bank's management rested on a matrix, which linked together the full set of players (governmental actors and civil society, multilateral and regional agencies, bilateral partners), factors (domestic institutions and policy systems, infrastructures, country-specific issues) and, last, policies. All these elements were retained as essential in the creation of 'a summary management tool', to provide 'a holistic and strategic approach to development based on country ownership and partnership' (Wolfensohn 1999, 23). The CDF approach addressed development issues through the entire country system (as opposed to the previous SALs' targeting of selected economic sectors), including it in a complex web of development networks. This implied aligning the preferences and strategies of a broad range of actors, domestic and foreign, international and bilateral in nature, public and private. Prominence was given to poverty reduction, to which, at least formally, all else was subordinated, and to good governance: apparently, aid effectiveness was crucially influenced by the type and quality of institutions and policies of partner countries (Burnside and Dollar 2000 and 2004). In the case of least developed countries, PRSPs replaced SAPs, calling for the inclusion and participation of different actors in partner countries, and urging coordination and alignment with other donors. In spite of the numerous obstacles encountered along the way, the Bank has pursued its CDF/PRSP approach further, adjusting the trajectory incrementally, but confirming its trust in a systemic (thereby inescapably political) approach to poverty reduction to improve aid effectiveness. Indeed, in 2004, the Bank adopted a new, comprehensive framework for development policy lending (DPL).[7]

Additionally, it has also revised its hallmark core business, i.e. lending to finance investment operations.[8] Collectively, the five key pillars that underpin the Investment Lending Reform (greater focus on results and risk; emphasis on implementation support as opposed to supervision, new lending options and tighter links between disbursements and results; creation of an enabling environment to implement reforms; revising the policy framework for investment lending to a simpler, principle-based one) signal a shift to increased flexibility towards local or country-specific needs, as well as an emphasis on a more careful management of risks to achieve better results. Support to the country's own implementation capacity has explicitly substituted for the earlier supervision by Bank's officials, thanks to the recommitment of IDA resources and the wider discretionary margins allowed for project restructuring. Through the setting of 'intermediate and monitorable... indicators', reformers in the Bank hope, result-based lending should encourage the improvement of accountability chains both on the side of the WB management with respect to the Board, and on the side of the implementing agencies within partner countries.[9] Similar to the links between the World Bank poverty turn and Third Way discourse,[10] the World Bank's emphasis on result-based management owes much to OECD-adapted principles from New Public Management experiments (Murphy 2008, 64). The multiple reverberation effects between domestic and multilateral environments (Putnam 1988), particularly through the circulation of ideas and high level officials across posts in the two contexts, confirm the relevance of the interaction between domestic, international and transnational levels in the formation of the consensus on result-based management of development policies.

Overall, the shift from the Washington Consensus to the post-Washington Consensus across the turn of the new millennium has marked for the World Bank a full-scale policy change: instruments, goals, strategies, as well as the political and normative foundations of its action have been reoriented (Kleistra and Mayer 2001, 393; Hermann 1990, 5–6). Since the mid-1990s the Bank has responded to past failures and critical feedbacks, through the diversification of its 'products' (from SALs to DPLs) and the redefinition of its core tools. On the one side, it has adopted reforms to make investment lending more flexible, and more tightly tied to performance. On the other side, however, it has also tried to gradually reduce its supervision on partner countries through support to implementation and improved risk management. The softening of its top-down technocratic culture towards a participatory lending model is evident, whatever the discrepancy between official changes and actual performance (Stiglitz 2002a; Woods 2006; Easterly 2007; Weaver 2008; Murphy 2008). Two aspects of those transformations are singled out here: the politicization of the World Bank's approach to development lending, through its targeting of institutional and social goals in partner countries, and its enhanced focus on management for results. As discussed in the next section, both were to become crucial for the evolution of the EU's own aid policy in the new millennium.

3.3 From assistance to development to policy coherence: the long road travelled by Brussels

In its early years, the EU approach to aid was essentially modeled on the special relationships between its founding fathers and their former colonies. Formally, it was based on unilateral and reciprocal free trade agreements with third countries, the Association Agreements, provided for in the Treaty of Rome (Arts 131–136). Through the Yaoundé Convention of 1968, the Agreements have become voluntary and negotiated, as well as non-reciprocal and stable, since the Lomé Convention of 1974. The EU has also broadened the geographical reach of its development policy. In addition to the relations with the African, Caribbean and Pacific Group (ACP), formed in 1975, and covered under the Yaoundé and Lomé Conventions, the EU has struck partnership agreements with Latin American and Asian countries (ALA). An important turning point came about with the Maastricht Treaty, signed in 1992 and in force from 1993, which provided for an explicit EC competence in development cooperation

(Art. 177). In 2000, the Lomé framework was replaced by the Cotonou Partnership Agreement, which emphasized the contractual nature of the ACP–EU relations, but increased the range of political conditionalities and pushed the envelope of trade liberalization as a tool for development (Bretherton and Vogler 2006, 122–127). Most importantly, since the 1990s the Union has expanded the reach of its development policy, to include the Southern Mediterranean Partners (through the Barcelona Process in 1995, then changed into the European Mediterranean Partnership), and, particularly, the Eastern Partners after the end of the Cold War. Since 2004, the two groups have been merged under the label of 'neighboring countries', and their relations with the EU managed through a new framework, the European Neighborhood Policy. The increased importance of neighborhood countries and the relevance of security and foreign policy objectives in the EU's aid policy have been reflected in the trends of EC Official Development Aid (ODA). In spite of the emphasis on poverty reduction (in both Title XVII of the Maastricht Treaty, and Art. 177 of the Amsterdam Treaty) between 1980 and 2000, the share of the (increased) amount of official development aid by the EC to Part II neighbors (Central and Eastern European, as well as Newly Independent Countries from the former Soviet Union) equaled that devoted to other middle-income and, most notably, LDCs (Least Developed Countries) (Bonaglia et al. 2006, 176–177). At the end of the 2000s, the EU channeled almost 60% of its development resources to middle-income countries (ODI 2009). Yet, notwithstanding the drive provided towards joint efforts through the 2006 European Consensus, the Lisbon Treaty has left the competence on development cooperation a shared one, between the Union and MS.

EU studies on aid and development have noted the Union's efforts to reconcile both altruistic and opportunistic goals in a better devised strategy, to improve performance in aid delivery, and promote a more coherent image in the external world.[11] Since the adoption of the Treaty of Maastricht, sustainability and human dimensions have gained prominence in EU aid policy, and so have the promotion of democracy and the respect for human rights (European Commission 2000b, 2000c). Political conditionality has been officially endorsed in the EU Association Agreements since 1995,[12] while the promotion of peace and security have become pivotal aspects of the EU self-claimed foreign policy role through the Cotonou Partnership Agreement and the Everything-but-Arms (EBA) initiative.[13] In 1996, the Commission first acknowledged the need to link aid disbursement to performance assessment, turning from the 'paternalism' of the first three Lomé Agreements towards a more technical, performance-based approach (Bonaglia et al. 2006, 172). As discussed above, the emphasis on result-based performance was part of a broader ideational change supported by national and transnational elites, linked to the result-based .management reform of public sectors in several major OECD countries (notably the UK, New Zealand and the US), and closely connected with the Third way discourse. Subsequent evolutions indicate that the Union has fully embraced such post-Washington consensus values, as ownership, partnership, inclusion ('participation') of civil society into political dialogue, gender equality and action to address security and state fragility issues (European Consensus on Development Policy 2006). The analysis conducted here on the EU–WB interaction in the two decades across the turn of the third millennium, indicates that imitation dynamics and adaptive learning have been accompanied by innovative processes on the EU side (Argyris and Schön 1978, 2–3; Levy 1994, 285). Emphasis on the normative and altruistic dimension of development promotion, as well as a preference for positive conditionality, as opposed to negative sanctions, have in fact supported the emergence of the 'first Brussels Consensus' in 2006, which has led, according to some, to a peculiarly distinct EU approach to aid policy (Carbone 2007, 55).[14] These results have also gained the EU a leading role in advancing the implementation of the Paris–Accra Agenda on aid harmonization and donor coordination. The New Consensus on Development (2017) witnesses an enhanced effort by the EU and its member states to implement the objectives of Agenda 2030. While strengthening the commitments of the 2006 Consensus (including reaching the ODA/GNI 0.7 target originally set via the MDGs, within the deadline of the 2030 Agenda), the New EU Consensus on Development (2017) sets the implementation of the 2015 SDGs as one of its core goals.

In the war on terror launched after the attacks against the US on 9/11, a wide – though not consensual – coalition compacted behind the idea that aid should prioritize countries whose strategic relevance and institutional stability were considered particularly at risk. Earlier calls for 'comprehensive' development approaches were then coupled with a new emphasis on the virtuosity of the prosperity–security link. The correlation had been dear to the US liberal thought since the rise of totalitarian regimes in European war-torn economies after the Great War (Hull 1948), providing a policy template over which consensus would periodically re-emerge, with the unfolding of military conflicts in poor areas of the world. In 2005, the Commission succeeded in conveying the idea that both MS and EU institutions should improve their effort to make non-aid policies coherent with development objectives. In turn, the Council later affirmed that security priorities should also be taken into consideration in EU aid policy. Since the adoption of the EU Consensus on Development in 2006, policy coherence for development has become an official target of the EU development policy.[15]

A decisive move towards improved coherence between aid and other EU policies had however occurred some six years before, under the Prodi Commission, reformed in 1999, upon the drive provided by Commissioner Nielson (Carbone 2008, 332).[16] The relevance of such a turn lies more in the process through which it came about, and in the consequences it has generated, than in its innovative potential. Even before the launch of the World Bank's CDF in 1999, there was hardly anything new in the idea that, to maximize chances of being successful, aid policy should factor in donor- and recipient-specific contextual variables. Across decades of controversies (Papanek 1973; Mosley 1980; Boone 1996), studies on the aid–growth link have discussed multiple conditions that are supposed to increase aid effectiveness (Burnside and Dollar 2000 and 2004; Easterly et al. 2004). By the end of the millennium, the World Bank had endorsed the emphasis on policy selectivity as a key driver of aid effectiveness (World Bank 1999), fueling a debate on the appropriateness of specific policy criteria to guide lending (Easterly 2007; Rajan and Subramanian 2008; Clemens et al. 2011).

Yet, ideas take time to circulate, and they get incorporated into actual policies only under peculiar conditions.[17] In 2000, the special consideration of the poverty effects of non-aid policies to ensure coherence rallied most donors, developing agencies and several, though not all (conspicuously not the US), major states under the same flag, behind the UN launch of the Millennium Development Goals. The idea behind the Goals was not a new one, and had earlier roots in the OECD and World Bank's blueprints for a post-Washington Consensus. The result-based approach behind the MDGs, eight goals to reach by 2015, and 18 indicators to monitor along the way, was indeed drawn from a previous OECD plan for International Development Targets (IDT), which, while launched in 1996, had not been incorporated into actual policies. Even before that, the OECD had sponsored reforms in MS to modernize their public sectors along the lines of the New Public Management (NPM) approach, under the guidance of the OECD Public Management Committee (PUMA). The endorsement of NPM by the OECD, and its critical stance on EU's development policies some years later (OECD 1998) provided the basis for the Union's initial internal debate on coherence, which, as hinted above, took some time before being genuinely reflected in official positions. Thus, the traction exerted by domestic political shifts in key OECD donor countries interacted with new economic ideas and organizational concepts that were being suitably mobilized by pro-poor advocacies, to provide key input into the redefinition of development policies across the turn of the millennium. Factual stimuli (policy failures, systemic shocks) and normative transformations (NPM, inclusive approach to poverty reduction based on policy selectivity) have resulted in a major ideational shift away from the earlier Washington Consensus, and have brought about significant policy changes for both the EU and the World Bank.[18]

Overall, the EU's development policy has gone a long way since its early days. In addition to having become a leading actor in promoting the agenda of aid effectiveness, and a pivotal leader in the Monterrey and Doha Conferences on FfD and in the Paris–Accra process, in 2007 the Union has also issued its own guidelines on how the 2006 Consensus on development should be implemented, releasing a Code of Conduct on Complementarity and Division of Labour in Development Policy.[19] Finally, the EU 2017 Consensus includes among the new priorities: mainstreaming inequality reduction into EU and MS development policies, tackling youth unemployment, as well as addressing fragility, environmental and migration threats. While a core innovation in the SDGs is their applicability to both developed and developing countries, the key structural change in the text of the EU Consensus of 2017 is its unified structure, and the elaboration of a single set of priorities and commitments for both the EU and its member states (ODI 2017).

It remains to be seen however, whether, in the absence of political will from the major MS, the shift to comprehensive and coherent anti-poverty orientation of the World Bank and EU development efforts could lead to a transformation in the 'constitutive politics' of either organization. At the beginning of the new millennium, hope was put on the progressive mechanisms triggered by the institutional innovations brought about by the Lisbon Treaty in matters of EU external representation, and on the World Bank's 'voice and participation reform', to which the next two sections are devoted.

3.4 The post-Lisbon landscape and the EU at the World Bank[20]

A recurring theme in the literature on the Union's role in international affairs, the discussion on the composite nature and roles of the EU polity (Elgström and Smith 2006b, 1–4) re-emerged in the scholarship on the complex post-Lisbon landscape. Omnipresent in most EU-commissioned studies has been the argument of an apparent unsuitability of the current governance of most among the existing multilaterals to the legal personality that the EU has acquired through the Lisbon Treaty. A hybrid political entity (King 1999, 313 cited in Manners 2002, 240), the Union operates as a supranational actor in some matters, intergovernmental in others, but without a clearly defined stateness, or features comparable to those of existing federal states.

Since 2011, the upgrade to an 'enhanced observer status' for the EU in the UN General Assembly (UNGA) indicates however that, in the post-Lisbon era, Brussels has obtained the right to speak with one voice in what is an essentially intergovernmental framework. The change has led other regional groupings to apply for a similar upgrade.[21] While such compacting may lower transaction costs compared to the 193-members-sized UNGA, internalizing potentially diverging preferences that are only partially covered by EU competence may not facilitate decision making, either from the standpoint of the EU–MS dynamics, or from that of the UNGA overall process (Miller 2011). The trial-and-error path through which Brussels has obtained its new status at the UN indicates that consolidating the EU's ability to act externally as a unified actor in other IOs upon the principles premised after Lisbon has been very much an incremental process.[22]

Parallel to the emerging EU drive towards 'effective multilateralism', a disconnection has materialized between the evolving EU structure and allegedly 'unsuitable' governance frameworks in other international *fora*. Relative to the Bretton Woods institutions, which came into being before the EEC was created, timing has not been on the EU's side.[23] In the Lisbon Treaty the EU constituents have chosen to refer specifically to the UN law (Wessel 2011, 14–17) to model the EU's external representation in a number of policy areas, including development cooperation.[24] However, such qualifications are not accompanied in the Treaties by provisions that specifically legislate on adapting the hybrid nature of the EU to the governance structures of other existing international organizations. While the goal to 'promote an international system based on stronger multilateral cooperation and good global governance' has been institutionalized in the post-Lisbon TFEU (Art. 21, 2, h), an exceptionally wide margin of discretion has been left to the Union and its MS 'in certain aspects relating to the powers and external representation of the EU' (European Parliament 2011b, 8).

At present, the EU representation in IOs that operate in areas falling into shared competences is to a wide extent left to ad hoc, discretionary implementation. Projections on the evolution of the EU's position at the World Bank post-Lisbon are therefore highly conjectural. Some considerations however can be made on its expected direction, and related implications for the future of EU–World Bank partnership. Two different but complementary perspectives are discussed here: institutional evolutions (on either side), and related developments in the day-to-day practice.

Under the first angle, three different issues appear particularly relevant: the provision of new roles and responsibilities pursuant to the changes in EU external representation in the Lisbon Treaty (1); the permanence of development cooperation as a shared-parallel competence, against a background of increased EU proactivity in these matters (2); and the current representation system within the World Bank (3). Taken together, these elements point to few changes in the existing system for coordination of EU MS at the Bank, but suggest that some potential could be further developed. In the policy practice, the current unofficial formula is based on the mix between the 'sectoral' competence of the Development Commissioner in high level meetings, and the routine coordinating role played at the Board by the ED (Alternate or Advisor) of the country holding the Rotating Presidency of the Council (RP), premised on the pre-Lisbon practice of external representation in shared competence matters.

The post-Lisbon formal provisions on external representation, particularly through the creation of the HR for Foreign Affairs and Security Policy, and the EEAS, have radically downsized the role of the RP in the making of the Common European Foreign and Security Policy (CFSP) (Bunse and Klein 2013; Vanhoonacker et al. 2010). However, the new provisions on the EU external representation have only partially modified the role played by the RP in the coordination of EU EDs at the World Bank's Board. Based on the Treaty of Amsterdam, the RP was entitled to formally represent the Union in CFSP matters and to express the EU's position in international organizations.[25] The Treaty of Amsterdam (TEU Title V, Art. 19) also called on the MS to coordinate their action within such *fora* and to uphold their common positions. The Council (Rotating) Presidency has in practice fulfilled this task at both the World Bank and IMF Boards.[26]

Pre-Lisbon, the Community and the MS were required to 'coordinate their policies on development cooperation' and to 'consult each other on their aid programmes, including in international organisations' (Art. 180 TEC, as amended by the Amsterdam Treaty), and had the option to 'undertake joint action' (Ibid.), with the possibility for the Commission to 'take any useful initiative to promote' such coordination. Art. 302 of the Amsterdam Treaty (part Six, General and Final Provisions), entitled the Commission to maintain relations with international organizations. The provision has been modified post-Lisbon, delegating to the Union the authority to 'maintain. . .relations as are appropriate with. . .international organisations' (Art. 220, 1, Part V, External Action by the Union, Title VI, The Union's relation with International Organisations and third countries and the Union delegations), and entitling both the HR and the Commission to implementation rights (Art. 220, 2). Yet, the representation of the Union in IOs is attributed to EU delegations (Art. 221, 1). While formally under the authority of the HR, they are bound to act in close cooperation with MS diplomatic and consular missions (Art. 221, 2).

A disconnection exists between external representation and competence in shared matters, the second feature of the post-Lisbon institutional evolutions discussed here. The tension stems from the hybrid nature of development policy, which falls in between technical-economic (and perhaps more likely to be communitarized in the future), and quintessentially political matters. By definition (Art. 4.1 and 4.4 TFEU), development cooperation and the provision of humanitarian aid are parallel competences, a sub-section of the wider group of matters falling into shared competences: EU action in these areas cannot prevent MS from exercising their competences.[27] Arguably, development cooperation could be considered a matter falling into 'shared-to-coordinated competences', depending on the relative strength of its ties, with either exclusive-shared (agriculture, trade, environment, fisheries) or fully coordinated matters (health, industry, culture). It can be argued that when the 'attraction' occurs towards the exclusive-shared extreme, MS 'can exercise shared competence until the EU intervenes in the matter for the first time' (which should be based on subsidiarity, however). Conversely, when attraction occurs towards the shared-coordinated extreme, the EU can only intervene to supplement a predominantly national competence. While in the first case MS have a residual competence with respect to the Union, in the second case it is the EU whose competences are residual with respect to those of MS. The authority to implement such competences in the relations between the Union and other IOs is attributed to both the HR and the Commission (Art. 220 (2) TFEU). However, as noted above, the representation of the EU in IOs is attributed to EU delegations under the authority of the HR (Art. 221, 1 TFEU).

What are the implications of the changes in external representation, and the tension between representation and competence issues, for the EU's presence at the Bank, under the current World Bank's governance system, the third facet of institutional evolutions analyzed here? As recalled earlier, in regular Board meetings the EU can speak through its MS, depending on the EU EDs' willingness to coordinate (technically, but not necessarily in the followed practice, when shared competence prevails over parallel one, as discussed above). During the Annual Meetings the EU can also take advantage of informal fixes. Absent an EU formal membership to the World Bank, the EU delegation to the US and the other Washington-based IFIs can only liaise between the ED (alternate or else) of the country holding the RP and the other EU EDs at the Board, on the one side, and the Commission, and the EEAS (ultimately the HR) in Brussels, on the other. In the practice, the RP and the other EU MS are still the ultimate leaders of the 'EU game' at the Board.

Based on Art. 47 TEU of the Lisbon Treaty, the Union enjoys consolidated external legal personality: it can become full contracting party, and acquire membership, in international organizations. However, the World Bank Articles of Agreement do not envisage the possibility of accession by shareholders other than states. While there is no formal obstacle to their revision, the amendments that would be necessary to accept the EU as a member call for a redefinition of the existing constituency-based system. This spells long negotiations and, arguably, cross-pressuring from different sides by current shareholders. The evidence presented in Chapter 5 points to the existence of support from several sources in the Commission, as well as from selected non-EU shareholders and sections of WB management in Washington, to compact the current eight-constituency representation into a single EU seat. A different picture has emerged, however, based on inputs from most – though not all – the EU EDs, who seemed reluctant to discuss changes in the WB governance system that could lead to a compression of 'their' seats and shares.

As discussed in the previous section, the EU development policy has progressed, but is still very much a process in the making.[28] The issue at stake here is the absence of provisions on intermediation between the EU's post-Lisbon system of external representation (HR-cum-EEAS) and the current constituency system of the Washington-based IFIs. The vacuum left (particularly relative to the RP role in coordinating over the formation of common positions) is symptomatic of the wider uncertainty on the respective roles of HR–EEAS, Commission, RP and MS in *fora* where shared competences prevail (Barkowski and Wiatr 2012). Post-Lisbon, development has emerged as a doubly doomed policy for the EU: highly divisive, and therefore easily captured by MS' domestic priorities, but minimally salient, and therefore deprived of the political traction that would be needed to build consensus around compacting an 'EU voice' at the Bank.

Finally, in practice, the current situation has led to *ad hoc* informal solutions, especially in the day-to-day decision-making at the Board. Before Lisbon, an EU observer was admitted to the Development Committee at the Annual Spring Meetings of the World Bank and IMF (a similar exception being made within the Financial Committee). In lieu of the RP, and in light of the high relevance of decisions taken there, the position was normally occupied by the Development Commissioner. Since Lisbon, external representation in IOs has been attributed to EU delegations under the HR authority: the observer seat in the Development Committee should be ultimately reserved for the HR position. To date, the HR has continued along the pre-Lisbon practice, so that it is the Development Commissioner who represents the EU twice a year at the Annual Meetings. On the one side, this precedent signals that the HR and the Commission have found a successful way to deal with the formal disempowerment of the RP in CFSP matters, along the lines of past routines of EU representation in the IFIs.[29] On the other side, the additional level of intermediation has not uniformly helped to smooth things out.[30] In practice the RP still coordinates EU EDs in relevant matters at the Board and liaises with the relevant DGs in Brussels and with the EU delegation in Washington (currently integrated through the newly created EEAS, and accountable to the HR).

Further developments have strengthened the role of the Commission in supervising the work of delegations operating at IOs on development matters. Post-Lisbon, former DG DEV has been merged with EuropeAid into DG Development and Cooperation-EuropeAid. Designed along partially different lines compared to the previous DG DEV, DG DEVCO-EuropeAid featured a 'Task force for an enhanced dialogue with International Organisations' directly reporting to the Director General. In 2011, sources internal to the Task Force acknowledged that its activities were specifically devoted to improve the cooperation only with International financial institutions (IMF, WB, AfDB, ADB, IADB), making it clear that cooperation with the UN (and its specialized development agencies, arguably) fell within the preserve of the HR and the EEAS. In the light of combined provisions of Art. 210 (1) and Art. 210 (2) TFEU, the role that the new Task Force and, more broadly DG DEVCO-EuropeAid could play, appeared crucial.[31] As of 2018, DG DEVCO features a dedicated Unit on International Organisation and Development Dialogue with Other Donors within Directorate A, devoted to general and sectoral policy issues in the area of International Cooperation and Development Policy. The new Unit deals with relations with all the development-relevant multilaterals – with several posts devoted to EU–UN relations, and a single post allocated to the EU–IMF/WB relations.

While the role of the HR and the creation of the EEAS have been instrumental to enhance the coherence and consistency of the EU's external action, multiple doubts have emerged about how such task would impact the Union's development policy, and how the rivalries between the Commission and the EEAS staff could be reconciled (Henökl 2013, 14–15). Concern has been expressed about a securitization of aid, or, on the contrary, a developmentalization of security policy (Smith 2013). It remains to be seen, however, whether the additional levels of intermediation generated by the re-configuration of posts and responsibilities in the post-Lisbon EU–World Bank environment will improve the coherence of Brussels' external policies, and enhance its ability to contribute to the pursuit of development goals with the Washington-based institution. In the daily routines of the World Bank's Board, the RP chairmanship of the Eurogroup is likely to remain the default practice for a while.

3.5 Accountability, effectiveness and the World Bank 'voice reform'

The debate on compacting the EU's representation at the World Bank's Board is closely connected with the reform of the internal governance of the Bretton Wood institution.[32] A change from the current system, in which the EU MS are spread across six to ten different voting directorates (depending on which alternate/advisor chairs the directorate, based on the rotation schedules in mixed groups[33]) should involve the creation of fewer, EU-homogeneous, constituencies.

The reform of the governance of the Washington IFIs has been discussed in the economics and IPE literatures (Woods 2001, 2006; Truman 2006; Ahearne and Eichengreen 2007). The theme is part of the wider debate on the feasibility and advisability of transposing democratic criteria from domestic to international contexts (Archibugi and Held 1995 and 2011; Zürn 2000). For the purpose of the present analysis, it is important to single out a particular aspect of that otherwise thick and ramified debate, which echoes the discussion on the tradeoff between effectiveness and legitimacy in consociational vs majoritarian democracies (Lijphart 2008, 13, 16, 168, 270), centered on the relative merits of expanding the representativeness of IO boards.

On the one side, the advocates of cosmopolitan democracy support the replication of delegation chains typical of liberal democracies at the level of international *fora*. In their opinion, the process would be both beneficial, to improve the IOs' responsiveness to those affected by their decisions (Held 2002, 26), and feasible, based on the expansion of voice rights for a growing number of stakeholders, among whom NGOs and transnational advocacy coalitions (Kaldor 2003; Macdonald 2012). On the other side, hard-core skeptics have questioned both the advisability and feasibility of such replication. Independent sectoral authorities, such as central banks or other regulatory agencies, have been the norm in most liberal democracies. Yet, their very performance has crucially depended on their autonomy from the circuits of input legitimacy typical of democratic systems (Kahler 2004). Expanding access rights to a higher number of (supposedly) non-representative NGOs – the skeptics' camp maintains – would not only hamper the cause of transposing democracy to the global level, but also shake the very foundations of democratic principles at the domestic level (Schmitter 2000, 216, quoted in Kahler 2004, 154–155).

IR realists have warned against the epistemological risks of applying the domestic analogy to the study of institutionalized cooperation at the international level, as done by cosmopolitans and neo-Kantians. Absent a global *polis* – the realist argument goes – there is no space for the formation of a global *demos*.[34] IR and IPE research has acknowledged the relevance of these realist critiques (particularly with respect to endogeneity between states' interests and institutional performance of the delegated organization; Mitchell, 2009; Stone 2009 and 2011), exploring avenues to increase IOs' accountability vis à vis different categories of affected stakeholders (Archibugi and Held 2011; and, specifically on the World Bank, Woods 2006, 2007, 2008a and 2008b), but also questioning the relevance of democratic responsiveness criteria when applied to international financial institutions (Vreeland 2006).

Entrenched in theoretical debates, the legitimacy–effectiveness quandary has several policy-relevant implications. A major one refers to the advantages and disadvantages of reforms that enhance IO responsiveness to an expanded set of stakeholders (gaining in legitimacy, but bearing some loss in effectiveness, according to some), on the one side, and options that increase an IO's relative autonomy (particularly, but not solely) from new stakeholders, to improve its delivering on an existing mission, on the other. The extent to which the two run parallel to each other, diverge as horns of a true dilemma, or, rather, constitute complementary aspects of a more complex, but eventually synergistic process, is the object of an ongoing debate.[35] The plurality of stances points to the absence of a scholarly consensus on what constitutes legitimacy in an intergovernmental context (transparency, accountability and responsiveness have much in common with, but are by no means coincident with democratic representativeness, which implies a complex set of elements, relative to both horizontal and vertical ties), and the difficulty to achieve convergence on a universally valid definition of effective performance.[36]

Enhanced access to the World Bank by new stakeholders has been granted through numerous initiatives aimed at increasing transparency.[37] Yet, in spite of those efforts, the increase in the World Bank's operational costs in the past three decades has been mostly reflected in higher interests paid by borrowers, raising doubts about the accountability of the Executive Board to the Bank's poorer members. Capital increases, shifts from European to US bond markets with shorter term maturities in the 1990s, and the choice to lend at variable rates, have to a non-negligible extent been passed through on borrowers' fees (Woods 2006). So have the costs from the expansion of activities of the Bank (safeguard measures, new trust funds, special programs for former USSR and fragile countries, to name only a few). A typical borrower wound indeed pay 0.5 interest fee on a loan contracted in 1979. Three years later the fee had tripled to 1.5. In 2008 (fiscal year), 25% of the IBRD's gross income was accounted for by the Bank's net loan margin, worth USD 624 million (Zedillo 2009, 26 fn 42).

Originally, the poorer members were granted minimal voice rights beyond their subscriptions through an even-handed distribution of basic votes. Allocated to each new member in a fixed quantity upon membership acquisition, basic votes accounted originally for approximately 10.8% of the total World Bank shares. In 2006, they covered a mere 2.8% (Woods 2006, 206). Pursuant to Phase I of the 2008–2010 voice reform, the IBRD share of basic votes in total votes has been doubled to 5.5%. However, none of the two further proposed changes to either 8.11% ('tripling option') or 10.78% (restoring the 1944 ratio), envisaged to enhance the voice of the poorest, have been taken up in Phase 2 of that reform (Vestergaard 2011, 34). In such a case, accountability through a revised distribution of votes and shares would not be required on 'merely' democratic criteria, but, more broadly, on grounds of equity and operational best practices. According to Harry Dexter White, the rationale behind basic votes (he referred to the Fund system) was indeed more than a simple egalitarian move: the wellbeing of the institution depended on its legitimacy to all its members, creditors and borrowers alike.

In defense of the existing allocation of votes, however, others have observed how shifting to the criterion 'one country one vote' could in fact be more discriminatory, as it would bias formal representation to the advantage of smaller and/or poorer countries, without in fact changing much in terms of coalitional equilibria, that are often forged in other *fora* by the larger lenders anyway (Kahler 2004, 136–137).[38] The creation of alternative contexts where development policies are, to a variable extent, contested and negotiated has widened the options available to the poorest borrowers (Avant et al. 2010). Such a change, however, may not have improved coordination dynamics: empirical evidence from the ever-increasing reach of negotiations on trade-and-development related issues has shown that moving around (or on the borders) of a higher number of *fora* does represent in fact a burden for the poorer countries (Finger and Schuler 2002; Latif 2005).[39]

Conservatives further argue that a strategy of redistributing shares incrementally would risk being both unfair and ineffective. Changes in voting powers of even a few percentage points may indeed make a substantial difference in constituencies with a particularly high share-to-country ratio. If the US voting share were reduced from its current 16.39 to a share below 15 percent, the change would deprive the country of the veto power that it currently enjoys over decisions requiring an 85% majority. Conversely, marginal redistributions to the advantage of constituencies with a disproportionately low share-to-countries ratio, such as the African constituencies composed of 22 and 23 member countries (which currently yield 1.92% and 1.80% voting powers, respectively)[40] would bring very limited gains to their members anyway.[41] Both sides, 'conservatives' and 'reformists', agree that continued action by the Bank must rest on a solid support by its major shareholders, among which are now the large middle-income economies of China, India, and Russia.[42] Such support should be, however, supplemented with a more diffuse, possibly strengthened trust from its borrowers.

To address the concerns of the poorest and least represented countries, some have suggested introducing the requirement of double majority (votes and countries), particularly on the most sensitive issues (Jakobeit 2005; Strand and Rapkin 2005; Woods 2006, 2010; Birdsall 2009).[43] The change would compensate the current asymmetry in voting shares – whose revision in favour of the poorest borrowers would be difficult to justify to both large lenders and emerging and transition economies. Such a change has not however been incorporated in the 2008–2010 World Bank 'voice reform'. Most noticeably, new voting rules may not get reflected easily in organizational practice, depriving the reform of its expected benefits, on both equity and accountability terms. Indeed, the World Bank has long been informed by an established corporate culture of consensus, upon which proposals that have not been previously agreed on through informal channels, are rarely subject to vote before the Board. Voted decisions have been a rather singular occurrence in decades of practice, as detailed in Section 6 of Chapter 5 of this volume.

It is against this background, external to the Union, but internal to the Bank, and therefore to a large extent endogenous to the interactional context between the two IOs, that the options for a more compact representation of the Union at the World Bank's Board should be considered.

3.6 Fewer seats, more influence?

Currently there are eight constituencies with an EU ED at the Board, out of an overall total of six to ten constituencies that can be potentially led by an EU MS (Table 3.1). Their current cumulated power amounts to 753,400 votes, equivalent to 32.06% of total Board votes. The total however also includes votes provided by

Table 3.1 The current representation of the EU MS at the Board, votes by constituency

*EU MS voting power at WB Board by constituency**		
	N. votes	*% votes*
Germany (ED)	97264	**4.14**
France (ED)	91094	**3.88**
United Kingdom (ED)	91094	**3.88**
Belgium (ED)–Austria (AED)	38103	1.62
Austria	15301	0.65
Belarus	4901	0.21
Czech Republic	8683	0.37
Hungary	11483	0.49
Kosovo	1656	0.07
Luxembourg	2979	0.13
Slovak Republic	4765	0.2
Slovenia	2399	0.1
Turkey	26333	1.12
Constituency	**116603**	**4.76**
Spain (ED)–Venezuela (AED)	44849	1.91
Costa Rica	1813	0.08
El Salvador	831	0.04
Guatemala	2691	0.11
Honduras	1331	0.06
Mexico	35515	1.51
Nicaragua	1563	0.07
Venezuela	21051	0.9
Constituency	**109644**	**4.67**
Netherlands (ED)–Ukraine (AED)	46519	1.98
Armenia	2336	0.1
Bosnia and Herzegovina	1343	0.06
Bulgaria	7298	0.31
Croatia	3596	0.15

(*Continued*)

Table 3.1 (Continued)

*EU MS voting power at WB Board by constituency**		
	N. votes	*% votes*
Cyprus	2151	0.09
Georgia	2485	0.11
Israel	6709	0.29
Macedonia, FYRoM	1117	0.05
Moldova	2256	0.10
Montenegro	1378	0.06
Romania	7556	0.32
Ukraine	11667	0.50
Constituency	**96411**	**4.10**
Italy (ED)–Portugal (AED)	61593	2.62
Albania	1627	0.07
Malta	1764	0.08
Greece	2538	0.11
Portugal	6617	0.28
San Marino	1285	0.05
Timor-Leste	1284	0.05
Constituency	**76708**	**3.26**
Denmark (ED)–Sweden (AED)	18486	0.79
Estonia	1860	0.08
Finland	12129	0.52
Iceland	2432	0.10
Latvia	2444	0.10
Lithuania	2600	0.11
Norway	14108	0.60
Sweden	20523	0.87
Constituency	**74582**	**3.17**
Total EU MS-led constituencies	**753400**	**32.06**
Canada (ED)–Ireland (AED)	59044	2.51
Antigua and Barbuda	1210	0.05
Bahamas, The	1761	0.07
Barbados	1638	0.07
Belize	1276	0.05
Dominica	1194	0.05
Grenada	1221	0.05
Guyana	2216	0.09
Ireland	8477	0.36
Jamaica	3874	0.16
St Kitts and Nevis	965	0.04
St Lucia	1242	0.05
St Vincent and the Grenadines	968	0.04
Constituency	**85086**	**3.62**

(*Continued*)

*EU MS voting power at WB Board by constituency**		
	N. votes	*% votes*
Switzerland (ED)–Poland (AED)	35350	1.50
Azerbaijan	3061	0.13
Kazakhstan	5263	0.22
Kyrgyz Republic	1797	0.08
Poland	17819	0.76
Serbia	3536	0.15
Tajikistan	1894	0.08
Turkmenistan	1317	0.06
Uzbekistan	3433	0.15
Constituency	**73470**	**3.13**
EU MS-led +Canada and Switzerland-led	**911956**	**38.80**

Source: Aidflows, Revised March 29, 2017

non EU MS, such as the Latin and Central American partners, in the constituency led by Spain, and the Northern, Central and Southern European, as well as Central Asian partners, in the groups led by the Netherlands, Belgium, Italy and Denmark, respectively.[44] Under a 'maximum weight' ten-EDs scenario, i.e. including the votes allocated to the constituency currently under the Swiss and Canadian EDs, the collective weight of the EU member states would amount, in the present distribution, to 38.80% of the total World Bank votes.

This instant picture points to an overrepresentation of the EU, which, when able to speak with one voice, can build on the additional votes brought by non EU MS in EU-led mixed constituencies. Whenever possible the benefits of such over-representation have been spent wisely on building consensus around EU-core goals, as discussed in Chapter 5. Yet, intra-constituency negotiations have also led to opposite results, whereby countries which do not hold the ED post during the semester of their Presidency (i.e. while retaining the RP) may even have to abstain from advancing proposals that would otherwise obtain a consensus within the Eurogroup, if the proposal is not backed by their overall constituency.

Last, under a 'minimum weight' six-EDs scenario, within the current voting distribution, the EU EDs can mobilize approximately 23% in voting power. Out of the seven mixed constituencies, two are typically hegemonic, i.e. those chaired by Canada and Italy; three are basically hegemonic, i.e. those chaired by Switzerland, Austria and the Netherlands; one is tripolar (that chaired by Spain) and, finally, one is in between a tripolar and a quadripolar structure (the Nordic-Baltic Constituency, where the voting shares of Sweden, Norway and Denmark are closely followed by that of Finland, as shown in Table 3.1).

If all the EU MS were to be grouped into the same constituency, their aggregate voting power at the Board would diminish from approximately 32% to 26.89% (see Table 3.2). Still, such percentage would outperform the influence mobilized under a 'minimum weight' six-EDs scenario. More relevantly, pooling the EU countries behind a single ED with a voting share of 26.89% would create by far the most powerful constituency at the Board, followed by the two members with the largest numbers of shares, the US and Japan, with 16.39% and 7.07% relative voting power, respectively.

The scenarios sketched above incorporate the changes introduced through the 'voice reform' of the World Bank's internal governance. Following the Monterrey Consensus of 2002, which encouraged the World Bank and IMF to 'continue to enhance participation of all developing countries and countries with economies in transition (DTC)' (World Bank 2010a, 1), the World Bank's Board agreed in

Table 3.2 EU MS representation under a single EU constituency scenario

EU MS	*No. votes*	*% total votes*
Germany	97264	4.14
France	91094	3.88
United Kingdom	91094	3.88
Italy	61593	2.62
Netherlands	46519	1.98
Spain	44849	1.91
Belgium	38103	1.62
Sweden	20523	0.87
Denmark	18486	0.79
Poland	17819	0.76
Austria	15301	0.65
Finland	12129	0.52
Hungary	11483	0.49
Czech Republic	8683	0.37
Ireland	8477	0.36
Romania	7556	0.32
Bulgaria	7298	0.31
Portugal	6617	0.28
Slovak Republic	4765	0.20
Croatia	3596	0.15
Luxembourg	2979	0.13
Lithuania	2600	0.11
Greece	2538	0.11
Latvia	2444	0.10
Slovenia	2399	0.10
Cyprus	2151	0.09
Estonia	1860	0.08
Malta	1764	0.08
EU MS total	631984	26.89

Source: Aidflows, Revised March 29, 2017

2008 on a two-phase package of reforms to increase DTCs' voice and participation. During phase 1, the DTCs' voting power in IBRD was increased from 42.6% to 44.1%, and an elected Executive Director for Sub-Saharan Africa (SSA) was added to the WBG Boards (Ibid., 2). Phase 2, which was agreed on at the WB Spring Meetings 2010, produced a 3.13% increase in the (collective) voting power of DTCs at IBRD, bringing it to 47.19% (World Bank 2010b). The approach used for the shareholding and voting power realignment has also been the basis for a selective capital increase of USD 27.8 billion.

As a result of this process, shown in Table 3.3, some of the EU MS, namely France, Germany and the United Kingdom, have witnessed a relative decrease in their voting power (Bretton Woods Project 2010). The same applies to the Netherlands, Belgium, Italy, Denmark, and Sweden which all rank among the 20 countries that lost most of their pre-reform voting power. On the other hand, countries such as Greece, Romania, Spain and Poland (within Europe) are among those that gained the most from the voice reform, and in some cases (Turkey) even doubled their share of votes. With the full implementation of the voice reform, and under the present constituency system, the collective weight of the EU MS on total World Bank's votes has thus decreased from 32.97% to 32.38% (Table 3.5). As seen above, subsequent shareholding revisions have brought that total further down to 32.06%.

Under a single-constituency scenario, the completion of the 2008–2010 voice reform was expected to bring the aggregate voting power of EU MS down from

Table 3.3 The variation in EU constituencies' voting shares from phases 1 and 2 of the 'voice reform'

	Percentage of voting power (as of August 1, 2011)	*Percentage of voting power after voice reform Phase-2*[1]	*Variation*
Germany (ED)	4.40	4.00	–0.40
France (ED)	4.22	3.75	–0.47
United Kingdom (ED)	4.22	3.75	–0.47
Austria (ED)–Belgium (AED)	4.58	4.96	0.38
Austria	0.68	0.63	–0.05
Belarus	0.22	0.20	–0.02
Belgium	1.77	1.57	–0.20
Czech Republic	0.40	0.36	–0.04
Hungary	0.50	0.47	0.03
Kosovo	0.07	0.09	0.02
Luxembourg	0.11	0.12	0.01
Slovak Republic	0.21	0.20	–0.01
Slovenia	0.09	0.10	0.01

(*Continued*)

Table 3.3 (Continued)

	Percentage of voting power (as of August 1, 2011)	*Percentage of voting power after voice reform Phase-2*[1]	*Variation*
Turkey	0.52	1.08	0.56
Netherlands (ED)–Ukraine (AED)	4.43	4.18	–0.25
Armenia	0.08	0.10	0.02
Bosnia and Herzegovina	0.05	0.06	0.01
Bulgaria	0.33	0.30	–0.03
Croatia	0.15	0.15	0.00
Cyprus	0.10	0.11	0.01
Georgia	0.11	0.12	0.01
Israel	0.30	0.28	–0.02
Macedonia	0.04	0.05	0.01
Moldova	0.10	0.11	0.01
Montenegro	0.06	0.07	0.01
Netherlands	2.16	1.92	–0.24
Romania	0.26	0.31	0.05
Ukraine	0.67	0.60	–0.07
Spain (ED)–Venezuela (AED)	4.41	5.06	0.65
Costa Rica	0.03	0.08	0.05
El Selvador	0.02	0.07	0.05
Guatemala	0.14	0.15	0.01
Honduras	0.05	0.07	0.02
Mexico	1.15	1.68	0.53
Nicaragua	0.05	0.07	0.02
Spain	1.71	1.85	0.14
Venezuela	1.25	1.11	–0.14
Italy (ED)–Portugal (AED)	3.44	3.60	0.16
Albania	0.07	0.08	0.01
Greece	0.12	0.33	0.21
Italy	2.72	2.64	–0.08
Malta	0.08	0.09	0.01
Portugal	0.35	0.34	–0.01
San Marino	0.05	0.06	0.01
Timor-Leste	0.05	0.06	0.01
Sweden (ED)–Denmark (AED)	3.27	3.08	–0.19
Denmark	0.83	0.76	–0.07
Estonia	0.07	0.08	0.01
Finland	0.53	0.50	–0.03
Iceland	0.09	0.10	0.01
Latvia	0.10	0.10	0.00
Lithuania	0.11	0.11	0.00
Norway	0.62	0.58	–0.04
Sweden	0.92	0.85	–0.07
Total	**32.97**	**32.38**	**–0.59**

[1] Phase 2 currently under implementation as the Bank Selective Capital Increase (SCI) subscription period is open until March 2015; see DC 2011-0005 Modernizing the World Bank Group: An Update, p. 13 http://siteresources.worldbank.org/DEVCOMMINT/Documentation/22885417/DC2011-0005%28E%29Modernization.pdf

Table 3.4 The variation in EU MS voting power from phases 1 and 2 of the 'voice reform'

	Percentage of voting power (as of August 1, 2011)	*Percentage of voting power after voice reform Phase-2*	*Variation*
Austria	0.68	0.63	−0.05
Belgium	1.77	1.57	−0.2
Denmark	0.83	0.76	−0.07
Estonia	0.07	0.08	0.01
Finland	0.53	0.50	−0.03
France	4.21	3.75	−0.46
Germany	4.39	4.00	−0.39
Greece	0.12	0.33	0.21
Ireland	0.33	0.35	0.02
Italy	2.72	2.64	−0.08
Latvia	0.10	0.10	0
Luxembourg	0.11	0.12	0.01
Netherlands	2.16	1.92	−0.24
Portugal	0.35	0.34	−0.01
Slovenia	0.09	0.10	0.01
Spain	1.71	1.85	0.14
Sweden	0.92	0.85	−0.07
United Kingdom	4.21	3.75	−0.46
Cyprus	0.10	0.11	0.01
Czech Republic	0.40	0.36	−0.04
Hungary	0.50	0.47	−0.03
Poland	0.67	0.73	0.06
Slovak Republic	0.21	0.20	−0.01
Malta	0.08	0.09	0.01
Romania	0.26	0.31	0.05
Bulgaria	0.33	0.30	−0.03
Lithuania	0.11	0.11	0
Total	**27.96**	**26.32**	**−1.64**

Source: World Bank Corporate Secretariat, August 2011

approximately pre-reform 27.96 to 26.32 in percentage terms (Table 3.4). As seen above, however, while the EU MS have experienced a contraction in their relative voting power, the decline has been less steep at the margin (26.89% instead of 26.32%).[45] Moreover, even discounting for the rise of China, now the third largest subscriber to WB shares, and the enduring primacy of the US, followed by Japan, the EU MS collective voting power still outperforms that of the Bank's three top shareholders.[46]

The 'institutional anomaly' upon which the EU, 'a bigger aid donor than any of its member states', who has 'important operation partnerships with the Bank in European and African regions' (European Parliament 2011b, 11–12), does not even have an observer status at the WB Executive Board has been raised several times, in the academic literature and policy circles (Bini Smaghi 2004 and 2006; Woods and Lombardi 2006, Phillips 2006, Pisani-Ferry 2005). As investigated in

Table 3.5 The voice and participation reform 2008–2010

	*Number of votes (as of August 1, 2011)****	*Percentage of voting power (as of August 1, 2011)****	*Percentage of voting power after voice reform Phase-2*	*Variation*
EU direct representation under current system******	544,269	32.97	32.38	−0.59
United States	265,219	16.07	15.85	−0.22
Japan	158,654	9.61	6.84	−2.77
G7*	330,865	20.05	18.68	−1.37
DTCs**		44.06	47.19	3.13
17 non-G7 industrialized economies	234,583	14.19	13.40	−0.79
Australia	26,153	1.60	1.33	−0.27
Austria	11,313	0.68	0.63	−0.05
Belgium	29,233	1.77	1.57	−0.2
Denmark	13,701	0.83	0.76	−0.07
Finland	8,81	0.53	0.50	−0.03
Greece	1,934	0.12	0.33	0.21
Ireland	5,521	0.33	0.35	0.02
Iceland	1,508	0.09	0.10	0.01
Israel	5,000	0.30	0.28	−0.02
Luxembourg	1,902	0.11	0.12	0.01
Netherlands	35,753	2.16	1.92	−0.24
New Zealand	7,486	0.45	0.43	−0.02
Norway	10,232	0.62	0.58	−0.04
Portugal	5,710	0.35	0.34	−0.01
Spain	28,247	1.71	1.85	0.14
Sweden	15,224	0.92	0.85	−0.07
Switzerland	26,856	1.62	1.46	−0.16

*This includes the aggregate voting power of the constituencies led by Canada and Italy

**Developing countries and countries with economies in transition

***World Bank Corporate Secretariat, August 2011

****Germany, France, United Kingdom, Austria–Belgium, Netherlands–Ukraine, Spain–Venezuela, Italy-Portugal, Sweden–Denmark

Chapter 5, consultation over matters of joint interest has been the main dimension along which the EU EDs have built their cooperation at the World Bank's Board. Since 2003, under the auspices of the Italian ED's office, the EU EDs and Alternates have started to meet informally every Friday morning, creating their Eurogroup, to consult over matters of common interest. Ad hoc meetings have also been held, and several joint positions have been issued. Progress on coordination has come along, with informal rules on methods and matters.

However, the anomaly is such 'only' from the point of view of a – hypothetical – collective principal. Undisputable on grounds of net (EU) welfare, such stance overshadows the enduring absence of an exclusive EU competence in development cooperation, including post-Lisbon, as well as the differences in the bilateral aid policies of the EU MS, which are reflected in their practice at the Board and in the different geographical and thematic contexts. Empirical records indicate that there is no consensus on the issue of compacting the representation of the EU at the World Bank's Board, even in what should be one among the most 'supranational' of the EU institutions, the EU Parliament (European Parliament 2011b). As detailed later in the book, instances of intra-institutional divergence further question the strength of an EU-wide drive towards compact representation in multilateral organizations. Institutionally, different EU external policies are associated to different intensities in EU competences (and, as seen above, they are not always consistently reflected in the Lisbon provisions on external representation). Politically, they are subject to a variety of sector-specific captures within the EU.

For practical purposes, each of the adjustments that have been suggested to support the case of pooling the influence of EU MS has its merits. Within the 'maximalist' options for reform, plans for a single EU constituency envisage a rotation of EU MS as chairs, with the possibility of a Commission representative acting as an alternate (European Parliament 2011b, 21). Alternatively, a transition towards two EU constituencies is suggested, one chaired by EU MS along rotating patterns, albeit with terms longer than the current six months, the other under the Commission authority, on grounds of the substantial amount of funds channeled by that EU institution through the World Bank.[47] Intermediate solutions point to the upgrade of the Union to a status of enhanced permanent observer, along the lines of the upgrade in the UNGA. By so doing, the Union would be able to present its positions with a single voice at each Board meeting, without having to wait to be (informally) convened at the Development Committee during the Annual Meetings, twice a year. Minimalist suggestions note the relevance of an enhanced coordination among EU EDs within the current constituency system, particularly through the creation of a Brussels-based forum, along the lines of the SCIMF, to structure coordination of the EU positions in the different *fora* for development financing, such as the World Bank and the other major regional development banks. The creation of an 'EU Platform on development' pointed precisely to that direction (idem 21, 28).

The different outcomes on the hypothetical continuum, between the maximalist and minimalist voting reform options, have implications on the relative concentration of shares. However, it does not necessarily follow that a more compact representation is associated with increased effectiveness of the EU's performance at the Board, as discussed in Chapter 5. For a joint EU seat to be conducive to EU-own goals it is also important that centrifugal forces and latent cleavages that have been slowing down the Europeanization of MS development policies so far are not simply internalized in a new institutional 'cage' at the World Bank's

Board, but are debated and reconciled at deeper levels within the Union. Creating a single EU constituency would be tantamount to a full delegation of authority in development matters from MS to the Union, which is currently impossible given the absence of EU exclusive competence. This said, not all the scenarios described above are mutually exclusive, and some could be indeed successive steps along a mid-term frame, as in the case of the proposed 'EU platform on development'.

3.7 Conclusions

The WB late 1990s 'poverty turn' and the adoption of the 'Brussels Consensus' of 2006 by the EU, respectively, embody changes in both organization's non-constituent policies. Both transformations responded to the critical feedbacks advanced by the OECD and civil society on WB and EU performances, respectively: the poor achievements of SAPs modeled on the Washington Consensus template, and the scant attention to results of the EU development policy before the new millennium. Coupled with a renewed accent on result-based management (an input received from the OECD-sponsored Third way approach), the World Bank emphasis on comprehensiveness and the EU's call to policy coherence were two key normative innovations developed to address those concerns. Both organizations re-oriented their policies and programs accordingly, targeting poverty eradication (whereas previous approaches had focused mostly on growth support) and good governance promotion, inaugurating (allegedly) more participatory models. Acknowledging the importance of alignment and coordination among donors, the EU and the WB strove to improve their cooperation along the Paris–Accra process. Post-9/11, the normative emphasis on policy comprehensiveness was reinforced by a resurgent securitization of aid, so that security and development policies became two complementary aspects in the multilateral quest for a prosperous peace. These ideational and material incentives were taken up by key leaders and staff internal to the two organizations and contributed significantly to foster normative and policy change. Corroborated by substantive evidence from official documents and feedbacks from policy practitioners, the timing of those changes in each organization suggest that reverberation effects from the World Bank's adoption of the CDF–PRSP framework played a key role in the EU's own policy change, through both adaptive and complex learning, often according to logics that also responded to appropriateness needs.

Ideational triggers, however, did not produce change at the level of constituent policies in either organization: the redistribution of shares in the World Bank's 2008–2010 'voice reform', and the post-Lisbon creation of a single EU-legal personality in international *fora*, have not been reflected in changes of the EU's representation at the WB Board so far.[48] Very little transformation occurred in 'second order rules' as a result of the post-Washington Consensus reforms in the World Bank, or after the implementation of the first Brussels Consensus in the post-Lisbon scenario by the EU. Alternative solutions have been debated, but only informal fixes have been devised in practice. Development policy has remained a shared competence, and more symmetric representation at the WB Board has a long way to go, with the US still retaining the option to veto decisions that need a qualified majority of 85%.

There are obvious differences in the mechanisms through which inter-organizational relations influence change in constituent and non-constituent policies, respectively. Result-based, comprehensive development and multi-stakeholder models have been recalled several times by the two governors in their new policy templates, but these normative evolutions have not touched the substance of their second-order rules, in terms of radically redistributing either shareholding rights at the World Bank's Boards, and competences between the EU and MS. To explain the stasis that has infused the EU and the World Bank in their respective attempts at 'constitutional changes' one must look beyond the boundaries of the standard constructivist toolbox, and engage both institutional and power-based approaches.

So far, policy change has been reconstructed largely through a diachronic observation of organization – and policy-specific transformations on either side, with reference primarily to official records about how each multilateral received the evolutions experienced by its 'significant other'. Inputs on the micro-evidence of the EU–WB relations across the same period, discussed in the following chapter, suggest that own and alter beliefs (conceptions and expectations) have exerted a discernible influence on the redefinition of the missions and (non-constituent) policies of the two organizations. How has the Bank received the change in the EU's approach to development policymaking? To what extent have the two organizations recognized each other as complementary, and to what extent have they seen the other in competitive terms, across those developments? The next chapter answers these questions by exploring change in non-constituent policies by the two global governors with the help of role theory. Chapter 5 in turn investigates attempts at change in constitutive politics, and their stasis, under the hybrid accountability ties that connect the EU and the World Bank.

Notes

1 The following pages provide new ground to analyze the effect of inter-organizational relations on IOs' change, touching on the strengths and weaknesses of rationalist and reflectivist approaches to that endeavor. Additionally, the chapter delves into the analysis of change in both constituent and non-constituent policies, or, following a different classification, it looks at institutional vs non-institutional change. On the difference between constituent and non-constituent policies, in addition to the seminal Löwi (1972), see Tsebelis (1990), Pollack (1994) and Bulmer (1994), who refers to the concept through the terms 'constitutive politics' and 'constitutive decisions'.'Constituent' and 'constitutive' qualifiers are used interchangeably in this book.

2 The analysis does not assert the theoretical primacy of either unit-level or systemic factors in the study of IOs' political and policy change. Along a similar line see the reappraisal of the core IR debate on the appropriate level(s) of analysis by Rosecrance (2008). The literature on foreign policy analysis (FPA), which has a well established lineage within IR and public policy scholarships, has provided relevant contributions on (foreign) policy change, investigating the interplay between analytical levels on the one side (Gustavsson 1999), and the interaction between rational and non-rational

logics on the other (Carlsnaes 1987; Wæver 1990). On the importance of non-material dynamics in the relation between an IO and its environment see Stetter (2013), on the EU. On inter-organizational relations see Bierman (2008).

3 See the World Bank 'A Note on Program Lending' (SecM80–150), February 29, 1980; as well as its Structural Adjustment Lending (R80–122), May 9, 1980.

4 As discussed in Chapters 7 and 8, similar criticisms have been expressed by the Bank about the EU, on grounds of discrimination among different developing partners.

5 The picture presented here is necessarily a synthesis of a much denser process, which also entailed a profound rethinking of theories, tools and strategies within the economic and managerial Anglo-Saxon-socialized intelligentsia. Rich policy oriented reviews, focused specifically on the World Bank across almost two crucial decades, are presented in Mosley et al. (1991) and Easterly (2007). For a critical reading of the emergence of the World Bank's new poverty approach to development as caused by a deliberate transnational managerial design see Murphy (2008). In the constructivist vein see Weaver (2008), as well as selected chapters in Park and Vetterlein (2010).

6 Highly synergic, the relation between Stiglitz and Wolfensohn eventually culminated in Stiglitz's firing by Wolfensohn under the pressure of the then Secretary of the US Treasury Larry Summers. See Mallaby (2004). A constructivist interpretation of their individual roles in leading change in the World Bank's mission over those years is provided by Weaver and Park (2012).

7 World Bank (2004). On the implications of the different World Bank's operational policies under international law see Tan (2010, 184–187). For a recent review of the Bank's results from the DPL approach see OPCS (World Bank, Operations Policy and Country Services 2012a).

8 'Investment Lending Reform: Concept Note', World Bank OPCS, January 29, 2009. The reform has further proceeded, as discussed in OPCS (World Bank, Operations Policy and Country Services 2012b).

9 Since January 2012, the Bank has introduced a third instrument, 'Program-for-Result Financing', to support entire programs led by the client country without the restrictions usually attached to traditional investment lending (World Bank, Operations Policy and Country Services 2011). Result-based disbursement, inclusion and flexibility to adapt to local needs are some of the improvements on the previous investment lending template.

10 On the links between Stiglitz's research and the third way philosophy see Stiglitz (2002b).

11 See among others Holland (2004), Elgström (2006), Bretherton and Vogler (2006), Orbie and Versluys (2009).

12 Political conditionality entered the Union's development toolkits first in the IV Lomé Convention in 1995, where the respect of human rights, democracy and the rule of law became, at least nominally, official benchmarks in the Union's aid allocation criteria.

13 The Cotonou Partnership Agreement was signed on June 23, 2000 and entered into force in April 2003. Revised for the first time in 2005, 'to enhance the effectiveness and quality of the ACP-EU partnership', the current version has been implemented since July 2008, with amendments in 2010 and 2014 (European Commission–DG Development and Cooperation–EuropeAid 2012). The EBA initiative was launched in 2001 to remove quotas and duties on all imported goods from 48 world LDCs except arms and ammunitions. Both frameworks are further discussed in Chapter 9 of the book.

14 Relevant achievements were also made in the area of Financing for Development (FfD), since the Monterrey consensus of 2002, and the successful pressuring that led the Commission to have MS increase their ODA/GNI levels.

15 While relevant as a watershed of EU normative transformation, the concept of policy coherence for development seems to suffer from several weaknesses (Carbone 2009).

16 The links between coherence, consistency and performance are addressed in Chapters 5 and 6 of this book.

17 The constructivist view of epistemic communities, whereby technical ideas succeed in being incorporated into actual policies under conditions of shared consensus among experts, and in times of critical uncertainty among political elites (Adler and Haas 1992), has been further qualified in the literature. Particularly relevant for our purpose is the role played at particular points in time by social, organizational and political needs of key actors operating at different governance levels. The idea is that policy change may be either triggered by a crisis of some kind (Gustavsson 1999, 86–87), or that the opening of a 'window of opportunity' gets skillfully manipulated by policy (or norm) entrepreneurs who are able to identify and couple streams of policies and problems, respectively (Kingdon 1995).

18 On the roots of these ideational shifts and their connection to role changes see Chapter 4.

19 Along the way, several limitations have however impaired the achievement of a more effective EU approach to development policymaking. With respect to the EU Aid Effectiveness Agenda, in 2009 the cost of EU weaknesses was estimated to be between 25 and 30 bn Euros from 2010 to 2015, equivalent to 10% of the total spending on aid (European Commission 2009c).

20 The Lisbon Treaty was signed on December 3, 2007 in Lisbon and entered into force on December 1, 2009, after some protocols were added mainly to facilitate ratification from Ireland, which had rejected the 2007 version through a referendum, in June 2008. The text contains the consolidated versions of the Treaty on European Union (TEU) and of the Treaty on the Functioning of the European Union (TFEU), and includes protocols, declarations and the Charter of Fundamental Rights of the European Union, as amended after the reform draft in Lisbon.

21 See UNGA A/Res/65/276 of May 3, 2011. Before the upgrade the EU was represented by the Commission, as a permanent observer since 1974 (UNGA Resolution 3208 (XXIX), October 11, 1974).

22 On September 14, 2010 a majority compacted at the UNGA to defer voting on granting the Union 'enhanced observer status'. The diplomatic debacle undergone by then-HR Baroness Catherine Ashton was worsened by her – allegedly – too timid stance on the EU's position with respect to the Arab Spring. With an External Action Service (EEAS) in its infancy at the time, the learning process undergone by the HR in the UNGA did not appear easily replicable at the World Bank's Board.

23 A counterfactual is provided by the EU's representation in the WTO, where the Union is a full member along with MS, and either one of the two participates to the – rare – voting sessions, depending on issues. In obvious addition to the fact that the EU retains exclusive competence in trade matters, time also played a role to explain Brussels' membership in the WTO, as evident when considering the effort contributed by the Union (Community) during the Uruguay Round in founding the new organization (Wessel 2011, 12).

24 See Art. 208 TFEU (Title 3, Ch.1, Development cooperation), which calls for both EU and MS compliance and conformity with commitments taken and objectives approved 'in the context of the United Nations and other competent international organisations'.

25 Art. 18, Title V of the Provisions on a Common Foreign and Security Policy of the TEU, as amended by the Treaty of Amsterdam (1997) reads: 'The Presidency shall represent the Union in matters coming within the common foreign and security policy'. Differently, according to the Lisbon Treaty (TEU Ch.2 Art. 27, par 2), it is now up to the HR to represent the Union and implement the CFSP, with the support of the EEAS. Art. 34 (TEU ch. 2, par 1) in the Lisbon Treaty reiterates the provisions of the Treaty of Amsterdam by calling on the MS to coordinate their action within international organizations and to uphold the Union's positions in such *fora*. The RP, though, is not tasked anymore with expressing the position of the Union, which has been attributed to the HR, along with the formal responsibility to organize the coordination of MS.

26 In addition to the recent evolutions at the UN General Assembly, the graduation of monetary affairs into an exclusive competence of the EU since the implementation of the Euro in 1999 has also provided the basis for a sustained call towards compacting

the EU's seats in the IMF Board (Bini Smaghi 2004 and 2006; Truman 2006; Ahearne and Eichengreen 2007). Post-Lisbon developments on the EU's legal standing in international *fora* are discussed, among others, in Wessel (2011) and Emerson et al. (2011). On performance aspects see Jørgensen et al. (2011a), on foreign policy implications see Missiroli (2011) and Vanhoonacker and Pomorska (2013).

27 Art 4.4 of the TFEU reads: 'In the areas of development cooperation and humanitarian aid, the Union shall have competence to carry out activities and conduct a common policy; however, the exercise of that competence shall not result in member states being prevented from exercising theirs.' Art. 21 (3) (TEU) calls on the Council and the Commission, assisted by the HR, to cooperate to ensure consistency between the different areas of the EU's external action (and between the latter and the EU other policies). Art. 22 (Ibid.) entitles the European Council, on a recommendation by the Council, to identify – by unanimity – strategic interests and objectives of the Union's External action, attributing to the Commission the discretion to submit joint proposals on, inter alia, development issues.

28 It has not materialized through exclusive competence at the EU level (communitarization), and it has only partially developed through an adaptation of EU member states' national approaches to development (Europeanization). However, as discussed in Chapter 4, it has taken place through the external diffusion of (selected) European norms (Laatikainen and Smith 2006b, 9).

29 Formally, such cooperation has been reinforced in the Lisbon Treaty through the attribution to the HR of the Commission's Vice-Presidency (Art. 17 (4) and Art. 18 (4) TEU).

30 Evidence from the first Revision (2013) has suggested that 'turf wars' prevailed between the HR/VP and other Commissioners, and only a few EEAS staff was devoted to coordinate work with the Commission's DG DEVCO.

31 Art. 210 (1) TFEU makes coordination and consultation between the EU and MS in the field of development cooperation (including in International Organizations) a legal obligation, and Art. 210 (2) TFEU enables the Commission to take any useful initiative to promote such coordination. As seen above, the New EU Consensus on Development (2017) is broadly informed by a structural commitment for the EU MS and institutions to act jointly in development policy.

32 While first appearing in the official agenda of the World Bank in a background paper prepared for the 2003 Spring Meetings, the 'voice issue' had been latent on the radar screen since earlier calls on the Bank to improve its internal governance. The UN Millennium General Assembly of 2000, and, more evidently, the Monterrey Consensus of 2002 first listed enhanced voice and participation of developing countries as priorities for multilateral institutions (Jakobeit 2005; Vestergaard 2011, 20).

33 I.e. constituencies composed by EU and non-EU MS.

34 A vast number of contributions exist on a debate which has spanned across almost two decades (see Archibugi 2004), and where the boundary positions presented here (hard realists–rational institutionalists vs cosmopolitans–neo-Kantians) are in fact in good company with other stances along a nuanced continuum. Among them, the skeptical optimism of democracy theorist Robert Dahl, who believed in the virtues of global democracy, doubting however about its practical feasibility (Dahl 1999). Along this line also see Koenig-Archibugi (2011).

35 Namely, authors in the cosmopolitan vein disagree with the dilemmatic reading, and see the two horns as rather complementary aspects of what is considered a better system altogether. This echoes Lijphart's results about the positive correlation between democratic quality and policy effectiveness as representativeness increases in democratic regimes – so that better results are obtained in consociational democracies, as opposed to majoritarian, on both quality and effectiveness counts. Institutionalists, on the contrary, frame the discourse in terms of a trade-off between accountability to an increasing number of stakeholders and the ability that an organization has to deliver effectively on a stated set of policy objectives/mission. According to Keohane (2003),

the issue is fundamentally a normative one, so that boundaries of external accountability (where does the buck stop?) can be set ultimately only based on ethical a-prioris.

36 See Woods (2008b, 16), Gutner and Thompson (2010), and Chapters 5 and 6 in this book.

37 An example, discussed in Chapter 2, is the WB recent Open Data Initiative and Access to Information Policy.

38 A similar point on the competition between the Bretton Woods institutions and other *fora* is advanced by Woods (2008a, 10–11), who, as discussed above, reaches however opposite conclusions on the need to expand the voting powers of the poorest.

39 A burden which existing IOs have accepted to share, however, through the launching of 'capacity building' and 'integrated framework' programs to enhance the abilities of less resourceful partners.

40 As of March 16, 2018, they have been increased to 2.08% and 1.95% of total votes.

41 As of March 29 (2017), there are three all-African constituencies: a roughly bipolar one, Africa Group 3, created in October 2010, composed by Angola, Nigeria and South Africa, under a South African Executive Director; a 22-countries constituency named Africa Group 1, composed by English-speaking African countries, Botswana, Burundi, Eritrea, Ethiopia, The Gambia, Kenya, Lesotho, Liberia, Malawi, Mozambique, Namibia, Rwanda, Seychelles, Sierra Leone, Somalia, South Sudan, Sudan, Swaziland, Tanzania, Uganda, Zambia, and Zimbabwe, currently led by Zimbabwe; and a 23-countries constituency, Africa Group 2, mostly composed by French- or Portuguese-speaking African states, Benin, Burkina Faso, Cameroon, Cabo Verde, Central African Republic, Chad, Comoros, Ivory Coast, Democratic Republic of Congo, Djibouti, Equatorial Guinea, Gabon, Guinea, Guinea-Bissau, Madagascar, Mali, Mauritania, Mauritius, Niger, Republic of Congo, São Tomé & Principe, Senegal, and Togo, currently led by Burkina Faso.

42 China is the third largest shareholder to the IBRD, with its single-country constituency holding 107,284 votes; Russia occupies the 9th position, in terms of voting power, with 67,195 votes, to which the 3,145 votes held by Syria, recently added to Russia's previously single-country constituency must be added. India has 70,613 votes, but guides a constituency (Bangladesh, Bhutan and Sri Lanka) able to mobilize 84,997 votes. Their three constituencies are collectively worth slightly more than 11% of total IBRD voting power. The other single major players among the developing world are Brazil (43,151 votes, in a nearly-hegemonic constituency, worth 3.33% of total WB votes) and Saudi Arabia, commanding slightly 67,195 votes in its single-country constituency, or 2.86% of total votes.

43 In fact, a proposal advanced by Jakobeit in his study for the German Ministry for Cooperation and Development (BMZ) (2005) envisaged the possibility of double majority only for operational decisions (projects and personnel), leaving financial and strategic matters to the existing system. Also see Birdsall (2009).

44 These groups include Timor-Leste and San Marino, within the constituency led by Italy/Portugal.

45 The discrepancy is partly accounted for by the entry of Croatia as a new EU MS in 2013, which has brought EU27 to EU28, bringing some 0.15% in voting shares. Additionally, a selective capital increase has been completed in 2015, and shares are constantly updated, as the live update of shares and subscription in the World Bank Data.

46 As of March 2017, the US retained 16.39% in total Board votes (with 385,192 votes), with Japan holding 7.07% of voting power (166,134 votes). China in turn could wield 4.56% in total votes (with a total of 107,284 votes), ranking third above Germany, the first among EU contributors to the Bank's shares, holding 97,264 votes, or 4.14% of total IBRD votes (Aidflows data 2017).

47 Among the intermediate solutions, that proposed in the Zedillo Report envisaged a reduction of a least four of the eight currently EU-chaired constituencies (Zedillo 2009, 29, 37).

4 The EU's development policy and the EU–World Bank relations

The contribution of role theories

4.1 Introduction

Studying the evolution of the EU development policy cuts across multiple, interconnected dimensions, that are empirical, analytical as well as theoretical in nature: the peculiarity of the Union's 'external action', the relation between internal and external incentives (and particularly the interplay between the Union and its 'significant others' in that policy area), the balance between material and non material factors, rational and non rational logics, involved in these processes across time.[1]

This chapter investigates policy change in the EU development cooperation by looking at two of those macro-dimensions, the internal–external nexus, on the one side, and the ideational–material balance of potential causal factors respectively, on the other. It does so by tracking the influence of self- and alter-perceptions of specific EU foreign policy roles on the EU's (non-constituent) policy change that occurred in development cooperation across the turn of the millennium, as reconstructed in the previous chapter. This latter is thus observed in the context of the interplay between the Union's role conceptions and World Bank's expectations, and complemented with prima-facie evidence on the EU's role enactment. The focus on social and ideational mechanisms does not rule out the relevance of material factors and rational logics, which are in fact largely intermixed in the practice. Yet, it highlights the relevance of those mechanisms to study changes in non-constituent policies effected by imperfectly overlapping, interacting IOs, discussed here and in Chapter 3.

The chapter is organized as follows: the next section contains a brief review of the academic EU and IR literatures relevant for the analysis of EU development policy. Tracing a genealogy of role theory in IR studies, Section 4.3 addresses the relation between foreign policy analysis and role theory, while section 4.4 introduces the theoretical elements on role conception and expectation employed in this analysis. Section 4.5 reconstructs the evolution of the EU's role conceptions in development policy, investigating the influence of external expectations from the World Band and other significant actors in development policymaking. Role theory is engaged to investigate the influence of these external ideational elements on the changes that have occurred in the EU's development policy roles since the new millennium. Section 4.6 complements such diachronic analysis with an update on role expectations held by the World Bank on the EU, by looking at views from EDs and management at various levels, based on results from a research survey conducted between 2008 and 2011. Together, the two sections bring forth analytical and empirical elements to reconstruct and interpret the current EU's role at the World Bank and in multilateral development in the post-Lisbon era. Section 4.7 looks at the mismatch between current World Bank's expectations and the EU's role claims, advancing preliminary insights on role and policy performance, which is specifically targeted in the analysis of performance-as-effectiveness, presented in Chapters 5 and 6 of the book. Section 4.8 concludes.

4.2 Studying the EU development policy: EU studies, IR and the advantages of role theories

In the scholarly literature, the EU's aid policy has been explored through a plurality of lenses: political-economic (Grilli 1993; Santiso 2002), policy-analytic (Holland 2002; Hoebink and Stokke 2005; Carbone 2007), and social-constructivist (Bretherton and Vogler 2006; Orbie and Versluys 2009). Recent research has emphasized the importance of different approaches to explain sector-specific outcomes of the EU development policy and the relevance of the regional factor (Söderbaum and Stålgren 2010; Holland and Doidge 2012; Carbone 2013b). Such a variety echoes previous analyses of EU trade, monetary and investment policies, which have contributed with crucial insights to the broader academic research on the EU external action in economic matters, based on institutional, ideational and power-based approaches (Patterson 1997; Collinson 1999; Meunier and Nicolaidïs 1999; Meunier 2000; Knodt 2004; Damro 2006; Taylor 2006; Young 2007; Baroncelli 2008a).

Based on sociological role theories of foreign policy (Elgström and Smith 2006b), scholarly research on the EU's external role has analyzed the external perceptions on the EU policy role in multilateral trade and environmental negotiations (Elgström 2006), pioneering the exploration of images on the EU from the outside world (Lucarelli and Fioramonti 2010). It is to these studies in the constructivist vein that we owe the early research on the EU's images on development policy (Bonaglia et al. 2006), as well as the early calls for further analysis on the interplay between own images and others' expectations in the definition of the EU foreign policy roles (Elgström 2006, 37). Within the broader research agenda on the EU's global identity, actorness and role, findings from both the institutionalist and constructivist Schools, have fed into a strand within the literature on intersecting multilateralisms, focused on the EU and multilateral institutions (Laatikainen and Smith 2006a; Jørgensen 2009; Jørgensen et al. 2011a; Costa and Jørgensen 2012). These investigations have confirmed how, in the policy practice, the EU's role(s) enactment in, and relation with international institutions is often a mix between ideational and material factors, with own and others' behavior responding to both rationalist and reflectivist logics.

Change by IOs in the era of global politics has been authoritatively analyzed by both IR constructivists and institutionalists. Yet their respective findings have not always been analytically commensurable. Radically different takes on the level-of-analysis problem, and a generalized indifference for the material–ideational balance within each camp have contributed to widen the gap. In turn, studies in foreign policy analysis have provided ground to bridge the split: the links between ideational processes (such as complex learning and identity changes), behavioral responses and policy changes have been the object of an ongoing debate, which has long since called attention to the interaction effects between individual cognitive processes and political variables at both the systemic and domestic levels (Levy 1994, 306). While not specifically delving into the processes through which own and others' expectations are created, evolve and influence the interactions between large IOs and their policies, this chapter provides a theoretical elaboration of composite aspects of the EU's policy role in development issues, at the World Bank and with the World Bank. In addition, it looks at its evolution through the help of role theory, advancing a preliminary assessment of its practical implications.

First, it adds fresh insights to assess the importance of ideational components (both internal and external to the EU) in the understanding of the evolution of the EU's roles in development policy across the past 20 years. It then matches such evidence with views from other core external stakeholders (OECD, selected NGOs and specialized press), whose cross-time implications have been anticipated in the previous chapter. A case is made about the influence that these external inputs, often expressed as performance assessments, had on the EU's redefinition of its development policy, as well as on its assumption of new roles, in the post-Washington Consensus era. Finally, it engages evidence on (EU's) role conceptions and (WB) expectations in development policies, to set the context for the analysis of the EU's performance-as-effectiveness that will follow in Chapters 5 and 6.

In addition to being relevant to identify gaps between normative aspirations and others' expectations – the chapter suggests – role theory sheds light on (role and) policy change across time, unveiling the sources of general policy orientation beyond the micro-evidence of rule-constrained negotiations based on strategic bargaining. The reference to (role) performance and (role) impact dimensions adds plasticity to an otherwise purely ideational framework. When the task is one of analyzing complex unintentional outcomes, however, such reference bears the limitations of approaches that are based exclusively on the premises of ideational primacy (constructivism) and methodological individualism (foreign policy analysis). The role of ideational variables in the understanding of policy changes must therefore be circumscribed, particularly with respect to cases of change in constituent politics. Role theory is to be complemented with other approaches to understand complex policy results, or to explain performance outcomes that are neither primarily related to ideational dynamics nor visibly respond to discursive practices typical of structurationist settings (Giddens 1984; Wendt 1994; Bretherton and Vogler 2006, 26). As previously noted in this book, most notable examples are outcomes in 'second-order rule making', such as the difficult coordination on the redefinition of shareholding rights in the Eurogroup, on the occasion of the World Bank's 2008–2010 'voice and participation reform', anticipated in the previous chapter and investigated in Chapter 5.

4.3 The evolution of the EU's development role and the World Bank's post-Washington Consensus: foreign policy analysis and role theory

Through his seminal research, Kalevi Holsti (1970) incorporated sociological role theory in the IR analysis of foreign policy. In contrast to the holism of structural-systemic approaches,[2] Holsti believed that 'national role conceptions' were largely shaped by historical, cultural and societal processes in which perceptions of individual policymakers played a key part. His idea was a distinctive comeback to the methodological individualism of the liberal, classical realist and English IR Schools. The emphasis on the subjective component of foreign policy seemed to be confirmed by empirical evidence (Holsti 1970/1987; Wish 1987), whereby the patterns of states' foreign policy behavior (decisions and actions) appeared correlated to the role conceptions held by decision makers. Based upon such evidence, Holsti concluded that foreign policy (role) conceptions heavily influenced the foreign policy performance of states. Since then, the naiveté of the early mechanical correspondence between decision makers' beliefs and a country's foreign policy behavior has been refined, and the relevance of contextual incentives, material, institutional and ideational, duly acknowledged (Searing 1991). However, Holsti's earlier intuition that roles influence the making of the foreign policies of states still holds true. The relevant qualification here is that a variety of actors may intervene, through different processes and at multiple levels, in the formation and change of such roles.

Among them, socialization and learning have been accorded a particular relevance by IR constructivist analyses on the structuration of informal rules in international politics (Wendt 1992, 1999). Based on the insights of symbolic interactionism (Mead 1934), IR constructivist role theory has investigated how roles emerge from processes of states' interaction (i.e. multiple agency networks), studying their effects (role enactment, policy performance), and detailing their feedbacks from reverberation on inter-state relations. Structural incentives (such as institutions, short of constitutional redefinition, or systemic changes, whether material or normative) influence the choices of individual actors and groups, when creating roles, projecting them or taking them up, but their effect varies, across time and contexts. As reconstructed in the previous chapter and elsewhere (Baroncelli 2009; 2010), the dynamics of the World Bank's shaping of the post-Washington consensus, as well as its influence on the redefinition of the EU's own approach to development policy, suggest that external ideational triggers, from concerned NGOs and progressive OECD members, have gained increased normative strength, impacting in relevant ways on the norm and policy changes experienced – and projected in the outside world – by the two large multilaterals.

Relative to the redefinition of the EU's development policy in the new millennium, the focus on role theory provides unique insights on changes whose *primum movens* cannot be tracked back solely, or primarily, to structural (either power-based or institutional) inducements, and that are more appropriately reconstructed through instances of role-informed networks of agency. Additionally, neither institutional nor power-based approaches can shed much light on the gaps between the EU's normative aspirations and the external expectations retained by relevant others on what it should do. The analysis of the EU's behavior at the World Bank through the lens of role theory, then, assesses the significance of specific role expectations (retained by World Bank's officers) for the processes of the Union's role taking in its development policy. Furthermore, it brings new insights to the wider debate on the EU's role in the world.

The combination of concepts from role theory and foreign policy analysis takes on additional relevance when applied to the EU case. Based on the transitioning nature of the EU polity and compared to states' foreign policy roles, the EU's roles appear – if possible – more fluid and malleable. By virtue of its peculiar nature, 'more than an intergovernmental organization, less than a state' (Bretherton and Vogler 2006, 21–22) the EU possesses, as noted here and elsewhere, multiple – and highly contested – roles, some of which are context-specific, such as 'leader in trade negotiations' or 'development promoter', others with wider reach, as in the case of its 'role sets' defined under the labels of 'normative' and 'civilian' power (Manners 2002; Aggestam 2006). In this respect, its foreign policy behaviors are for most part a work-in-progress, as they add a good dose of institutional vagueness, particularly in matters falling under shared and parallel competence. While role theory allows one to reconstruct multiple role claims from different agents, to look at the structuration of such roles in an interactional context, foreign policy analysis helps to clarify time, logics and causal nexuses involved in these processes (Baroncelli 2013b).

The creation of those roles, and, to some extent, their enactment by the EU through its actual policies, has evolved across time, responding to the effects of the interaction between EU-internal drives, on the one side, and to the incentives, either positive or negative, from the external environment, on the other. The World Bank's role as the EU's 'most significant other' in the group of aid multilaterals, makes it imperative to look at how the two IOs' respective role claims have influenced their interaction and their own role and policy changes.[3]

The chapter focuses primarily on images, statements and clearly identifiable policy decisions that are attributable to the Union, the Bank and other external stakeholders, leaving to subsequent chapters the discussion on the impact of the interplay among these decisions on the actual policies targeted at developing countries. Here a difference is drawn between role performance and policy performance: while the former refers to the foreign policy behavior of a specific actor (say EU inputs to increase aid volumes or to launch the Eurogroup), the latter refers to complex policy outcomes (say results obtained in policy coordination along the Accra Agenda or relative success in advancing the EU's preferential EPA system in SSA).

4.4 Role: conceptions and expectations

Across time, academic research has offered multiple interpretations for the concept of foreign policy role. The IR power transition literature has often associated it with that of status, stressing the 'emanation' effect from material power dynamics to the sphere of political and normative recognition by other major actors in the international system, warning against the risks implicit in instances of 'delayed recognition' (Gilpin 1981; Doran 1989). While some have identified foreign policy role with a given set of behavioral regularities (Knodt and Princen 2003) others have used the term to indicate the ability to influence policy courses (Hill 1990; Bretherton and Vogler 1999). Reference to role concepts serves a bridging purpose, between structural and institutional features on the one side, and purposive action by individuals and groups on the other. Roles would therefore 'unlock the door between institutional structure and individual behavior' (Searing 1991, 1249).

Role conceptions originally pertain to the 'subjective dimension of national foreign policy', and are composed by 'normative expectations that the role beholder expresses towards itself' (Aggestam 2006, 19). Empirically, the extent to which [role conception] 'tends to reveal the intentions and motives of the foreign-policy actor, in other words the meaning of action' (ibid.) varies greatly, according to a number of different factors (not least cognitive dissonances between different discourses). At the theoretical level, compared to other components of the notion of role, conception is the closest to individual agency: as such, it potentially allows the highest degree of intentionality in the analysis of foreign policy.

Role expectations specifically refer to images (norms, values, principles, intentions, descriptions of reality) that other actors retain with reference to the role beholder. As such, they draw on both own position in the relevant reference structure (international system, policy contexts, organization) and on the position occupied by the role beholder (again, possibly in a multiplicity of different contexts). For our purpose, role expectations depend on what the others think of the EU, which in turn also depends on what they think of themselves, in the overall relevant context. While analytical and space reasons suggest to circumscribe the notion of 'relevant context' here, one should always keep in mind the element of multiplicity (contexts and expectations) when aiming at tracking back a comprehensive EU foreign policy role-set (Aggestam 2006).

The investigation on the EU's role in hybrid delegation follows the conceptual framework elaborated by Elgström and Smith (2006b). The status, behavioral regularity and influence meanings each stress separately important constituent elements of the concept of role. Yet, the composite nature of the definition by Elgström and Smith captures simultaneously several other components of the concept of role, adding flexibility to the operationalization and retaining relevant information from the empirical analysis of foreign policymaking. On the theoretical side, as aptly noted elsewhere (Aggestam 2006; Elgström and Smith 2006b), the agency component, or 'subjective dimension' of foreign policy analysis (Holsti

1972), inherent in the idea of 'role conception' appears fruitfully integrated with the context-component – integral to the idea of 'role expectation' – from theories of complex organization. Dynamic elements are added to the picture through the incorporation of learning and socialization dimensions from the study of role taking, through the interaction among actors and institutionalization processes (Wendt 1992). Finally, while role performance is also included in the original definition provided by Elgström and Smith (actual foreign policy behavior, Aggestam 2006, 20), here a difference is made between role and policy (performance and impact, respectively), two concepts that do not always coincide in practice.[4]

As discussed in Chapter 3, PA and bargaining models centered on strategic decision-making help to explain change, or its absence, in two key cases of EU and WB constituent politics. Differently, other major transformations of the two IOs in their non-constituent politics have responded to ideational dynamics and non-rational logics, entailing a complex mixture of agent-induced judgment, structural constraints and role expectation. This chapter contends that role theory potentially brings insightful elements to the analysis of the EU's making of its development policy, at the Bank and through the Bank.[5] As discussed below, own and others' images, especially when expressed in the form of performance assessments, appear to influence the way decision-makers shape the policy agenda, and may ultimately have a tangible impact on both policy outputs and outcomes. Relevant from an IR–IPE perspective, is the interactive nature of these processes, whereby others' views happen to feedback into own views, at times being percolated in re-definitions of own role conceptions and, under specific conditions, translated into consistent role performances and turned into actual policies.

4.5 The evolution of EU's role conceptions in development policy and the influence of external expectations: the World Bank and the others

The EU's claim to support development through a foreign policy of solidarity (European Commission 2000b) has gradually evolved out of an original – internal – solidarity plan (Nielson 2001).[6] The attainment of an 'ever closer union among the peoples of Europe'[7] was coupled in the original text of the Treaty of Rome with the call to concerted action towards, *inter alia*, 'balanced trade and fair competition', in order for the common commercial policy to serve as a stepping stone to gradually remove the existing barriers to international trade. Additionally, the founding fathers worked to strengthen the 'solidarity' ties between Europe and 'the overseas countries', towards the 'development of their prosperity'.[8] The path that led to such evolution has not however been a linear one.

Since the inclusion of international cooperation among the goals of the CFSP in the Maastricht Treaty,[9] the EU has incorporated in its role conceptions an emphasis on the promotion of 'sustainable' and 'human' dimensions of development. Consistent with its political mission, the Union has also clearly linked the promotion of development in the world outside to the attainment of other EU foreign policy goals. Encouraging development has been acknowledged as part of a wider 'political plan' to integrate developing partner countries in the global economy and to 'help reinforce democracy and the rule of law, whilst promoting respect for human rights and basic freedoms' (European Commission 2000, quoted in Bonaglia et al. 2006, 170). Democracy promotion and the respect for human rights were reaffirmed in EU regulations in the early 1990s (Olsen 2000; Youngs 2001; Santiso 2003), and inclusion of political conditionality clauses in association agreements became a common feature after the Barcelona Process was launched in 1995.[10] As discussed in Chapter 3, a major turning point occurred in the mid-1990s, when the Commission called for a revision of the criteria that had informed its 'paternalistic' modes of aid allocation under Lomé, towards a more objective performance-based approach (European Commission 1996).

Since the 1990s, development promoter, active democracy supporter, human rights defender and facilitator of further integration in the world economy have then emerged as the main EU role conceptions in development policymaking. At the end of that decade other significant shifts took place in the Union's conception of foreign policy role in the areas of development and development-related policies (namely trade and security). A major turning point was marked by the Cotonou Agreement of 2000, through which the promotion of peace and security functions gained further prominence in the foreign policy role conception of the Union, with additional references to migration and trade-security links (European Commission 2002; EBA Initiative).[11]

The new millennium also witnessed a broader redefinition of the values informing the EU's approach to development cooperation. Inputs for a 'more globally-minded Europe' gained further strength in European cabinets, following the change that occurred in world politics after the Al Qaeda attacks to the Twin towers on 9/11, causing at times tension with the American ally, and unfolding a lively debate on the redefinition of the EU's external role in world affairs.[12] The Commission successfully worked towards forging an EU own Consensus on development, based on the idea that aid policies, now primarily targeted at reducing poverty, should be 'owned' by all the potentially relevant stakeholders, including Civil Society Organizations (CSOs) in partner countries, which ought to be engaged in political dialogue. The emphasis on promoting different goals through supporting development (from dealing with political fragility to engendering development) was accompanied by a conscious search for coherence on the side of the Union (Dearden 2003; Hoebink 2004; Carbone 2008, 334). A genuine belief in the virtues of scaling up was conveyed by the Commission's effort to enlist EU MS towards reaching the 0.7 ODA/GNI target. In the discourse on improving aid effectiveness, the EU also claimed a leading role in advancing the implementation of the Paris Declaration on aid harmonization.[13]

Evidence from third-parties provides core inputs to reconstruct the dynamics of the EU's role formation and role taking in development policy across this period (Baroncelli 2009). The influence of systemic factors and the relevance of interactions between the EU and other external actors, in shaping the evolution of the EU development policy, appear largely confirmed when looking at long-term trends. The adoption of adjustment conditionality in World Bank's SAPs witnessed a broader shift that had invested the donors' community after the catastrophic effects on most developing countries of the debt crisis in the early 1980s. In the Fourth Lomé Convention (signed in 1989), the EU ended up replicating the World Bank's adjustment conditionality template, though in a modified version, with considerable costs to its earlier pledges to non-conditionality and non-interference. Lacking financial resources, expertise, and the support from MS, comparable to those available to the two Bretton Woods IFIs at the time, the EU could not conceivably challenge their dominance (Brown 2004, 18–24). A similar trajectory seems to have occurred with respect to the incorporation of the human, sustainability and governance dimension in the EU's aid policies. Emphasis on human and sustainable development had achieved particular prominence since the mid-1960s in the development literature (Arndt 1987). Yet, it was only at the end of the 1980s, when the adverse effects of several World Bank and IMF first generation adjustment programs became known to the world of development practitioners (Cornia et al. 1987), that the importance of the human dimension of aid financing re-emerged powerfully. While the European Council itself openly supported the need to overcome these limits (Council of the European Communities 1988), the EU was not able to set a course independent from that pursued by the World Bank.

The shift from Lomé to Cotonou, and the EU's new claim to a role of poverty reducer through positive inclusion, its aspiration to become promoter of good governance and human security, reconstructed in Chapter 3, have responded to critical stimuli, developed amidst the broader changes that had taken place in the development community since the late 1990s. Indeed, in 1998, through its DAC peer review mechanism, the OECD had expressed its concern on strategic and implementation aspects of the EU development policy (OECD 1998). The Bank itself had emphasized the risks inherent in EU aid programs that did not take into account governance benchmarks (World Bank 1999). While these specific recommendations were targeted to EU supposed flaws, the overall failure of the WTO Ministerial Meeting of Seattle in 1999 showed how developing countries were increasingly compact in voicing their dissent to the industrialized countries, donors and partners (Panagariya 2002). Insights from the development literature (Stiglitz 2002a; Woods 2006; Greig et al. 2007), as well as remarks from top World Bank officials (Baroncelli 2010), indicate that these and other recommendations from development agencies were themselves a normative response to the concerns advanced by developing countries, part of the overall debate on the Washington Consensus (Oxfam 2002). The launch of the Millennium Development Goals, along with the creation of the development agenda in trade negotiations (the Doha Development Agenda) were perhaps the most visible among the remedial actions undertaken by the major donors.

Relevantly, the Commission also took up the challenge of improving EU aid delivery, through internal reorganization and better coordination with other donors, to better meet partner countries' needs. To be sure, the EU was undergoing its own, serious, internal crisis, as shown by the collective resignation of the Santer Commission in 1999, after accusation of briberies and corruption.[14] Amidst the broader reconsideration of the Washington Consensus, the new Commission, led by Romano Prodi, initiated a redefinition of the EU's development policy. The window of opportunity that had opened through the failure of the Bank's sponsored structural adjustment approach was exploited by the Union at several stages.

Showing considerable institutional resiliency, the Prodi Commission produced a profusion of documents to build a new framework for the Community development policy, to mark a change with the previous Commission and to promote a new system of external relations (see among others European Commission 2000a, 2000b, 2000c). With the launch of the Cotonou Agreements in 2000, the Union responded to the critiques against the way it had managed its relations with the ACP countries. Brussels took on a higher responsibility to promote cross-policy strategies in those countries, linking aid allocation to the respect of human rights and to the attainment of governance benchmarks, and adding a clear security dimension to its development assistance under critical conditions, in fragile and terror-torn states. In January 2001 the EuropeAid External Cooperation Office (AIDCO) was created, to coordinate the implementation of development financing tools through the European Development Fund (EDF) and the EC budget.[15] Efforts at reducing the gap between emergency aid (managed by Directorate-General for European Civil Protection and Humanitarian Aid Operations (ECHO) since 1992) and development aid were also included in the reform, and so were provisions to stimulate the dialogue with CSOs, and to enhance the EU's impact on the UN framework of multilateral development agencies. The new Commission successfully supported the scaling up agenda at Monterrey in 2002, while the proactiveness of the succeeding Commission (which took office in 2004 under the guidance of President Barroso), culminated in the EU Consensus on Development of 2006 (Carbone 2007). Subsequently, a peculiar emphasis was put on improving the division of labor among donors through the harmonization of respective aid policies, through the Commission's Code of Conduct on Complementarity and Division of Labour in Development Policy (2007). While factors internal to the EU have undoubtedly contributed to such policy changes,[16] the normative and policy developments reviewed above, which took place in the World Bank and in the broader aid, trade and security communities, have exerted a crucial influence on the content and direction of the EU's choices, encouraging Brussels to take on new roles in development financing. In 2000 the Luxembourg Process was launched, to guide the cooperation between the Union and the Bank in the promotion of development in the MENA region, while the Limelette Process provided the institutional umbrella for their collaboration in the Africa region. In 2005, the Commission and the Council released two communications on Africa, both endorsed by the Council, and the first EU-led Trust Fund, the Africa Infrastructure Trust Fund (EU-AITF), was launched in 2007.

To what extent have World Bank perceptions of the EU matched the new role claims by the Union? To what extent do they add elements to reconstruct the foreign policy roles of the post-Lisbon Union? It is precisely on role expectations and preliminary evidence on role performance that the focus is now turned.

4.6 Expectations from the World Bank[17]

Not surprisingly, most of the World Bank's role expectations of the EU refer to its economic policies (particularly development and trade) and, when mentioning roles in other policy areas, exhibit an explicit connection with their economic dimension. However, allusions to EU's roles in policy areas other than development or to overall role-sets cutting across policy domains are not infrequent, suggesting that several apexes at the World Bank expect a more synergic, multifaceted and composite foreign policy role for the Union.

A large majority among the World Bank interviewed officers see the EU as an international power. Yet, the concept is qualified under multiple counts, and several nuances added when the category is referred to the EU. The multifaceted role, expressed in the own EU conception of 'peace, prosperity and freedom' builder appear to be a generally received one at the Bank, but broadly positive views on role performance (the degree to which the EU is perceived to have fulfilled its claims) lose their commendatory connotation when referred to the attainment of specific goals. Indeed, the multiplicity of foreign policy objectives endorsed by the Union, and the feeble influence of the Commission in foreign affairs – compared to the weight of leaders from EU MS – have been connected to instances of the EU's poor role performance (introduced in section 4.6 below) and, more broadly, to instances of flimsy role and policy impact (which is the subject of Chapters 5 through 9).[18]

In the eyes of the World Bank, the domestic analogy of a 'Union of the Third Millennium', able to project externally the pursuit of domestic values of freedom and prosperity, is a distinctive trait that differentiates the EU from other political-economic unions. However, variations in perceptions exist on this point, with beliefs from Bank units that specifically focus on social issues pointing to opposing views, of a Union that uses double standards and that has not consistently promoted its core social internal values in the outside world.

World Bank officers also clearly appreciate the political mission of the EU – a trait that differentiates it from the (officially) a-political mission of the Bank – and even appear to commend Brussels' opportunity to normatively advance the promotion of political values through the EU's economic policies. On the matter, most have praised the non-coercive EU's approach to foreign economic policymaking, contrasting it with the more aggressive US approach, positively acknowledging the EU 'unselfish' methods, and the linkages between economic and security goals in Brussels' foreign policy.

On the role of the Union as 'supporter of free trade', perceptions from the Bank seem to be fairly in line with findings from other studies (Elgström 2006; Fioramonti 2007; Poletti 2007). The view of a 'Community' that 'will assist developing countries on trade and regional integration through fostering equitable and environmentally sustainable growth, smooth and gradual integration into the world economy, and linking trade and poverty reduction or equivalent strategies' (European Parliament, Council, Commission 2006, 11) does not appear to be a shared one in the Bank. 'Protectionism', 'preaching', 'agricultural subsidies', 'unfair manipulation of ROOs issues' are recurrent images. In trade matters, the Bank sees the EU as a strategically minded defender of its own interests, rather than an altruistic facilitator of the integration of developing countries into the world economy. Numerous technical criticisms have emerged relative to the non-pro development nature of the EU 'ultimatums' to its ACP partners in the post-Cotonou phase of the EPA negotiations. In contrast to the roles that the EU has claimed for itself in the Brussels Consensus of 2006, these criticisms also clash against the EU's role conceptions in trade matters, which portray Brussels as a major promoter of development through both vertical and horizontal trade integration.[19]

The 'facilitator' role in poverty eradication and economic integration is however confirmed by World Bank views on aid provision in sheer financial terms. While the virtuosity of the Nordic group has clearly emerged in several instances, the overall Union is singled out in the donor community for its generosity, and its commitment to reach the 0.7 ODA/GNI target praised across the board. Comparisons with the US and China indicate that the EU is seen as playing a distinct role in development, less constrained by national political concerns (compared to the US) and more informed by ethical values (compared to China). The EU's role as a major collective donor is therefore duly acknowledged by the Bank, even if the tension between bilaterals and the Commission is also a recurrent theme.

Overall, on leadership issues the most frequent image at the Bank returns the EU as a very important player in shaping trade policies in the world, likely to grow in this role in the future, a relevant actor in development issues, but only a minor, in some cases virtually non-existent player in shaping security equilibria. On the one side, views based on the day-to-day organizational practices, whereby the Bank's staff deals with EU MS, point to some vagueness as to whether the EU is seen as a unitary actor. On the other side, when it comes to views on broader policy matters, there appears to be a widespread image of the EU as relatively independent from the other major donors, with its own distinctive policy style, able to provide a viable alternative to compensate the US preference for mainly market-based solutions to development problems.

4.7 Views on the EU's role and policy performance: the external–internal mismatch

Different from research on role characteristics of the EU in multilateral negotiations (Elgström 2006), and similar to studies of the EU in IOs (Laatikainen and Smith 2006a, Elgström and Smith 2006a), this chapter focuses on role expectations from a single multilateral organization. Compared to the former seminal study by Elgström (2006) the difference implies that some candidate explanations for the type and variation of role expectations are to be found in the characteristics of the World Bank's organizational context. While this research is not primarily aimed at theorizing on the origins of role images, a few observations are advanced relative to the ties that connect organizational rank to role images, to qualify the analysis on policy performance that is done in the second part of the book.

Evidence from the survey indicates that the organizational role and function of World Bank officials contributes significantly to orient their images of the EU. While the top management is in charge of pursuing Bank-wide goals, EDs are collectively accountable to the Board of Governors, and individually to their national governments (in single-country constituencies) or constituency of members (in multi-country constituencies). In this latter capacity, they have a duty to advance the specific priorities of their constituency (all the member countries in the group). Secondly, as the difference in roles and functions between these two groups (EDs on the one side, management and staff on the other) is reflected in their behavior, the interaction with different actors also influences their perceptions of the EU. In their capacity, Vice-Presidents (VPs) have a higher chance to interface with EU representatives in client countries, in addition to EU MS at the Board and EU officers in Brussels. As a consequence, they have frequently referred to how the EU and its policies are perceived in partner countries, rather than at the Bank's Headquarters (HQ) in Washington. Differently, the EDs, while also having – from prior exposure or current briefing from their staff – experience on the EU–WB interaction in client countries, tend to focus more on the interactions that take place either in HQ DC, Brussels and other EU capitals, or in world top-level meetings. Thus, to understand role and policy change, the analytical focus has been widened to policy practice (role enactment and policy performance), investigating specific negotiation processes that have occurred between the two organizations.

At the end of the 2000s, views on the EU's role and policy performance by the top World Bank political management (EDs), portray a less-than-smooth strategic coordination between the Bank and the EU in goal setting, on the one side, and speak of difficult coordination of EU Members at the Board, as well as in client countries. The first issue directly points to an image of the EU that 'is still grappling with what its strategic role is', which has been quoted by one top political official as to 'why a strategic partnership [between the Bank and the EU] is missing'.[20] In this respect, among the retained 'EU's greatest weaknesses' the same top political official went so far as quoting explicitly the 'unwillingness to discuss the shape of the EU influence in international institutions'. The reasons behind such unwillingness (confidentially confirmed by interviews and documents from the Commission[21]), and its extent are specifically addressed in the next chapters. Here it is important to note the potential reputational loss carried by the EU's lack of clarity on its future strategies. The mere fact that the EU is seen by these top Bank apexes as not having been fully able to define its goals so far, then, risks becoming a key motivation behind the difficulty of moving from the current ad hoc, point specific cooperation between the two institutions to a strategic partnership (a 'master plan' would be missing, as well as a clear vision on the future of aid architecture).

Specifically relative to the second issue, coordination of EU EDs at the Board and EU MS in client countries, several points have been raised. On the one side, the long lamented lack of internal EU cohesion is supposed to have detrimental effects on the assertiveness with which EU MS are able to coordinate and support common EU positions at the Board consistently throughout a range of decision processes. The perspective from interviewed EU EDs is one of fragmented action. The fact that the EU MS are currently spread over eight different constituencies (out of which three are single-country constituencies, and the other five are mixed constituencies) is seen by top EU EDs at the Bank as if sometimes there were 'eight different Europeans'. Add to this that a recurrent element in the interviews, common to both technical and political top staff as seen above, is that 'The EU is not a member of the World Bank'. Given the majoritarian contribution to the overall Bank's budget provided by the EU MS and the EU institutions (the Commission, among the quoted actors in the interviews), the net effect is often interpreted as one of 'under-representation'. As discussed in Chapter 3, such expectation has been matched by the permanence, post-Lisbon, of development cooperation as a shared competence. The ability of the Eurogroup to coordinate and influence meaningfully decisions taken at the Board depends crucially on which issues are on the agenda (constituent vs non constituent politics), and on the degree of homogeneity of the EU EDs' preferences on the matter at stake, as discussed in Chapter 5, about internal and external effectiveness dimensions of the Eurogroup's performance at the Board.

Over the turn of the first decade of the new millennium, the EU broad claims to increased transparency and effectiveness in its development cooperation policy, advanced in the Consensus on Development of 2006 appeared shared only to a limited extent and with high geographical variability, as discussed in Chapters 7, 8 and 9. While views from World Bank officers in the ECA region have been mostly positive, pointing only to the risks of the EU (conscious) neglect of CIS and Central Asian countries, views of and from the World Bank officers active in the Sub-Saharan Africa and MENA regions have returned a mixed image of the EU transparency and effectiveness in its development policy role. Progress achieved through the Luxembourg (MENA) and Limelette (Africa) Processes has been fully acknowledged, as has been the participation of the Union to the Paris Process.[22] However, the EU's self-claimed leading role in implementation has not been reflected in the Bank perceptions. Role expectations also hoped for a Union that would be faster in matching economic support with political and moral influence, as well as more careful to minimize the risk that goal attainment were subverted downstream in the policy process, either through minimizing the lack of consensus among MS and with the Commission, or by anticipating excessive pressuring from partner countries once the objectives had already been set and funds disbursed. Well into the first decade of the new millennium, the EU claims to transparency and effectiveness did not appear to be fully matched by views from non-European World Bank officers, both management (VPs and Senior Officials) and political (EDs), that pictured the EU as often unclear in goal setting and difficult to deal with, on grounds of excessive bureaucratization, slowness and lack of technical competence.

4.8 Conclusions

This chapter has looked at the EU–WB relations through the lens of role theory, focusing on the EU's role conceptions and World Bank's expectations, and introducing the World Bank's views on the broader issue of the EU's performance in development. Perceptual insights from World Bank officials, based on a research survey conducted in 2008, have been relied on to reconstruct the image of the EU from the Washington-based IFI. Complemented with inputs from third parties, these findings suggest that ideational triggers, in the form of role expectations from the Union's (most) significant other among development multilaterals, may have played a role in the redefinition of the EU's role in development policy across the turn of the century.

Relative to role expectations, the empirical findings from the survey on the EU's image at the World Bank confirm the results of previous studies on IOs, pointing to the acknowledgement of the EU 'presence' through references to its size and positional importance in the global economy. Considered as a leader in trade matters, the Union is seen by the World Bank as gaining a growing influence in development issues. Its presence in security affairs, however, is largely regarded as negligible. With respect to the intersection between the two multilateral contexts, EU MS are retained to have a low joint institutional impact at the Board. The dual nature of the EU, which is regarded by World Bank interviewees as both a multilateral and a bilateral donor, magnifies images of disunity and low coordination. In the absence of a single seat, the hypotheses on the strength of 'tied hands negotiator' often spell inconsistent position across constituencies, and splits between large and small EU MS. The extent to which these perceptions are matched by actual practice, and the relative effectiveness of the Eurogroup's coordination at the Board is in turn investigated in Chapter 5 below.

Role expectations from Bank officials also confirm the datum of low 'horizontal policy coherence' reported elsewhere (Elgström 2006) relative to the trade-development link, as well as of low effectiveness in tapping the full potential of the aid-security link. Different from previous findings on the EU policy role in other multilateral contexts, and in clear contrast with the emphasis put by the Union on the concepts of transparency and effectiveness, perceptions from World Bank officers have also conveyed images of competence that is low, and of slowness and excessive bureaucratization in the planning and implementation of its development policy. These images also conflict with the emphasis on decentralization and better coordination, incorporated by the EU Consensus on Development of 2006.[23]

As noted above in Section 4.6, expectations from the Bank contain a normative component, and attach an innovative potential to the EU in the fulfillment of its complex political-economic role. The 'Union of the Third Millennium' could become 'what the Bank will never be', by its very nature and mission, i.e. an external agent able to support openly political and economic transitions at once. The Union's 'soft diplomatic approach' is contrasted with the more militarized USAID take to development. The high content in ideals of the EU development strategies is compared to the new, apparently 'value-free' (but interest-based) Chinese approach to aid policy. Interestingly, but somehow consistent with its formally a-political mission, views from several Bank officials do not generally claim a strong leadership role for the Washington-based IFI, and rather see the organization as a key partner of the EU and other major players in the development community.

Connections between role conceptions and role expectations, as well as consequentiality between images and behavior, depend on a multitude of factors. So does the validity of role theory when applied to the understanding of role performance and policy impact in the context of inter-organizational relations. Accordingly, this chapter has also touched on the role that external voices of dissent from developing countries and NGOs, critical of the performance of multilateral aid projects modeled on the Washington Consensus template, played on the redefinition of the overall development architecture since the end of the 1990s. OECD–DAC and World Bank own recommendations have plausibly influenced the EU's redefinition of its development policy, encouraging Brussels to improve coordination with partner countries and international agencies, as the Luxembourg and Limelette Processes appear to suggest. In the latter case, a learning process has been underway, where the perceptual filter of the Bank, the institutionally chosen partner of the Union, seems to be received as a positive policy input by a number of EU-Brussels and EU-field based actors. To be sure, both processes are two-way, with Bank actors quoting several cases of fruitful interaction with EU colleagues, especially on the side of social and political issues, such as security and human rights, democracy and gender issues. Yet, the lamented 'lack of courage' of the Union, which is perceived as often too timid in taking up its role of democracy promoter and human rights defender, resonates somewhat disturbingly of the 'capabilities-expectation gap' from earlier times (Hill 1993).

Voices from the Bank convey a distinct awareness of the EU's ongoing effort to endorse a complex leadership role in world affairs, and of Brussels' commitment to fully support the substantive values informing that effort. The ability of the Union to adapt its development policy role through change, responding to the challenges of the late 1990s, depended both on its internal resiliency and on the impact of others' role expectations. As discussed in this book, EU adaptation also responded to broader system-wide transformations. In this respect, the role theory perspective should be circumscribed under several dimensions. Its usefulness is maximum when employed to study foreign policy behavior, indeed the goal towards which it was originally designed by Holsti, or to investigate 'general policy orientations' (Aggestam 2006, 21). Yet, not surprisingly, it declines when employed to explain complex policy outcomes (i.e. international politics as opposed to foreign policies). Specifically, it loses traction when employed to investigate the influence of inter-organizational relations on game-changing policies (constituent politics) pursued by IOs. The analysis of the post-Lisbon permanent gap between the EU external representation and its development competence, on the one side, and of the World Bank's debate on the 2008–2010 voice reform, on the other, indicate that interest and power-based strategic incentives have crucially influenced the outcomes achieved in those cases by either IO (the permanence of major asymmetries in the World Bank's internal governance, the permanently shared nature of the EU's competence in development cooperation, the enduring absence of EU membership to the World Bank). The Eurogroup's low influence on decision making at the Board when shareholding rights are on the agenda, a topic investigated in Chapter 5, confirms this reading. The rules and stakes of each game, and potentially the identity of change agents within the same IO, are different in the two spheres of constituent and non-constituent politics, respectively.[24] The disaggregation between shareholders and management, or between political and technical actors within each IO, which is usually more visible and impactful in instances of non-constituent policy changes, tends to be overshadowed by the power and interest considerations of shareholders (MS) in constituent policy changes. Substantially different is also the degree of each institution's permeability to external influences, which, in the cases analyzed here, appears lower in constituent politics, compared to non-constituent types.

Finally, development policies are now formulated in a context that is denser, in terms of both actors and interactions (number and type), compared to even the recent past. Contacts between the Union and the Bank have increased substantially, and the quality of their interactions has markedly improved since the new millennium. Cooperative experiences in Central, Eastern and Southern Europe have opened the way to sustained partnerships also in the MENA and Africa regions. However, several voices in the World Bank have cast a mixed light on Brussels' role performance. In the eyes of the Bank, if not coupled with higher effectiveness, the EU attempts at increasing its visibility in world affairs may also have adverse reputational consequences. From horizontal policy inconsistency in the trade–aid links, to the weak coordination at the Board, or in instances of dualism between MS and the Union, some coherence seems to be missing at the planning and implementation levels. It is precisely to the investigation of these issues that the rest of the book is devoted.

Notes

1 On the need to look at both inside-out and outside-in logics in the formulation of EU development policy, taking into account identity issues across the post-Lisbon turn, see Smith (2013).

2 Systemic approaches had been transferred to the social sciences through the 'cybernetic revolution' some 15 years earlier, and would become the dominant approach in IR studies almost ten years later in Waltz's Theory of International Politics (1979).

3 The case is based on both normative and material grounds, as argued among others by Brown (2004) and Farrell (2008). Compared to the World Bank Group (in fact itself an agency in the UN family, but largely autonomous in terms of mission, programs and resources), the UN system could be a potential competitor in the group of the EU's 'most significant others', due to the slightly higher amount of EU channelled development funds to the whole UN (Euros 6.6 bn allocated through the UN system between 2002 and 2016, vis à vis Euros 2.2 bn allocated to the World Bank over the same

period). Yet, such total should in fact be disaggregated by each target agency (UNDP, UNEP, FAO, UNICEF and others), whose relative weight in the allocation of resources towards poverty reduction and operational practices is often less relevant compared to that of the World Bank Group. Recent evidence relative to allocations to Multidonor Trust Funds also points to a preference for the EU to allocate resources through the World Bank Group (for contracts spanning between 2002 and 2025, Euros 2.524 billion, or 53% of total EuropeAid allocations through multilateral agencies) relative to channeling to the UN-specialized agencies (for contracts spanning from 2003 to 2020, Euros 1.636 bn, or 34% of EuropeAid channeled funds to multilaterals) (European Commission–DG DEVCO-EuropeAid 2016).

4 While role taking might be successful and have an impact, there is always the possibility that the policies adopted through role conformity – or successful fulfillment – do not meet the needs of the recipients (i.e. that the policy has been either badly designed or poorly implemented: two outcomes that are chiefly policy- more than role-specific).

5 Also see Baroncelli (2008b; 2013a).

6 On a different count, as discussed below, the application of the domestic analogy to the making and study of EU foreign policy is a contested issue.

7 Preamble to the EEC Treaty (Rome Treaty), accessed at http://europa.eu/scadplus/treaties/eec_en.htm.

8 Ibid.

9 The Treaty of Maastricht was signed on February 1, 1992 1992 and entered into force on November 1, 1993.

10 Political conditionality entered the Union's development toolkits first in the IV Lomé Convention in 1995, where the respect of human rights, democracy and the rule of law became, at least nominally, official benchmarks in the Union's aid allocation criteria.

11 The basis for the EBA initiative was the EU generalized system of tariff preferences (2001–2004), as laid out in Council Regulation 2501/2001 (European Council 2001b). Under the special treatment granted to least developed beneficiaries, the Regulation fully incorporates the 'Everything But Arms' (EBA) initiative (European Council 2001a).

12 Connected to the debate on burdensharing, and the advisability of contributions of the European allies to NATO out-of-area operations, the frictions between Washington and the European capitals had been an ongoing issue in EU–US relations. See *The Economist*, Facing responsibility, Special Report on Europe in the world, November 23, 2002. US Edition. Post-Lisbon, the EU has attempted a cross-pillarization of its external action, further developing the links between trade, security, migration and development policies within the broad area of external action. An analysis of the results of such attempt for the EU development policy is in Carbone (2013a).

13 The Paris Declaration, produced in 2005 at the Paris High-Level Forum on Aid Effectiveness, which brought together 30 donors, 60 partner countries and 30 development agencies, called for a redefinition in the global effort to improve aid effectiveness. Explicit affirmation of role taking with respect to the implementation of the Paris Declaration is found in the First Part of the European Consensus on Development: 'The EU will take a lead role in implementing the Paris Declaration commitments on improving aid delivery and has in this context made four additional commitments: to provide all capacity building assistance through coordinated programs with an increasing use of multi-donors arrangements; to channel 50% of government-to-government assistance through country systems, including by increasing the percentage of our assistance provided through budget support or sector-wide approaches; to avoid the establishment of any new project implementation units; to reduce the number of un-coordinated missions by 50%' (p.21, Part I).

14 Since the post-Santer redefinition, in 1999, the Commission has worked towards improving the EU's aid delivery, through the creation of EuropeAid, to implement its

programs, and by an attempt to delegate to field offices (through a policy of 'deconcentration'). While not claiming analytical precedence of internal re-organization over other external triggers, the datum indicates the importance of co-evolution of different processes in the change in the EU's development policy. On the matter see Gustavsson (1999).

15 Chaired by the President of the EU Commission, the EuropeAid Co-operation Office was originally supervised by DG Relex and DG Development, and reported to a joint Group of Commissioners responsible for external relations, including, along with DG Relex and DG Development, also DG Trade, DG Enlargement and DG ECFIN Commissioners. Post-Lisbon, EuropeAid has been fully integrated with DG DEV in the new DG Development and Cooperation – EuropeAid. Since 2015, the full name of DG DEVCO has become Directorate General for International Cooperation and Development.

16 In addition to the post-Santer reorganization, other EU internal factors taking place across the same span of time were the broader enlargement drive and the pursuit of the 'constitutional envelope', which was concluded with the adoption of the Lisbon Treaty in 2009.

17 The analysis of the EU's role at the World Bank and with the World Bank is based on evidence gathered through a research survey, conducted with political apexes, top management and staff at the IBRD, as well as through official IBRD and IDA documents. The survey was part of a broader research project on 'The External Image of the EU'–Survey II, sponsored by the EU DG Research under the 6th Framework Programme, as well as by the GARNET Network of Excellence. Conducted by the Author at the World Bank, through a semi-structured questionnaire in January 2008, the survey covers several aspects of the EU–World Bank relations, including EU's performance at the Board and in the field, two topics that have been further investigated through additional interviews with both World Bank and EU officials, as detailed in Section 3 of Chapter 5 of this book. This chapter elaborates the output of selected answers on the EU's role from the questionnaire that was submitted to 18 IBRD officers (management, staff and EDs). In-depth interviews have complemented the role-portion of the survey, providing additional elements to complete the picture described above. Out of a total of 18 semi-structured interviews, 11 were given to senior management and technical staff (VPs, Sector Directors, Senior Consultants, Lead and Senior Economists), and seven to political staff (EDs and Alternate EDs). Consequently, reference in this and other chapters to 'views from the World Bank' only applies to the opinions of the interviewed officers, and does not in any way constitute an official view of the IBRD or The World Bank Group. Additional references to the survey are in Baroncelli (2009, 22–23) and Baroncelli (2010). References to the broader 'External Image of the EU' research project are in Lucarelli and Fioramonti (2010).

18 'If Merkel, Sarkozy and Brown come out and say something jointly they will have far more impact than the Commissioners or the Head of the Commission. . .' (Author's interview, Washington, January 2008). In addition to the expectation-performance gap, caution should be exerted in differentiating between role expectations (what others think about the role beholder) and views on role expectations (what others say they think about the role beholder). In practice, measuring the gaps between the former and the latter may not always be possible. Empirical research on foreign policy roles must confront the same problems of positivist research in the social sciences based on data retrieved from interviews and subjective claims. The analysis on performance presented in the second part of this book addresses this issue through evidence from third-party sources.

19 These perceptions do not correspond to a monolithic view on the EU's role, and in fact display an evident regional variation. The analysis on the outcome dimensions of the

EU's development policy conducted in Chapter 7 seems to confirm Brussels' ability to positively link trade and development objectives in the Balkans, while exposing however the discrepancy in the EU's approach to trade liberalization in the MENA and SSA regions, investigated in Chapters 8 and 9, respectively.

20 Author's interview, Washington DC, World Bank HQ, January 16 2008. As seen in Chapter 2, across time, the strategic nature of the EU–WB partnership has been gradually acknowledged, through multiple revisions of the Trust Funds Framework Agreement and through the creation of a Task Force for the relations with the IFIs in DG DEVCO, now included in a broader Unit on International Organisation and Development Dialogue with Other Donors.

21 Author's phone interview, 2011.

22 As discussed in Chapter 9, within the Paris Process, the Limelette Process is indeed regarded by most top officials as an unprecedented step, which brings the Bank and the Union 'under the same umbrella for the first time'.

23 The factual implications of these expectations on performance are in turn analyzed with the help of evidence from other sources on performance-related issues, by looking at the EU's contribution to the pursuit of development goals, through the Bank and with the Bank in the field, as discussed in Chapter 5 and, more specifically, in Chapter 6.

24 Relative to the IBRD context, management and staff may get their way when the change is (perceived by shareholders as) an issue mostly cosmetic in nature, while shareholders would not allow a revision in the organization's governance rules that risks undermining their power and position.

5 Analyzing performance I

The Eurogroup and its effectiveness at the World Bank's Board[1]

5.1 Introduction

Under the Prodi Commission, Brussels had pushed successfully for closer coordination among the EU EDs at the World Bank's Board, and the informal practice of meeting every Friday morning to discuss matters of EU interest became a consolidated habit. Through the consultation routine of the Eurogroup in 2003, a vertical, yet informal and mediated, link was thus developed between the two organizations. Two years before, the direct, horizontal link between the two governors, via Brussels' channeling through different WB managed TFs, had been formalized under the FA. Chapters 2, 3 and 4 have analyzed the shape of these ties (hybrid delegation), deepening the focus on specific sets of variables, logics and dynamics behind their stasis and change across time.

This chapter focuses in turn on the effects of hybrid delegation, exploring different aspects of performance-as-effectiveness through an original analytical framework. IR and EU studies have typically explored IOs' performance at the institutional level. In the second part of this book the focus is, conversely, on IOs' performance in both decision-making and implementation stages. The analysis of the EU's performance at the World Bank and with the World Bank offered here relies on a purposefully 'thick' conceptualization of effectiveness, unpacked into three main components and related sub-components. In addition to investigating performance at different phases of the policy process of a single IO (the EU), the analytical setup advanced here is applied to complex performance outcomes, i.e. to results from the joint performance of large intersecting multilaterals that cooperate in the same issue area.

The chapter is organized as follows: against the background of the EU, IR and policy analysis relevant literatures, section 5.2 introduces the analytical framework, detailing its different components. A case is made to support the choice for a primarily process-based research strategy to investigate inter-organizational performance. Issues pertaining to the empirical methodology and data gathering are the subject of section 5.3. The relative effectiveness of the Eurogroup to advance the goals of the new EU approach to development at the World Bank's Board is discussed in sections 5.4 and 5.5. Based on data on the procedural workings of the

Group, these sections look at coordination among EU EDs at the Board, addressing internal effectiveness. Section 5.6 focuses on the core components of the EU's external effectiveness at the Board, reviewing selected cases of successful coordination, such as the debate on development promotion in fragile states, and the coordination of the EU EDs on matters of interest to the three African constituencies at the IBRD Board. Section 5.7 investigates performance issues in 'constituent policy', focusing on the Eurogroup coordination over the 2008–2010 World Bank 'voice reform'. Section 5.8 concludes, discussing the potential determinants of the EU's performance, and advancing selected policy inputs by the Union to play a development-enhancing role via the Eurogroup at the Board.

5.2 Hybrid delegation and complex performance-as-effectiveness: a framework for analysis

The essence of hybrid delegation[2] raises both theoretical and operational issues, about the conceptualization of performance, what exactly is meant by effectiveness, the identification of appropriate levels of analysis, channels of influence, and potential benchmarks. Consistent benefits can be derived by broadening the scope of the existing IR scholarship on IOs' performance, to study the relative influence of intersecting multilateral institutions in high level *fora*, on the one side, and the result of their joint efforts in the field, on the other.

Academic work on IOs' performance/effectiveness[3] is to a large extent tributary to research on evaluation in administration sciences and public policy (Helm and Sprinz 2000, 631). Mirroring the debate that has developed in those fields between outcome and process based approaches, respectively, IR scholarship has argued that the appropriateness of quantitative, result-based large-N strategies is conditional on the relative autonomy of the performing organization, its centrality within a given regime, and, not least, the eligibility of achieved solutions to objective measurement (Gutner and Thompson 2010, 235). Under low organizational autonomy, low centrality and weak outcome quantification, an opposite case supports contextual assessments of performance, which privilege process-behavioral variables, and investigate IOs' achievements by looking at multiple series of micro-level decisions (ibid.).

Relevant for the study of the EU's performance at the World Bank and through the World Bank, outcome-based quantitative approaches have potentially serious limitations, some of which can be overcome through process based-strategies. Primarily quantitative approaches account for the EU-cum-MS impressive financial effort. Yet, they would not do justice to the results achieved by the EU and the World Bank through their cooperation under hybrid delegation. A quantitative aggregation of its different components into a summary measure of effectiveness would return a rather crude – and mostly inaccurate – assessment of the EU's performance at the Bank and with the Bank.

Process-based strategies have at least two advantages in the study of contributed (joint and parallel) performance. First, they are better suited to identify constraints that span beyond a single organizational context, as they encompass overlapping arenas and extended policy networks. Second, weaker under standardization and quantitative measuring criteria compared to outcome-based methodologies, process-based approaches offer however a firmer ground to hypothesize causal inferences to explain complex performance from hybrid delegation across long chains, particularly under high uncertainty on either (true) agent or (true) principal type.

Covering different stages in the making of a policy,[4] the framework articulated here disaggregates the performance components of the EU's behavior into three macro-indicators: internal, external and contributed effectiveness (see Table 5.1). Returning a 'thick' reconstruction of performance, the tri-partition encompasses the complexity of inter-organizational relations, compared to evaluating the performance of a single IO. The wide focus on processes that are both internal to the Eurogroup and external to it, allows the framework to identify and interpret both micro-decisions at group level and broader coalitional dynamics at the Board. Additionally, the incorporation of different policy stages (including implementation and monitoring) renders the quintessential dilemma of performance evaluation explicit (effective for whom?), by building it into the analytical setup.

Internal effectiveness gauges the cohesion of the Eurogroup and its ability to reach an agreement on matters of EU interest. External effectiveness accounts for the ability of the Eurogroup to influence decision making at the Board. Contributed effectiveness proxies the consistency between the EU official goals and its channeling through the WB TF system, on the one side (policy consistency), and evaluates the extent to which the EU–World Bank joint and parallel programs and projects have met the needs of the citizens at whom they were originally targeted, on the other (policy impact).

Internal and external effectiveness refer to the EU's performance at the World Bank through the Eurogroup. Based on Laatikainen and Smith (2006b), internal effectiveness has been further disaggregated here, and operationalized by way of two indicators: cohesion and coordination of EU MS at the Board.[5] Internal to the dynamics of the Eurogroup, cohesion refers here to the relative shielding

Table 5.1 The EU at the Bank, the EU with the Bank: exploring effectiveness

INTERNAL		*EXTERNAL*		*CONTRIBUTED*					
Cohesion	Co-ordination	External Independence	Influence on DMaking	Policy Consistency					Policy Impact
				Vertical–Institutional	Horizontal–Sectoral	Horizontal–Geographical	Internal–External	Technical	Outcome Analysis

of a 'united EU' against centrifugal forces from single EU MS. As such, it also includes self-identification processes between MS and EU institutions. Coordination, in turn, is investigated by looking at dynamics of mediation within the Eurogroup and refers to the ability of the EU EDs to present common positions at the Board. Proxying features of actorness of the Union at the Bank, cohesion and coordination are related to each other in different ways, though they are not necessarily coterminous (as discussed later in this chapter, about the discrepancy between perceived cohesion and the ability of the Eurogroup to coordinate over strategic issues).

External effectiveness proxies the ability of the Eurogroup to project its influence on non-EU MS at the Board. The 'external' label refers to the relational nature of such dimension, compared to the within-group qualities of internal effectiveness as conceptualized above. External effectiveness has in turn been disaggregated into two sub-components: external independence and influence on decision making. The former proxies the degree to which the EU MS are able to lead the debate according to Brussels' desiderata, when they do not coincide with those of other major shareholders. Influence on decision making refers to the Eurogroup's relative ability to steer the Bank's decisions towards Brussels' preferred ends.[6]

Last, through the lens of contributed effectiveness, the framework assesses the EU's ability to contribute to the attainment of the goals that it shares with the Bank. To what extent does the EU participation help in the achievement of joint development goals? How has hybrid delegation and its evolution impacted on their attainment?[7] These questions are answered in the following chapter, which also delves into the analytical priors to the conceptualization of contributed (outcome) effectiveness. The following section, in turn, describes the empirical methodology that has guided the overall investigation on performance presented in these two chapters, as well as the data gathered from World Bank, EU and third party sources.

5.3 The data and empirical methodology

As anticipated, the analysis of performance advanced here is informed by a primarily qualitative, process-based approach. To reduce the bias from subjective components, relevant information provided through the interviews has been triangulated with feedbacks on the same issues from a variety of sources. First, views from WB non-EU EDs, management and staff have been collected, to differentiate the sources on the dynamics of the Eurogroup towards the reconstruction of internal and external effectiveness. Second, relative to all three types of effectiveness, information on EU stances has been gathered through interviews with EU officials. Third, a thorough examination of primary, secondary and gray literature, including inputs from selected relevant media and NGOs, has been also carried out.[8] Increasing the number, and more relevant, the variety of data sources over the same phenomena both generates new observations and new ways of looking at the chosen *explanandum*. Process tracing along such triangulation has corroborated the descriptive generalizations advanced in the book about the EU's performance at the Bank and with the Bank. Moreover, it has helped to generate preliminary hypotheses on causal mechanisms that have informed the dynamic of hybrid delegation across the surveyed period.

The multi-faceted prism described in the previous section has thus been applied to different typologies of data, primarily of qualitative nature, with some minor quantitative elements (relative to term positions of the Eurogroup in the first half of 2011). Performance has been analyzed based on documentary evidence, on the one side, and interviews with World Bank and EU officials, on the other. The documentary evidence is comprised of EU and World Bank official and non-official documents, such as formal communications, memos, briefings and, respectively, reports, working papers and newsletters. Third party documents (articles from newspapers, academic and research papers, reports from various sources) further integrate the off-the-shelves component of the data.[9] In total 33 interviews were conducted between January 2008 and August 2011, of which 23 with World Bank and ten with EU officers. The first round of interviews, based on the survey discussed in Chapter 4, collected views from 18 officers at the World Bank HQ in DC and at the World Bank's office, in Brussels, in 2008. Subsequently, control interviews were carried out with other World Bank's officers at later points in time (2009, 2011), including interviews with staff deployed in the regions. Finally, EU interviews were conducted, based on the same questionnaire devised for World Bank's staff, and specifically devoted to provide a mirror perspective on the World Bank from European sources (2011).[10]

In the absence of comprehensive data on joint positions, to assess the cohesion and coordination of the Eurogroup (internal effectiveness), point data on term positions (mid-term assessment of the Rotating Presidency during the first trimester of 2011) has been complemented with inputs from in-depth interviews with Executive Directors, which have also yielded primary information for the investigation on the external effectiveness of the Eurogroup.

Through the survey component of the analysis, consistency issues have been approached mainly from a sectoral angle, focusing on the perceived fit between stated and achieved objectives of the EU in the interviewees' respective areas of competence (i.e. regions or functions, for technical management staff, and constituencies, for political staff). Cross-checks have been provided by submitting the same questions to EU officers, and by complementing the evidence thus obtained with inputs from diversified sets of third party sources (evaluation studies from independent think tanks, press briefs from NGOs and relevant media, interviews with third-party practitioners and, when available, feedbacks from voices in partner countries, in addition to secondary academic literature).

Finally, policy impact has been similarly reconstructed through triangulation based on World Bank, EU and third party sources. The fit between policy results and the units' (regional, functional) and constituencies' demands, respectively, has been investigated primarily on the basis of in-depth interviews with top- and high-rank officers, covering both political (EDs) and management (VPs, Sector Directors) positions in the Bank. Third party documentary evidence, particularly independent evaluation reports, has been extensively used to qualify the findings from the World Bank survey and EU feedbacks on the overall assessment of the EU's policy impact through contributed effectiveness.

The high organizational rank of most among the World Bank's interviewees tends to bias answers on the neutral side. However, the distortion appears compensated by the breadth in strategic visions entailed by their top positions. While lower staff is closer to counterparts in partner countries, and highly familiar with program-specific details, it also tends to be on average less knowledgeable on the IO's overall performance. Most World Bank managers and staff persons, and a number of political representatives who participated in the survey have served in other lower technical positions in the Bank in the past, which has allowed them to return substantive comments on evaluation issues. Finally, the total number of WB political (EDs) and management (VPs) apexes in service at the time was approximately twice the number of WB interviewees. While lacking the significance of a statistical sampling, the ratio strengthens the results presented here on the EU's performance in the EU–WB context of hybrid delegation.

5.4 The EU and its member states: internal effectiveness through cohesion and coordination

Agreement among the EU EDs may or may not get reflected via Eurogroup's joint statements, which, in addition, are neither formal nor binding in character, in a way that makes procedural aspects of EU cooperation at the Board less tractable for empirical purposes. To this discrepancy, the limited availability of records on informal meetings (either of the Board in plenary session or of the Eurogroup) adds a further layer of complexity: missing coordination may therefore be either the result of missing records or evidence of divergent stances. To solve the puzzle of 'missing data–missing coordination' a mixed strategy has been followed. First, the disaggregation of internal effectiveness into two subcomponents has allowed to retain potentially relevant information on informal dynamics in the Eurogroup, nuancing between cohesion (identification with the EU, short of joint positions) and coordination (primarily emerging from common positions, official statements, reported stances). Second, records on the coordination of EU EDs through the Eurogroup have been complemented with relevant information from interviews with other key World Bank officers (non EU-EDs, top management and staff).

While not conducive to *measures* of the EU's effectiveness at the Board, views on cohesion and coordination have returned prima-facie evidence on the existence of a distinctive EU-specific approach at the Bank and in development financing, as opposed to divergent national approaches adopted by individual EU MS. As shown in Figure 5.1, a relative majority (almost 39%) among the World Bank

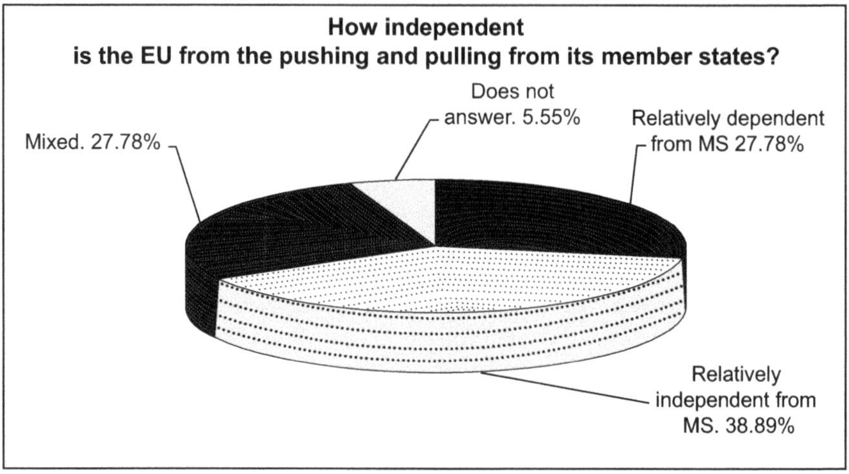

Figure 5.1 Internal effectiveness: perceived cohesion of the Eurogroup

Note: N=18

Sample composition: seven EDs (four EU, three non-EU), 11 managers and staff (four VPs, five senior managers and economists, one residential representative, one OED consultant: five EU and six non-EU).

officials who were interviewed sees the EU as relatively 'independent from particular pressures' from its MS, considering the EU's common positions as the result of genuinely mediated interests, often in the direction of a multilateral approach to development. Almost 28% of respondents see the relation between EU MS and EU institutions as a mixture of particular interests and genuinely common intents. Interestingly, the same proportion unequivocally believe that joint statements are the result of mini-lateral pressures from specific EU MS at the Board, rather than the effect of a Brussels' led consensus.

Elements on the side of relative independence of the Eurogroup from minilateral captures comprise the joint statements by EU EDs, which, albeit not formal in nature, are seen as carrying moral and signaling weight in the eyes of non-EU members at the Bank. Also, customary Friday meetings of EU EDs (the Eurogroup practice) do reinforce the perception that the EU is more than the mere sum of its constituent parts.

On the side of mixed opinions, the role played by statements and values visibly pursued by individual EU MS has been mentioned to explain how, in the evaluation of the cohesion of the Union at the Bank, the image is perhaps one of 'half empty–half full' glass. On the side of relative dependence, the lack of a unified seat at the Board is regarded as a main determinant of Brussels' inability to shape majorities, while the lack of harmonization among different bilateral agencies in the field has been mentioned as an example of 'perverse independence'. The basis of such perception is most likely placed in the organizational structure and praxis of the Bank, which only counts states as shareholders. The majority of World Bank staff is indeed exposed more frequently to EU MS, than to representatives of the EU institutions, even if trips to and from Brussels have substantially increased since 2008, along with joint staff training and staff exchange programs.

Relative to coordination, the creation of the Eurogroup at the Board has substantially enhanced the ability of the EU MS to consult and potentially agree on joint positions. In spite of its relative recency, the Eurogroup has been unequivocally praised for its gradual improvement, compared with the situation at the Fund, where, albeit with a higher degree of formalization, the level of coordination is perceived by some as being lower. Critical voices have however lamented the fragmentation of the action of EU MS, even venturing to claim an inability or 'unwillingness [of the Union] to discuss the shape of its influence in international organizations'.[11] Larger EU MS are sometimes seen as 'more European than others', as they do not appear particularly keen on promoting common initiatives at the Bank, but have at times elected other *fora* to discuss coordination issues, such as the G-7, for HIPC and MDRI in the past, without previous consultation with other EU MS. Friday meetings are regarded as an opportunity for the regular exchange of information on different national priorities, and, in case of divergent opinions, as a forum to seek compromise. However, EDs are briefed by their respective Ministries from national capitals, not by the EU authorities, even if trips to Brussels occur at least once a year. Compared to the SCIMF-EURIMF mechanism[12] for coordination at the IMF, the informal Eurogroup practice is surely less demanding in organizational terms.[13] The fact that the chairmanship of the Eurogroup follows the six-months rotation of the EU Presidency makes coordination at the Bank on EU issues more dependent on changes occurring in Brussels, and thus, according to some, potentially more difficult to achieve. Coordination issues, as perceived by some EU EDs, are perhaps less problematic at the IMF, due to the longer duration of the SCIMF Presidency, which, albeit not set in advance, spanned over four years in the past (in the case of Mr Bini Smaghi). On the other side, contrary to their colleagues at the IMF, and in spite of the lower institutionalization of EU coordination mechanisms at the Bank, it is to be acknowledged that EU EDs at the Bank have already succeeded in reaching a notably high number of common positions.[14]

5.5 The Eurogroup and coordination at the Board

Coordination of the EU MS at the Bank emerged in the early 2000s, and was given its current form in 2003, when the Italian Presidency sponsored the institutionalization of the Eurogroup's Friday meetings (among EU EDs, Alternates or Advisors). Built on a matrix of issues of EU interest, the Eurogroup's procedural workings were designed to stimulate intra-EU discussion at the Board, and possibly forge consensual positions to issue joint statements. While coordination had occurred since the 1990s, its shape and frequency (particularly common positions of the EU EDs on Board decisions) have been defined as more sporadic and less visible compared to the post-2003 period.

Several elements concur to explain the timing of those developments. On the one side, first-image inputs, from both the Commission and World Bank's sides, point to the role played by a critical mass of decidedly pro-European personalities (in Brussels and Washington) in those years. On the other side, EU- and system-specific variables had also been at work. The preparatory ground for the Brussels Consensus of 2006, with the Commission's effort to create an EU-wide template for development coordination was well known to executives in Washington.[15] The coordinating nature of the proposed mechanisms was perceived as respectful of the sovereignty of EU MS. The Benelux countries appeared particularly in favor of moving to a denser approach to coordination. Germany shifted from initial reticence to a leading role, also thanks to its first-rate personnel in Washington. France seemed to orient its actions more along ad hoc, nationally strategic lines, adhering to the coordination game when convenient, and taking some distance when not advantageous. Italy was diplomatically supportive even if financially weak on committing resources through the Bank.

As detailed in the previous chapters, significant changes had also occurred since the mid-1990s in the system of multilateral finance for development. Critiques from several sources had put under severe strain the very nature of the Washington Consensus. A radical redefinition of the World Bank's priorities and approaches had followed, under the Presidency of James Wolfensohn. In turn, that change had influenced the EU's elaboration of its new approach to development policy. During such major reshaping of the World Bank's identity, awareness had grown in Europe that a window of opportunity had just opened to forge a new role for Brussels' approach to development policy.[16]

Across time the Eurogroup has refined the original coordination matrix. General principles and procedural issues have been laid out, on how discussion should be structured, up to the drafting of joint statements (see Table 5.2). Relative to 2008 and 2011, the evidence indicates a generalized interest on the side of EU MS to promote coordination at the Board, with ability to release joint statements varying across different RPs. Interviews with EDs have provided inputs towards a – partial – reconstruction of such institutional memory. Since the launching of the Eurogroup under the Italian Presidency, the Swedish, Danish and Belgian Presidencies appear to have been particularly effective in promoting EU-wide goals while, on average, larger EU MS have tended to be less proactive in pushing EU-wide envelopes through the Group. Plausibly, the former have put a higher premium on the possibility to voice EU preferences through the Eurogroup, compared to the latter, that had the option to resort to other *fora* (such as the G7) to express their views. Additionally, and different from EU MS sitting in multi-country constituencies, the 'big three' (Germany, the UK and France), which have their own, single country, constituencies, were spared the effort to build a 'within-constituency-consensus' towards EU-joint positions. Conversely,

Table 5.2 Procedural workings of the Eurogroup

Frequency of European Group Meetings	• Every week
Types of issues for discussion	• Steering Committee Preparation • Strategy and Policy Papers/Issues • CASes/Major Adjustment Operations • Other issues (i.e. issues of special interest to members or having a EU dimension)
Criteria for selection of specific CASes/ adjustment operations	• Accession countries • Major borrowers • EU dimension (e.g. large EU program) • Issues of special interest
Joint statements	• Only on points on which there is an agreement among Group members • *Procedure:* The Presidency would circulate a draft for comments by the members. The statements would be issued in the names of those who wish to endorse it.

Source: Courtesy of the Hungarian Presidency representatives at the World Bank's Executive Board (Jan–June 2011), April 2011

for smaller EU MS, the Eurogroup became a strategic resource to rally other non-EU partners in respective constituencies around their preferred options. As a consequence, their RPs have been particularly keen to support coordination in the Group.

While the Eurogroup's coordination is based on informal consultation, the EU MS have agreed to a set of common principles to guide their weekly practice: clarity, concision, timeliness, selectivity, pragmatism and honesty. First, the Group should be selective in deciding which issues have a truly collective relevance, to limit ex ante the burden to essential matters, increasing the 'credibility and effectiveness' and limiting 'fatigue' perception by non-European chairs and management' (Hungarian Presidency at the World Bank 2011a). Second, a responsibility is also placed on the Group collectively to ensure timeliness and pragmatism on three dimensions. The Group should determine agendas ahead of time (at least one month), to allow longer time horizons to the discussion. Also, the Group is required to adopt a pragmatic approach and assess – during the coordination meetings – whether the issues on the table have a reasonable chance to 'reach a sufficiently strong and broad consensus', and to evaluate the possible need to withdraw early from discussion when chances of success are patently dim. Finally, members of the Group should notify their interest in co-signing a joint statement, or lack thereof, in a strictly timely fashion. Third, the Group should also limit suggestions to necessary provisions, to arrive at joint statements that are 'concise and clear', avoiding 'Christmas tree' statements (ibid.). Fourth, Group members should keep each other informed, as early as possible of parallel drafting efforts 'in which European Chairs other than the Presidency are involved' (ibid.). Fifth, to avoid sabotaging a negotiation process, the Group advises those members that do not feel enough commitment to stay out from the early stages of discussion. Additional pledges refer, respectively, to the encouragement of Part II EU MS (borrowers) to enhance their participation to the discussions; to the open nature of the Group with respect to leader selection along interest/knowledge/comparative advantage; and to the possibility that the Presidency withdrew altogether from its steering role when receiving non-negotiable instructions (including from non-EU countries in cases of Presidencies from mixed constituencies). Outreach has been incorporated as a further principle in the guidelines, whereby the Group also agrees 'when appropriate, to reach out to other constituencies/groupings without forgetting to reach out to other Europeans in conformity with the spirit of the Lisbon Treaty' (ibid.).

The endorsement of these principles and related practices is completely voluntary. The Hungarian Terms of Reference on the EU coordination principles at the Board, as its predecessors, the Belgian Rules of Engagement, and the Italian Matrix, are gentlemen's agreements. As such, they do not formally constrain any of the EU MS. Their behavior at the Board is regulated under the World Bank Articles of Agreement, and its constituency system, in matters falling under MS competence, which, according to conservative readings, constitute the vast majority of development issues that are discussed in that venue.[17] As noted above, the informal nature of these provisions may explain the – relatively – higher coordination outputs reached by World Bank EDs compared to their counterparts in the IMF.

The steps taken to encourage coordination at the Board suggest that EU MS have gone a long way. Arguably, these achievements may have different motivations and, over the longer term, strive at different goals. Initial efforts have come from medium or small-sized MS in mixed constituencies, with inputs from the Commission. Even discounting the somehow shallow participation of some MS at certain times (most particularly the three big ones and new entrants), the fact that cooperation is now in place, indicates that a consensus has been reached among EU MS on the existence of an operational EU dimension – albeit limited to consultation matters – in their behavior at the World Bank's Board.

Even discounting the limited availability of information on consultations in the Eurogroup, some important elements have emerged to reconstruct its main achievements. Quantitatively, the Group has been particularly active, releasing 20 joint positions during the first trimester of 2011, out of approximately 30 coordination meetings.[18] Of these latter, a slightly higher majority was composed of *ad hoc* meetings, which may signal the proactive stance of the Group to consult on issues beyond routine coordination, usually dealt with in the weekly Friday meetings. Far from offering a comprehensive picture of the Group's praxis, the datum indicates however a particularly high frequency in the issuing of joint positions over that period. The informal rules have it that joint statements are issued 'only in the names of those who wish to endorse [them]' (Hungarian Presidency at the WB 2011a, 1), but preferred praxis is that no joint statements are produced in case unanimity is not reached. Thus, 20 joint positions out of 30 coordination meetings, out of which a majority is of the *ad hoc* sort, i.e. on non-routine issues, may come quite close to reflect a consensus among EU MS at the Board.[19]

As part of its amelioration process, the Group has agreed to submit itself to three-month performance assessments, an indication that EU MS are keen on monitoring themselves on how well they coordinate on matters of EU joint interest. As anticipated, the records discussed below cannot obviously account for the Group's performance across time. Nonetheless, they provide point evidence on qualitative aspects of its cohesion and coordination dimensions. As shown in Table 5.3, the sample on internal feedbacks on the work of the Presidency covers approximately 85% of the expected range of respondents (23 out of 27). Overall, out of a rating range from poor-1- to good-5-, the Group rates the Presidency's performance at 4.41 points, setting it highly above the average (3). Also the total average calculated over the group of itemized scores, 4.20 points, signals a tangibly high degree of internal consistency among the different answers per respondent. Even if the overall perception of the Presidency's performance is higher than the calculated mean over detailed assessments on specific aspects of coordination and cohesion, the deviation (0.16 points) is not dramatically large with respect to the intervals between each evaluation rank (1 point). While group-think dynamics may be (and most likely are) at work, this last point provides a rule-of-thumb indication that such an assessment has a reasonable degree of internal coherence. Apparently the best achievements have been recorded on the implementation of

Table 5.3 Half-term assessment of Presidency performance by Eurogroup

Item	*Score (1 poor–5 good) range*
1. Overall Presidency performance so far	4.41
2. Presidency's effort in planning issues for discussion ahead of time	4.36
3. Presidency's effort in selecting 'candidate joint statements'	4.32
4. Presidency's efforts to ensure decision taken/course of action chosen are clear	4.14
5. Presidency's efforts to assess chances for sufficiently strong and broad consensus	4.36
6. Presidency's efforts to organize the annual Brussels trip?	4.27
7. Overall experience in the Brussels trip?	4.07
8. Presidency's efforts to promote its thematic priorities (such as the Roma inclusion in Europe)	4.18
9. Presidency's efforts to reach out to other constituencies	3.91
Average calculated performance (items 2–9)	*4.20*

Source: Courtesy of the Hungarian Advisor at the World Bank (2011), under Hungarian Presidency term (Jan-June 2011). N= 23. Last row integrated by the Author.

timeliness, pragmatism and selectivity criteria, in the planning and discussion phases. The Presidency is considered particularly effective in ensuring appropriate information ahead of time, pre-selecting 'candidate joint statements', and in saving time and effort during meetings, towards maximizing the chances to 'reach a sufficiently strong and broad consensus' (Mid-term Performance Review, Hungarian Presidency 2011b). Next come the Presidency's efforts in ensuring that decisions or 'courses of action decided during ... the meetings' are clear (ibid.), as well as the organization of the annual Brussels trip. The promotion of own thematic priorities by the Presidency is rated at lower, though still above-average levels, leaving the lowest assessment to the Presidency's effort to reach out to other constituencies (3.91 points out of the 1–5 range).

Other aspects have been identified as somewhat more challenging, with issues ranging from collective principality problems, to informational asymmetries compounded with time-related concerns, with respect to both WB and Brussels' managements. More particularly, EU EDs have suggested longer term horizons for the consultations in the Eurogroup, particularly in the pre-selection phase of issues eligible for common consultation from the World Bank Outlook agenda, to allow the Group a longer period to develop a common view. Also, an intensification of the dialogue with the EU delegations, in Washington and elsewhere, has been quoted as a step in the right direction. In essence, interviewed EDs believe that the Group could perform better by improving the quality, type and quantity of informational inputs into its decision-making process. Transparency on the input side, demanded by the Group from both the Bank's management and EU delegations, appears to work at the level of internal dynamics as well, where reciprocal requests of openness among EU MS are coupled with advice to increase honesty and frankness ('differences of views. . .[should be] acknowledged more candidly at coordination meetings'), to ease the task of assessing 'the likelihood of arriving at consensus' and to make sure that 'the drafting [is] not so cumbersome' (Hungarian Presidency 2011b).

With respect to internal effectiveness (cohesion and coordination), the Group should then technically operate as an agent for the EU, as it strives to implement the duty to ensure coordination on shared competence matters. The EU EDs wear two hats, and have to mediate between their 'Bank-wide' and 'EU-specific' collective principalities, respectively (the latter being proven by the agreement on abstaining from issuing joint statements that are not backed by unanimous consent). In addition to balancing their national mandates with the inputs from the WB management (including the informational cost of gathering information on the WB Outlook ahead of time, in the example), EU EDs also bear the cost of obtaining clear guidelines from Brussels (or the Washington/regional EEAS delegations). Several elements in the survey conducted for this study, as well as from the mid-term performance review quoted above, suggest that clearer inputs and information could be provided by EU institutions.[20]

These holdups compound political, organizational and communicational obstacles. In light of the absence of an EU seat, and notwithstanding the post-Lisbon efforts towards a unified external representation of the Union, the setup and improvement of the Eurogroup's informal practice marks a significant progress. The case rests on the particular relevance of coordination within a decision-making system which is informally, but routinely, based on consensus. From 1996 to 2000, only four formal votes were reported at the Board.[21] Equity and efficiency considerations have been raised for and against the current practice followed at the WB Board, but, to date, virtually 99% decisions are still taken by consensus.

From the EU standpoint, informal coordination to speak with one voice appears of paramount importance in a context where consensus is the norm in practice, such as in the World Bank's Board, compared to a system where majoritarian rules are also binding in the practice of decision making (so that proposals are actually put to vote).[22] Indeed, if voting were the followed practice, the effort and manoeuvring put in place by major diplomatic brokers (usually those EDs that can wield substantial shares) could be lost behind the evidence of vote counts, most of the time reflecting Bank-wide cleavages beyond the EU–non EU dimension (such as borrowers–lenders, or other thematic or geographical cleavages). In such a case, the EU's role would most likely be lumped together with that of the US or other major lenders, which, as discussed in next section, are perceived as less supportive than the Union on gender, environmental and social issues. Conversely, in the current consensus system in place at the Bank, and provided that it is able to speak with one voice, the Eurogroup sponsored-coordination method provides a further visibility bonus to enhance the EU's influence. This puts a higher value on the progress made by EU EDs in structuring coordination at the Board on matters of EU interest since the early 2000s. However, it also puts a stronger responsibility on their shoulders to further proceed along that track, attaching a higher burden to instances of missed coordination.

5.6 The Eurogroup and the others: external effectiveness through independence and influence

Beyond issues of coordination within the Eurogroup, evidence from the survey indicates that the EU is able to project a peculiar style through its MS at the Board, which is clearly distinguishable from that of other influential donors. While both independence and influence very much vary across issue areas, the overall EU's approach is considered as being more altruistic, as well as softer (with respect to both labor market and security policies) compared to that adopted by the United States. In some instances, the EU's behavior, both at the Bank, through the Eurogroup, and in the field, has been referred to as a counterbalance to the perceived narrowness of US development strategies, that appear to be too tightly linked to that donor's foreign policy interests. In climate change and energy matters, the Eurogroup has played along common EU guidelines. Another instance of a clearly impactful action of the Eurogroup has been its successful pressure on the need for the Bank to produce an agreed strategy on capital increase. While different EU MS had different views on who should give to whom, and how much, the level of tactical coordination on these matters was substantial during the consultation that were held prior to the release of the World Bank's strategy for recapitalization after the crisis of 2008.

Specifically relative to the first component of external effectiveness, independence, EU EDs have been speaking with one voice on the results expected from the Bank in countries where the EU has a record of past engagement or ongoing political dialogue. Major instances are the positions taken by EU EDs on Sub-Saharan African countries, as well as, more generally, on fragile and conflict-torn states. Commenting the World Bank 2011 World Development Report (WDR) on Conflict, Security and Development, the Eurogroup clearly sided with the Commission, questioning the World Bank's risk averse approach in fragile states, and suggesting that WB management ended it altogether (DELUSW E-note, March 29, 2011, 1). At the same time, the Eurogroup encouraged the Bank to 'further explore what success looks like in a higher risk environment including how procurement and fiduciary systems could better suit fragile states' (World Bank 2011a, 1–2). Inquiries emerged about how the World Bank management intended to operationalize its conclusions, particularly with respect to the repeated emphasis on the need to build partnerships with all the main players in fragile situations.[23] Overall, the EU MS emerged as a group able to speak with one compact, critical voice about what they perceived as an opportunity for further improvement by the Bank's management. Relative to development promotion in fragile contexts, the EU MS also asked that TFs be aligned with the WB Country Assistance Strategy (CAS) as well as, in its absence, the Interim Strategy Note (ISN) for fragile states. That joint position resonated a similar concern by EU institutions and stakeholders, with respect to channeling methods and tools through the World Bank managed TFs, as detailed in Chapters 7 to 9.

On these geographic and thematic issues both the Commission and the Parliament expressed matching self-acknowledgment of their special expertise and involvement, claiming a leading role for the Union in keeping political dialogue open even under conditions of extreme political duress. The frictions between the Union and the Bank about the respective accountability systems in the management of co-financed projects in Zimbabwe and the oPt, detailed in Chapters 8 and 9, respectively, exemplify at the highest the dilemmas of promotion of multiple complex goals from the outside through primarily economic incentives. The fact that EU MS at the Board made a priority of pushing the EU envelope on these issues, taking a critical stance vis à vis the Bank's management, show that coordination may succeed even in the absence of exclusive EU development competence and of exclusively EU-homogenous seats at the Board.

In other instances, however, distinctiveness played against the Union, and the adoption of the North American model in private sector development was quoted as more beneficial compared to the 'statist' approach of continental European models. Additionally, the – otherwise positive – opinions on the EU's role in trade negotiations and development policy have been nuanced by several impeding factors, among which Brussels' supposedly adverse selection of non-pro development trade policies, particularly evident in the case of CAP-trade issues and EPAs, discussed in Chapter 9.[24] Critical feedbacks on the implications of the EU's distinct approach to development policymaking have also emerged with respect to its – allegedly – too timid support to spreading democratic values through development aid, in the MENA region and in the Balkans, investigated in Chapter 8 and Chapter 7, respectively. Last but not least, non-EU voices from the World Bank also confirmed the evidence that emerged from the analysis of the Eurogroup workings, about an apparent lack of clarity in selecting and communicating the Group's strategic goals to the other Bank members.

Relative to influence, the second component of external effectiveness, the EU is seen as a potentially impactful player in the decision-making process at the Bank, although its leverage (32.06%) is retained as too low compared to its contributed resources (subscriptions and TFs). In the Bank, some sources relate such low leverage to the absence of one or more EU-homogeneous seats: in their opinion, the fact that the EU's weight is currently spread over 8 chairs,[25] without an EU-unified seat and a Commission that is not a formal party to the process, leaves little hope that the EU will speak with one voice at the Bank. VPs and EDs from developing countries have not raised the issues of change in internal governance and representation, rather focusing on the EU ability to coordinate in the field. At the beginning of the 2010s, dealing with (supposed) ineffective representation was not perceived as a priority by the Eurogroup's Presidency, speaking for the overall Group, which considered the existing shares and voting system as fair in the context of the overall World Bank internal governance.[26] Out of the interviewed EDs, only one of the two EU EDs from single-country constituencies who have accepted to participate in the survey, mentioned representation as an issue of particular concern. Most of the others lamented the absence of cohesion (i.e. a low degree of internal effectiveness) in the Eurogroup vis à vis other members of the Bank (especially large donors from the G7, such as the US or Japan). They did not relate the weakness of the Group to the absence of EU-homogeneous constituencies, complaining instead about the Eurogroup low ability to compact solid voting coalitions across constituencies, often due to centrifugal blows by large EU MS. While these remarks refer mostly to poor, and poorly – or only weakly – timed, consultation of larger to smaller EU MS,[27] other issues seem to have also impaired the possibility of the Eurogroup's influence on decision-making at the Board.

From the side of larger EU MS, weak strategic coordination on sensitive issues, particularly shareholder matters, has been a major factor behind the achievement of less-than-optimal achievements. The outcome has been credited to adverse negotiation timings on specific occasions, with last minute revealing of countries' true preferences, after several months of cosmetic discussions, which was reflected in patching up different positions and offering a weak, interlocutory side, rather than a proactive, coherent and shared strategy to the Bank's management.

Into the second decade of the new millennium the Eurogroup's consultation practice has contributed to structure views at the World Bank of the EU as a large donor, both collectively and through the Commission, marked by its own peculiar approach to development promotion. Conversely, contradictory inputs have emerged on the Eurogroup's external effectiveness, i.e. its ability to consistently influence decision making at the Board: aside from the exception noted above (the large EU single-country constituency among the 'big three', voicing its hope for a unified EU voice at the Board), influence matters were rarely related to representation issues, somewhat of a taboo, and broader (in)effectiveness issues were mostly framed in terms of consultation deficits. These latter proved particularly serious for the Eurogroup, in the 2008–2010 debate on the voice and participation reform, which is the subject of the next section.

5.7 The EU influence on strategic Board decisions: the Eurogroup, IDA contributions and the debate on the 'voice reform'[28]

Historically, several EU MS have been very generous donors to IDA, the WBG concessional agency, most notably the Nordics and the 'big three', France, Germany and the UK. The inclusion of a component on IDA contributions in the formula to reallocate IBRD shares devised during the 2008–2010 World Bank 'voice and participation reform' has been quoted by some of the EU EDs as an example of impactful cooperation of the Eurogroup decisions taken at the Board. Positions were different early on, with Spain particularly diffident about including past IDA contributions. However, under converging interests of key EU players, intense consultations led the Eurogroup to eventually issue a common position.[29] Allegedly, the EU's influence was crucial in advancing the proposal to include a tangible acknowledgement of lenders' past IDA commitments in the new quota formula to be adopted for the IBRD. Into the second year since the initiation of the reform, the achievement was quoted as an indication that EU MS had been able to coordinate on strategic matters and purposively influence key decisions at the Board.

A deeper insight into the broader Eurogroup's coordination process on the 'voice and participation reform' reveals however a nuanced picture. In the 2010 Annual Report of the Nordic–Baltic constituency, the ED Anna Brandt in service at the time explicitly referred to the 'responsibility of coordinating European positions in the Board, including some divisive and difficult issues, like voice reform' (Nordic–Baltic Constituency Office, 2010, Foreword). Frank consultations among EU EDs however, appear to have been held only in the final stages of the reform, very much under external pressure.[30] While to some extent commendable, the results of such consultations seem to show that the informality of the Eurogroup's practice has played in that case against the EU cause.

As detailed in Chapter 3, several steps have been taken since 2008 through the second phase of the 'voice reform'. At the Spring meetings of April 2010 a capital increase of 58 USD bn was agreed (the so-called General capital increase – GCI), in addition to the voice component, 'shifting 3.1% of voting shares from developed to developing countries, resulting in a total shift of 4.6% of voting power since 2008, bringing developing countries' voting share to 47% in IBRD... through a Selective Capital Increase (SCI) of USD 28 bn' (Idem). Once the reform was implemented, summing up increases in basic votes and quota-related votes (and including the effect of income-group reshapings, described below), the group of developing and transition economies (DTCs) had gained 7.19 % in aggregate voting power.

Overall, DTCs have gained, yet some countries and constituencies in that group have seen a deterioration of their previous position. Changing the system then in place at the Bank, upon which countries were ranked by aggregate income (high, middle, low), on the occasion of the 2008–2010 'voice reform' it was decided to reshape groupings into two broader camps, industrialized countries and DTCs, respectively. Additionally, three high-income economies (South Korea, Singapore and Malta) were moved to the DTC group, which included only middle and low income countries. Other, less patent, questionable reclassifications have been effected, justified under the general rule that the IMF system (World Economic Indicators – WEO) was chosen over the WB system (World Development Indicators – WDI). Most notably, several WDI-high income countries had been in fact classified as developed and emerging economies in the WEO system (Bahamas, Bahrain, Barbados, Brunei, Darussalam, Croatia, Equatorial Guinea, Estonia, Hungary, Kuwait, Latvia, Oman, Poland, Qatar, Saudi Arabia, Trinidad & Tobago, United Arab Emirates). Finally, in spite of being ranked as high-income economies in both WDI and WEO systems, but perhaps based on their post-transition situations, the Czech Republic, Slovak Republic and Slovenia, were also reclassified in the DTC group. These reshufflings resulted in a pure reclassification effect worth of 3.48%: netting this out of the 7.19% total increase, the real shift for middle and low income (WDI) countries amounted to only 3.71% voting power in percentage terms (Vestergaard 2011, 53).

Within the Eurogroup, assessments on the accomplishments of the 'voice reform' cross a wide spectrum. On the one side, the reform was seen as a well rounded achievement, to rebalance of voting powers in favor of DTCs, while reasonably preserving the relative strength of the EU MS.[31] On the other side, alternative readings have judged the reform's results as sub-optimal, and the negotiation dynamics in the Eurogroup as being outmanoeuvred by non EU MS, who could bank on the EU MS reportedly low level of – timely – frankness on respective objectives and priorities. When negotiations started, EU MS supported the increase of voting power for DTCs, but also tried to contain the potential losses to their own national shareholding rights. EU membership could have represented a tactical advantage on both fronts. EU MS preferences converged on DTCs voice increase, and the consultation opportunity offered by the Eurogroup could do nothing but improve the chances to coordinate on the redistribution of voting powers, to articulate an EU coherent position at the Board. However, the advantage turned into a backlog. Several months into the negotiations, the Eurogroup meetings amounted to little more than opportunities to advance surface 'Christmas Tree' statements about principles to be incorporated in the reform, which were left aside once the discussion proceeded further, as the matter came to be framed in more pressing, opportunistic terms.[32]

France had already publicly expressed its opinion on the fact that 'Europeans are not overrepresented at the WB and IMF. They are the main contributors, thus they need to preserve a certain voting weight which allows for taking the right decisions and properly account for them to their own countries' taxpayers' (French ED at the EP on February 2007, quoted in Eurodad 2007, 6). In spite of alluding to 'Europeans' (not EU, though) then, the French ED had clearly referred to national accountabilities through EU MS fiscal systems. Down along the road of more concrete discussions on redistributing shares and voting powers, the consultation in the Eurogrop shifted gradually on national, as opposed to EU-wide, priorities, and the discussion on expected gains was framed in openly relative, as opposed to absolute, terms. The French ED made it subsequently clear that, irrespective of the implications of the reform on the DTCs redistributing issue, France's goal was to preserve its voting rights to a level that was not inferior to that of the UK.[33]

Other EU EDs strove to attain more principled solutions. In phase 1 of the reform, the Nordic–Baltic constituency pushed successfully to create an additional African chair.[34] The Nordic–Baltic countries were also particularly vocal on the need that the second phase of the reform should not reduce the benefits accrued to the poorest shareholders to the advantage of stronger middle-income and transitioning economies (Nordic–Baltic Constituency Office 2010, 2). While insisting on the need to increase the DTCs' voice, however, the Nordics also spelled out their objection to incorporate absolute (as opposed to relative) measures of the IDA contribution into the voting formula, opening a cleavage within the EU broad consensus on that matter. To their credit, indeed, it should be said that their IDA contributions as a share of GDP makes them by far the most generous donors across the Bank. While certainly motivated by their past performance on IDA/GDP shares, in development terms their request to have an IDA relative component in the voting formula was not completely off the ground.

In turn, the UK and Germany came about with two different strategies to revise the quota formula. The UK's position was informed by an inclusive view on how the role that borrowing countries, and their experience as clients of the Bank, should be reflected in the voting formula.[35] The German position, perhaps less principled and more technical-mathematical, was nonetheless aimed at reaching an outcome that could be acceptable to others (Stumm 2011). Among the Mediterranean EU MS, less vocal on the issue, Spain abstained from siding with the more poverty oriented options, pushing instead to advance the demands of its middle-income Latin American partners in the constituency.[36] Italy has generally supported EU-led proposals, taking however the backseat during the turning points of the voice reform. Both Spain and Italy had however expressed their skepticism over the medium-term feasibility of a seat-compacting plan for the EU (Eurodad 2007, 6–7).

While not overlapping, the priorities of EU MS could have been made more compatible on several counts (inclusion of the IDA component, increasing the voice of DTCs, preserving reasonable shares in light of EU contributed resources), had consultations been more open and timely. The outcome, on the contrary, was that the EU partners stopped considering principles and quickly moved to discussing shares and voting power issues when faced with the reality of other constituencies that had been faster to coalesce and present their clearer agendas to the management. Overall, the EU MS succeeded in having the IDA contribution component finally included in the new quota framework, but they lagged behind in broad terms on the redistribution of voting power: overall, they lost 0.60 % in voting shares (from 32.97 to 32.38), while the US maintained its veto power with a 15.85 voting share.[37] As seen above, in spite of the EU supporting a large portion of the redistribution, the real gain for the middle and, particularly, low income countries has been much more modest than what is purported in World Bank official documents.

Beyond face value events, the unresolved tension between two different goals accounts for the mixed results obtained by the Eurogroup in the overall World Bank's 'voice and participation reform' of 2008–2010. On the one side, compacting support to enhance the voice of DTCs at the Board was essentially an issue in regime preservation for the EU MS, as the effort was key to increase the World Bank's legitimacy, thus benefitting the whole institution. On the other side, the consultations in the Eurogroup on how to contain vote losses for EU MS exhibited several features of an iterated prisoner's dilemma game, with efforts to reach (mere) Pareto-optimality, loosely defined as an outcome of vote gains for some, with no loss for any of the others in the group.[38] Eventually, the Eurogroup consultations on the voice and participation reform achieved suboptimal records on both counts. The public goods supply game (adjusting the World Bank internal governance to widen voting powers of the DTC group) featured for a long time as the main issue in the agenda of the Eurogroup. Conversely, the matter of shares redistribution and reconfiguration of voting power (along with its implications for intra-group relative gains) had to be rushed into the Group consultations at the very last minute, under the pressure of other, non-EU shareholders. In the end, the advantage of an additional informal consultation forum offered by the Eurogroup became both a hindrance to effective decision making (due to additional, group-specific, transaction costs under time constraints), and a lightning rod to channel pressures from non-EU MS, concerned about the issue of European overrepresentation at the Board.

5.8 Conclusions

In the preceding sections, the focus has been moved from conceptualizing the broad relation between the EU and the Bank's respective systems, to analyzing the achievements of EU MS at the Board in matters of EU relevance. Through the lenses of an original analytical framework, the chapter has conceptualized the EU performance, looking at how and how well EU MS coordinate with each other at the World Bank's Board, and gauging the ability of the Eurogroup to follow along courses of action suggested by Brussels. While both self-perceptions and views from other actors in the Bank point to a good degree of internal cohesion of the Eurogroup, the analysis of its origins and of its performance in specific instances has shown that internal coordination suffers from several problems (limited transparency, high costs to obtain timely relevant information from EU and WB managements, time consistency problems in revealing national priorities along the consultation process). Still, the number of joint positions produced (particularly notable, in the absence of an exclusive EU competence and Commission presence at the Board) suggest that the current consultation-through-coordination system may bring higher benefits compared to a more compact alternative, in the context of informal consensus approach that characterizes decision making at the IBRD Executive Board.

The overall effectiveness of the Eurogroup depends on a variety of factors. National preferences expressed by EU EDs matter, but their influence varies across multiple dimensions, which include availability of information from Brussels and Washington managements, as well as policy-specific determinants, as crucially shown in the case of the debate about the voice reform. When divisive issues are under discussion, i.e. under potential changes in 'constituent politics' – the case of substantial redistribution in shareholding rights – collective action problems are magnified, and the opportunity offered by informal consultation through the Eurogroup may turn into a burden. In the first phase of the voice reform, the Eurogroup has been particularly effective in pushing for an additional African Chair (much along the pressures from the Nordic–Baltic constituency). Also, the inclusion of the IDA component in the final quota framework has been substantially influenced by the compact backing of the Eurogroup, where opposition from middle-income Spanish-led constituency was successfully overcome through consultation inside the Group. However, on shares and votes redistribution, the Eurogroup has remained caught in less principled debates at the very last minute, and MS have in the end rushed towards maximizing their respective national shares on a group-basis, thus weakening the Group to external pressures from non-EU EDs on burden-sharing issues at the Board. The absence of an EU-led coalition to end the US veto power at the Board, when qualified majority is required, is probably motivated by the unwillingness of the Europeans to oppose their main Atlantic partner, and, at that time, to jeopardize the overall voice reform. Nonetheless, the emphasis on preserving national shares and voting powers has led the EU EDs to focus on narrow intra-group maximization of relative gains, detracting energies from the pursuit of development and EU goals (wider voice rights to the poorest, preservation of higher shares for the EU group as a whole).

Notes

1 Earlier analyses on the performance of the EU at the World Bank have appeared in Baroncelli (2011) and (2013a).

2 As discussed in Chapter 2, the label captures the informal dynamics of the Eurogroup at the Board and between EU EDs and the EU institutions in Brussels, on the one side, as well as the transactions between the EU and the World Bank under the Framework Agreement, in selected Association Agreements and relative Trust Fund Boards, on the other.

3 In their framework to analyze IOs' performance, Gutner and Thompson (2010, 232) differentiate between 'effectiveness' and 'performance', preferring the latter over the former, for its being 'more contingent and complex', compared to the – supposedly – endogenous references (organizational resources, abilities) inherent in the concept of effectiveness. While their choice points to a need to get closer to a 'holistic measure' (Ibid.) of IOs' accomplishments, taking into account externally set parameters for evaluation, the issue is mainly a definitional one. As detailed throughout this chapter, effectiveness can be conceptualized as an essentially thick quality of organizational behavior, encompassing the top-down meaning of implementation as conformance, the bottom-up connotation speaking to outcome analyses, as well as meanings related to the efficacy of group dynamics (at both the intra- and inter-organizational levels).

4 The importance of tracking performance across multiple stages had been discussed in the policy analysis literature by Easton (1965), Pressman and Wildavsky (1973), Van Meter and Van Horn (1975).

5 According to Laatikainen and Smith (2006b, 9–10) internal effectiveness embodies 'more than just [demonstrating] cohesion in voting on UN resolution', and refers to the willingness of EU MS to act collectively at the UN through the EU, rather than independently, as well as to their ability 'to reach agreement on positions, policies, statements, etc.'

6 External effectiveness in Latikaainen and Smith's work is mainly related to the ability of the Union to achieve its objectives and influence the debate at the UN. In the words of the authors, it also pertains to 'Europeanization as external diffusion of European norms and forms of political organization' (Laatikainen and Smith 2006b, 9–10).

7 The literature on outcome evaluation is wide and ramified. Early references to the topic in the implementation literature are Mountjoy and O'Toole (1979), Nixon (1980).

8 While less serious, due to the higher availability of information on policies and programs in the regions, the potential bias also applies to the analysis on contributed effectiveness. The same triangulation strategy has therefore also been followed to contain the subjective elements of data reported through interviews in the analysis on contributed effectiveness, as discussed in Chapters 7, 8 and 9, featuring selected case studies in the ECA, SSA and MENA regions.

9 For a detailed analysis and discussion of these sources see Baroncelli (2009, 12–15).

10 In the first half of 2011, ten in-depth interviews were conducted with EU officials, from the EU Commission (DEVCO, RELEX) and the EU Parliament, who provided the key elements needed to reconstruct the main dynamics at play and to symmetrically double-check World Bank's feedbacks on specific programs and policy courses.

11 Interview with top-level World Bank Official (EU ED, Washington January 2008).

12 The Brussels-based SCIMF is a sub-committee of the Economic and Financial Committee of the EU, that interacts with the Washington-based EURIMF (formed by EU MS representatives to the IMF) to coordinate on matters of EU and IMF interest.

13 See Bini Smaghi (2004) and Eurodad (2006).

14 Bini Smaghi (2004) notes how excessive institutionalization of coordination may induce perverse effects, increasing divisiveness among EU EDs. In the IMF, the 'Euro divide' has represented an additional source of potential difficulty to strengthen coordination at the Board (European Parliament 2011, 21)

15 Former high-level European officials in service at the World Bank's Board at the time have referred to a clearly perceived 'Lisbon trend' (Author's interview, 2011).

16 Author's interview with EU Commission's official (2011).

17 Technically, the exceptions to such a reading vary in grades, rather than in type, with the degree of coverage of development-related matters combined with the area-specific nature of the project. As noted in section 5 of Chapter 2 and section 4 of Chapter 3, the Union does not have an exclusive competence in development matters, which remain

largely in the hands of MS. However, according to the duty to act in conformity with the principle of unity of external representation of the Union, MS are required to coordinate on issues under discussion at the Board that impinge on aspects of development policies that are closely connected with matters where the EU has exclusive competence (especially referring to trade, agricultural, fisheries and environmental policies). Similarly, MS have a duty to coordinate on World Bank project financing in countries/regions covered by EU schemes (such as candidate and potential candidate countries, ENP and SSA countries (under the EPA scheme), as well as in priority areas for the Commission (prominent examples in the period under study are Iraq, West Bank and Gaza/oPt, or global funds against pandemics such as the Global Fund to fight AIDS, Tuberculosis and Malaria - GFATM).

18 The Author is grateful to the then Hungarian Advisor at the World Bank Executive Board, who kindly shared such assessment with her, during the six-months Hungarian Presidency of the EU in the first half of 2011.

19 Nine out of 20 positions refer to either region- or country-specific strategies and programs, another nine to Bank-wide items (from specific internal issues, such as reforms of corporate management practices to updates on the reform of the Bank's internal governance, to flagship publications, as the WDR, recurring twice, or GMR) and two to Bank-wide issues that have a clear outreach dimension (use of country procurement system and response to global food price volatility, a key topic in 2011).

20 Issues emerged about the poor briefing of the Directors by the EU delegation in DC on matters to be discussed in Brussels in the first semester of 2011. More particularly, and relative to their Brussels trip, reference was made to the proliferation of many short, not always focused meetings with Commissioners and DGs in Brussels, and to the absence of lower-level focused meetings, to inform EDs of technical issues at stake during the subsequent high-level meetings.

21 More specifically, matters under discussion at the Board were 'constitutional issues', such as IBRD capital increase (according to Art.2, sec.2, b) of the Articles of Agreement) and adjustments to IBRD loan rates, but also contested projects, such as, in the 1996–2000 period, the Chad–Cameroon pipeline, or the Western Poverty Reduction Project. On the latter see World Bank 2000; Wade 2000; Woods 2001.

22 Article 5, section 3 b) states that 'Except as otherwise specifically provided, all matters before the Bank shall be decided by a majority of the votes cast'. Section 3 in that article is devoted specifically to voting, and immediately follows a section on the Board of Governors. Furthermore, under a), section 3 establishes the stock of basic votes allotted to each member state (250), irrespective of economic weight or contributed shares to the Bank's pool of resources. In essence, even in the absence of a 'covering provision' that specifically requires Executive Directors to decide by majority voting, a majoritarian obligation does exist with respect to 'the Bank' under section 3 b) of Article 5. Additionally, disseminated throughout the text there are several instances in which different majorities are required according to matters under discussion (see, among many others, Art.2 sec.2 b), quoted above; Art.2 sec.4 on issue price of shares when different from par value; Art.2 sec.4, on specific issues regarding payments for direct loans, or, again in Art 4, sec.8, iv to buy and sell different sorts of securities.

23 Yet, similar remarks could be advanced about the vagueness of the Commission's Code of Conduct on Complementarity and Division of Labour in Development Policy (2007), where the extant neglect of actors other than the Commission, MS or other EU institutions suggested that the issue was originally left underdetermined on the EU's side as well.

24 As discussed in Chapter 4, the EU is retained to play a negligible role in security affairs, where its low assertiveness is almost uniformly questioned across the Bank.

25 See Table 3.1 Chapter 3, on current EU EDs representation at the Board.

26 Author's interview with EU ED (April 2011).

27 Interestingly, issues of representation at the Board have emerged as concerns primarily among EU EDs from small member states, or EDs from neighboring countries, somehow different from the debate on the same issue at the Fund.
28 Key empirical inputs into this section are interviews with a few EU EDs and Alternates at the World Bank's Board, held in late 2009 and mid-2011. Upon confidentiality request of the interviewees, anonymity is maintained throughout the text. The implications on the changes of voting power brought about by the reform have been discussed in section 6 of Chapter 3 of this book.
29 The issue was critically raised in the Zedillo Report: 'While some European countries are generous donors to IDA, it is not clear why this should translate into chairs in the IBRD, IFC and MIGA boards. The larger problem is the absence of transparent, and fair principles to govern the distribution of chairs on the [WBG] Board. If IDA contributions are to determine the allocation of chairs on the IDA Executive Board, this principle should be made explicit' (Zedillo 2009, 29).
30 Interview with top political WB officer, 2011.
31 With respect to consensus within the Eurogroup, German sources have praised the role of their home country in supplying the pooling model that would form the basis for the quota formula negotiated at the Board, but have also reported 'different interests' and the need of an 'intense debate' before the presentation of the common Eurogroup's proposal to the Board (Stumm 2011).
32 Author's Interview with top WB political officer (2011).
33 Author's Interview with top WB political officer (2011).
34 Which brought the chairs for African countries to three, and the overall number of chairs to 25, thus overcoming the advice of reducing the total number of chairs to 20, advanced in the Zedillo Report.
35 The UK's more pro-development stance must however be qualified under several respects. Relative to the quota formula, its behavior at the 2007 Spring Meetings (when developing countries first pushed to have the PPP criterion passed for weighting the GDP term) has been defined as one of 'blocking attempts at meaningful reforms [of] the IMF's governance structure' (Eurodad 2006, 6). Relative to the chairs issue, while in principle favorable to compact the Eurogroup into a single seat, the UK never openly suggested to be ready to relinquish its single-country appointed directorate at the Bank.
36 There are no low income countries in the constituency led by Spain. Apart from Nicaragua, El Salvador and Guatemala, which are currently classified as lower-middle income economies, all the other constituency members belong to the group of higher-middle income countries. For a brief discussion on the composition of EU constituencies see section 6 in Chapter 3. On World Bank country classification see http://data.worldbank.org/about/country-classifications/country-and-lending-groups.
37 Data referred to the completed Phase 2. Current shares and voting power (32.06% for EU-led constituencies, 16.39% for the US constituency, as of March 2017) include further adjustments and shareholding revisions, as detailed in Chapter 3, section 6.
38 The distinction is made by Cohen (1993).

6 Analyzing performance II

The EU's contributed effectiveness to the World Bank's programs

6.1 Introduction

The analysis on the EU internal and external effectiveness conducted in Chapter 5 indicates that Brussels' influence on decisions taken at the IBRD Board is much dependent on the nature of the issue and the type of policy at stake. While decision making in constituent politics, such as changes to shareholding rights, largely responds to incentives dictated by national priorities, on other sector- and region-specific issues of common EU interest, MS have been able to better coordinate. The extent to which such coordination has been turned into higher contributed effectiveness to support development has varied widely, along a host of factors, including program- and partner-specific dimensions. This chapter deepens the focus on those components, analyzing consistency (between stated and achieved objectives) and impact (policy outcome) dimensions of the EU's development efforts when cooperating with the World Bank and through Bank-sponsored or managed programs. Detailed investigations are in turn presented in Chapters 7, 8 and 9, where the general evidence provided here is deepened with the help of case-studies relative to the ECA, MENA and SSA regions, and analyzed through the lenses of role theory, inter-institutional bargaining and effectiveness frameworks advanced in the book.

Analyzing consistency and impact through the lens of 'contributed effectiveness' has required to expand the set of EU-specific goals, to include World Bank's own aims (as noted in Chapter 2 the two sets overlap on several – but not all – counts), towards a preliminary understanding of the main inter-organizational dynamics behind their joint performance. Also, due to the public nature of both organizations, the higher politicization of their shared goals has called for particular caution in reconstructing practices from official documents and interviews, compared to analyses of inter-organizational performance of private organizations. A further cautionary note is advanced to guard against the risk of 'functionalist entrapment' inherent in the analysis of long and highly disaggregated delegation chains. As suggested in Chapter 5, the thick conceptualization of performance articulated here is intended as a heuristic device, and should not be used as a model to infer causality between the three types of effectiveness conceptualized in Chapter 5. While links do indeed exist, there are several reasons that suggest particular caution in functionally relating internal and external effectiveness, on the one side, to contributed effectiveness on the other. As discussed at several junctures, EU EDs take on multiple roles so that it is not a foregone conclusion that successful coordination within the Eurogroup is the main determinant, say, of effective implementation of a specific program in the field. Equally, even under Eurogroup-led impactful decision making at the Board, multiple factors intervene along the delegation chains and within the broader development networks surrounding the two organizations. Pressures from the European Parliament or EU CSOs, or managerial initiative on the side of either of the two organizations are two cases in point. Predictably, the causal processes identified by this performance analysis are by and large highly spurious. Finally, an EU consensus may not necessarily work towards a development-friendly outcome.[1] With no prejudice for the positive implications of the Eurogroup's successful coordination at the Board, from a development perspective these considerations further support the case for widening the focus of performance analysis to the broader EU–World Bank inter-organizational and policy spaces.

While policy impact appears to be one among the most visible features of performance, and a salient theme in the policy-oriented literature on IOs, the identification (and, more so, the evaluation) of 'what has been achieved', by whom and exactly under which institutional framework is by no means univocal.[2] The next section situates the conceptualization of contributed performance presented here in the policy and development literatures, to set the context for the analysis that will follow. To what extent are plans followed by facts? Additionally, to what extent are implemented blueprints responding to the needs of supported groups in partner countries? The former question has guided the analysis of consistency, here conceptualized as the relative absence of gap between EU official goals and achieved results, that is discussed in section 6.2 below. The latter has informed the investigation on policy impact, which is the subject of Section 6.4. Section 6.5 in turn connects the evidence on contributed effectiveness with the two organizations' respective views on the nexuses between political and economic elements in the promotion of development, to introduce the investigation of the EU–World Bank relations in Europe and Central Asia, Middle East and North Africa, and Sub-Saharan Africa presented in chapters 7, 8 and 9, respectively. The concluding section summarizes the main findings on contributed effectiveness, reflecting on selected EU and World Bank performance strengths and weaknesses, in light of their past cooperation and in view of their efforts to support the attainment of the United Nations Sustainable Development Goals.

6.2 Contributed effectiveness I: policy consistency

Academic research has variously debated the dynamics of inter-organizational cooperation, looking at both the congruence between planned and achieved objectives (policy consistency), and at the ability of such goal attainment to effectively solve problems on the ground (policy impact). A particular concern for the EU academic and policy communities is the degree of coherence, often 'used interchangeably with consistency' (Carbone 2008, 323) that the Union displays across the multiple policy areas of its external action, and the inherently problematic processes to achieve such coherence. From a development perspective, however, consistency implies a plurality of dimensions that go beyond the EU-own shaping of that concept, whether under the label of development-oriented coherence or not.[3]

In this framework, policy consistency proxies the degree with which action has occurred in accordance with pre-set policy targets and standards, including, but not limited to, the – relative – absence of contradictions between the EU foreign policies in different domains. The development perspective adopted here looks at consistency in terms of the relative gap (or absence thereof) between what the EU has committed itself to achieve in terms of development aims and what it has been able to reach through its policies and frameworks, on the one side, and through the collaboration with the World Bank, in traditional trust fund channeling, new own blending facilities and various ad hoc programs on the other.

In the words of public policy studies, policy consistency captures here the relative fit between expected and achieved aims, mirroring early conceptualizations of 'performance as conformance' aspects of implementation (Barrett 1981). In the analytical framework presented in Chapter 5 such relative fit is played across five different dimensions, or five consistency components: vertical-institutional (1), horizontal-sectoral (2), horizontal-geographical (3), internal-external (4) and technical (5). The five-fold disaggregation helps to identify, respectively, the relative harmony across statements and policies of EU MS and institutions (both vertical and horizontal 'institutional consistency'); the degree of the EU's 'traditional' horizontal consistency (the EU 'policy coherence, across different external policies); Brussels' congruity at the horizontal-geographical level (i.e. the coherence of its approach towards different partner countries, based on the EU's official frameworks); the accord between what the EU does internally and what it pursues externally (in selected policy areas); and, finally, the Union's 'technical consistency' (i.e. the ability to employ self-claimed expertise in specific issues).

Aside from terminological debates, the EU literature has largely focused on the internal sources of the EU's consistency deficits (Hoebink 2004; Carbone 2008). The analysis conducted here incorporates these insightful inputs, but situates them within the broader networks of development policymaking. Conceptually, it widens the focus to incorporate complex aspects of interactive performance. Empirically, it investigates consistency through feedbacks from the World Bank, officers in partner countries (which are shareholders to the Bank), and other relevant stakeholders (regional banks, such as the EIB, or CSOs which regularly assess the development achievements of both multilaterals).[4]

As shown in Figure 6.1, 49% of the World Bank's respondents express positive or generally positive assessment of the EU's overall consistency, while 39% of the interviewees voice their concern with respect to correspondence between the Union's official statements, on the one side, and its actions and policies, on the

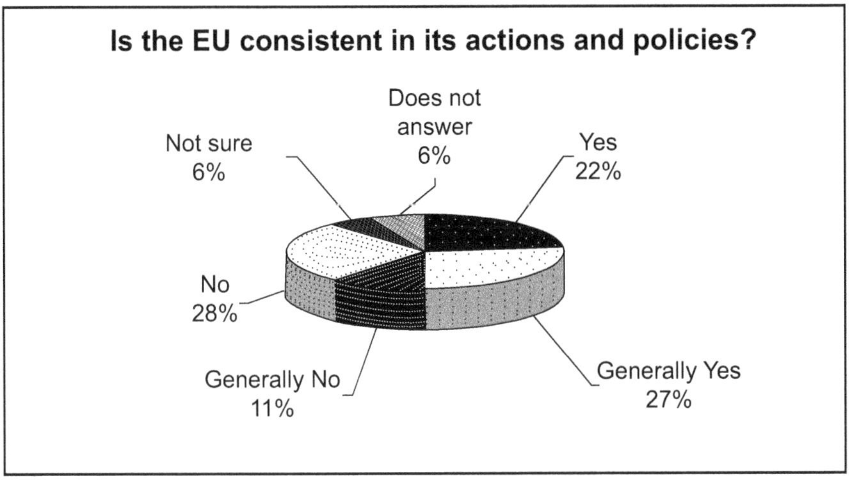

Figure 6.1 The EU policy consistency

Q: Do you believe that the EU is consistent in its actions and policies?

Note: The question was asked with reference to pertinent constituencies to EDs, and to relevant units to VPs and technical staff.

other. Indeed 28% of the respondents believe that the Union suffers from a serious consistency deficit, while some 11% nuance this stark negative assessment, but still deem the EU's implemented actions and policies as largely contradictory of its statements.

With respect to the past, the EU appears to have improved its policy consistency across the board under the Barroso Commission. The establishment of a good dialogue process in the Balkans was quoted among the most visible examples of such progress, and the Union's innovative approach to security through economic cooperation with the Stability Pact countries was unambiguously praised. Both cases are analyzed in Chapter 7, where the positive views expressed by World Bank counterparts are contextualized in the broader framework of the EU–World Bank relations in the Balkans, against a more mixed evidence of lower geographical consistency on the EU's side.

Several feedbacks were however given on the critical side. Deficits in institutional consistency were mentioned, particularly relative to divergences between the Commission and MS, among MS, or within the EU institutions. Weak coordination across policy sectors was also quoted, with deficits in horizontal policy consistency. However, by and large one of the Union's most often quoted weakness, was the perceived EU contradictory approach to development assistance in different countries, i.e. low horizontal coherence on the external side. Critiques were raised on the wavering coherence apparently displayed by the EU in its internal policies on migration and social inclusion vis-à-vis its external actions in those areas. Finally, several respondents have particularly questioned the EU's technical ability to implement its policies on the ground, mentioning also performance weaknesses in the monitoring and evaluation of its own programs and actions.

Relative to institutional consistency (1), the EU passivity in OECD discussions was quoted, as well as divergences between the Commission and the bilateral agencies of member states. Indeed, assessments of the 'general consistency' of EU policies, seem to emphasize how behind the surface of harmonious statements may lie different understandings of goals and strategies, by member states' bilaterals and the Commission, respectively. A similar case regards inconsistencies within the EU institutions, which appear to have varied according to different cleavages. A fault line has been identified in certain areas between interactions and official statements at the top level (Commissioners, World Bank's President and VPs), on the one side, and its equivalents at lower organizational levels, on the other. More precisely, as better detailed in Chapter 7, in spite of the official invitations by several EU Commissioners to the World Bank to enter boards and committees of EU-sponsored funding facilities, particularly in the Western Balkans and neighborhood countries (such as the WBIF), the follow up from the side of lower Commission staff appears to have been particularly slow or, at times, even absent. In the view of World Bank's staff, mid-level Commission staff does not seem to feel empowered to make the envisaged changes happen. A similar evidence has been gathered on EU–EIB relations: at the end of the 2000s, and in spite of improved relations between the ECA VP and the EIB President, turf battles at lower floors between the two sides were quoted as hindrances to the cooperation between EU institutions and the World Bank. On the other side, horizontal cleavages (among different EU institutions) have emerged, along issue-specific preferences in Parliamentary committees, as documented about the debate on the creation of an EU-joint constituency at the World Bank's Board, warmly sponsored by the EU Parliamentary Committee on Development, but openly opposed by the EP Trade Committee. With respect to top-down discrepancies within the Commission, the difficulty appears to stem from defensive posture of lower staff, perhaps due to a lack of incentive mechanisms to increase the participation and motivation in key changes decided at the top. With respect to cleavages among parliamentary committees, what appears as an inconsistency from a purely organizational perspective becomes instead a virtue of democratic debate. Such 'inconsistency' then ultimately reflects the unique nature of the Union, not an international organization, not a state, but a mixture of the two, embodying the potential to develop the strengths retained by either of them, but also carrying the burden of managing the tensions from their otherness.

With respect to horizontal-sectoral consistency (2), the trade-poverty 'missed link' appeared a matter of particular concern. The EU was particularly blamed for not having – supposedly – taken full advantage of trade negotiations (especially with the African partners, before and after the launch of the EPA process, as discussed at length in Chapter 9, and with the MENA partners, as shown in Chapter 8) as an antipoverty tool. Similar difficulties emerged with respect to the implications of the trade–energy link, with special reference to the EU's approach towards the Eastern Europe and Central Asian CIS partners, which also appears as a prominent issue in horizontal geographical consistency (3), relative to the – alleged – geographical discrimination, analyzed with more depth in Chapter 7. Also, the EU's actions have at times seemed to contradict its statements on the use of economic incentives (and disincentives) towards stabilization and democratization in the Middle Eastern partner countries, a case investigated in Chapter 8. Relative to internal–external policy consistency (4), a rather negative judgment has been voiced on the discrepancy between what the EU does internally, especially in the areas of social inclusion, poverty reduction and integration, and its external behavior in the same policy areas.

Weak horizontal-geographical consistency (3) embodies the recurrent theme of the EU's perceived low policy coherence across different areas of the globe. A general consensus exists on the fact that the EU's approach to development has long prioritized countries in the Neigborhood, particularly in some parts of the ECA (Europe and Central Asia) and, to a lesser extent, MENA (Middle East and North Africa) regions, leaving Sub-Saharan African countries on the side, until recently, and, still to this date, devoting only minimal attention to poverty eradication in Asian, Pacific and Latin American countries. While no one would dispute that the difference in the respective missions of the two organizations by and large accounts for the high geographical diversification in the EU approach to development, still voices from – and on – these latter three regions report somehow discomfortingly about the EU's neglect. As further elaborated in Chapter 7, the perceived EU's discrimination between different countries in the ECA region, and between countries supposedly belonging to the same EU-sponsored groupings has been an additional obstacle to the effectiveness of its programs in that region.

Several voices also questioned the EU's different methods for policy evaluation, their high variability across DGs ('each DG has its methods to assess its policies'), as well as the dubious EU incentive systems for external consultants (systematic renewal of hirings in exchange for positive 'external' evaluations). With respect to the latter aspect, feedbacks from the World Bank country offices also pointed to difficulties in relating to their counterparts in the (then) Commission delegations. Inputs from posts in the MENA (current) and SSA regions (2008) indicated that, even when their Commission colleagues on the ground exhibited high levels in competence and preparation, their ability to tackle technical issues arising in the day-to-day working, especially those involving economic analyses or rapid evaluation of economic proposals/requests, was often below average. A need to prior consulting with offices in Brussels, as well as a most frequent reliance on the work of external advisors to prepare technical reports, or to provide feedbacks when asked, appeared the norm rather than the exception. Experts from academic institutions that were hired to produce Commission-financed preparatory studies have reported duplication (apparently two different DGs, DEVCO and RELEX, respectively, had been working on the same subject in parallel) and difficulty in obtaining information from their commissioning sources.[5]

In an attempt to increase transparency, the Parliament has targeted its concerns to the expenses incurred by the Union to pay external advisers on EU programs in emerging and developing countries. Replying to a question by the Parliamentary Committee on Budget Control about the exact amount devoted to fund external experts, the then Commissioner to Development, Andris Piebalgs, replied by candidly asserting his inability to provide either a quote for the overall costs from external experts, their total number (referring to then DG DEVCO–EuropeAid), or a range for their hourly wage (European Parliament 2011c). The availability of this piece of information to address a parliamentary written question is, technically, an issue of internal inter-institutional accountability, and, to some extent, a potentially irrelevant element towards result-based effectiveness. As reconstructed in Chapter 4, on the evolutions of the EU–WB relations through successive revisions of the Framework Agreement, the EU has taken up a more assertive stance on the matter, particularly through a systematically active involvement of the Parliamentary Committee on budgetary control and an enhanced role for the European Court of Auditors, including through the adoption of more rigorous Financial Regulation in 2012.

In the light of the increased financial effort, actual and expected, that the EU has sustained to promote development, particularly since the global economic crisis, amelioration of technical preparedness to guarantee the consistency between stated goals and achieved results has become even more relevant. In addition to the fit between expected and achieved objectives, however, assessing the outcomes of the EU's development efforts, through the Bank and with the Bank, takes on additional significance. As exemplified by the parliamentary question on the fees paid to development consultants, legitimate concerns on financial transparency witness a physiological utilization of institutional accountability rights within the EU. However, from an outcome-oriented and development-minded perspective, an excessive emphasis on conformance controls may divert energies away from the core goals of Brussels' development policy: improving the lives of those who are most in need.

6.3 Contributed effectiveness II: policy impact

In our analytical framework to analyze performance, contributed effectiveness also incorporates the policy impact of Brussels' development efforts, a proxy for the outcomes on the ground of the whole policy process, assessed (ideally) against the needs of the 'end receivers'. The impact dimension refers to the concept of policy outcome, as derived from the policy analysis literature, and it is employed here to assess the degree to which the overall policy process has provided satisfactory solutions for the problems that it was designed/implemented to address. Owing to outcome analyses in implementation studies, this inquiry refers to 'building, bottom-up, a picture of the particular "implementation structure", the network structure of actors and parts of organizations as well as their relationships and interactions in influencing outcomes' (Barrett 2004, 254, in Hjern and Porter (1981)). Along the conceptual vein of development studies, 'impact' is therefore related to the degree to which a policy 'meets the needs' of those at whom the policy is targeted.

There is a solid, though not consensual, bulk of studies on the impact of aid and aid policies on development. Debates have divided academics and practitioners in opposing camps, based on different opinions on methods, indicators and timing (Easterly et al. 2004; Easterly 2007; Clemens et al. 2011; Kaufmann et al. 2009 Banerjee and Duflo 2013). Early policy studies on implementation had already warned against the risks of making evaluation criteria a policy end in itself (Williams 1971 in Barrett 2004, 255), collapsing performance analysis on performance achievements intended as conformance. Such an occurrence has been and will inevitably be to a certain extent part of the policy game, particularly when high-level knowledge-producing institutions, such as the World Bank or the OECD, are involved.[6] In the development community, change in evaluation systems has occurred along discontinuous paths, often triggered by exogenous factors. The evolution of new evaluation criteria, and their feedback into policy adjustments has often been a long-term process.[7]

In the IR literature on regime effectiveness, the outcome dimension has been at times conflated with what is defined here as consistency, with some confusion between the problem-solving and conformance metrics.[8] The reference to formal objectives, and the resort to gap-gauging against an ideal baseline scenario, clearly point to a genealogy that is closer to top-down implementation studies, and early analyses of management performance in the business literature. While important in several respects, sticking to the sole consistency dimension bears the many limitations of 'performance as conformance' analyses. Additionally, it potentially carries a self-referential element that downplays the importance of inter-institutional dynamics, which are crucial in the study of contributed performance from the cooperation among global governors.

The way in which (outcome) performance is assessed has evident implications for the options that are available to theorize about its roots. Policy impact has indeed been shown to depend on the outcomes of the policy-action dialectic at field level (Strauss 1978; Lipsky 1980). A whole generation of studies assessing aid effectiveness has followed along this path, theorizing about the need to assess aid effectiveness, and plan about future allocation, primarily conditioned on the quality of institutions and policies in the receiving country (Burnside and Dollar 2000).[9] Warnings about the drawbacks of strictly quantitative benchmarking, particularly regarding the different implications of measuring regimes' vs IOs' effectiveness have been expressed in the IR debate on IOs' performance (Gutner and Thompson 2010, 230–231). Along a similar vein, in his *The White Man's Burden* (2007), an extensive and sanguine review about the achievements of multilateral aid policies and studies over the past 60 decades, the economist William Easterly has persuasively argued about the need to seriously reassert the relevance of case studies and micro-analytical strategies to assess the impact of aid policies. Compact benchmarks, including quantitative ones, are handy reference points but they are not immune to criticism and subjectivity: their usefulness should be necessarily complemented with other inputs. Studies in the institutionalist vein have similarly explained specific cases of poor IOs' performance on the basis of weak or adverse conditions in the field (Gutner 2005; Howard 2008). While the debate on 'conditional aid' is still very much an open issue (Deaton 2013), the influence on aid effectiveness exerted by actors other than IOs and their member states (borrowers and lenders) has become a topic of enhanced salience. Following the empirical methodology outlined in Chapter 5, policy impact has therefore been reconstructed qualitatively through a triangulation process, based on World Bank, EU and third party sources.

As a first step, the opinion of a variety of World Bank internal actors has been obtained, about the EU's ability to effectively operate towards achieving shared goals, either across the board, or specific to the respondents' area of expertise/functional unit.

The snapshot sketched in Figure 6.2 indicates that a relative majority of respondents among World Bank officers (44%) considered the EU as only moderately impactful in meeting the needs of developing partner countries through its development policy. However, this less-than-satisfactory assessment was counterbalanced somehow by the datum on high and very high policy impact, whereby 39% of respondents retained the Union able to attain its policy goals in a way that was satisfactory also for aid recipients.

Among the highlights, the results of several initiatives on development coordination and assistance that the EU has taken since the beginning of the new century have been quoted. With respect to cooperation between the Commission and the Bank, the Limelette Process, kicked off in 2003 for SSA partner countries, now subsumed in the wider Paris Agenda,[10] and the Luxemburg Process, initiated in 2000 for the MENA partner countries,[11] have been mentioned among the most

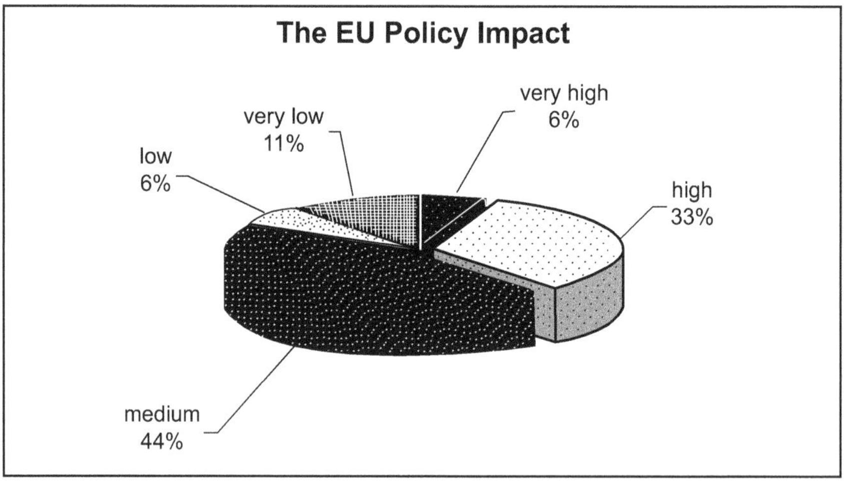

Figure 6.2 The EU policy impact

Q: What is your opinion on the effectiveness of the EU policies with respect to your region/functional unit/constituency?

prominent examples. While institutional evolutions have pointed to an enhanced dialogue and more structured cooperation between the two organizations, field impact has varied over that period, as discussed in Chapters 8 and 9. The outcomes of the cooperation between the EU and the Bank in the Balkans initiated in 1999 under the formal mandate provided by the Stability Pact for South East Europe, and structured through a World Bank–EC Joint Office for South East Europe Reconstruction in Brussels, have been particularly praised, for their ability to raise resources and promote development and democracy opportunities in the region.[12]

On the side of lowlights, a critical or highly critical opinion on the Union's effective contribution to reduce poverty and promote development has been shared by 17% of the respondents. An overview of the empirical references that were more frequently associated to these below-average achievements, indicates that functional ties with consistency issues have been at work in specific cases, though not always being systematically connected to poor outcomes in the field.

Cases where consistency issues compounded with impact ones related to poor institutional coordination, both at the horizontal (inter-agency) and vertical (MS-Commission and Brussels-field) levels. With respect to the latter aspect, i.e. vertical deficits, in several instances the EU was criticized for its supposedly poor approach to capacity building, especially in new member countries, which, in their simultaneous roles as recipients and donors, have lamented the EU's lack of assistance and have relied on the Bank's expertise to develop minimum abilities to cope with their new responsibilities, as discussed in Chapter 7 on the World Bank–Bulgaria and World Bank–Romania MoUs on the absorption of EU structural funds. In other cases, the weak development impact of EU programs has been related to a deliberately deficient antipoverty strategy. Cases in point link those unconvincing results to poor consistency between trade and development policies, as shown by critical positions in the debate on the EPA negotiations with Sub-Saharan partners, or in other dialogues with Associated MENA partners, both relative to the thorny issue of the revision of the Rules of Origin (ROOs) systems, discussed in detail in Chapters 8 and 9, respectively.[13]

Still, in other cases the poor outcome of EU's policies was not functionally related to consistency issues. In a number of instances poor field performance was linked to the EU's excessively bureaucratic system, apparently plagued by mushrooming programs in an overburdened agenda. Additionally, the slowness of the EU finance system, and the excessively politicized process of aid allocation have emerged as key constraints on the EU ability to impact positively on its aid delivery, even in the presence of a clear commitment.

To sum up, in policy processes where both the EU and the Bank have collaborated, World Bank's feedbacks painted a moderately performing Union. The relative majority of answers pointed indeed to an evaluation of average effectiveness in contributed terms, praising the role of the Union in raising awareness on the trade and development agendas, but criticizing its less than effective approach in delivering aid in trade issues.

6.4 Contributed effectiveness and inter-organizational performance: World Bank and EU's views on the link between political and economic drivers in the promotion of development

On the one side, the hindrances that have been identified to higher EU policy effectiveness pertain to difficulties in coordination, financing, delivery, monitoring and evaluation functions. As such they may appear as mainly technical in nature, and perhaps may have technical (as opposed to political) origins. Other sources of the deficits in the EU contributed policy effectiveness have emerged, however, from both the documentary evidence and the interviews, reflecting the differences that exist in the missions, goals and strategies that the Union and the Bank respectively pursue. Linking to the analysis on roles presented in Chapter 4, this section connects the two organizations' respective views on the nexuses between political and economic elements in the promotion of development, to consistency and impact dimensions in the attainment of respective missions.

In the economics and political science empirical literatures, as well as in policy oriented development studies, the debate is still open on the specific relation that exists between economic choices and socio-political values and institutions in the promotion of development, both in terms of sign and direction (see among others North 1990; Barro 1997; Boix and Stokes 2003; Açemoglu et al. 2005; Gerring et al. 2005; Easterly 2007). Methods and indicators abound, proving how specific types of institutions are conducive to different levels of development, and how, on the contrary, initial economic conditions impact on subsequent political development paths, variously discounting for the role of domestic and external factors. To the cleavage between political and economic factors, then, these contributions add an explicit external–internal dimension, which has gained prominence in policy circles since the revision of the early inward looking approaches in the modernization vein (Rostow 1960), through the pushes towards outward-oriented development strategies (Krueger 1997; Burnside and Dollar 2000; Dollar and Kraay 2002).

To this day, evaluation methods are constantly scrutinized, and the evidence is still mixed, on the impact of aid, and the effect of domestic policies on the opportunities for development. Beyond the 'micro-macro paradox' (records of encouraging results at the micro-level against negative evidence at the macro-level; Clemens et al. 2011; Rajan and Subramanian 2008), the few elements on which there seems to be agreement, according to our survey, are that evaluations on performance should be carried on in terms of specific actions and contexts, and that caution should be exerted in establishing any fixed relation between aid flows and domestic institutions in partner countries, as the two are obviously linked through multiple, highly spurious, channels.[14]

Reflecting the divergence in the academic and policy literatures, when World Bank practitioners are asked about the benefits attached to economic tools in the promotion of specific social and political values, their opinions diverge.[15] On the one side, according to some of the respondents, the Bank has a responsibility to administer, invest and redistribute resources for its member countries, but it should do so according to its own organizational values. These do not include the possibility of making principled statements on preferred political systems, but may well have close relation with key rule of law features that are incorporated in substantial democracies (such as the preservation of human dignity and the protection of basic political and civil rights). On the other side, others opt for a more restrictive interpretation of the organization's mission, and recall that the Bank acts on the requests of countries, and is therefore bound by its chiefly economic mission to 'only' reduce poverty and promote development in those partner countries that require its support. By organizational design, therefore, the active support to values and aims other than the twin goals of poverty eradication and inequality reduction occurs in the Bank either as a side effect, or through aid allocated on the basis of benchmarking exercises on different governance and investment climate national systems. Against this background, World Bank respondents, particularly the management and staff persons among them, have often framed the discourse on policy impact in technical, as opposed to political, terms.

The same issues have different implications when considered from the standpoint of the EU. As introduced in Chapter 2, compared to the World Bank's mandate, the EU wider and more complex mission entails at the same time a larger scope for action, a higher political leverage, and higher responsibilities. The diversity in development philosophies and foreign policy goals of the EU MS require substantial efforts in coordination and composition, efforts that have not always been consistent, as discussed above. A complex mission coexists with a multitude of strategies, that are political and economic (and also social and environmental), internal and external, as well as plural, as they stem out of the combination of the different MS priorities. Increased complexity brings higher degrees of freedom, but it also widens the margin for mistakes. Brussels' 'moral obligation' to pursue the common goals incorporated in the Union's complex mission does not face the obstacles of primarily economic organizations, such as the World Bank. The EU is a political actor, and a very generous donor altogether, less constrained in linking the attainment of political objectives to the provision of economic support, albeit more exposed to allegations of performance gaps, on both consistency and impact grounds.

Brussels has indeed used its leverage to advocate the respect of human rights conditionally, even if the same benchmarking criteria have been applied differently to institutions, political and economic, in different countries.[16] As discussed more in depth in Chapters 7 and 8, the EU's rigorous application of conditionality clauses in Pre-accession Agreements with ECA partners has been contrasted against the low enforcement of similar clauses in Association Agreements with MENA countries, respectively. Past colonial experiences in North Africa and current security interests in the Balkans and in the Middle East concur to account for these differences. So does the rationale of the EU enlargement strategy, whereby prospective members have been monitored more closely, and more often offered positive or negative incentives, compared to associated partners.

However, cases of successful use of political leverage, short of immediate economic gains, to obtain an improvement in the political situation of partner countries do exist, as shown by the EU tough stance on the protection of human rights issues in Haiti. Increased aid and a sustained effort to harmonize donors' actions has been the hallmark of the 2005 EU strategy to fight poverty in Sub-Saharan Africa, the region that has perhaps gathered the most vocal support from the development community towards increased aid against poverty. EU initiatives in that region since the beginning of the new millennium have definitely pointed to a more proactive stance in development terms, particularly compared to previous approaches (European Commission 2005). Nonetheless, as discussed in Chapter 9, the Union's contributed effectiveness in advancing development in Sub-Saharan African Countries should be carefully balanced by taking into account the controversial role of the EPAs. Trade and Agricultural priorities, as advanced by DG Trade and DG Agriculture, have appeared to be in conflict with development goals, as pursued by DG Development at the time. True, the Europe–Africa Summits, as well as the sustained emphasis that the then-Development Commissioner Michel put on scaling up and coordinating aid flows to Africa did provide clear incentives to enhance the development impact of the EU's role in the region. The high variability among different countries, however, as well as the changing dynamics in African politics have made it more difficult for the Union to pursue its goals consistently.

In strictly 'contributed terms', i.e. relative to the Bank's goals (originally the promotion of development, currently the eradication of poverty and the reduction of inequality) the EU's records appear, at best, mixed. The cases of new member countries in Central and Eastern Europe stand out as examples of relatively successful economic and political simultaneous progressions (albeit differences exist among them, also depending on differential performances), and so does the linking of economic, security and political conditionality in the partnerships established through the Stability Pact in the Balkans, a theme approached in Chapter 7. As shown in Chapter 8, the EU's development accomplishments are less evident with respect to Association partners in North Africa, such as Tunisia or Morocco (best performers in the MENA region but often behind their counterparts in Eastern Europe and the Balkans). Similarly, as discussed in Chapter 7, the EU's approach to development promotion in Central Asian Republics, such as Kazakhstan, Belarus and Kyrgyzstan, seems to pay tribute more to respecting the primacy of Russian tutelage and preserving the EU's own energy interests than to promoting development and governance goals.

The picture is different if one looks at a single organizational performance, considering the EU's effectiveness in reaching its own goals. At times these have been largely shared with the Bank, as in the cases of new members in the group of transition countries in Central and Eastern Europe, where economic development and political transition have proceeded somehow simultaneously.[17] When related to the specific EU goals of diffusion of democratic values and protection of human rights, political conditionality appears to have yielded fruits, at least in the countries that were monitored consistently as they proceeded in their paths towards accession. Yet, when Brussels' foreign policy interests are factored in, results achieved by the Union in the MENA region before the eruption of the Arab Spring, in March 2011, appear less questionable compared to their assessment under a purely development-oriented perspective. If the rationale of the EU action plans was one of promoting cooperation between EU domestic firms and partners in North African countries, in a way that preserved political stability in the region, then the EU reached, at least in part, its expected goals.

Finally, a comparison between the EU and the World Bank in the pursuit of the joint targets in poverty reduction and development promotion indicates that the EU's more balanced approach to conditionality has enjoyed a relatively higher success, compared to the Bank's initial emphasis on structural adjustment. As proven by a number of studies, tied aid has been a recipe for disaster from a development perspective.[18] Structural Adjustment Programs have been gradually abandoned by the Bank, after the fiascoes that, since the Asian crisis, were exposed to the world public opinion, as discussed in Chapter 3. In this respect, the simultaneous existence of multiple, at times contrasting national approaches to development has been a strength, rather than a liability, for the EU. At the beginning of the new millennium, and compared to the Bank, which had to counterbalance the negative experiences of SAPs conditionalities, the EU has benefitted from an enhanced 'moral credibility bonus'. In the eyes of third parties, the EU shift from earlier process (policy)-based conditionality to outcome-based conditionality to assess performance in partner countries has further tipped towards the positive the balance of Brussels' contributed effectiveness.[19]

6.5 Conclusions

To complete the analysis of the EU's performance under the framework presented in Chapter 5, this chapter has looked at Brussels' contributed effectiveness, on the basis of first-hand inputs provided by World Bank's officers. The empirical evidence points to five major clusters around which feedbacks emerged on the EU's policy consistency and on the broader implications of the EU's development policies for the needs of partner countries. Problems of institutional coordination (vertical, between EU institutions and MS, and inter-institutional), as well as horizontal-geographical and horizontal-sectoral inconsistencies have been singled out as areas of particular concern, potentially exacting a toll on the credibility and field performance of Brussels' development policy, particularly in light of the EU effort to project externally a good reputation as a standard bearer of the causes of poverty reduction and development promotion. The partnerships with the Bank for Southern and Eastern European countries, the Limelette and Luxembourg Processes, and the effort put in bringing forward the Paris Agenda are witness to such progress. Less importance has apparently been devoted by the Union to develop focused communication and training strategies, particularly towards new MS, according to Bank officials, who have lamented Brussels' emphasis on a generic, external projection of positive images, in the absence of a clear strategy for inter-organizational cooperation. Adding to coordination deficits (both among DGs and between bilaterals and the Commission), problems have emerged relative to the EU's low ability in streamlining financing procedures, and developing a reliable system for monitoring and evaluating the results of its policies.

Both organizations, however, have learnt from past difficulties, as shown by the policy changes that have occurred since the early critiques to the Washington Consensus in the late 1990s, and after the debates on the Paris Agenda and the EU 'one size fits all' EPA recipe for Africa. The incorporation of conditionality clauses in cooperation agreements or programs, and the linkage of economic benefits to the attainment of specific political (governance, in the Bank's jargon) goals, only work in the longer term if conditions are acceptable also to the weaker party in the agreement. As it has been long shown in the Bank's practice, development happens only when, at critical junctures, donors and recipients agree. Therefore, forcing unnatural grouping of countries, as in Sub-Saharan Africa, to carve economic areas that are overburdened by red-tape adjustment requirements, that are beneficial to the EU production and export interests, may not be the most credible way to promote development and fight poverty.

The multiple souls coexisting in the European Union have put it at both an advantage and a disadvantage with respect to supporting development. As noted by one World Bank respondent, the 'mere existence of the EU contributes to the effectiveness of the overall development process, as it provides a pole of attraction. . .to give hope to countries who are in need'.[20] The emulation capital is no doubt there, and progress has occurred, via the EU support to the Agenda 2030 and to the attainment of the SDGs, as reaffirmed by Brussels in the 2017 New Consensus on Development. The evolving context of the EU–World Bank cooperation, detailed in Chapter 3, is also a witness of the EU's and World Bank's will to enhance the effectiveness of their partnership. Further efforts however are needed to improve the consistency and outcomes of their cooperation in the third millennium, as detailed in the remaining chapters of this book.

Notes

1 A notable example, discussed in Chapter 9, being the ambiguous effects of the EU trade policy on development in several Sub-Saharan partners.

2 Definitional and identification problems of this sort have been discussed by Barrett and Fudge (1981) in their seminal contribution to the study of policy implementation networks in domestic contexts. In turn, multi-stakeholder models in the literature on organizational performance have addressed strategies of welfare maximization by principals under conflicting claims by multiple stakeholders (Holmstrom and Milgrom 1991; Tirole 2001). Multi-stakeholder approaches in development policymaking have come to the fore particularly since the new millennium, even if the label has been used in the practice to lump together a wide variety of partnerships (Martens 2007).

3 On the different meanings of consistency, and on the confusion with the twin concept of coherence, both in the academic literature and in the EU official documents, see Carbone (2008), who specifically analyzes the EU own concept of 'policy coherence for development' (PCD).

4 The choice implies that EU consistency is analyzed by looking at its interaction with the Bank and via empirical inputs from the Bank on that interaction. As detailed in

Section 5.3 of Chapter 5 on data and empirical methodology, third party inputs have been included to reduce bias from correlation between observed phenomena and the source of inputs on those same phenomena. More particularly, consistency issues have been approached mainly from a sectoral angle, i.e. by asking the interviewees their opinion on the fit between stated and achieved objectives of the EU in their respective areas of action (i.e. regions or functions, for technical management staff, and constituencies, for political staff). Subsequently, cross-checks have been provided by submitting the same questions to EU officers, and by complementing the evidence thus obtained with inputs from diversified sets of third party sources (evaluation studies from independent think tanks, press briefs from NGOs and relevant media, interviews with third-party practicioners and, when available, feedbacks from partner countries, in addition to secondary academic literature).

5 Interviews with academicians who have played leading roles in the preparation of DG DEV financed-reports suggested that duplication of work has happened, and that after several months of commissioned work the hired team of external experts was invited to dissemination events for very similar research outputs apparently produced by other Commission DGs (namely RELEX). Author's interview (2008).

6 Thus, effectiveness has been employed to capture the extent to which a regime 'solves the problem that motivated its establishment' (Underdal 2002, 11), and to assess the gap between the achieved result and the optimal solution to the problem (Helm and Sprinz 2000). Gutner and Thompson make this point about the generality of IOs (2010, 233).

7 An example is the correlation between the refinement of several approaches to evaluation of development programs and the circulation of technical elites from key World Bank posts to prominent external think tanks and academic institutions, as in the cases of Joseph Stiglitz, Nancy Birdsall, Paul Collier and William Easterly.

8 Both references are quoted in Gutner and Thompson (2010, 230).

9 From a practitioner's point of view, a plausible objection to the substance of this line of reasoning is that, within degrees, IOs should be specifically, and particularly, equipped to tackle issues of capacity building at the implementation level.

10 The Limelette Process was created to support harmonization between the EU Strategy for Africa and WB Action Plan (World Bank 2005a), coupling scaling up with enhanced coordination to pursue the attainment of the MDGs. Performance issues relative to the EU–WB cooperation under the Limelette process, including recent developments, are discussed in Chapter 9.

11 The Luxemburg Process is a high-level policy dialogue initiated in 2000, which also includes the EIB and, with an advisory role, the IMF.

12 See 'The World Bank in Brussels', June 2007, prepared by the World Bank Office in Brussels, http://www.worldbank.org/eu. Additional information on the World Bank–EC Joint Office for South East Europe Reconstruction can be found at www.seerecon.org.

13 See Brenton and Ikezuki (2005) and Hoppe (2007). This assessment appears largely confirmed by third party sources. See, among others, Oxfam (2005, 2006a, 2006b, 2007a), ODI (2007), Open Europe (2008), the *Financial Times*, 'Crying wolf over aid and trade?', May 16, 2007; 'Africa–EU tariff proposal raises concerns', November 23, 2007; 'Brussels reaches deal with East Africa Bloc', November 28, 2007; 'Tariffs will rupture relations, Africa warns EU', December 9, 2007.

14 Sharing a similar concern, the next three chapters focus on the EU's performance through selected case-studies.

15 Critical IPE has interpreted the resemblance between the academic and practitioners' thought as a physiological outcome of the horizontal links between elites in the two camps (Murphy 2008). However, a plurality of views within the same organization may simply be the result of – honestly reported, even though subjectively filtered – different experiences of staff members in a variety of contexts (project, country, time).

16 Conditionality has been the subject of extensive research, especially since the emergence of the anti-global movement in the late 1990s. On the EU and conditionality see, among others, Youngs (2001); Smith, K. (2004); Magen and Morlino (2008). On the WB and conditionality see, among others, the seminal Mosley et al. (1991); Koeberle et al. (2005); Woods (2006).
17 As noted above, this is a broad comparison among regional impacts: in this particular instance, the EU's policy effectiveness in the ECA region is considered against the EU's policy effectiveness in all the other partner countries. Differences in EU's performance exist vis à vis different 'European transitioners'. See Chapter 7.
18 The analysis of security-targeted economic incentives (both positive and negative) is beyond the scope of this chapter. It is however important to recall that the multiplicity of foreign policy objectives carried on by the EU obviously requires that its overall effectiveness be assessed through a balanced, inter-sectoral policy approach.
19 See Molina (2008).
20 Interview with World Bank ED, January 16, 2008, Washington DC.

7 Europe, Central Asia and the challenge of double transitions

7.1 Introduction

EU–WB cooperation in the ECA (Europe and Central Asia) region is different from all the other instances of joint EU–WB action: there the Bank very frequently operates within the EU or in the EU immediate neighborhood.[1] With the exception of Russia and the five Central Asian partners, reference has been made to the existence of a 'triangular relationship', encompassing the partner country, the Bank and the Union (World Bank ECA 2011, 12). Supporting simultaneous transitions to democracy and market-based systems has confronted the two organizations with exceptional challenges. The balancing of security, energy and development goals in the EU external agenda on the one side, and the restructuring of the WB programs in the new EU MS,[2] on the other, have multiplied the layers of the EU–WB hybrid delegation. Yet they have also created the potential to pool expertise and resources to help accession in candidates and potential candidates, and to support sustainable development throughout the region. Since the end of the Cold War, these challenges have proven to be the catalyzer of what is perhaps the thickest set of EU–WB region-based initiatives to date, including the setup of a joint EU–World Bank office in the aftermath of the Kosovo crisis, active between 1999 and 2008.

Views from the World Bank have pointed to an 'excellent and cooperative dialogue', supported by regular contacts with the Commission, EU MS bilateral donors, the EIB and the EBRD. At times, these highly positive instances were contrasted with less successful occurrences, with the EU–World Bank relation burdened by region- and country-specific fragmentation as well as by 'lack of strategic vision'.[3]

More particularly, voices from the World Bank management qualify the EU policies as broadly effective in the Balkans, and, by and large, in all non-CIS countries (Commonwealth Independent States). At the end of the 2000s, the EU's approach to the Balkans appeared 'innovative' and 'fast' in reacting to the multiple changes that had occurred in the 1990s. The launch of the Stabilization and Association Agreements, the support given to trade integration in the area, as well as the reliance on non-governmental instruments to advance the governance agenda stand out – in the eyes of the Bank – as notable EU successes in ensuring coherence between the political and the economic tracks of its composite mission.[4] Some concern has emerged however about the development implications of Brussels' differential treatment of partners in the ECA region. Echoing feedbacks from national authorities, voices from the World Bank quoted the partial exclusion of CIS and Central Asian partners from the EU development effort, noting how the latter were either approached by the Union with a subservient tone (Russia), or an altogether lecturing attitude. Allegedly, the inconsistency matched the EU fluctuating approach to development, at times highly political, at times more prone to the economic side of the matter. The duty to support partner countries ('clients') in their quest for development, has made it easier for some, in the Bank's management and staff, to relate to critical comments from national elites that were either uneasy with the EU, when that was perceived as too intrusive (as in the case of some Central Asian republics), or felt discriminated against 'privileged' neighbors (as in the case of Macedonia and Bosnia and Herzegovina).

To what extent have these World Bank's views and expectations on EU's role performance been matched by actual achievements? Conversely, what is the view of the EU on the World Bank's role in the region, particularly in new EU MS and candidate countries? How has the relation between the two IOs evolved across time, and how has their cooperation navigated the challenges posed by the momentous transformations that have occurred in the region? Within the context of hybrid delegation described in Chapters 2 and 3, and along the role and performance analyses conceptualized in Chapter 4, 5 and 6, this chapter seeks to answer these questions. Additionally, it investigates the extent to which the recent transformations in the 'division of labor' between the EU and the Bank have prompted a change in the organizations' respective roles in the region, looking at the implications of these evolutions for the future of both EU enlargement on the one side, and of development financing on the other.

By way of a targeted review of the democratization literature on the role of external actors, section 7.2 summarizes the main challenges faced by the EU and the WB to support double transitions in post-Soviet systems. In section 7.3 the differences between the EU's and World Bank's respective 'maps' of the wide ECA region at the beginning of the new millennium are fleshed out, to ground the discussion on the inconsistencies (perceived and realized) of the EU's approach to former CIS vs non-CIS countries against the background of EU enlargement. Section 7.4 analyzes the effectiveness of the EU's programs in the Western Balkans from both development and democracy promotion perspectives. While the EU has not always followed coherent strategies to pursue its multiple goals in the region, the analysis of cooperation entertained since 1999 with the World Bank, conducted in section 7.5, shows how, under the UN pressure to help with stabilization and reconstruction in the aftermath of the Kosovo War, promising knowledge transfer has occurred between the two organizations in the area of development financing, leading to the creation of EU own blending facilities for the Balkans and the Neighborhood countries. The EU innovation in development financing has impacted on the Bank's role in the region, but the change has not uniformly resulted in a downsizing of the latter's activities, as discussed in section 7.6, on the new challenges posed by the global economic crisis of 2008 and on the difficulties of new members to absorb the EU structural funds by 2013. The concluding section sums up findings on role change and performance, discussing their implications for the effectiveness of the EU–World Bank cooperation in European and Central Asian partners.

7.2 The EU and the World Bank in Europe and Central Asia: enlarging development and accompanying transition

Whether synergistic or antagonistic, the links between political and economic transition in the post-Soviet space have been investigated at length by scholars in comparative politics (Linz and Stepan 1996).[5] A debate first emerged about the relative benefits that early changes in either the economic or the political system of a country could bring to democratization. Robust economic fundamentals, it was argued, should come prior to political opening, even if that meant tolerating longer periods of non-democratic rule (Myrdal 1968; Huntington 1991). Counterpoints have noted how, on the contrary, deferring democracy in the name of abstract time-sequencings might in fact curtail the evolution of bottom-up drives towards representative institutions (Berman 2007; Carothers 2007). An alternative case has supported the cause of simultaneity of democratic political transition and radical reforms of the economic system (Diamond and Plattner 1995; Bunce 1999; McFaul 2002). As shown by reversed political transition in Russia, sequencing issues interact with the challenges of balancing economic and political transitions in ways that are inherently complex, country-specific, and that may block or turn around democratic consolidation (Baroncelli 2010). The trajectories followed by several ECA countries have further guarded against sticking to pre-designed templates to support transitions. Neither the thesis of the necessary primacy of political transitions, nor its alternative, privileging economic satisfaction over democratic consolidation, are immune from criticism. The regress in both growth rates and democratic consolidation experienced, post-accession, by Poland and Hungary, indicates that prioritizing socio-political concerns over balanced budgets may not be an entirely viable recipe either.

Such deterioration appears somewhat problematic when considering that other incentives to democratization were available to these countries, namely their prior democratic experiences and the 'shield' of the EU accession perspective.[6] Yet, the EU carrots have not uniformly acted as welfare maximizers for these new members, initially cushioning them against the backdrop of the Russian economic collapse of 1998, but also discouraging reforms of their overinflated, and often corrupt, large public sectors (Åslund and Jenish 2007). Burdened by the costs of sticky labor markets and growing public deficits, the Czech Republic, Hungary, Poland and the Slovak Republic experienced major economic slowdowns between 1999 and 2004. More worrisomely, – well before the populist wave of the 2010s – social dissatisfaction had emerged in several new members against policies decided in Brussels, and a shift had occurred towards intransigent conservatism that went beyond traditional European right-wing liberalism. The World Bank responded by advising cuts in the public expenditures of countries that endured growth stagnation. In turn, the good economic performance achieved under markedly authoritarian regimes in several CIS countries alerted both IOs against the adoption of rigid sequencing templates to support transition in post-Communist systems.

In the early 1990s neither the EU nor the WB were experts in supporting simultaneous transitions, which, among other things, included coping with the effects of the implosion of the Soviet Union and the demise of the Council for Mutual Economic Assistance (CMEA). Additionally, there was the assumption that post-Soviet states were somewhat mature economies, particularly if compared to the developing systems that had previously emerged from decolonization in other parts of the world. The corollary, correct only in part, was that as external agents of change, neither the Bank nor the Union should be concerned with supporting state-building processes. Initially, the Bank focused its efforts on supporting transition from planned to market economies. It soon became evident, however, that the interest of several transitioners in EU accession required officers in Washington to coordinate more closely with their counterparts in the EU, which in turn had become a 'magnet' due to the social, political and economic attractiveness that it possessed in the eyes of its neighbors. As a result, the Bank turned into a partner for new and prospective EU members to support reforms necessary to comply with accession and pre-accession requirements and to implement the *acquis*.

In addition to widening the Union's political reach, enlargement has influenced Brussels' approach to inequality. Since the 1970s, disparities between current and new members have been smoothed with the help of the EU (EC) Structural Funds. Through their reform in 1988–1993, with the creation of the Cohesion Fund, the EU (then EC) shifted from what had been up to then flat financing, to targeted support and quantifiable benchmarks to promote cohesion in different parts of the internal market.[7] Since the two enlargement rounds of 2004 and 2007,[8] Brussels has engaged in a learning process on supporting transition-cum-development of systems that were radically different from those that had entered in previous rounds.[9] Further discussed below, such learning has supported changes in the EU's enlargement strategy in an attempt to temper the negative effects of 'fatigue'. Enshrined in the Stabilization and Association Agreements, and 'augmented' with the enlargement criteria set out for the Western Balkans after 2007, the EU 'thick' approach to graduation has sought to develop synergies between accession targets, market access and support to democracy. Yet, as discussed below, Brussels' ambitious effort has not been immune from inconsistencies.

Ultimately the post-Cold war enlargements have also prompted a shift in the Commission's approach to development policy. This particularly influenced the redefinition of the Union's strategies towards partner countries, to the point that currently the neighborhood is conceived, at least formally in the revised Lisbon Treaty, as a single wide vicinity, stretching from the Southern Caucasus, to include

Middle-eastern partners from the Mashreq such as Lebanon and Palestine, up to the Maghreb countries.

On the other side of the Atlantic, these developments have prompted a redefinition in the own mission of the World Bank in ECA countries, including some drastic reorganization, for both Washington HQ and resident offices in the region. In the 2000s, these adaptive restructurings have certainly challenged the Bank's role in the region. Disengagement has been, however, only part of the story. Fears that the Bank would 'go out of business' there have not been fully matched by subsequent evolutions. Overall, learning has occurred on both sides, and enhanced cooperation has ensued between the EU and the WB in several ECA countries.

7.3 Two different maps?

The complexity of the EU–WB interaction and several of their past difficulties to cooperate effectively in the ECA region owe much to the fact that, in the early stages of the post-Soviet enlargement process, the two organizations viewed the countries in the wider Eurasian space through less-than-identical maps, and had different ideas on how to best approach development-cum-transition issues in the region. Differences in respective missions concur to explain that divergence. However, more intense development preferences by the EU post-enlargement, with respect to vast portions of the Eurasian continent (new members and neighbors) added salience to otherwise physiological idiosyncrasies. On the one side the redefinition of the EU's policy goals in the region raised the constraints on the World Bank to adapt to what became new priorities for its members. On the other side it opened the way to new coordination frameworks for the Union and the Bank, which entailed innovative self-redefinition from both actors.

According to their EU or EU-related status, countries regrouped in the ECA region belong to one out of these five categories: EU members, candidates, potential candidates, neighbors or, finally, partners. EU–WB cooperation in new MS (including Malta and Cyprus), and in candidate and potential candidate countries is covered by an MoU, originally signed in 1998 and revised in 2000 and 2006.[10] The memorandum regulates cooperation between the Union and the other multilateral development banks that operate in the region, among which, in addition to the World Bank, the EIB ('in liaison' with the EC) and the EBRD.[11] Leaving to future specific agreements the details of co-financing solutions (including the thorny issue of audit rights by the EU institutions), the MoU significantly provided for the Commission the possibility to delegate to the IFIs the administration and/or supervision responsibility over the own Commission's financial contributions, particularly in the case of parallel co-financing (European Commission in liaison with the EIB, and other relevant IFIs, 2006, 6).

New members from the 2004 and 2007 enlargements were further differentiated according to their relations with the WB: EU MS that were still benefitting from

World Bank loans (Bulgaria, Poland, Romania), EU MS that had stopped borrowing, but where the Bank was still active through technical or analytical services (Czech Republic, Estonia, Lithuania, Slovenia, Slovak Republic), and non-borrowers which requested new loans to face the 2008 global crisis (Latvia, Hungary).

In spite of the multiple country classifications, the ECA region is considered by the Bank as a whole, receiving loans worth USD 10 billion-plus, or 18% of the World Bank's overall lending volume in 2010 (World Bank ECA 2011; World Bank ECA Brussels 2011b, 4). The Bank has emphasized the tailor-made character of projects and programs financed with that budget, around country- and sector-specific needs, highlighting however the global reach of its mission, with respect to non-discrimination in the opportunities offered to all potential borrowers. Overall, the Bank purports an a-political approach to tackling development needs of all its partners, claiming the neutrality and best practices as defining hallmarks of its lending activity.

Conversely, the EU's differentiated approach to the various countries/groups in the ECA region has at times appeared as contradictory, leading to the geographical and sectoral horizontal inconsistencies anticipated in Chapters 5 and 6. Divergences between the EU and the WB have emerged, particularly, on how to best support development in Central Asian countries and in Russia. Preferential access granted in the 1990s to candidate countries in Central and Eastern Europe resulted in discrimination against CIS partners, which could not experience the expansion in export shares enjoyed by former CMEA members then in the EU10 group (Åslund and Warner 2004). The Union took some time to redress the balance through a unitary approach to the CIS group, eventually producing a strategy at the end of the 2000s.[12] Discontent was voiced with World Bank top managers, however, by some Central Asian leaders about the allegedly lecturing attitude with which the emerging EU Central Asia Strategy was presented to them by the EU German Presidency.[13] The EU conveyed the impression of operating under the assumption that Russia and Central Asian partners had a priority interest to join over time in a wider European space, and consequently adopted a diplomatic (though not financial) approach that was more similar to that followed with neighbors and candidate countries. Conversely, neither the regional leader, Russia, nor the other Central Asian partners, seemed to be interested in getting closer to the EU *acquis*. In the eyes of World Bank respondents, the EU appeared to have somewhat crossed the line between projecting soft power in a convincing manner (particularly in small countries) and taking up a 'do-as-we-do' overly assertive posture with external partners. While other views from the World Bank top management pointed to European integration after World War II as an amazing success story in overcoming deep seated animosity, the inconsistent projection of the EU's soft power in Central Asia appeared particularly problematic from a development perspective.

The contradictions of the EU's approach to development in Central Asia and Russia are closely related to the Union's weak conditionalities and the pursuit of its political, energy and security priorities in the region (Hoffmann 2010). The quest has been marred by the difficulties faced by Brussels in reconciling contrasting national priorities of some MS, particularly the diverging views of Germany and Poland on how to engage with Russia. Contributing to a less-than-effective role of the Union in former CIS countries has also been the clash between the EU interest-based search for an energy partnership with Russia and Central Asian partners, on the one side, and its aspiration to become a normative pole of attraction, on the other. Apparently, Brussels has struggled to acknowledge how most Central Asian countries have so far preferred to rely on China and Russia as their reference partners: the absence of social or political conditionalities, and the (relatively higher) similarity between those countries and the Russian and Chinese regimes on several counts (not least the emphasis on non-interference in sovereign matters), has further discouraged them from 'shifting westwards' towards the EU.

Addressing the core issue of the merits and limitations of exporting the EU model to best support democracy-cum-development in post-Soviet countries, voices from the World Bank have suggested that 'less EU' in Central Asian partners may have been better than 'more EU' in Central European states. The economic decline in the latter after the Russian crash of 1998 has been contrasted with the positive performances of their Central Asian neighbors in the early 2000s. While also badly hurt by the Russian default, Central Asian countries had little possibility to resort to the EU market, and chose to drastically reform their budget policies (Åslund and Jenish 2007). Post-crisis suggestions to rethink the European growth model have also come from WB (ECA) studies, which assert the need for Europe to reform its social security and pension systems, and to improve investment climate in Southern MS (Gill and Raiser 2012).

Differences exist, however, within the broad approach adopted by the Union towards former CIS countries that are part of the EU neighborhood, and that for some time have been considered for inclusion among potential candidates, with access to ENPI facilities.[14] Upon specific requests from Georgia, Moldova, Armenia and Ukraine, the Bank has aligned its Strategy papers and programs to the EU's Action Plans, cooperating with the Commission to assist those partners in the definition of reform priorities. Among them, Georgia and Ukraine have openly resorted to the EU and NATO in an attempt to counterbalance Russian influence. In their eyes, the EU attraction provided an incentive to unilaterally approximate the *acquis*.[15] Even discounting the delicate diplomatic equilibria in the Caucasus, and the subsequent conflict between Russia and Ukraine (2014), the Bank's expectations on the EU's role in the area have been very much consistent with EU's own role conceptions, particularly as a leader in exporting norms through leading by example. Initial progress made by Ukraine in the 2000s has emerged prominently as a bench for comparison with the (comparatively) slower progress achieved by Southern neighbors in the MENA region (a topic discussed in Chapter 8). While domestic drives to autonomous take-up of the *acquis* account for that progress, the superior performance by EU's Eastern Neighbors was also motivated by the expectation that the EU might one day offer them membership. Ultimately, the deterioration of the Arab Springs into 'Arab Falls', the war between Russia and Ukraine and the Syrian conflict, have relegated enlargement fatigue and related EU consistency deficits in the region to the bottom of Brussels' development agenda. Those same issues have emerged however over the course of the EU–World Bank cooperation in the Balkans, which is discussed in the next section.

7.4 Leading transition and accession in the Western Balkans: the EU's role between innovative synergies and horizontal inconsistencies

In Western Balkan countries the Union underwent some serious tensions between its value- and interest-based personae (Bretherton and Vogler 2006), incurring an utmost failure in conflict prevention and management.[16] Yet, it also experimented new financial solutions, supporting political transition through the provision of economic incentives and, ultimately, the perspective of accession. Currently all countries in the area have moved to either candidate or potential candidate status.[17] The replicability of successful Central and Eastern European enlargement has however been debated. While ethnic and religious cleavages have been called into question to explain the wavering compliance by Balkan partners (Freyburg and Richter 2010 on Croatia, as well as Türkes and Gökgöz 2006), weaknesses in EU policy consistency and impact have also emerged, linked by some to an overburdened EU agenda (Elbasani 2008), pursued less than reliably, and often prey to MS mini-lateral pressures.[18] The politicization of domestic cleavages accounts for country-specific evolutions, and so do the regressive interactions between ethnic factionalism and development needs experienced in post-conflict contexts hindered by stateness and regime-transition problems. However, the 'Balkan blues' (Füle 2010, in Friends of Europe and Konrad Adenauer Stiftung) has at times appeared as a scapegoat for the wavering effectiveness of EU programs. Overlooking that datum greatly underestimates the role played by external actors in supporting development in the Balkans. On the contrary, and in addition to providing a key test for the quality of their relations, the EU–WB interaction has catalyzed multiple energies to project stability and support development-cum-democracy transitions in the region.

In the aftermath of the 1999 Kosovo crisis, along the lines sketched by the UN resolution 1244, the European Commission coordinated an ambitious initiative to promote 'peace, stability and economic cooperation' in the Balkans: the Stability Pact for South East Europe (SP-SEE). The World Bank also joined in the new framework, along with the UN, NATO, the Council of Europe, the US, Canada, Turkey, Russia and Japan. Following the intervention of NATO in Kosovo, the SP-SEE was the first step towards an EU-sponsored, comprehensive approach to the Western Balkans, regrouping 40 countries and seven major multilateral organizations. The idea was to first stabilize and then offer associate partnership to the Balkan countries, with accession as the final goal of a gradual integration process.[19]

The SP-SEE was to develop synergies between financial support, regional trade integration, security stabilization and support to democratization, with expected spillovers from the involvement of all the major multilaterals (Welfens 2001). Ultimately, however, it was the perspective of accession that offered partner governments the key incentive to cooperate.

A joint EC–WB office was set up in Brussels in the summer of 1999, with a mandate from the SP-SEE members to mobilize and coordinate international financial assistance for the reconstruction and development of South East Europe.[20] Staffed by EU officers seconded by DG Enlargement and by World Bank personnel, the Office was jointly financed by the two institutions, even if the bulk of expenses was covered by EU resources, that also paid for half of the operational costs of World Bank personnel. During its early years, the Office coordinated donors through conferences and the creation of a High Level Steering Group, raising some 10 billion Euros in financial assistance to the region.

The own EU-sponsored Stabilization and Association Process (SAP), which should have supported the SP-SEE, became instead the core driver of change in the Western Balkans, with progress made by partner countries measured through their ability to sign and implement the Stabilization and Association Agreements (SAAs), offered within that framework (Bechev 2006).[21] While the variation in compliance with EU conditionalities has been explored from different angles in the EU literature (Schimmelfennig et al. 2005; Freyburg and Richter 2010), the evidence also points to the EU's inconsistent assessment of such compliance, and related inconsistent rewarding/punishing of good and bad performers by Brussels. A sub-type of the more general 'selectivity dilemma' of aid policymaking (Burnside and Dollar 2000; Easterly et al. 2004), the 'stabilization dilemma' faced by the Union in the SAP (Kramer 2000) allocated resources to partners that were (*ex ante*) more stable and showed pre-existing (acceptable) levels of what the Union considered to be requirements for its envisaged path of stabilization and association. At times, such an approach obscured the dense interactional effects that were activated under the simultaneous support to political stabilization and economic development (Türkes and Gökgöz 2006).

Similar views were conveyed by World Bank's ECA top managers, who noted how the innovative potential of the SAP process was hindered at times by Brussels' difficulty in assessing progress along the association path via the EU own pre-defined benchmarks. The main inconsistencies seemed to lay in the EU-internal delicate political equilibria on what became, through time, the third round of post-Soviet accessions. The EU enlargement plans suffered a major setback in 2005–2006, when the negative outcomes of the Dutch and French referenda on ratifying the Constitutional Treaty unequivocally signaled that new accession paths would be put under tightened scrutiny by EU MS. In the summer of 2006, public opinions in MS unmistakably shifted against further enlargement (Germany reached a record 66% opposition to widening; opposing majorities also compacted in France, the Netherlands, Belgium, Luxembourg, Austria and Finland) with narrower pro-enlargement majorities reached in Greece, Ireland and Italy. The Commission produced a New Strategy on

Enlargement for 2006–2007: political uneasiness and declining public support to further enlargement in the Western Balkans were reflected through a careful re-wording of the commitments taken at the Thessaloniki Summit of 2003. While reaffirming the EU's broad pledge to enlargement, the Commission made progress on membership conditional upon new elements. Consolidation of the enlargement agenda became a priority: while it honored existing commitments with countries already in the process of accession (namely Croatia and Turkey), the Union would be cautious in assuming new ones. Stricter conditionality criteria were also adopted to assess progress during the pre-accession phase, including, particularly, progress in reforming the rule of law. Before being granted candidate status, countries would have to pass tests designed according to newly defined benchmarks ('introduced' as a 'new tool' after 'lessons learnt from the fifth enlargement', COM (2006) 649, 23).

Overall the financial generosity of the EU's programs in the Western Balkans seems undisputable.[22] Their effectiveness however has been informally questioned by voices from the World Bank on grounds of low geographical policy consistency. The complaints of Macedonia and Bosnia and Herzegovina emerged with particular emphasis, as their leaderships felt discriminated against other countries in the group, perceived as enjoying a privileged status in the path towards EU accession. Allegedly, as shown by the slowdown in the pace of enlargement after 2006–2007, the Western Balkans were somehow paying the price of higher EU conditionality bars, due to Romania and Bulgaria's uneven implementation of accession requirements. Uneasiness has developed about how progress is differentially assessed even by the countries that have participated in various roles to the enlargement round (Devrim and Maršić 2009). Worries about the creation of a 'Balkan ghetto' had already surfaced in the Anglo-Saxon specialized press (*The Economist* 14 January 2006), where the risk was discussed that the new EU approach could end up in splitting, rather than modernizing, the region along the cleavage of privileged candidates (Bulgaria, Romania and Croatia, originally) versus countries that seemed somehow doomed to remain in a 'pre-accession limbo' (Macedonia, Serbia, Montenegro, Albania, Bosnia and Herzegovina and Kosovo). Subsequent evolutions, such as the launching of the accession process for Montenegro (in December 2011), the confirmation of Serbia as a candidate country (European 2012), and the granting of candidate status to Albania in 2014 seem to challenge this belief, tempering the dim views on the post-2007 EU's enlargement fatigue. However, as proven by the many holdups in the relations between the EU and Macedonia (a candidate since 2005), the concern from a development perspective is that new, ever changing obstacles may arise to slow down, and ultimately block accession, irrespective of progress made by candidates in meeting EU requirements.

In spite of three positive progress reports, Macedonia has not started negotiations for accession.[23] The Greek formal opposition on the matter of the country name, even after a favorable verdict of the International Court of Justice (ICJ), certainly bears the main responsibility (ICJ 2011). The European Parliament called for the negotiations to begin 'with no further delay' (European Parliament 2012, Resolution 14 March 2012 on the 2011 progress report on the former Yugoslav Republic of Macedonia), as repeatedly recommended by the Commission, yet with no formal EU proposal to officially start them. The advice given by the EP's Chairman of the delegation for relations with Albania, Bosnia and Herzegovina, Serbia, Montenegro and Kosovo, Mr. Kukan, is that Macedonian leadership 'should be broadminded in accepting compromise proposals for the name, with a geographical reference like Upper or Northern, some adjective maybe. . .if there is a Greek proposal, Macedonia should be broadminded in trying to accept it. However, first they have to receive a proposal!' (Balkanalysis 11 April 2012). Even if discussion about the implementation of chapter 23 and 24 still lies ahead,[24] the real dealbreaker is Greece's hesitancy towards making an offer.[25]

The risks connected to the upward revision of EU benchmarks have also emerged on the occasion of the pre-accession negotiations with Bosnia and Herzegovina (BiH). The country is still coping with multiple challenges. Managing the tensions between the Republika Sprska (RS) and the Muslim-Croat Federation (FBiH) has been particularly difficult: the country's weak rule of law and worrisome corruption levels have substantially hindered the implementation of provisions on democratic rights (FreedomHouse, various years). Since the Dayton Agreement of 1995 and the ensuing 'Bonn Powers' from the Bonn conference of 1997, a High Representative is authorized to remove officials and pass laws, whose constitutionality may however be reviewed by the Constitutional Court).[26] The consociational BiH regime has been enmeshed in ethnic polarization and war-time rhetoric, ending up in a de facto veto system, whereby required unanimity threatens stability at both federal and state levels (Maršić and Marko 2007).[27] The persistence of many among these obstacles has made the way to accession both harder and longer than expected. However, the EU inconsistencies in assessing the progress made by BiH have allegedly strengthened the role of domestic veto players against a credible commitment towards reform (Batt 2009). Apparently, BiH difficulties in complying with conditions set by the Office of the EU High Representative for the police reforms were judged with particular harshness by Brussels. The last country to have signed an SAA, in June 2008 BiH was still waiting for the entry into force of the agreement. While ratified by all EU MS, its enforcement has been made conditional on Bosnia and Herzegovina's changing its constitution, according to the 2009 ruling of the European Court of Human Rights, whereby equal opportunities to run for political offices should be granted to all Bosnian citizens, irrespective of their national or ethnic origins. Conversely, the signing of the EU–Serbia SAA in April 2008, its ratification, initiated in June 2010, and the granting of candidate status in 2012, have raised doubts about the EU using double standards in its approach to the region, and particularly towards BiH (Ducasse-Rogiers 2012, 32). Particular concerns have emerged relative to an allegedly selective application of conditionality criteria on international commitments as judged by the ICTY (International Criminal Tribunal for the former Yugoslavia)

(Balfour 2008, 39). Incorporating feedbacks from Bosnian civil servants in both FBiH and RS, subsequent appraisals suggest that the introduction post-2007 of new political criteria for accession may be a potentially destabilizing factor for the country (Bercio and Böttger 2012, 5). Projecting the 'Turkey syndrome of delayed and postponed integration' onto Bosnia and Herzegovina's existing fragilities through ongoing ambivalence, may have particularly adverse implications (Bărbulescu and Troncotă 2012, 22), both for the country and for the EU's own credibility in the region.

The belief that, in spite of adjustments to new, more stringent EU benchmarks, some countries in the Western Balkans 'will never make it', seems hard to eradicate. Growing frustration in partner countries in turn contributes to undermine achieved stability. The point is proven by results from opinion polls in the region, about the chances that peaceful relations are maintained even in the absence of EU membership (Devrim and Maršić 2009).

Since the global economic crisis of 2008, some EU MS already suffering from enlargement fatigue have taken further distance from what they defined as 'second rate enlargement', supporting a 'triple-A process' which now prioritizes the absorption capacity of the Union (de Groot in Lagendijk and Wiersma 2012, 1). Stricter conditionalities on Chapters 23 and 24 are openly called for, also through a change in the order of the negotiation agenda ('put the difficult stuff on the table right from the start', idem 2), and so is the alignment of potential candidates with new post-crisis EU rules for budgetary coordination, to implement chapters 9 (EMU) and 17 (financial services and supervision). While setbacks on the second track are beyond counting in both member and candidate countries, the worrisome *revirements* on chapters 23 and 24 from the controversial reforms in Hungary (EC Press Rapid Release IP/12/24, 17 January 2012) have added to the list of post-accession EU second-guessing. These developments have encouraged further benchmark revision for candidates and potential candidates. An evident instance at higher bar setting, the evolutions reconstructed above reinforce the perception that the Union may have a higher than normal propensity to change the rules of the game multiple times along the way.

Such evidence corroborates the remarks from World Bank voices on Brussels' lack of courage, its being too timid in simultaneously pursuing the EU political and economic goals, of supporting stability and democratic transition through economic assistance and market access on a regional basis. Although not entirely misplaced, these expectations often underestimate the difficulties in balancing the attainment of such diverse goals by a polity whose external powers are still regulated under different power-sharing schemes, varying across those very policy areas whose synergy should count most for the success of EU-sponsored actions (most relevantly, trade, development and humanitarian aid, support towards democratic transition, foreign and security policy). Relevant for our purpose, the WB critical remarks on the mixed achievements of EU policies in the Western Balkans must be put in the wider context of EU–WB cooperation in the region. Critiques have worked towards strengthening the predictability of the EU's policies, often stimulating learning from the interaction with the Bank, and triggering the assumption of a more autonomous EU role, in the region and in the wider neighborhood, through the creation of EU blending instruments, the Western Balkans Investment Framework (WBIF) and the Neighborhood Investment Facility (NIF).

7.5 The EU–World Bank relations and the future of cooperation in ECA countries: from ad hoc opportunism to strategic partnership

Since the days of the Stability Pact and the establishment of the EU–WB Joint Office, learning has occurred on both sides, with notable achievements in development, security and governance. The Bank has aligned its tools (namely CASes – Country Assistance Strategies, CPSs – country partnership strategies, and CEMs – country economic memoranda, reshaped as Programmatic EU Accession CEMs) with the EU pre-accession and accession priorities as – currently – set by the EU through the IPA. Specifically, it has targeted its policy-based lending, technical assistance and sector programs to support clients in the implementation of the reforms required for EU membership or for closer integration, regularly discussing these matters with EU (Commission) counterparts in the 'ECA country days' (World Bank ECA Brussels, 2011b, 7). As shown in Table 7.1, between 2000 and 2010, out of the 11.4 billion Euros of the ECA co-financing portfolio, the Bank accounted for more than 40%, while EU financial institutions covered approximately 29%.[28] In country programs the ratio of complementary (separate) vs co-financing (joint) schemes has varied (by countries and needs), while in regional programs complementarity has mostly been the norm, as in the cases of the Energy Community of South East Europe or in the Trade and Transport Facilitation in Southeast Europe Project.

On top of the exceptionally high support provided along its own tracks[29] the EU has cofinanced many World Bank projects and programs with grant elements

Table 7.1 Cofinancing development in the ECA region, 2000–2010*

		%
WB	4833	42.44
EBRD	592	5.20
CEB	598	5.25
EIB	2179	19.13
Others	3186	27.98
Total	11388	100

*Million Euros

Source: Author elaboration from World Bank ECA Brussels (2011b, 10)

Table 7.2 EC contributions to the World Bank's ECA Trust Funds in 2010

IPA	33.90
Regional	29.30
Central Asia	26.90
ENP	18.90
Total	108.79

* Million USD

Source: World Bank ECA Brussels (2011b, 8)

provided by the Commission. In 2010, the EC accounted for approximately 10% of the overall World Bank ECA Trust Fund portfolio (i.e. with USD 109 million – including however multidonor trust funds – out of a total 1.1 billion). As shown in Table 7.2, its geographical composition privileged the IPA countries (USD 33.9 million) and regional programs overall (USD 29.3 million).

In spite of such interpenetration, the EU–WB cooperation in ECA has often proceeded along ad hoc tracks, with stops-and-go cycles of sharing in the strategic direction towards common regional or sub-regional goals. At times wary of new approaches suggested by the Bank, the Commission has however been able to turn inputs from Washington into assets to improve the EU approach to financing development-cum-transition in the region, while still keeping the lead on donors' coordination in the Western Balkans.

Through time the emphasis on programs under the EC–WB Joint Office has shifted to regional cooperation on three infrastructural areas (energy, transport and, to a lesser extent, environmental issues). While the Joint Office was still serving its early purpose of facilitating EU–WB cooperation, its role had become increasingly ancillary to the IFIs (International Financial Institutions) Advisory Group established in March 2007, chaired by the Commission and including, in addition to the WB, the EIB, EBRD, CEB, IFC and other major regional development partners active in the region (Black Sea Trade and Development Bank, German KfW, and the other members to the SP-SEE), for which it then served as a secretariat. At the end of 2008, the Office was closed, officially 'because it had completed its mandate to raise funds for the Western Balkans'. That success, however, entailed that 'it was not really justified to keep [the Office] running under EC funding, given the many new important partners that had joined along towards financing development and accession in the Western Balkans'.[30] Since then, the World Bank ECA Brussels Unit has been established, to coordinate with EU institutions on cooperation in the region.

While still benefitting from the World Bank expertise in lending operations,[31] since 2007 the Union has developed its own tools to blend loans and grants instruments for project financing, through setting up the NIF in 2008, and the WBIF in December 2009, along the template devised for the Africa Infrastructure Trust Fund, launched in 2007.[32] The main goal behind these instruments is to lever grants with loans to increase financial impact and coordination, ideally through bringing around the table all the potentially interested donors, including, particularly, the private sector. The new EU blending facilities also aim at empowering beneficiaries in partner countries early on, to avoid proliferation of projects and sub-optimal use of the countries' already scarce capacities. The elaboration of a structured procedure, consistent across the years, and valid for all the potential donors, under the Commission's 'grant umbrella' should also increase predictability and therefore facilitate implementation by partner countries.[33] The World Bank was not within the group of founders (which comprises, along with the Commission, the CEB – Council of Europe Development Bank, the EIB and the EBRD, called 'partner IFIs') of either the NIF or the WBIF, which bore a chiefly EU hallmark and regional focus, and, up to June 2011 has participated to the facilities as an 'active observer'.[34]

In the case of the WBIF, however, after a year of operational work and an internal review commissioned by founding members in December 2010, a request came, particularly from some MS, but also supported from the Commission, to upgrade the Bank's role to associate membership, with a status closer to partner European IFIs. The change eventually occurred in June 2011, on the occasion of the WBIF Steering Committee meeting.[35] World Bank sources claimed that an upgrade to 'associated IFI' (as opposed to full membership, i.e. arguably 'partner IFI') would be more consistent with its ongoing effort in the WBIF, given that 'the WBG is not in a position to provide additional grant resources to the WBIF in cash' (World Bank ECA Brussels 2011a). Operationally, the difference is that associate financial institutions in countries where other European IFIs operate, cannot work alone, and must cooperate, through cofinancing, with the EU IFIs. In the words of a Commission officer, 'the logic of the mechanism is precisely this, to involve several donors to add their loans to the grants provided to these countries by the Commission'. The World Bank is a de facto partner member: its representatives sit on all the steering committees, give advice on how to best proceed, and also screen projects in selected cases.

The associate role has come with two (suggested) exceptions on the side of the Bank, leaning on the 'full partnership' status, that have encountered criticism from some WBIF members. While under 'associate membership' the Bank may not 'act as a lead IFI on any project submitted to the Project Financiers group', there are exceptional circumstances under which it may take such capacity: in WBIF-funded projects in Kosovo – 'when no other IFI would be in a position to take the lead' – and 'in sector development projects', funded under the IPA scheme, basis for the World Bank-sponsored sector-wide approaches (idem, 2). Similar to the EU–WB coordination in the occupied Palestinian territories, discussed in Chapter 8, development financing in Kosovo has proven the comparative advantage of Brussels' close cooperation with the Bank. In that context, the pursuit of political dialogue under particularly challenging diplomatic conditions has combined with urgent development priorities. Based on its formally apolitical mandate and faster disbursement process, the World Bank has appeared as better suited to manage projects in post-conflict contexts through relatively easier procedures (see European Commission, Directorate General for Enlargement 2007, 5).

Conversely, some WBIF members have questioned the eligibility of the WBG to assume a leading role in financing sector development projects under SWAs (Sector Wide Approaches) supported through EU funds (IPAs). More particularly, voices from the World Bank suggested widening the scope of the WBIF technical assistance and co-financing through 'sector development projects' (SDPs), whereby analytical work, policy reform and capacity building could be focused on the development of sectors (as opposed to stand-alone projects), deemed to be strategic to support a partner's broader development needs. SDPs are generally regarded as potentially helpful to lay the foundations of broader sector-based approaches to be implemented under the Instrument for Pre-Accession (IPA), and to also fulfill their more traditional 'WBIF'-function as levers for additional loans by new financing partners. In the mind of the Bank's officers, both full-members and associate IFIs could share in the lead of SDPs, which would find their natural financing partners in regional bodies such as SEETO (South East Europe Transport Observatory) or the Energy Community Secretariat. The extent to which such 'leadership sharing' occurs in a welfare-enhancing fashion has been debated, considering that the process is part of a system (trust-funded development) originally developed by the World Bank, and now financed through starting EU grants within the context of an EU-sponsored facility. While some disagreement has emerged on the new division of labour, in its capacity as 'Associate IFI' the World Bank has also obtained a formal remit to lead projects on 'sector development work' (Western Balkans Investment Framework (WBIF) 2011, 20).

The upgrade to associate membership in an EU-created investment facility marks a notable progress for the EU–WB cooperation. The fact that the EBRD and the EIB (the latter, as seen above, a historical antagonist of the Bank in projects within the EU) are among the founding agencies with full partnership status in the WBIF Board suggests that past divergences may be substantially overcome through pragmatic solutions to improve transition and development opportunities in the Western Balkans. Discussion between World Bank officers and EEAS and DEVCO representatives about the possibility of a similar upgrade of the World Bank's role in the NIF and Investment Facility for Central Asia indicate that other attempts at further approximating the two organizations' financing systems are currently underway to support development in the overall ECA region.[36] The degree to which these interpenetrations (EU contributing to World Bank's Trust Funds on the one side, World Bank's participating to EU blending facilities on the other) are likely to improve the existing schemes to finance development will emerge through time. Beyond their success in raising funds around the Commission's grant components, particularly from the private sector and most notably in the post-2008 context of increased financial instability, the EU blending facilities have been questioned for their loose accountabilities and opaque decision making sub-systems (European Think Tanks Group 2011). As discussed above, milestones have been reached only after sustained effort, with diffidence from some parts of the EU against opening the WBIF to World Bank's associate membership. Sources from WBIF have also hinted at the need of an intense diplomatic working on the sector approaches, to smooth the diffidence often surfacing on the side of some parts of the Commission towards the World Bank's style, at times perceived as too blunt. These inputs have been matched by an acknowledgement from the Bank's side that a somewhat excessive managerialism may have raised justified concerns on the EU's side. The matter however, has been treated most as an issue of poor communication skills, rather than a serious fault in advancing proposals to the Commission.[37]

Overall, however, interaction in the WBIF has improved the EU and WB knowledge of respective project cycles and internal practices. The new EU blending facilities have provided an additional track to structure an otherwise loose set of different co-financing schemes, complementing the WB Trust Fund option. From the EU standpoint, they have strengthened Brussels' leverage on the definition of broader World Bank strategies and projects in areas of common interest. Finally, anticipating the emphasis put by the SDGs and Agenda 2030 on the role of the private sector in financing development, the creation of EU blending facilities has supported the evolution towards a more autonomous, and technically denser, approach of the Union to development financing. Further enhanced by the launch of an ambitious EU External Investment Plan at the end of 2016, the EU's blending facilities complement the political primacy and the financial weight of the Union in the Western Balkans and in the Neighborhood, widening its reach in Africa, Central Asia and Latin America.

7.6 Brussels, Washington and the new EU members: helping them to help themselves

A core element of the engagement of the EU and the World Bank in a large portion of the ECA region has been the peculiar nature of triangular relations developed in new member states, particularly those who have not yet graduated out of their borrower's status. An MoU was signed between the Bulgarian Government and the World Bank to accelerate absorption of EU funds (2012).[38] At five years since the country's accession to the Union, assistance from third parties was still required to support capacity building, lest for the remaining 7 mn Euros in EU funds be lost to administrative failures, apparently due – among other things – to extremely complex EU requirements for the utilization of structural funds. A similar agreement was signed between the World Bank and Romania. Subsequently, new MoUs have been signed by the World Bank with Bulgaria (2015) and Romania (2016) to provide continued support on the implementation of the EU Structural and Investment Funds (2014–2020).

Behind the low utilization rates of EU structural funds lay prohibitive red tape costs (apparently from both EU and domestic regulations), lack of institutional capacity and, in the cases of Bulgaria and Romania, a risk of diversion to the advantage of corrupt domestic elites. Compared to development partners that are not EU members or privileged neighbors, national interlocutors in Sofia and Bucharest represent a peculiar sort of recipient: (formally) entitled to accession benefits yet not fully able to relate to Brussels as experienced counterparts on fund use and absorption. 'Untangling the maze of EU funds' appeared problematic before Bulgaria's accession (Andronova and Vassileva 2006), and the cohesion-cum-development effectiveness of EU structural funds has remained a sensitive issue (*Financial Times* 2 December 2010).[39] Subsequent evidence on absorption rates by all EU MS in the two rounds of allocation of cohesion and structural funds (2000–2006 and 2007–2013) indicates that domestic fiscal constraints, whether accompanied by systemic shocks or not, may not always be the main culprit (Marzinotto 2011, 5). Also, the issue of short-term negative fiscal impact in new members upon their accession is not a new one (Backé 2002; Kopits and Székely 2002), and does not seem to have constituted a long term challenge for countries such as Poland or Estonia, where immediate negative impacts were also expected. What does make the World Bank's action so relevant, in the cases of Bulgaria and Romania?

Lessons from new members from the first round of post-Soviet accessions seemed to show that a more effective budgeting process and reduction in public expenditures have been a constant of their exercises in fiscal consolidation (Meth-Cohn and Shields 2005). However, the cases of the two South-Eastern members acceded in 2007 pose substantially higher institutional challenges, not least due to their notably weaker and highly variable administrative capacities. Conservative projections estimated the average deterioration in Bulgaria's fiscal position at -1.6% of its GDP over the period 2007–2009 (Andronova and Vassileva 2006). The risk that funds were not spent effectively by the 2013 deadline has entailed potentially higher losses, namely limited demand-driven growth, persistently weak administrative capacity and, ultimately, ongoing dependency from foreign aid. Domestic reforms and simplification of EU procedures have appeared as ineludible steps to ensure a proper implementation of the funds.[40] As a matter of fact, much of the pressure has rested on Bulgaria and Romania to adapt through capacity building. Apparently, the World Bank (now also joined by the EIB and the EBRD) is still retained by the two EU MS as the most effective provider of support on overcoming weak fiscal capacity, a constraint that goes beyond austerity caps (Marzinotto 2011, 6).

Conversely, critical voices have noted how the two MoUs may have served the somewhat less-than-noble purpose of helping the World Bank to maintain control on disbursed tranches, as projected budget deficits in the two countries also impact on their ability to implement Bank's projects and pay outstanding loans back) (Marini and Kovacheva 2010). On a different ground, the evidence also points to an 'excessive interventionism' by both the EU and the WB, one helping partner countries about the implementation of funds provided by the other. The issue obviously touches on the long-time need to rationalize Brussels' bureaucratic intricacies as well as on the usual stabilization necessities of borrowing countries. However, particularly since the Euro crisis and the uncertainties about the economic future of other EU members, absorption difficulties pose a challenge that will need to be addressed in a coordinated fashion: that of sequential interventions to tackle cohesion needs of countries that are members of – and receive support from – both the Union and the World Bank.

On the EU side, the MoUs have been considered as strategic moves made by the Bank, to enhance its visibility in the eyes of new EU members, that needed support to implement the *acquis* and further smooth transition. This EU role expectation has been mirrored by a – more positive – role conception by the Bank, which frames the downsizing of its traditional lending role by strengthening its long-standing role as a knowledge and services provider (World Bank 2012).[41] EU expectations such as the – above quoted – uneasiness with the emergent role of the Bank in new MS carry an undeniably competitive nuance, and frame the World Bank as a somewhat intrusive contender in a European domain. According to this view, the World Bank's presence in these EU countries would be increasingly redundant. Coordination problems have also emerged at the staff level with respect to the World Bank's allegedly go-it-alone approach, which, according to this view, has not always taken into account the role of other European IFIs active in the area, most notably the EIB.[42]

Alternative views from the EU have remarked how the Bank has, in this particular instance, been able to redefine its role, complementing rather than thwarting the Union's effort in the ECA region. Matching its comparative advantage in disbursement under particularly challenging constraints, the Bank's assistance to support new MS in fund absorption has been acknowledged at the high level, by Secretary Generals of both DG ECFIN and DG REGIO, who have asked the Bank to step in to help new members meeting the 2013 deadline.[43] The effect of the Bank's new fee-based services provided to Romania and Bulgaria is to be fully assessed yet. However, it is a fact that the Union has not directly been able to intervene with effective in-house knowledge support, and that, in the end, it has chosen to rely on the services provided by financial intermediaries (among which also the EIB and the EBRD, which are, noticeably, part of the EU framework). 'Reimbursable technical assistance' is the practical way through which the World Bank has supported Bulgaria and Romania to absorb the EU structural funds. Different from the Trust Fund channel, the Bank is hired directly by the EU Member state (or IPA Member state, in the case of candidates and prospective candidates) to provide consultancy services: while the general use of these World Bank 'fee-based services' is a widespread practice among several middle-income shareholders (Gulf States, Russia, Chile to name a few), resorting to these services to help EU Members to absorb EU structural and cohesion funds under official EU endorsement appears as a stepchange in the overall EU–World Bank relations in the region.

7.7 Conclusions

The EU and the World Bank started with two radically different 'maps' of the region: the enlargement process, and the building of a new circle of EU neighbors had a momentous impact on both the EU's relations with these countries and its interactions with the World Bank, influencing the Bank's conception of its changing role in the region and its perceptions of the unanswered needs in Central Asian partners. By and large, the evidence discussed in this chapter lends some support to the WB critical views on the EU's approach to Central Asian partners, particularly comparing their autonomous growth progress with the slowdowns experienced post-2004 by several EU10 countries. Contrasting the EU's deficits in sectoral and geographic horizontal consistency in contributed effectiveness, voices from the World Bank have on the contrary praised Brussels' policies for Central European and Balkan countries.

Yet, these broadly positive views have been qualified in several respects. While marked by higher, generalized effectiveness, the consistency in the EU policy in the Western Balkans has been highly variable, in general, and with particular concern in the cases of Bosnia and Herzegovina and Macedonia. National authorities in the region have voiced their preoccupation with the EU's apparent use of a 'double standard' to benchmarking progress in governance issues towards potential accession. These concerns are particularly relevant for the credibility enjoyed by the Union in Sarajevo and Skopje. In the fashion of the 'Achilles and the tortoise' paradox, these countries feel that 'they may never be able to ultimately accede, no matter how deep their effort is' to comply with the EU's constantly moving targets. The empirical evidence discussed above for the cases of Macedonian and Bosnian SAP processes indicates that the ultimate political *placet* by MS has hindered the own EU goal setting, upstream, and Brussels' implementation efforts, downstream. A major determinant of this inconsistency is the multiplicity of roles that the EU institutions-cum-MS play in the region.

In the past 20 years, however, a change has taken place, in the respective EU's and World Bank's roles in the region, in ways that countered the existing 'technical vs political' division of labour. Since the establishment of the Joint Office for South East Europe and the Balkans in 1999, the EU–World Bank cooperation has evolved, particularly after the creation of EU facilities for the Neighborhood (NIF) and for the Western Balkans (WBIF), in 2008 and 2009, respectively. These instruments have demonstrated the Union's willingness to take up increasingly autonomous roles in blending, proving its ability to lead pooling efforts independently from the World Bank, and relying on EU-based IFIs, such as the EBRD and EIB. As discussed above, the WBIF has internalized, and partially solved, some of the past tensions between the Bank and the EIB, even if, for the time being, the divergent opinions about the recent upgrade of the World Bank to associate member, and the opaque net of new, multiple accountabilities, have relegated effectiveness issues beyond fund pooling somewhat on the side. A growing interpenetration of roles has resulted, with the EU taking part in World Bank's managed Trust Funds, and a World Bank's contribution to EU blending facilities, alongside EU IFIs and private donors.

Explicitly acknowledging the core political and economic role that the Union has taken up in the candidate and Neighborhood countries, including the upgraded EU leadership on the strategic side of financing, the Bank has gradually repositioned itself in the provision of complementary services (technical assistance, fee based services) along with its traditional lending track. The move has been criticized by some in the Commission, according to which the Bank would be seeking new visibility to compensate for scaling down in new EU MS. Alleged Bank interferences with the political strategy of the Commission, through going bilaterally and downplaying the EU regional approach, or through skipping coordination 'steps' with the EIB, have raised the issue of new competition fault lines between the two organizations. At the high level, however, both sides have been working to strengthen cooperation. Positive comments by EU Commissioners about the MoUs between the World Bank and Bulgaria and Romania, respectively, indicate that Brussels sees its role as complementary to that of the Washington-based IFI, and that it considers the Bank an ally in the process of ensuring a balanced consolidation of enlargement gains.

The complementarities existing between a large financier and agent of political change (the EU), and a chiefly technical provider of development loans and knowledge (the Bank), have not been superseded. In spite of the evolving division of labor between the two IOs, role change has been incremental, with a lag between newly performed functions and official status. Whether the growing interpenetration between EU and WB roles in respective financing facilities (WB trust funds, EU blending facilities) will lead to a development-enhancing infra-sectoral exchange, or will on the contrary end up in magnifying turf battles between increasingly substitutable agents, is an open issue. It remains however important to note how since the late 1990s the two IOs have shifted from an ad hoc cooperation towards an increasingly coordinated approach to support development in the many contexts of the post-Soviet space.

Notes

1 In 2008, the World Bank ECA regional unit covered 30 countries: Albania, Armenia, Azerbaijan, Belarus, Bosnia and Herzegovina, Bulgaria, Croatia, Czech Republic, Estonia, Georgia, Hungary, Kazakhstan, Kosovo, Kyrgyz Republic, Latvia, Lithuania, FYR Macedonia, Moldova, Montenegro, Poland, Romania, Russian Federation, Serbia, Slovak Republic, Slovenia, Tajikistan, Turkey, Turkmenistan, Ukraine, Uzbekistan. New EU member states were however considered separately, under the EU10 label Currently the unit operates in 23 countries, as the Czech Republic, Estonia, Hungary, Latvia, Lithuania, the Slovak Republic and Slovenia have graduated out of ECA lending portfolio.

2 The emphasis is here on the EU10 group, which refers to the ten new members that have acceded the EU between 2004 and 2007 and have been – and in some cases still are – World Bank's borrowers, with different graduation schedules: Czech Republic, Estonia, Hungary, Latvia, Lithuania, Poland, Slovak Republic, Slovenia, Bulgaria and

Romania. Between the end of the 1980s and early 2007, the group collectively received USD 11.1 bn in World Bank loans, for a total of 143 operations, not including technical assistance, which was also supplied by the Bank at the countries' request (World Bank 2007d, 3)

3 Author's interview with World Bank top management officer, January 2008.
4 Author's interview with World Bank top management officer, January 2008.
5 With respect to post-Communist transitions in Europe and Central Asia, Linz and Stepan endorse the primacy of political change, criticizing the alternative line of legitimation, a sort of reversed 'pyramid of legitimacy', from economic satisfaction to democratic consolidation (1996, 435–439).
6 In their analysis on the rule of law reforms pursued by Central and Eastern European countries, Magen and Morlino (2008) focus specifically on the effects of the interaction between EU incentives and domestic conditions.
7 While the European Regional Development Fund (ERDF) had been created in 1975, to reduce regional disparities after the entry of Denmark, Ireland and the UK, in 1973, internal cohesion was given priority since membership was widened to include the Greece in 1981, and then Spain and Portugal in 1986. The European Social Fund (ESF) and the European Agricultural Guidance and Guarantee Fund (EAGGF) had existed since 1958, but their cohesion dimension was particularly strengthened by the reform of 1988–1993. On that occasion, a seminal debate emerged on the nature and effects of the EU cohesion policy. Early core references include Anderson (1990), Marks (1993) and Pollack (1995).
8 Croatia joined in 2013.
9 While different in their goals and target countries, the EU instruments to support candidate and potential candidate countries along the Stabilization and Association Process all share an emphasis on regionalization, partnership and programming towards increased cohesion. The first three pre-accession incentives launched in 1999 were the Instrument for Structural Policies for Pre-accession (ISPA), the 'Poland–Hungary: Actions for Economic Reconstruction (PHARE), and the Special Accession Programme for Agricultural and Rural Development (SAPARD), subsequently extended to the countries of 2007 enlargement. Additionally, the Community Assistance for Reconstruction, Development and Stabilisation (CARDS) was established in 2000, to rationalize support to the Western Balkans transitions. Since 2007, all these four funds have been replaced by the single framework provided by the Instrument for Pre-Accession (IPA). While differentiating between candidate and potential candidate countries, IPA aims at providing 'a unique and rationalized framework for the 2007–2013 financial envelope'. See http://europa.eu/legislation_summaries/agriculture/enlargement/e50020_en.htm
10 As of May 2012, candidate countries were Croatia (since 2013 an EU member), Turkey, Montenegro, Serbia and FYR Macedonia. Potential candidates were Albania (graduated to candidate since 2014), Bosnia and Herzegovina, and Kosovo. The first revision amended the MoU to cover the newly created EU pre-accession instrument ISPA and SAPARD. The second revision took into account the 2004 enlargement and the graduation of Western Balkan partners to potential candidate countries.
11 The exact nature of the relation between the EU and the EIB (established through article 9 of the EC Treaty in 1958, as well as endowed with autonomous legal personality under article 266 of the same treaty) has been a matter of contention, see EP DG Research (2003) for a summary of case laws and opinions. It is now acknowledged that the EIB, providing long and medium-term loans, is an organ (body) of the EU, 'owned by EU member states', but not an independent institution within the group of EU institutions. The EU (through the Commission) has a seat on the Board of Directors, but not on the Board of Governors (composed by the 28 EU member states), and one on the Board of Directors of the EIF (European Investment Fund, the component of the EIB Group specialized in venture capital operations and guarantees for SMEs), where

it owns 30% of shares (the EIB owing 69.1% of its shares, and other EU FIs holding the remaining 8.1%). Currently the Deputy Director General of DG ECFIN is also the Director to the EIB. The EBRD was established in 1991 to help post-Soviet countries in the transition from command economy systems to market-based ones. The signatories of its founding Articles were 40 states (EU members, the US, Canada, Japan and a number of others, including countries from the Soviet space), the EU (through the Commission) and the EIB. As of 2018, the EU and the EIB have subscribed capital for 900.44 million Euros each, and each have one Director on the Board.

12 Relative to the period 2007–2010, the EU provided support worth Euros 719 million to Central Asian partners and 120 million to Russia (World Bank ECA Brussels 2011b, 12; EU Council 2007a).

13 Interview with top WB manager (2008).

14 For the period 2007–2013, support to Eastern Neighbors amounted to Euros 2 billion. On the implications of the new financing facilities for the ENP countries see Section 7.5.

15 The role played by the Union in these countries has been much debated, however. On Ukraine see Casier (2011), and Gawrich, Melnykovska and Schweickert (2010).

16 See Phinnemore and Siani-Davies (2003). Only after the NATO intervention to end the Kosovo crisis in 1999 did the EU adopt a comprehensive approach to the Western Balkans, leading in the launch the Stability Pact for South East Europe (SP-SEE), discussed below.

17 In April 2012, Croatia, Montenegro, Serbia and Macedonia had candidate status, while Bosnia and Herzegovina, Albania and Kosovo (under Security Council Res 1244/99) had potential candidate status. See COM (2011) 666 final. In 2013 Croatia became an EU member state, while Albania graduated to the status of candidate country in 2014.

18 While this applied to other donors active in the region (Gligorov 2001), the heterogeneity of MS preferences on how to proceed in the Balkans was all the more serious given the prominent role that the Union, through the German Presidency, had taken up as a leader in the creation of the Stability Pact.

19 Early on the perspective was offered to five countries: Croatia, Serbia, Bosnia and Herzegovina, Macedonia, with Albania joining later, and Montenegro and Kosovo being also included after their independence (2006) and quest for international recognition (1999), respectively.

20 Also see Section 2.2 of Chapter 2 of this book, as well as Hombach (2000), World Bank ECA Brussels (2011b, 5).

21 The core turning point in the EU approach, from a regional perspective to a framework of stabilization and association, occurred between 1999 and 2003, at the Feira Council and Zagreb summits in 2000, and, finally at the Thessaloniki summit of 2003. At Thessaloniki SAP became the policy framework for the accession of the South-Eastern European countries (European Commission 2003a).

22 The EU financial envelope for 2007–2013 in the Western Balkans and Turkey was up to Euros 11.5 billion.

23 See COM (2011) 666 Brussels 12 October 2011, COM (2010) 660 Brussels 9 October 2010, and COM (2009) 533 Brussels 14 October 2009.

24 Chapter 23 refers to the establishment of 'an independent and efficient judiciary', as well as to 'impartiality, integrity and a high standard of adjudication by the courts' towards 'safeguarding the rule of law'. 'A solid legal framework' towards deterring corruption and 'respect for fundamental rights and EU citizens' rights, as guaranteed by the *acquis* and by the Fundamental Rights Charter, are further required. Approximation to standards set in Chapter 24 requires candidates to implement the Schengen criteria on border control, visas and migration, including judicial and police cooperation in fighting organized crime and terrorism, even if substantial parts of the Schengen *acquis* are implemented following a separate Council Decision to be taken after accession. See https://ec.europa.eu/neighbourhood-enlargement/policy/conditions-membership/chapters-of-the-acquis_en

25 On June 17, 2018, an agreement was signed between the two countries' prime ministers, with the Balkan nation renamed 'Republic of North Macedonia'. At the time of this writing, the pact still has to be ratified the parliaments of either country.

26 See Maršić and Marko (2007, 1). Between 2002 and 2011, the HR post coincided with that of Special EU representative. The role played by the EU through its HR/EUSRs has been criticized for its lack of coherence and credibility, amidst a weakening of the Bonn's powers and a diminishing traction from the accession perspective (Batt 2009).

27 The regime allows the different groups (Bosniacs, Serbs, Croats) to be represented in central institutions along ethnic lines according to proportionality, along the principle of ethnic parity.

28 Relative to the overall World Bank's ECA portfolio (i.e. including own lending and other non-cofinanced activities) worth USD 53.5 billion over the same decade, the resources provided by the three EU IFIs cover a share of 8%.

29 SAP, ENP and Central Asian partnership, for a total envelope of Euros 13 bn for the 2007–2013 period, not including structural and cohesion funds for new members and EU lagging regions, worth of Euros 348 bn over the same period.

30 Interview with WB officer (July 2011).

31 Relative to the other five regional units in the World Bank organizational structure, ECA has been affected particularly badly by the 2008 global crisis (World Bank's estimates have identified it as the slowest to recover its pre-crisis records), almost doubling its projected lending needs (USD 6–8 billion from earlier USD 3–4 billion). ECA Brussels (2011b, 13).

32 In 2009, following the encouraging results achieved through the AITF (Africa Infrastructure Trust Fund), the EU has set up the Neighborhood Investment Facility (NIF), blending grants from the Commission and member states with loans from European IFIs, towards cofinancing large infrastructural projects in ENP partner countries. The World Bank may co-finance investments that receive support under the NIF, but can only step in provided that other regional IFIs are already active in that particular program. The implications of these EU new blending facilities are discussed with more detail in Chapter 9, where the pioneering creation of the AITF is analyzed in the context of the EU–WB relations and respective role changes since the second half of the 2000s.

33 Since 2007, the EU has further strengthened its approach to blending, creating facilities in all the regions covered by its external cooperation. Mostly financing infrastructural projects and the development of SMEs, the EU has blended grants (Euros 3.4 billion between 2007 and 2017) with loans from both public and private institutions equal to Euros 26.4 bn. Overall, the EU blending approach has mobilized an estimated volume of investment in partner countries equal to Euros 57.3 bn. See EU Commission–DG DEVCO (2017b).

34 More particularly, relative to the WBIF, the World Bank has played an active role as 'observer' in the IFI Advisory Group, Project Financier Group and Steering Committee (World Bank ECA Brussels 2011a), Courtesy of the World Bank ECA office in Brussels (2011).

35 Interview with officer from DG Enlargement, July 4, 2011. According to World Bank's sources, support to upgrading the World Bank's status in the WBIF was expressed by Commissioners Piebalgs (DEVCO-EuropeAid), Füle (Enlargement), Kallas (Transport), Oettinger (Energy). The closer association of the World Bank to the WBIF was substantiated by the latter's enhanced commitments (Euros 560 million in lending and

Euros 3 million in technical assistance, expected per annum, between 2010–2012) (World Bank ECA Brussels 2011a)

36 Interview with officer from WB-ECA Unit, July 2011. IFCA, the EU Investment Facility for Central Asia, was launched in 2010 (EC Decision C(2010)2314), modeled on the blending template set up through the NIF, and based on the EU Strategy for Central Asia (2007) and the DCI (Development Cooperation Instrument). Currently, aside from private and bilateral donors, IFCA admits the participation of 'other multilateral finance institutions' (in addition to the EIB, EBRD and the NIB, Nordic Investment Bank) after an examination done on a case by case basis (EuropeAid, Action Fiche for Central Asia, DCI-ASIE/2010/021–627 available at http://ec.europa.eu/europeaid/documents/aap/2010/af_aap_2010_central-asia.pdf).

37 Interview with EU officer, July 2011.

38 Government of Bulgaria and The World Bank, Memorandum of Understanding on Partnership and Support in the Implementation of the EU Structural Instruments (2012), available at http://siteresources.worldbank.org/BULGARIAEXTN/Resources/305438-1281638860598/7323821-1327250505847/MOU_ENG.pdf

39 The Bank has also helped candidates and new members with absorbing SAPARD (Special Accession Programme for Agriculture and Rural Development) funds when capacity hindrances or poor planning became particularly challenging. See World Bank Background Note (2007d, 15).

40 The EU has re-adjusted the targets by moving budget expenditures thresholds upward, and absorption deadlines forward, to cushion the effects of the global crisis. Low horizontal consistency has lingered on, however: Ireland was entitled to shift to a share of 60% of budget expenditures on GDP, well above the 40% ceiling originally agreed for Romania and Bulgaria.

41 Coming to the fore particularly under the Wolfensohn Presidency, the knowledge component of World Bank activities has been further qualified, through a radical reorganization and resolute emphasis on shared communication of best practices, in what has been described by its President Jim Yong Kim as a 'solutions bank' (Kim 2013).

42 In addition, and compared to the Bank, which tailors its projects to country- and sector-specific needs, the Union praises itself for approaching countries along the accession track in a coordinated fashion, eschewing bilateralism – a core weakness of the Bank's actions in the broad ECA region – as one among the least desirable outcomes. Interview with EU officer (2011).

43 The Bank has also provided budget support programs to Latvia, Bulgaria, Romania and Poland to cope with the effects of the global crisis.

8 Development, democracy and peace?

The EU–World Bank cooperation in the MENA region

8.1 Introduction

This chapter focuses on the EU–World Bank cooperation in the Middle East and North Africa (MENA), a region where great hopes have been matched by equally great disillusions. Against the background of hybrid delegation described in Chapters 2 and 3, the following pages rely on role theory to investigate role conceptions and expectations of the two organizations in MENA. Matching respective perceptions with third-party evidence, the EU's performance is then analyzed, along the framework presented in Chapters 5 and 6.[1] Identifying the main institutional incentives and external conditions that have influenced the EU–WB cooperation in MENA, the chapter explores Brussels' specific instances of contributed effectiveness to development aims in trade, democracy promotion, approximation to the *acquis* and support to the poor living in MENA conflict-affected areas.

Compared to the EU–WB relations in the ECA or SSA regions, the World Bank's expectations have exerted a milder influence on EU role change in the Maghreb. Also, transformation in EU–WB joint activities has been less evident compared to the parallel evolutions of their cooperation in those regions. The priority attached by the EU to stability (over domestic development and democratization), and the low leverage that either organization could exert on middle income resource-rich MENA partners, have at times resulted in relatively frictional interactions between the Union and the Bank. Diverging interests of EU MS have also hindered the political impact of the Commission's financial efforts. The absence of accession perspectives has, in turn, diminished the constraints on partner countries and, indirectly, on World Bank's programs, to align to the EU guidelines. However, the analysis of selected cases of EU–WB cooperation in non-routine contexts, such as the occupied Palestinian territories (West Bank–Gaza, in the WB country listing), or in MENA countries that have experienced actual and attempted regime transitions, suggests that the EU and the Bank have found practical solutions to approximate their respective accountability systems, and to work on a more effective approach to development promotion altogether.

Section 8.2 discusses the evolution of the EU's policies in the region since the Barcelona Process of 1995, focusing on the EU's approach to the Southern

Mediterranean countries in the context of its Neighborhood Policy. Section 8.3 in turn delves into World Bank expectations of the EU's role in political dialogue, trade liberalization and standard setting processes, against selected evidence on the EU's performance in the region. Section 8.4 explores issues in governance benchmarking for the EU–WB cooperation in MENA, highlighting the deficits in EU policy consistency, and the resetting in role expectation that has occurred on the side of the World Bank's management and staff. The section also briefly discusses the different factors that have been advanced, both in the literature and from World Bank and third parties, to explain the less than satisfactory EU development performance in the region. Feedbacks to these expectations from the Commission are then presented in Section 8.5, and specific instances of cooperation between the Union and the Bank in Morocco and Tunisia are discussed, respectively. Section 8.6 investigates the challenges of EU–WB coordination in parallel financing in West Bank and Gaza, exploring the outcome of hybrid delegation in fragile contexts, a theme that will be further discussed in Chapter 9 of this book. Section 8.7 concludes.

8.2 The EU and the World Bank in MENA: from Barcelona to the 'Arab Springs'

The EU institutions have been the single largest donor to the MENA region, with Euros 13,326 mn in cumulated commitments between 1995 and 2013.[2] While including countries that are either EU associates or partners within the European Neighborhood Policy (ENP), countries in the MENA World Bank regional unit do not have the perspective of full membership, or the incentives to reform that may be available to some of their ECA neighbors.[3] Yet, since the launch of the Barcelona Process in 1995 the EU explicitly singled out the relevance of political stability in neighboring MENA partners, a relevance that it has further restated since the terrorist attacks of 9/11.

Endorsed by 15 EU MS and 12 Mediterranean partners, in the context of the nascent Euro–Mediterranean Partnership (EMP), the Barcelona Declaration was adopted at the 1995 eponymous Conference, to establish a cooperative framework to promote peace, stability and security in the Mediterranean. These goals had to be attained, in principle, through the reinforcement of political dialogue, the definition of security partnership, the identification of areas of cooperation in the economic sphere (leading eventually to the establishment of an FTA between the EU and the Mediterranean countries), and the engagement in social, cultural and human collaborations.[4] Between 1995 and 2006, the Declaration has operated under the MEDA Regulation.[5] Over that period, MEDA financed the Barcelona Process with Euros 8.75 bn. Resources also originated from the EIB, and from the Facility for Euro–Mediterranean Investment and Partnership (FEMIP), expected to be the source of Euros 10 bn in loans for investment between 2002 and 2009. EC funds channeled through the EIB followed a discontinuous pattern from 1999 to 2006, initially increasing, and finally stopped in 2002. EC flows channeled through the EIB were subsequently resumed, totaling 519 million Euros over the full period.[6]

In 2004, parallel to the first round of post-Soviet enlargements, the European Neighborhood Policy (ENP) further transformed the EU approach to the Southern Mediterranean countries. Compared to the EMP multilateral approach, ENP partnerships (Action Plans) were defined on a bilateral basis, with positive conditionality being their chief characteristic (Del Sarto and Schumacher 2005, 22).[7] The change introduced a differential treatment based on the countries' readiness to pursue political and economic reforms, with best performers being offered strengthened partnerships with Brussels. Compared to the EMP, the ENP puts a higher emphasis on shared values, around which country-to-country approaches are to be developed, towards the pursuit of the EU's 'interests', most notably in security matters (ibid.). Somehow implicit in the EMP under the rubric of political and economic cooperation, security issues are a pivotal element of the ENP, under the heading of Justice and Home Affairs (which touches on migration issues and border security).[8]

A benchmarking approach was introduced, and the geographical scope of EU action was widened.[9] The conditions to obtain support through the ENP Instrument (ENPI) were meant as incentives for candidates to meet the requirements towards full membership. The ENPI replaced MEDA as the instrument for aid and technical assistance delivery, with the EIB and FEMIP maintaining their role. Out of the 13.4 bn Euros in the ENPI budget of 2007–2013 (Mediterranean countries and Eastern partners), around 90% was to be allocated on a bilateral basis, with the remaining funds devoted to Cross-Border Cooperation and the Neighbourhood Investment Facility (NIF). In 2008 a revival of the EMP came about with the creation of the Union for the Mediterranean (UfM), a multilateral forum for discussion and cooperation under the leadership of the then French President Sarkozy, and with the support of the leaders of 43 countries.[10]

In turn, between 1990 and 2010 the IBRD cumulated lending to the MENA region amounted to approximately USD 25 bn (World Bank 2010e).[11] The size of the World Bank commitments has also grown after the global crisis of 2008. Lending from IBRD increased from USD 1.6 bn (in 2009) to USD 3.5 bn (in 2010). IDA support, in the form of grants, rose by almost 25%, reaching USD 214 mn in 2010.[12] Compared to lending in other country groupings, the World Bank's MENA portfolio is among the lowest, however. IBRD cumulative lending to the MENA region between 1990 and 2010 amounted to USD 25 bn, or 7.1% of its total cumulative lending in the same period. Major recipient regions over the same span of time were Latin America and the Caribbeans, which accounted for 35% of the Bank's lending activities, and ECA, to which 24% of IBRD's lending was directed.[13]

Cooperation between the Union and the Bank in the MENA region takes place within the Luxemburg Process, a high-level policy dialogue initiated in 2000, which also includes the EIB and, with an advisory role, the IMF. A Strategic Partnership Agreement was signed in 2004, and the EC contribution to World Bank's managed projects in the region was substantially scaled up from less than USD 20 mn in 2003 to more than 120 mn in 2004. Joined by the IFC since 2007, the Luxembourg Group is convened twice a year to discuss country and sector strategies, and to work on thematic coordination. With respect to the former, the EU and the Bank have striven to harmonize their respective practices, while in the latter area they have cooperated on region-wide endeavors, focusing on energy, environment, private sector development and human development, particularly on migration issues.

The Bank frequently advises MENA partners on policy reform, and provides them with technical assistance to promote regulatory convergence within the ENP framework. Consultation between the Commission and the Bank at the strategic level occurs regularly on World Bank Country Strategy Papers, so that the Commission is fully updated on World Bank operations in partner countries. In the first decade of the new millennium, the major recipients of EU support through the Bank's managed Trust Funds in the region have been West Bank–Gaza and Iraq. The EU crucially cooperated with the Bank to support the former, with USD 65 mn in 2004, and to help the latter with USD 120 mn via the Iraq Trust Fund (ITF), to which the Union has been the largest contributor (33% in total ITF, World Bank Brussels Office 2007a, 4). Between 1999 and 2005, the Union channeled Euros 186 mn through the World Bank Trust Funds for West Bank and Gaza, of which 80 mn under the Public Financial Management Reform multidonor Trust Fund. In the oPt the Union has also contributed to the ESSP (Emergency Services Support Program) Trust Fund, which recorded USD 13 mn disbursement and 7 mn in cash contributions over FY 2009 (World Bank 2010f, 107). Between 1999 and 2005 a further Euros 20 mn were devoted to programs in countries within the MENA region (ADE 2008, Vol. I, 5). Not including trust funds managed by the IFC, or thematic trust funds, as of March 2010 the EU contributed to 3 WB–IDA managed Trust Funds with a specific focus on the MENA region (the ESSP MDTF (Multi-Donor Trust Fund) in Palestine, the IRTF in Iraq and the METAP for Mediterranean Environmental Technical Assistance). On the one side, it is important to acknowledge that the bulk of EU channeling in the MENA region has occurred mainly through the EIB (94.4 million Euros between 2003–2006 through the FEMIP technical assistance support fund; 200 million Euros from 2001–2006 to support risk capital investments, 68 million Euros from 2003–2005 to finance interest rate subsidies) (ADE 2008, Inventory Note, 34). On the other side, however, while ensuring a higher visibility to the Union, the EIB has not provided expertise in the management of development programs on a level comparable to that of the World Bank. Neither could it rely on the knowledge of country systems and established dialogue with local actors that have been developed across time by the World Bank (ADE 2008, Vol. II, Annex 8, Mission au Maroc).

8.3 Role expectations from the World Bank: political leader and standard setter in the making?

Voices from the World Bank consider the EU as a key interlocutor in the MENA region, with the EU-cum-MS as the most influential supporter in selected North African partner countries (notably Tunisia and Morocco), and the most generous donor to the occupied Palestinian territories. Role expectations mirror the potential voiced in various EU official documents since the Barcelona Process, but also reflect their vague formulations, and the mixed results of EU programs in the region. According to voices from the World Bank's management, the EU is a potentially powerful normative standard setter, particularly when it establishes specific governance criteria on which to benchmark rewards through positive conditionality. Views from the Bank have pointed to the EU as a 'Third Millennium' compact, a unique case at successful integration to advance internal prosperity and political freedom, and a stand-alone example at projecting the attainment of those same objectives onto its partners in the Neighborhood.[14] The EU approach to trade integration pursued in the 1990s in the Balkans stands out as a successful attempt at creative integration, where Brussels has wisely employed economic tools to build secure political environments. A similar approach has been advocated by Bank voices as potentially fruitful to also cope with the security instability and macroeconomic volatility in MENA, even if EU achievements there have not appeared up to that challenge yet.[15]

A major driver in supporting infrastructural projects in the Maghreb, in the 2000s the EU also emerged as a potential 'normative power bloc' for the region. Morocco's progress in regulatory approximation to the *acquis* is a case in point. Overall, however, the EU's leadership in norm setting for the MENA region has suffered from multiple weaknesses. While being one among the most important trade players, Brussels' leadership in development policies has appeared as highly below its potential in the region. At the end of the 2000s, voices from the World Bank suggested this to be a transitory deficit, ascribing it to the EU incomplete internal transition towards formulating coherent external policies beyond the economic sphere. Missing political evolution seemed to be closely connected with the different stances of EU MS vis à vis the different countries in the MENA region. In the following decade, the deepening divides among EU MS on evolving security and migration issues have further confirmed this expectation.

Doubts have been voiced, also, on the supposedly selfless nature of the EU's trade role in MENA (World Bank 2003), particularly in the light of the cumbersome and allegedly discriminatory evolution of the System of Pan-Euro-Mediterranean Cumulation towards a unified scheme for the whole neighborhood.[16] Similar to other World Bank's remarks on the EU's approach to trade liberalization in SSA, worries were expressed particularly regarding the exemption of sensitive products and the persistence of restrictive ROOs (Rules of Origin) in the Association Agreements between the EU and its Mediterranean Partners (Brenton et al. 2006, 21–22).[17] Trade trends indicate that a fall in the shares of MENA exports to the EU over total MENA exports occurred between 1995 and 2006 for most labor-abundant MENA countries, including those which had signed an Association Agreement with the EU (World Bank 2008b, 17, 27). Apparently, the persistence of bilateral cumulation in several AAs has prevented MENA producers from sourcing inputs from third countries. Sectoral findings suggest that the EU Association Agreements have actually impeded MENA's further integration into the world economy (World Bank 2008b, 28), forcing its producers to source less efficiently from the EU market, only to be able to re-export there.

Criticisms of the effects of EU trade policies in the region have been counterbalanced by perceptions in the Bank of broader policy effectiveness on the approximation of regulatory standards and on selected infrastructural projects. Voices from the Bank have, however, also pointed to existing gaps between the EU's role conception and performance on support to human rights and democracy, well before the bottom-up attempted democratizations that materialized through the 'Arab Springs'.

8.4 The EU's performance and the World Bank in the MENA region: governance benchmarking and credibility issues

A hiatus exists between the goals endorsed by the Union in its official documents, and the implementation criteria that Brussels sets for partner countries in the region, particularly with respect to the operationalization of benchmarking progress in governance, democracy and human rights protection. Pointing to gaps in vertical-and-institutional consistency, voices from the World Bank have questioned both the definition and the very incorporation of general norms into operational criteria by the EU.[18] In principle, the Action Plans are agreed only if a commitment to the pursuit of common values is identified in 'the fields of the rule of law, good governance, the respect for human rights, including minority rights, the promotion of good neighbourly relations, and the principles of market economy and sustainable development' (European Commission 2004). In practice, however, the EU has often banked on the vagueness of its own benchmarking criteria, applying conditionality only in the negotiating phases of its Action Plans, later to resort to often subjective, relation-specific evaluation on whether to push for more thorough application of political clauses on human rights or not. As with the EMP, resources within the ENPI have also been mainly allocated to governments, mostly leaving out the private sector and CSOs. Thus, while no gap existed between the EU's own role conception and that of the World Bank regarding the EU's role as a potential diplomatic leader and standard setter in several parts of the MENA region (notably the Maghreb, but, also, increasingly, the Middle East, with particular reference to West Bank and Gaza), it appears that Brussels' weak performance in setting its own benchmarks for political conditionality has led to a reconsideration about that potential.

Secondly, the enforcement of those very criteria appears also a sensitive issue. Evidence from both documental third party studies and World Bank's interviews has exposed a particularly low level in both institutional and horizontal geographical consistency of the EU in having the governance conditionalities of the Association and Partnership Agreements implemented. Apparently, the EU has never made use of the human rights provision, notwithstanding the multiple violations put in place by several neighbours (Vahl 2006, 10–11).

The internal inconsistency between the EU's stated goals and chosen policy courses appears particularly serious relative to pre-2011 Libya, which had been even offered a DCFTA (Deep and Comprehensive Free Trade Agreement) in 2008, in spite of its utmost disregard for human rights. While initially taking a tough stance to respond to the terrorist attacks perpetrated by Libyan alleged terrorists in Vienna, Rome and Berlin in 1986, the EU has radically softened the course of its approach to the protection of human rights and democratic values in that country. Pressures from Italy, interested in resuming relations with Libya, a former colony and an economic partner, have led the Union to bypass its own governance standards. 'One of the strangest things that the EU has done in recent years was to start negotiating a DCFTA with Libya in 2008' (Grant 2011, 11). Different from Eastern neighbors, 'No other country in North Africa had received this privilege, yet Libya's political and economic systems were the most backward in the region' (Grant 2011, 12). Other sources have concurred, concluding that the EU's 'wider foreign policy objectives (such as fighting terrorism and restricting illegal migration) and commercial interests (including Italy's dependence on Libyan energy resources) appear to have been prioritized over democratic reforms and respect for human rights' (Open Europe 2011, 8). While the Libyan example is perhaps one among the most visible, the Union has in fact kept channeling remarkable amounts of funds under its ENP Action Plans through several MENA governments. The Tunisian, Egyptian and Moroccan authorities are no exception: in spite of the numerous breaches to human rights and democratic conditionalities that occurred under the State of emergency in Egypt, and under the Ben Ali and Hassan II rules in Tunisia and Morocco, respectively, well before the spring of 2011, resources contributed to their regimes by the European Union have in fact grown as a share of contributions in previous years (Open Europe 2011, 7).

On the trade front, the situation has improved: the Union has gradually approximated the role of selfless trade liberalizer claimed since the launch of the Doha Development Round in 2001, with progress towards the establishment of a Mediterranean Free Trade Area pointing in that direction.[19] On the other side, however, the linkage between attaining political reform through the incentive of economic aid and the carrot of being integrated into the internal market has not borne the expected results. In the eyes of the Bank, the EU has been too timid in requesting that partner countries pursue significant reforms. The ENP country-specific approach was expected to improve things over the one-size-fits-all philosophy of the EMP (Kausch and Youngs 2009).[20] Its differential strategy might have allowed the EU to strengthen the existing relations with the most moderate countries, such as Morocco, Tunisia and Israel. At the same time, though, it has not seemed fully suitable to deal with the less moderate partners in the region.[21] As a matter of fact, the principled differentiation has not been applied in the policy practice for a long time, and very little emphasis has been put on conditions under Ferrero-Waldner's mandate as Commissioner for External Relations (2004–2009; Grant 2011, 3). In the pursuit of its political priorities, particularly ensuring border security, containing migration flows and combating terrorism, the EU has apparently lost sight of the constraints that it had set, often providing grants to countries that did not qualify under its benchmarking approach, to fulfil democracy, human rights and good governance conditions.[22] Finally, voices from the World Bank have cautioned against the potentially discriminatory – and counterproductive – nature of the ENP approach: by prioritizing candidates and potential candidates (particularly selected partners in the Balkans), Brussels has apparently downplayed the elaboration of an effective approach towards the MENA countries.[23] Following the deterioration in security and migration issues, in 2015 the EU launched a Review of the ENP, along its Global Strategy for the EU Foreign and Security Policy, putting a stronger emphasis on the synergies between prosperity, stability and security.

As in other instances of EU–WB cooperation, voices from the World Bank have acknowledged the peculiarity of the EU mission, whereby managing complex political equilibria often requires making choices on highly sensitive issues. Yet, reflecting on the EU's policies in the region at the end of the 2000s, the same voices suggested that the Union be more 'objective in assessing progress made in economic and political governance' and more transparent in its dialogue with partner countries. The examples of loose enforcement of political conditionalities in the Association Agreements of pre-2011 Tunisia and Morocco have been contrasted with the more assertive approach that the Union had adopted in the Balkans through the Stabilization and Association Pact, and the utilization of trade integration as a strategy to promote political dialogue in that region. Similar to the strategy of grouping several countries in the ENP, the UfM has appeared to some doomed to fail. Mixing candidate countries with other neighbors has replicated the ambiguity of a multi-speed neighborhood policy. In the eyes of the World Bank, and through the lenses of the analytical framework presented in Chapters 5 and 6, the different performance of the EU's programs in the MENA and ECA regions, respectively, is perhaps one of the most tangible cases of the EU's low geographical policy consistency.

Ex-ante disbursements in the presence of unattained political goals have lessened the credibility of the Union, both in the eyes of the Bank and of partner countries, whose leaderships have on the contrary been strengthened in their expectation of continued support from Brussels, irrespective of their progress towards democratization. In addition to not achieving its own goals, the EU passivity has also negatively impacted on the EU external image as a normative power in the setting and enforcement of high moral standards. Voices from the World Bank suggested that the EU could be faster in matching economic effort with political and moral influence in the MENA region, as well as more careful to minimize the risk that goal attainment be subverted downstream in the policy process.

Several explanations have been provided for the less than satisfactory approach of the Union to pursue its goals through political dialogue in the region. First, lack of consensus among MS and between them and the Commission on sensitive countries has substantially impaired the attainment of governance objectives.

The main cleavage appears to be between Northern EU MS, which have sponsored the promotion of democracy, human rights and social development in the Mediterranean partners, and Southern EU Members (namely France, Italy, Spain, Portugal, Greece and Malta), which have on the contrary pushed for a dilution of both the setting and enforcement of political conditionalities in the Association Agreements with Mediterranean partners, in the attempt to shield their pre-existing bilateral ties in the region. Well before the conflict that currently affects Syria, a World Bank top manager quoted the country as one among the main examples of EU's inconsistent policy in the region: while the EIB had already invested more than 1 million Euros by the end of 2007, divergences between France and the UK over what was the best course of action at that time, seem to have substantially impaired the possibility for the Union to fully bank on its channeled resources to the country. Second, both official documents and secondary literature indicate that the shift from the EMP to the ENP has not entailed a radical reorientation of the EU approach to development promotion in the Southern Mediterranean partners. According to EU studies on the subject, the reason should be sought in the roots of the ENP, originated by the EU need to redefine its borders after the first enlargement round (Del Sarto and Schumacher 2005, 26). Third, the poor results achieved under the ENP framework can also be attributed to successful pressuring by partner countries on the continuation of EU support once the objectives had been already set and the main portion of the funds disbursed. As noted above, conditionality has been mainly applied only in the negotiating phases of the Action Plans, so that Governments in partner countries have been given a clear strategic incentive to downplay the strength of EU commitment to enforce political conditionality through negative economic sanctioning. Fourth, and strictly linked to the previous point, successful pressuring, at least in the Maghreb, is due to the relatively higher contractual power enjoyed before the EU by partner countries such as Morocco, Tunisia and Egypt, which are middle-income economies with a key role in the political equilibria of the region. As repeatedly voiced by World Bank sources, before the outburst of the region-wide wave of revolts in support of democratization, interruption of cooperation programs by the EU with these Maghreb countries on grounds of breaching political conditionality had never been considered as a realistic option. With respect to democratization, the limits of the Neighborhood approach are evident across the majority of the MENA signatories of Association Agreements with the EU. Morocco pursued a reform path which, while satisfying the EU's minimal requirements, was in fact far from being truly meaningful:[24] doubts about the fairness and transparency of elections arose when the Islamist PJD party (*Parti de la justice et du développement*), favorite in the polls, did not fare well during the country's elections of 2007.

8.5 *Realpolitik* and reality checks: stability vs democracy and the EU–WB cooperation in the Maghreb

> First, we must show humility about the past. Europe was not vocal enough in defending human rights and local democratic forces in the region. Too many

> of us fell prey to the assumption that authoritarian regimes were a guarantee of stability in the region. This was not even Realpolitik. It was, at best, short-termism—and the kind of short-termism that makes the long term ever more difficult to build. I am not saying that everything we did was wrong, rather that Europe, at this particular moment more than ever before, must be faithful to its values and stand on the side of democracy and social justice. The crowds in the streets of Tunis, Cairo and elsewhere have been fighting in the name of our shared values. It is with them, and for them, that we must work today—not with dictators who are, as we speak, spilling the blood of their own people with utter disregard for human life.
>
> (Štefan Füle, EU Enlargement and Neighborhood Policy Commissioner 2011)[25]

Following the 2011 'Arab Springs' a major rethinking has taken place in the EU and within the Commission, particularly. Inputs from top-level administrative officials have pointed to a different reading of past policy courses followed by the Union with its MENA partners. Reacting to critical role expectations from the World Bank, high level management officials from the Commission have mentioned the differences between the two organizations, their missions, and incentive structures, repeatedly quoting the political constraints within which the EU operates, as opposed to the, comparatively, 'freer hands' conduit that can be pursued by the Bank.[26] In the eyes of the interviewed Commission's officers, compared to the situation in unstable Maghreb contexts, the relatively more effective EU performance in enforcing political conditionality in the Balkans can be explained through the presence of political and military support from both MS and the international community there. In retrospect, the ENP has not failed altogether in the Maghreb, voices from the EU claim, mentioning *Realpolitik* needs as inherent to political dialogue. In the words of a top-level Commission officer in service before the 2011 Arab wave of attempted democratization, at the end of the day 'You must talk with whomever is there, which is what we, and the World Bank, did then'.[27] The time lag partly explains the difference between this reading (referred to events that occurred before 2011) and the official comment by Commissioner Füle on the events of 2011, witnessing that adaptation has occurred on the EU side. However, their contrasting nature reveals the complex mission of the Union, which embodies potentially conflicting political objectives (promotion of democracy and stability in what were once authoritarian and relatively stable contexts), and must therefore wield potentially competing strategies to pursue them. The quintessentially political nature of the EU's external roles also exposes the tight connection between its development and foreign policies.

Particularly positive outcomes have been attained on the approximation of standards by Morocco, which has voluntarily initiated incorporation of the *acquis communautaire*, through a process similar to that initially undertaken by Ukraine (where political openness has however deteriorated, well before the conflict with Russia). Neither of the two countries is a candidate for accession. Political and security evolutions in the 2010s make remarks about their progress in approximating the EU *acquis* at best tentative. However, their early unilateral engagement with the EU *acquis* seems to prove that normative attraction can set imitation processes in motion irrespective of conditionality enforcement. What seems to be missing on the EU side is a drive to trigger spill-overs from standard approximation to the adoption of rule of law systems and democratic principles.

Inputs on segmented consultations have emerged, purposefully enacted by the Moroccan Government with specific donors one at a time, to obtain sizeable financial support from both sides. While not necessarily the norm, middle-income countries in politically sensitive areas have often succeeded in playing off donors against one another. The hope is that a more consistent EU approach to governance benchmarking and progress assessment will also stimulate higher accountability from governments in partner countries. The prominence of bilateralism, and the quiet downplaying of a regional approach inherent in the shift from the EMP to the ENP, is however a factor that may send contradictory signals to partners in the Maghreb, thus weakening the EU's contributed effectiveness. On the other side, and some years ahead of the 2015 SDGs' call for mutual responsibilities for developed and developing countries, the Commission's reliance on budget support has reinforced the concept of mutual accountability, calling on the duties of donors and recipients alike to ensure effective disbursement and implementation of EU funds (European Commission 2010b, 6, 13).

Enhanced cooperation between the Union and the Bank appears even more important in the case of Tunisia, the only country where the 2011 efforts at democratic transition have not been reverted to date. In the discussion over the possibility that the Bank participated with the AfDB (African Development Bank) and the FDA (French Development Agency) to a Governance and Opportunity (GO) Development Policy Lending (DPL) Program in 2011, some EU MS voiced their concerns at the World Bank Board, about the weak accountability by the Tunisian authorities. Indeed, at the time of the discussion, a new government had not been elected yet. In the end, MS reservations were lifted thanks to the news that the EU (Commission) was also a donor to the Program. Jointly prepared by the EU and the World Bank, along with the AfDB and FDA, the loan obtained the *placet* of the Board, with a starting amount of USD 500 mn. Memos of the EU delegation in Washington indicate that the uncertainties of some EU MS have been 'alleviated', during a coordination meeting of the Eurogroup in Washington, when 'it came to their attention that the EU (a political entity) jointly participates in this operation' (EU delegation to the US, 20 June 2011, 2). Plausibly, the coordination at the Board has benefited from liaising between EU delegations, in Washington and Tunis, respectively, which have provided each other with 'timely inputs' in these times of high political uncertainty.

The micro-evidence of the 2011 GO Tunisia DPL Program indicates that the gap between the World Bank's expectation on the role of the EU as an influential diplomatic actor, as well as its perplexity about the EU's ability to speak and act with one voice at the Board may not be as persistent a feature as it appears from the 'instantaneous picture' of the fragmentation of representation under the current World Bank's constituency system. As seen above in this chapter and in other parts of this volume, the World Bank's management and staff do perceive the Union as a clearly political, and, at times, unitary actor in highly sensitive diplomatic matters, an evidence that is reinforced by the action of the EU institutions, at different levels. As shown in the case of the discussion on the GO Tunisia DPL Program within the Eurogroup, this holds true even when doubts arise within the group of the EU agents at the Board, the EDs. In that particular instance, the role of the EU delegation in Washington (now managed by the HR and run through the EEAS) has been crucial in projecting its tasks into concrete liaising activities to support better coordination at the Board. Details on the negotiations on the Tunisia DPL Program also reveal that different stances among MS can be overcome when EU institutions are able to liaise effectively between Brussels and the EU delegation in Washington.[28]

The EU's own and contributed effectiveness seems to have improved also with respect to its trade policies in the MENA region. As briefly discussed above, World Bank research has supported the case for horizontal trade integration in the Maghreb and Mashrek-Mediterranean countries, advocating better conditions for market access from the EU and the US. Particular attention has been devoted to speaking against discriminatory rules of origin, so that MENA exporters could profit from both outlets without having to design different development and industrial strategies. Sectoral evidence on the adjustment to the post-Multifibre world of four MENA countries (Egypt, Jordan, Tunisia and Morocco) indicates that, compared to the EU, the US has granted relatively more favorable preferences to selected MENA countries. Export boosts in textile and clothing sectors for Egypt and Jordan have gained from the establishment of QIZ (Qualified Industrial Zones). In the US–Jordan FTA, a 'third party rule' has allowed Jordanian producers to freely source inputs from anywhere in the world (World Bank 2006b, 11). A similar rule is incorporated in the Morocco–US FTA, even if a quantitative limit (36 million square meter equivalents) is set, and the rule has only a ten-years duration (World Bank 2006b, 26).

At the time of this writing, only Algeria, Morocco and Tunisia enjoy, in principle, full cumulation status under the Pan-Euro-Mediterranean System (meaning that they can source from third countries, manufacture domestically, and export preferentially to the EU), while the other MENA countries that have an Association Agreement within the Barcelona–EMP–ENP process either have bilateral or diagonal cumulation.[29] In addition to the necessary progress in horizontal integration (which has evolved among the four Maghreb countries through the Agadir Agreement but is far from being complete), in order to be able to apply full cumulation, the Euro-Mediterranean partners will have to adjust their trade agreements to the requirements of the vertical AAs with the EU.[30] Given the red tape costs of the different certification systems of origin applied bilaterally by the Union, a question arises also with respect to take ups and utilization rates, a problem that also hampered progress on the EU's trade policy towards least developed ACP countries. Further improvement has occurred, however, in the simplification of the current System of Pan-Euro-Med cumulation,[31] currently resulting from more than 60 different bilateral protocols. The EU Council has launched a process to speed up the signing of the Convention on Pan-Euro-Mediterranean rules of origin (in force since May 2012), which will hopefully grant full cumulation to all the partners in the Euro-Mediterranean region. However, restrictions on sensitive products are still in place (tariff quotas are applied to 60 basic agricultural products, including key items in the formation of income in North African partners, such as fruits and vegetables; Open Europe 2011, 17 and European Council (2001b). The hope is that, similar to its rethinking of own governance benchmarking and enforcement, the EU will follow up also on World Bank inputs to pursue broader trade broader liberalization vis à vis the MENA partners, possibly removing the existing CAP restrictions against core MENA agricultural exports. As seen above, Brussels' reconsideration of its approach to democratic conditionality has occurred mainly as a result of the events following the Arab Spring. The hope is that a development-minded EU will adopt a genuinely liberal trade policy even in the absence of violent upheavals in partner countries.

Fragile institutions in other, highly securitized MENA contexts have long made enhanced cooperation between the EU and the World Bank a priority. Challenging contextual conditions provide higher incentives to improve donor coordination. However, those very conditions also raise the stakes of commitments for external actors, and increase the cost of trusting each other. Differences in respective EU and WB approaches to conditionality and budget support, which had remained latent in more stable Maghreb contexts, have emerged to their fullest on the occasion of the EU–WB cooperation in the occupied Palestinian territories, West Bank and Gaza Strip, to which we now turn.

8.6 Accountability and fragility: the EU and the World Bank in West Bank and Gaza

As in the case of the Tunisia Governance and Opportunity DPL, the accountability of partner countries is particularly relevant when funds are channeled through budget support, i.e. directly to a Government's budget, rather than through projects or programs under the direct supervision of a donor's agency.[32] While the method entails potentially higher risks of fraud and misuse if channeling does not occur along trusted routes (Barkan et al. 2004), budget support is key to improving capacity and building sustainability in partner countries (Oxfam 2010). Compared to other approaches, budget support is instrumental to fostering inclusion and participation of stakeholders, two core objectives embodied in the ownership principle, agreed upon in the Paris–Accra Agenda (European Parliament 2011a, 8). Yet, under conditions of fragility, i.e. when institutions are weak and public management practices well below average, delivering effective aid via partner country systems requires skillful political dialogue, a solid effort to support capacity building, as well as adaptability and creativity by both domestic and external actors.[33]

Institutional fragility has been variously defined in the literature, with different meanings attached to weak, fragile and, at the utmost extreme, failed states.

Rankings however converge on the classification of West Bank and Gaza territories.[34] Their contested sovereignty is reflected in terminological quarrels, so that while both the EU and the WB regard the Palestinian Authority (PA) as the country's legitimate government, the areas known as West Bank and Gaza are referred to as 'occupied Palestinian territories' (oPt), and in most datasets not counted as an independent unit, but as a part of the State of Israel. In the early 2010s, the oPt were regarded as less fragile compared to other conflict-ridden countries (Afghanistan, Iraq, Somalia and Ethiopia, coded as instances of highest institutional failure in most rankings). While the datum possibly reflected the mixing of Israel and Palestinian territories quoted above, reports from the World Bank indicated that

> Robust institutions of civil society have long been in place. The resilience of Palestinian society has repeatedly been tested under extreme conditions over the past decade, performing above and beyond any reasonable expectations. Palestinian institutions of state have developed rapidly and now have the capacity to provide satisfactory levels of service delivery to the Palestinian public.
>
> (World Bank Country Director for WBG, Mariam Sherman, 2010)

The early days of the Bank's development promotion under fragility owe much to its work in the Palestinian territories (World Bank 1993). Pursuant to the Oslo Agreements, the Bank launched its first post-conflict MDTF, the Holst Fund (active between 1994 and 2001), to finance the newly created Palestinian Authority. Further research ensued on the topic, with a seminal framework paper in 1997 on the 'Role of the World Bank in Post-conflict Reconstruction', providing the core input for the Bank's own Operational Policy and Bank's Procedures on 'Development Cooperation and Conflict' (Norad 2007, 214). In 2011, the Bank's World Development Report on Conflict, Security and Development (World Bank 2011a) directly addressed development promotion in conflict-ridden and insecure environments, further consolidating the organization's 20+ years long experience on the matter.

Validating the Bank's competence, voices from the Commission have unquestionably acknowledged the Washington-based IFI as a leader in promoting development in fragile countries.[35] On specific counts, however, Brussels has openly contested the Bank's management of some EU-contributed trust funds in conflict-affected contexts. In the oPt case, accountability emerged as a major challenge, while visibility issues were relatively less problematic, thanks to the prominent role of the Union in the Quartet.[36] Since the early 2000s, some MS (notably parliaments in the UK and the Netherlands), European media and NGOs have criticized the alleged fund transfers from the nascent Palestinian Authority to terrorist factions (both Hamas and Fatah-loyal militarized groups). Warning against the risks of financing terrorism, the EU Parliament, some NGOs and conservative sectors of EU MS domestic public opinions subsequently targeted the accountability of the Palestinian Authority, raising the issue of broader EU accountability vis à vis its taxpayers. Urging the Commission to avoid EU taxpayers' money being funneled to terrorist factions, those voices also questioned the ability of the World Bank to provide adequate guarantees to contributing donors.[37] Other inputs, instead, emerged to encourage major donors to prioritize support for the Palestinian people (Oxfam 2007b). Poverty-concerned NGOs focused on development challenges and the diversion of funds to unintended uses, over the rights of EU MS taxpayers. Overall, then, inside the EU multiple voices were raising the salience of diverging dimensions of accountability. Unfortunately, these discrepancies were often conflated under the labels of fiduciary and financial risks (the first referring to diversion of funds, according to the European Court of Auditors, the second to weak links between disbursements and fulfillment of agreed conditions by the partner authorities, according to the Commission) (Vanheukelom et al. 2011, 9). The Commission's identification of the World Bank as the guarantor of last resort also conflicted with the Bank's interpretation of own fiduciary accountability, whereby the ultimate responsibility for how funds are used is to be attributed to implementing agents in partner countries.[38]

The issue has gained further prominence in light of the EU's top position among the donors to the oPt through its own administered programs (worth Euros 4.26 bn from 1994 to 2009). After the worsening conditions of the Palestinian population since the second intifada, Brussels increased assistance from a yearly average of Euros 137 mn (1994–1999) to Euros 250 mn, financing the PA through direct budget support, upon requests for a comprehensive financial reform, which included, among other things, the creation of a single treasury account (STA) where donors' funds should be channeled. The Union called for the PA to set up an austerity, emergency budget, to which it attached conditionalities, supervised (but not audited) by the IMF[39] (European Parliament 2003, 'majority report'). Over time, however, the system was criticized for its low accountability to EU taxpayers, on grounds of alleged transfers to support the activities of Palestinian terrorist groups (Ehrenfeld 2003, 5–7). A Working Group, composed of Parliamentary Committees on Foreign Affairs (AFET), on Budgets (BUDG) and on Budgetary Control (CONT) supported by an OLAF (Office europeén de lutte anti-fraude) investigation, inquired on the matter finding no decisive evidence to prove the illegal nature of such transfers (European Parliament 2003).[40]

After the launch of the second intifada and the subsequent impossibility for the Commission to support the Palestinian Authority directly, Brussels opted for allocations through the World Bank Trust Fund system (ADE 2008, Vol. I, 32). Between 1999 and 2005, the EC has channeled Euros 186 mn through various WB managed West Bank and Gaza Trust Funds (ADE, 2008, Vol. I, 6), of which Euros 80 mn to finance reform of public financial management through a multi-donor Trust Fund (PFM TF), to which the EC was the main donor. Subsequently, the opening from the Israeli Prime Minister Sharon and the unilateral withdrawal of Israel from Gaza in August 2005, provided a window of opportunity to resume the earlier EU direct support to the PA. Through the appointment of James Wolfensohn, outgoing President of the Bank at that time, as the special envoy of the Quartet in the Territories, the main donors hoped that his relatively a-political brokerage could help to focus on the development and humanitarian emergency needs of the civilians in Palestine.[41] While not in service anymore, Wolfensohn was aware of the Bank's role as intermediary through which funds could be funneled to the PA without direct political involvement by the Commission. His diplomatic efforts appeared much in line with the assumption that a development-oriented solution could provide a way out of the crisis.

The situation worsened when, after the sudden illness of Sharon and the victory of Hamas in the elections of January 2006, fears of radicalization in the Territories grew out of proportion and donors decided to withdraw most of their support to the new government. Brussels suspended diplomatic relations with the PA as the Hamas-led government failed to meet the conditions set by the EU to guarantee assistance.[42] To sidestep the Hamas Government and reach the Palestinians, and upon request from the Quartet, the EU supported the launch of the Temporary International Mechanism (TIM) in the fall of 2006, a pooling facility through which donors could contribute to provide 'direct delivery assistance to the Palestinians' (TIM Factsheet, EuropeAid 2008a). In 2007, the Bank issued reports that showed how such bypassing had contributed to undermine the work that had been previously done by donors to support the creation of the STA, a backbone of the earlier fiscal reform (Nielson 2007). While the Bank openly stymied Israel's army's security operations and weak fiscal policies of both Hamas and Fatah-led Palestinian governments, it also called for the donors' community to sustain the reform of the Palestinian Finance Ministry, and pledged to them not to withdraw their support altogether. Within the TIM mechanism both the Union and the World Bank continued their cooperation over delivering aid to the Palestinians, yet the issue of accountability under direct delivery was not solved, as TIM itself took partial control on the funding for services and salaries of government workers, thus offering the Palestinian authorities an easy way out from being fully accountable to the donors.

Evidence from internal correspondence indicates that Commission desk officers fully acknowledged how serious the situation was. In a note to Commissioner Ferrero Waldner and World Bank's President Zoellick dated June 2007, the (then) Commission desk officer for the West Bank and Gaza reported his serious concerns about the evolution of the political and humanitarian situation in the territories, quoting the risks that an increased radicalization of political tensions would have on further bloodshed of civilian populations. The officer retained the Bank as having done 'excellent analytical work' on 'Movement and Access and Restrictions in the West Bank' (World Bank 2007c), but conveyed some apprehension over the possible suspension of the Bank's disbursements (including funds from the ESSP, under the Window I of the TIM mechanism), in case of default by the Palestinian Authority on their principal loan repayment. The follow up prepared by RELEX services for Commissioner Ferrero Waldner reveals a particularly cautious stance, and a request of further consultation with the Bank and the IMF, in the event that direct budget support to the National Unity Government was resumed. Anticipating the request from World Bank's officers, RELEX services also ruled out the possibility that the Commission stepped in to assist the repayment of the Palestinian Authority outstanding debts, or contribute to a multi-donor World Bank-managed trust fund, a move that would have warded off the much feared suspension of Bank's lending. Apparently, RELEX also lamented the slow pace of implementation of World Bank's managed Window I of the ESSP, exposing the bureaucratic obstacles in the Bank's procurement system.

While being instant images of complex dynamics, these elements disclose the difficult coordination between two different accountability systems, each with its own rationales and procedures, in a militarized context where multiple donors are involved. It also reveals how the EU wavering between explicit political involvement, on the one side, and supposedly neutral financial efforts ('aid to the Palestinians'), on the other, has strained coordination with the Bank, eventually weakening their development efforts. The EU's reliance on an allegedly lower profile via channeling through World Bank PFMTF responded to Parliamentary, NGOs and civil society concerns over domestic accountability of the PA governments, diminishing the visibility of the Commission in difficult times. Yet, relying on Bank-managed projects also weakened the influence that the EU could potentially exert through multilateral channeling. The setup of the TIM mechanism in June 2006, and the Commission's decision to resume budget support in June 2007, against the background of Blair's appointment as the Quartet's special envoy were clear moves to revitalize the EU's political leadership.

Across time, the Commission has negotiated to keep control of its channeled resources and secure Brussels' political leverage on World Bank-managed trust funds benefitting from substantial EU contributions. Additionally, it has worked to ensure consistency of action with EU MS. In the negotiations with the Bank, though most often quoted as a liability, frequently on grounds of divergences with bilaterals, the EU-MS shared development competence, has also been played as an asset. In a background note to a reply to the Bank's request to contribute with additional funding to the construction of a waste water treatment plant in Beit Lahia (an area north of Gaza where damages to a plant-supporting wall had caused flooding and several deaths), RELEX services openly advised the Bank to seek additional funding from EU MS involved in the area, such as France and Belgium. Rather than a recommendation from the most multilateral among the EU institutions, the Commission's stance appeared closer to a vested buckpassing move by the '29th donor'. The situation was resolved eventually when the EU resumed its direct assistance to the Palestinian Finance Ministry, led by Salam Fayyad, a member of the Third Way party, and former World Bank-officer endorsed by the Quartet, who committed to set up internal audit and control departments to monitor spending and implementation of the agreed reforms.

Overall, the donor community supported Fayyad's reorganization by assisting the three-year Palestinian Authority's Reform and Development Plan (PRDP), presented at the Paris Donor Conference of 17 December 2007. Between February and March 2008, the EU substituted TIM with the PEGASE mechanism, transitioning from emergency assistance to development aid: still open to all donors, PEGASE would cover reforms envisaged in the PA PDRP over a three-year period.[43] In March 2008, at the request of the PA and other donors, the Bank also set up its own PRDP-MDTF, to provide the Palestinians with 'an independently supervised mechanism for channeling budget support funds to West Bank and Gaza'.[44] Leaving joint co-financing only to the ESSP-TF, the EU and the Bank thus supported development in the oPt mainly through coordinated but independent mechanisms.[45] Frictions on slow disbursements by the Bank, as well as different perspectives on accountability and on advisability of further proceeding with direct budget support explain that separation.

Since 2014 a new deterioration in Gaza–Israel relations has led to a steep decline in budget support by the main donors, and a rise in the pre-eminence of Arab countries in supporting reconstruction in the territories. Despite the multiple tools available to the EU to engage in a constructive dialogue with Israel, and to support accountability improvement by the PA (Action Plans under the ENP, EU role in the Quartet and in the UfM), Brussels seems to have so far fallen short of matching its cooperation effort with effective results (DRN et al. 2014).

Against the backdrop of these contextual and relational challenges, however, the EU and the Bank have been able to cooperate to support civilians after the Israeli ground invasion of the Gaza Strip in the fall of 2008 (World Bank 2009). Cooperation through the Gaza Early Recovery and Reconstruction Plan (GERRP), initiated by the UNDP and the PA since March 2009, has indicated how under emergency circumstances both the EU and the WB are willing to join their efforts to consolidate donor responses to assess damages and support the PA in rebuilding where most needed (World Bank 2009). Progress on jointly supporting a PA cash transfer for the poorest also indicates that the EU and the Bank are willing and able to overcome the differences in their respective accountability systems to deliver basic aid. The subsequent merging of the World Bank SSNRP (Social Safety Net Reform) and the EU SHC (Special Hardship Case) to support reforms of the Palestinian social safety embodied in the Palestinian National Cash Transfer Program (PNCTP) shows that parallel financing can be fine-tuned, to the point of implementing a single financing scheme, especially when this is considered a main concern for authorities and citizens in partner countries, as is the case for the PNCTP, a priority cash transfer program.[46] The EU SHC and the World Bank SSNRP together have provided over USD 50 mn per annum to more than 50,000 poor households. Benefitting from resources and technical assistance provided by both institutions, the PNCTP has been regarded as one of the most advanced cash assistance programs in the whole MENA region (World Bank 2010c).

8.7 Conclusions

Against the overall background of the EU's role in the region, through its Neighborhood policy, and within the context of the EU–World Bank Luxembourg framework, this chapter has discussed EU role conceptions and World Bank's expectations of the EU in MENA, matching them with analyses on policy performance in specific cases of cooperation between the EU and the Bank, that emerged from the survey conducted for this study, particularly in the Maghreb and in the occupied Palestinian territories. Regarding contributed effectiveness, the EU displayed a combination of both proactive approaches and passive stances in its interaction with the Bank, narrowing the reach of the political dialogue fostered since the 1990s with its Mediterranean partners. Divergences among MS on preferred policy courses, issues of Commission own policy coherence and technical weaknesses have been identified as the main sources for such uneven achievements. All in all, World Bank expectations do not seem to have exerted a major influence, as role change on the side of the EU has taken place as a result of homegrown bottom-up attempts at democratization in some of the MENA countries. This confirms the overarching weight of security and political components of the Union's approach to promoting development in the region.

With respect to the Maghreb, diverging positions on trade issues have emerged, echoing the broader World Bank criticism against EU inconsistencies in Sub-Saharan Africa in pursuing opportunistic trade liberalization on the one side, and more altruistic development objectives on the other. Issues in governance benchmarking point to the EU's supposed geographical inconsistency, particularly with respect to other neighboring and potential candidate countries from the ECA region. Micro-evidence from support to macroeconomic stabilization in Morocco indicates that the EU and the Bank can engage in productive 'intra-sectoral' cooperation, and that coordination in parallel operations is crucial, to minimize the possibility that the authorities in partner countries play one donor off the other. The close-up on the negotiations behind the setup of the Governance and Opportunity DPL for Tunisia in 2011 indicates how the role of the Commission can be key to forging common positions among EU EDs at the Board, also providing evidence of an early example of successful diplomatic working by the EEAS. The case illustrates the influence of hybrid principals (the Commission indirectly playing such a role when matters covered by shared competence are discussed at the Bank's Executive Board) in helping actors who cover multiple roles (the EU EDs) to reduce the complexity of decisional processes, providing them with feasible alternatives.

Finally, the EU–WB frictions over budget support to the PA exemplify the coordination challenges faced by a political union and a development bank in a fragile and highly securitized context. While roles appear clearly defined in principle (political dialogue and grant financing on the side of the Commission, strategic support to development through loans and technical assistance on the side of the Bank), the evidence discussed in this chapter shows how the conflagration of military threats, humanitarian crises, political, economic and social shocks under serious stateness problems has extracted a heavy toll on routine coordination between the two organizations. Sources internal to the Commission, DG DEVCO–EuropeAid. have pointed out how one of the prioritized areas for dialogue between the newly established Task Force for an enhanced dialogue with the IFIs and the World Bank is indeed that of cooperation in fragile states (see Section 3.4 in Chapter 3). While it may be difficult to anticipate the full impact of such enhanced cooperation, the redefinition of EU–WB joint schemes in fragile, conflict-affected contexts has generated flexible arrangements to provide early relief to the poorest. The EU–WB cooperation in West Bank and Gaza bears similarities with other cases of EU–WB interaction in militarized contexts. This has been the case for some of the most conflict-ridden countries in Sub-Saharan Africa, such as Liberia, Eritrea, Mozambique and, discussed in the following chapter, Zimbabwe and Ethiopia.

Notes

1 Interviews with World Bank (Washington) and EU officers (Brussels) were conducted between 2008 and 2011.
2 Open Europe (2011, Annex 2). While different from actual disbursements, committments reported separately under MEDA I and II (8.75 bn Euros, between 1996 and 2006) and ENPI for the Mediterranean Countries (9.05 bn, 2007–2013) add to Euros 17.8 bn.
3 On this respect most analyses quote the words of the (then) President of the Commission Romano Prodi according to which the ENP implied 'sharing with the neighbours everything but institutions' (Prodi 2002). While the concept was restated in other official documents (European Council 2003b; European Commission 2004), readings pointing to the possibility of a 'hidden carrot' for some Eastern countries have also been advanced (Gsthöl 2007; Khasson et al. 2009).
4 There have been eight Euro–Med Foreign Ministers Conferences up to 2006, thereafter mainly conferences on specific topics, such as trade, tourism, culture, have been organized. In 2005, on the tenth anniversary, the participating countries met again at the Euro–Med Summit in Barcelona, agreeing on a Five-Year Work Program to foster the Euro–Med Partnership.
5 http://europa.eu/legislation_summaries/external_relations/relations_with_third_countries/mediterranean_partner_countries/r15006_en.htm
6 ADE (2008, Vol. I, 7).
7 As opposed to negative conditionality, which prevailed in the EMP.
8 European Commission (2004).
9 The EuroMed process comprises the EU members and ten Mediterranean Partners (Algeria, Egypt, Israel, Jordan, Lebanon, Morocco, Occupied Palestinian Territories, Syria, Tunisia and Turkey). With the exclusion of Turkey, which is a candidate country, the ENP also includes: Armenia, Azerbaijan, Belarus, Georgia, Moldova and Ukraine. The ENP has been revised in 2011 and 2015, listing four priority areas: good governance, democracy, rule of law and human rights (1); economic development for stabilization (2); security (3); migration and mobility (4).
10 These 43 include: the 28 EU member countries, plus Albania, Algeria, Croatia, Egypt, Israel, Jordan, Lebanon, Mauritania, Montenegro, Morocco, Occupied Palestinian Territories, Serbia, Syria, Tunisia, and the League of Arab Nations. Since 2011 Syria has suspended its membership. Libya has an observer status.
11 These figures pale in comparison with EU flows directed to the region. World Bank resources are loans to be repaid (IDA concessional portion, not included in the figure quoted in the text, amounts to 3,9 billion dollars for the same period), whereas the EU flows are mainly concessional, as their grant element represents a substantial portion of the quoted figures. Some criticism has been however raised by OECD evaluators relative to the inclusion of non-concessional lending by EIB under overall ODA by EU reporting institutions.
12 MENA region World Bank webpage at: http://web.worldbank.org/WBSITE/EXTERNAL/COUNTRIES/MENAEXT/0,,menuPK:247605~pagePK:146732~piPK:64003010~theSitePK:256299,00.html
13 The MENA partners, mostly middle-income countries, are at the bottom ranking of IDA lending, accounting for a little over 2% of its concessional loans between 1990 and 2010. Elaborated from World Bank (2010e).
14 Interview with WB VP (January 2008).

15 As discussed in Chapter 7 (Section 7.4), however, the EU's approach to the Balkans has not been immune from inconsistencies at several levels.
16 In place since 1997, the System includes the EU MS, the EFTA countries, the CEEC countries and the Baltic States. It was then widened to industrial products originating in Turkey (1999). In principle, it now includes the Barcelona–ENP countries (Algeria, Morocco, Tunisia, Egypt, Jordan, Israel, West Bank and Gaza, Lebanon, Syria) and, since April 2011 the Stabilization and Association partners, i.e. the Western Balkans. The ultimate goal is to create a free-trade area for the Mediterranean, with a unified system of rules of origin, allowing, in principle for full cumulation (i.e. free sourcing from lowest cost producers, whether internal or external to the FTA).
17 On the implications of the different cumulation systems see Brenton (2003, 13) as well as the EU taxation website, Common provisions on rules of origin, available at http://ec.europa.eu/taxation_customs/customs/customs_duties/rules_origin/preferential/article_774_en.htm#cumulation
18 See Chapters 5 and 6 on the conceptualization of the different components of effectiveness.
19 The liberalization of trade flows between the EU and neighbors such as Egypt, Israel, Jordan, Morocco and Tunisia is almost complete; moreover rules of origin have, for example, been streamlined and homogenized (Grant 2011, 4).
20 The main problems of the EMP and the UfM revolve around the lack of a conditionality system, and, especially in the in the case of the UfM, around the excessive focus on uncontroversial areas of cooperation (Kausch and Youngs 2009).
21 Del Sarto points out, and indeed it is hard to disagree, that such an approach is inappropriate when dealing with the MENA countries, which have no interest in joining the Union (Del Sarto and Schumacher 2005, 36).
22 Ibid.
23 Author's interview with MENA management, WB HQ 2008.
24 The EU has granted Morocco 50 million Euros under the 2007–2013 ENPI for governance reforms (Kausch and Youngs 2009).
25 Commissioner Füle's Speech on events in North Africa to the EP Committee on Foreign Affairs, 28 February 2011, available at: http://europa.eu/rapid/pressReleasesAction.do?reference=SPEECH/11/130
26 Author's interview (June 2011).
27 Author's interview (June 2011).
28 Overall, however, the contributed effectiveness of the GO DPL has been limited, with development impact rated as 'moderately unsatisfactory' (Independent Evaluation Group 2014).
29 Only in 2005 was a model protocol adopted along the lines discussed in 2002, with a view to gradually extending diagonal cumulation to all EuroMed partners. Its implementation started in 2007, limited to some areas of the MENA region (Augier et al. 2009).
30 On the Egyptian case see Ghoneim and Kheir-El-Din (2006).
31 See O'Brien (2009), and De Wulf and Malizsewska (2009).
32 In the Commission Green Paper on The future of EU budget support to third countries (COM (2010) 586 final) budget support is defined as: '...the **transfer of financial resources** of an external financing agency to the National Treasury of a partner country, following the respect by the latter of agreed **conditions** for payment. The financial resources thus received are part of the global resources of the partner country, and consequently used in accordance with the public financial management system of the partner country.' (European Commission 2010b, 3, bold in original text)
33 According to the World Bank, fragility applies to low income country or territory, IDA eligible (including those countries which may currently be in arrears), with a CPIA (Country Policy and Institutional Assessment) score of 3.2 or below. Countries are considered 'core' fragile states if their CPIA is below 3.0 or there is no data available. Countries are considered 'marginal' fragile states if their CPIA score is between

3.0 and 3.2. These designations are meant to provide guidance to policymakers in working with those countries with weak governance and limited institutional capacity for development. The CPIA scores provide guidance on the 'spectrum' of fragility and should not be interpreted as definitive, particularly as there is some variation and margin of uncertainty in the CPIA scores themselves (World Bank 2011c). Since 2011, CPIA have been continuously revised, to address the multifaceted nature of fragility, conflict and violence-affected contexts under new demographic surges, forced displacement and climate challenges.

34 In the Failed States Foreign Policy Index, Israel/West Bank (*sic!*) ranks 53rd (with a score of 84 over a range between 0 and 120) in a list of 60 countries in descending order from most (score of 120) to least fragile (0): http://www.foreignpolicy.com/articles/2011/06/17/2011_failed_states_index_interactive_map_and_rankings. In other datasets the Territories are not even mentioned, Center for Systemic Peace (2015) available at http://www.systemicpeace.org/inscr/SFImatrix2015c.pdf. The World Bank lists the oPt under the category 'fragile situations', but does not provide CPIA scores as, deprived of state sovereignty, the PA-Palestinian territories are not a member to the Bank, see World Bank (2011c).

35 Author's interviews with mid- and top-Commission's officers, 2011. See also ADE (2008, Vol. IIa, Annex 4, 61, 62, 64).

36 I.e. the mediating body composed of UN, US, EU and Russia, constituted in Madrid, in 2002 to broker the implementation of cease-fire agreements previously negotiated between Israel and the Palestinians under the diplomatic brokerage of the US.

37 See Ehrenfeld (2003). Between 2003 and 2007 EUfunding, a UK-based NGO, issued multiple briefs to alert on alleged misuse of EU support to the oPt. The IMF was also questioned, for its involvement in the general monitoring on the management of budget support.

38 A similar point is made in Slaughter (2005, 184), quoting Canada's Finance Minister Paul Martin, on the nuanced aspects of effectiveness of both institutionalized IOs, such as the IMF, and more informal networks such as the G20. In either case, it is believed, the ultimate accountability tie runs from national governments to their citizens.

39 'The IMF does not "monitor foreign assistance" to the Palestinian Authority. It simply provides the EU with information about broad developments related to its budget. It does not monitor or control every item in the budget' (Dawson 2002).

40 Another EP critical minority report was also issued, which pointed to payments made to Palestinian Leader Arafat that had not been accounted for in the majority report see Tannock (2004), as well as http://www.eufunding.org/accountability/EUWorkingGroupReport.html. The 'minority' report is available at http://eufunding.org.uk/accountability/DraftConclusionsLaschet.pdf.

41 '. . . the Quartet envoy has a very limited mandate. In my case I thought that the mandate was greater and for a time people humored me by pretending that I did in fact have a mandate to go beyond economic development. But if you read carefully the terms of the Quartet envoy, it is essentially an economic post. It is not a political post.' (Wolfensohn, 2011)

42 Comments from Wolfensohn are obviously his own, but his special position (former President of the World Bank, American citizen involved in the process under request from the US President) may help to put them into perspective: 'I personally don't think that Hamas at that time was setting out to blow the whole thing up. I think there were mutual mistakes made. Maybe the Gaza withdrawal was premature in terms of preparing the public. My own view was there was a tremendous desire on the part of the Palestinians who were in Gaza to have a peaceful and real economic development. I do not say for a moment that there were not extremists who would have wanted to blow it up, both emotionally and physically, and that there were not people who didn't want to see peace. I have no doubt that there were some, just as there were on the Israeli side who didn't want to see the development of this location.' (Friedson 2009)

43 Again, particularly after Hamas gained control of the Gaza Strip since June 2007, the PEGASE mechanism was also retained as safer and more accountable with respect to its predecessor TIM to avoid funds being transferred to Hamas loyals. Funds could be channeled either through the Central Treasury Account (CTA) or disbursed directly to final recipients.

44 In 2013, donors to the PRDP-MDTF were: Australia, France, Kuwait, Norway, Japan and the UK, with Poland, Canada and Finland having provided funds only until 2010. The PRDP-MDTF's mandate was further extended in 2011, with the last tranche disbursed in August 2017.

45 Macroeconomic and financial oversight of implementation of the PRDP reform by the PA was provided by the IMF and the World Bank. Additionally, between 2002 and 2010 the Bank supported the PA's emergency social sector program for over eight years through the ESSP MDTF, financed by the EU, DFID, Spain, Italy, France, Belgium, Norway, Sweden, Australia, Austria, and Switzerland.

46 Before the approval of the PA National Cash Transfer Strategy in May 2010, social assistance was provided through a complex web of organizations run by the PA, including at least three ministries, non-governmental organizations, and other external agencies implementing a series of uncoordinated initiatives including cash assistance and food aid. This has inevitably led to wastage of resources and poor targeting of assistance (World Bank 2010c). Currently, however, the impact of the new support scheme is limited to West Bank, as payments in Gaza are still made under the EU and WB respective systems (World Bank 2010d).

9 The EU and the World Bank in Sub-Saharan Africa

Declining trust, role change and the challenges of coordinating under fragility

9.1 Introduction

In the 1990s the EU shifted its external focus eastward, towards transitioning countries, and gave further impetus to the Association Agreements with partners in the Maghreb. The Commission also issued a Green Paper (1996), to deal with the unsatisfactory results of the non-reciprocal provisions of the Lomé process (Holland 2002). A redefinition of the EU relations with long-standing ACP partners, however, only came about in the new millennium, with the Cotonou Agreement. Entered into force in June 2000, the Cotonou framework provided for the creation of reciprocal trade-liberalizing European Partnership Agreements (EPAs) between the EU and individual African countries, to be implemented across an eight-year period. In March 2001 Brussels backed the launching of two initiatives, the African Union (AU, in 2002) and the NEPAD. Since 9/11, the Union has also given prominence to enhanced political dialogue with ACP partners, specifically focusing on security-related issues, particularly the fight against terrorism and weapons of mass destruction (Carbone 2008, 34–35). In 2005 the Union entered into a comprehensive partnership with the AU, through the Africa–EU Partnership, followed in 2007 by the Joint Africa EU Strategy (JAES).[1] Linking North and Sub-Saharan countries under the same comprehensive framework marked a major redefinition in EU–Africa relations, as did the support that Brussels provided to peace processes in conflict-ridden countries post-9/11. An extant example of North–South 'deep' preferential system, the EPA system was generally praised for its progressive and inclusionary nature. Overall, however, the the Economic Partnership Agreements have also undergone early criticism under multiple angles (Bilal and Stevens 2009).

Within the analytical framework described in Chapters 5 and 6, the following sections investigate the EU performance-as-effectiveness in two areas that have featured prominently in the EU–WB cooperation in the SSA regional unit: the trade-development track and coordination to deliver aid in highly fragile contexts, respectively. Based on the context of hybrid delegation described in Chapters 2 and 3, and relying on role theory concepts discussed in Chapter 4, the following pages explore the policy and institutional innovation introduced by the Commission through an interactive process of role change, as emerged in the EU–WB discussions about the launch of the EU–Africa Infrastructure Trust Fund.[2] Section 9.2 briefly sketches the EU–WB cooperation in the Africa region, arguing about its relevance and peculiarity, relative to EU–WB relations in ECA and MENA. Section 9.3 addresses performance issues, and investigates the EU's policy consistency in trade and development in the EPA negotiations, providing insight on Brussels' contributed effectiveness. The section employs the evidence from interviews with World Bank high level officers to refine the analysis provided in the literature on the negotiations of the EPAs, exploring the relative goodness of normative-institutionalist, bargaining-realist and persuasion-based constructivist interpretations of that process. Sections 9.4 and 9.5 move the focus on donor coordination in fragile contexts, examining the EU–WB frictions on respective missions and accountabilities in Zimbabwe and Ethiopia. The analysis illustrates the challenge of donor coordination in politically unstable contexts, assessing the costs and benefits of EU direct vs World Bank-mediated aid delivery. Investigating the first EU attempt to sponsor its own financing facility in SSA, Section 9.6 explores the EU–World Bank interactions surrounding the creation of the EU Africa Infrastructure Trust Fund, launched in 2007 after much tension between the Commission and the World Bank's management. The analysis suggests that the critical receiving by the World Bank may have in the end reinforced a process of role change on the side of the Commission. Section 9.7 summarizes the EU's development results in the region, particularly relative to contributed effectiveness under both consistency and impact dimensions, and draws theoretical and policy implications.

9.2 The Africa challenge: enhancing EU–WB cooperation between development and security concerns

The World Bank Group has been a major provider of concessional financing to African partners, even if the dismal results of SAPs in the 1980s and 1990s have fueled severe criticism. Stagnating growth and deteriorating poverty trends in the region have led critics to ask for a redefinition of the 'Washington Consensus', and have plausibly influenced the trend to increase aid volumes to the poorest in the new millennium (Easterly 2007). The EU has been at the core of that effort, with a notable influence played by the Commission's bold approach to stimulate ODA increases in the 2002 Monterrey Conference on Financing for Development. Within the debate on the MDGs, the EU and the Bank strengthened their efforts to take an active part in the Paris–Accra agenda, on both scaling up and donor coordination issues.[3] The two IOs identified non-synergic overlaps and shifting accountability systems as key obstacles to their cooperation in Sub-Saharan Africa. They also acknowledged how donors' conflicting schemes and uncoordinated priority benchmarking for SSA countries had too often led to weak results and unnecessary waste of resources, perpetuating low capacity and diffused exclusion of the poor.

Taken together, the EU MS and the Bank account for half of the ODA going to Africa. Since April 2003, the EU (Commission) and the Bank (via the Africa region and PREM units) inaugurated a round of annual consultations, the 'Limelette Process', named after the Brussels' neighborhood where the first meeting took place, to share strategies on key development goals for Sub-Saharan Africa (in the fields of adjustment policies, budget support, infrastructure development and governance).[4] A consensus on the need for both the Bank and the Union to 'improve coordination in client countries' and to better harmonize their efforts has emerged from both sides.[5] As expected, in the eyes of high level Bank management, efforts from the EU to sustain the Paris agenda have been a most welcome development, touching upon key aspects of the Bank's development mission, such as aid harmonization and alignment in donors' strategies (World Bank 2007a). However, these priorities have at times been neglected in the course of the EU–WB interactions on the ground. The elaboration of joint strategies was quoted by voices from the World Bank as a needed move to address concerns from partner countries and NGOs. In addition to softening conditionality, the drive to coordinate with the EU on 'how to distribute the aid that we each give', is considered by the Bank as a constructive course to 'find a middle ground' with Brussels, to close the gap that – allegedly – divided the EU and the Bank 'fifteen years ago', when they appeared to be as 'night and day' with respect to aid policy styles.[6] Tellingly, the Paris Process, and the Limelette Process within it, has been perceived by most top officials as an unprecedented step, that has brought the Bank and the Union 'under the same umbrella for the first time'. The result of a learning process, the Limelette framework has appeared as largely taught from recipient countries, for whom confusion, delays and poor implementation often meant piles of forms to fill in and regulations to comply with. The difficulty in dealing with different bureaucratic requirements, specific to multiple donors, before funds could be disbursed and projects completed, has often undermined the impact of development efforts on the ground. 'A road is a road', and it may not matter who builds it if you have to go to school or to work. A sense of urgency emerged from the World Bank's side on the need to devise a shared strategy with the EU for the region, most plausibly stimulated by the close contact with the reality of development needs in client countries. Additionally, the sense of urgency has loomed large since the entry of new actors with different goals and aid policy styles has changed the market for development financing (in the words of a World Bank's interviewee: 'now China comes in and disrupts the convergence that has been achieved with so much difficulty').[7]

The 'China factor' has not always been framed as a threat, but the country's enhanced shareholding rights at the Board have certainly changed the balance between the Bank and the EU, leading them to strengthen their efforts to coordinate along the Agenda 2030 and implementation of the SDGs. Nonetheless, EU–World Bank relations on aid harmonization and donor coordination in Sub-Saharan Africa have been often punctuated by frictions. The debate on aid effectiveness bears witness to differences and contentious issues, at the strategic, policy-design, disbursement and implementation levels. Similar to other cases of frictional dynamics in the EU–WB relations (discussed in Chapter 7), the smooth nature of high level contacts on donor coordination, between DC and Brussels, has been at times contrasted with a cumbersome EU approach to implementation. In the words of World Bank interviewees, 'overly bureaucratic' and 'slow' have been used to describe 'the nature of the beast: the EU is very bureaucratic, and foreign aid is not an exception'.[8]

Different from the MENA and ECA regions, Sub-Saharan African partners have never enjoyed the incentive of either accession or association. While better targeted since the EU Strategy for Africa (European Commission 2005), the EU relations with SSA do not entail the depth of engagement that characterize its ties with the candidate and neighboring countries. EU MS, particularly the UK and France, but also Belgium and to a smaller scale Italy, have paid special attention to consolidating their relations with former African colonies, often along national priorities. At times, this has spelled an alignment between EU delegates in the field with the policies and strategies of their countries of origin, rather than with Brussels. Finally, and particularly relevant for the EU–WB relations, donor coordination between the Union and the Bank is not bound to follow EU-predefined frameworks as in the Neighborhood and candidate countries. Higher flexibility exists, along with the potential to innovate on harmonization, as shown by the progress achieved under the Limelette process. The flip side of the coin is that such room for manoeuvre has opened the way to frictions when the two organizations' respective approaches have not appeared immediately compatible.

9.3 The debate on the EPAs: mistaking trade liberalization for development promotion?

Listed as trade agreements, the EPAs were originally intended to promote free trade between the EU and SSA partners, supplying a WTO-compatible framework to cushion the regressive impact from non-reciprocal treatment under the Lomé Conventions (Brenton et al. 2008, 3). Consistent with the Cotonou Framework, the EPAs lump together normative claims about free trade, security, development and good governance promotion. The involved DGs (particularly Agriculture on the one side, DG DEVCO and DG Trade on the other, respectively) held different views on which issues should receive priority. MS preferences also diverged. The UK and the Nordics sided in the pro-free trade–pro-development camps, opposed by the Southern and new members, who advocated for a more passive EU approach. France stood somewhat in the middle, endorsing a pro-development stance through continued protection, while Germany spoke for a pure free-trade approach. Different from past practice, according to which DG DEVCO (then DG VIII) would conduct negotiations with the ACP group, the mandate to negotiate the EPAs was given by the Council to DG Trade (Elgström 2008). The change was however compensated by a revision in the Directorate's organigramme, expanded to include a trade division, previously belonging to DG VIII. The rationale was to support a process where trade priorities, on top of the negotiating agenda of both the Commission and MS, could be realistically infused with development objectives, returning the image of an EU which was both a promoter of liberalism and a friendly supporter of development (idem, 11). Against the background of the ongoing war on terror, norms on human rights, governance and security were also included, to emphasize the political dimension of the process (Carbone 2008).

The Trade Group of the World Bank Research Unit (DECRG-Trade) and, later, a pool of trade specialists within the Anchor Unit PREM (Poverty Reduction and Economic Management), had worked for a while on the nature and implications of the early 1990s wave in regional trade integration (de Melo and Panagaryia 1992). Praising the beneficial aspects of 'deep' trade opening, their work qualified policy advice to the EU under several respects (Schiff 2002). Their conclusions also contributed to rebalance the image of the World Bank as an indefatigable supporter of trade liberalization. Their concerns about the EPAs, questioned the development implications of North–South agreements that expected joint negotiations with the EU from such a diverse set of country groupings. Warnings were voiced about the adverse effects from adding the requirements of vertical EU–SSA EPAs to those stemming from the 'spaghetti bowl'-like intricate network of horizontal RTAs already in place among the SSA partners (Winters 2002; De La Rocha 2003).

The pro-poor effect of the EU's trade policies in the region was also questioned, based on the meager outcomes of the special EU treatment granted to the group of least developed countries (LDCs) through the EBA (Everything But Arms) Scheme. Launched by the Union in 2000 to ameliorate the development effect of preference-granting under the GSP System, EBA has the undeniable merit of an indefinite duration, which entails the possibility of encouraged export diversification and a balanced integration into the wider world economy. Overall, the Scheme was criticized for exempting three products (sugar, bananas and rice) of particular importance to the non-ACP LDCs. The complexity of the EU regulations had raised the LDCs' cost of compliance to prohibitive levels, to the effect that utilization rates amounted only to 50% of EU imports from non-ACP LDCs, and were close to nil for the ACP group in the first year of implementation of the scheme (Brenton 2003). Apparently, most LDCs from the ACP group had preferred to rely on the existing Cotonou Framework, available to the overall ACP group, yet limited in duration, narrower in product coverage and costlier to implement. More relevant, the Cotonou Framework targeted sectors where the majority of ACP LDCs' exports already entered the EU under zero MFN tariff. Finally, the EBA Scheme had a more restrictive system of rules of origin (diagonal cumulation with value added requirement), compared to the Cotonou System which in fact granted the possibility to apply full cumulation rules to ACPs' exports to the Union.[9] While acknowledging the instrumental role played by EBA in opening the way to similar preferential systems (US AGOA – African Growth and Opportunity Act, and a similar Canadian system), World Bank trade studies returned a cautious view on the development implications of the EU's new approach to trade liberalization with the LDCs.

Overall, the EPAs have ingrained positive lock-in mechanisms in several African partners, allowing for a notable amount of flexibility (as acknowledged in the Agreements, recalling the 'variable geometry' metaphor). Trade research from World Bank experts on the subsequent evolutions of the EPA processes has also praised the eventual removal of restrictive ROOs in the interim agreements (IEPAs), identifying their high technicality as a major institutional impediment to developing competitive sectors in several African countries (Brenton, Newfarmer and Hoppe 2008). Notwithstanding these ameliorations, however, progress has stalled and negotiations have been marked by EU 'threats' against the countries that have not ratified their EPAs after the initialization of respective agreements.[10]

The EPAs' vague mandate and normative claims on trade liberalization as a development strategy have been explained by resorting to internal ('consensus norm') and external ('normative entrapment') factors (Elgström 2008). As discussed above, both sets of elements have been at play in the EPAs overall design and can account for its ambiguity. However, as discussed above, World Bank research and policy units (not its regional, operational units, however[11]) had since long issued critical reflections on the EU's envisaged trade schemes: not enough was done, so it was thought, to assess the implications of the proposed framework to support competitiveness in African Partners, in spite of the repeated references to reaching WTO-compatible agreements under reciprocal terms (Orbie and Faber 2011). By and large, the EPAs have raised doubts about the ability of the EU to ensure horizontal policy consistency, between its trade and development priorities.

Analyses on the IEPAs have also signaled a low level of EU inter-institutional consistency. Compromising between the earlier purist, liberalizing approach of DG Trade and a more development-friendly strategy, the EPA negotiations had to accommodate requests from the Nordics (plus the Netherlands and, particularly, the UK), also allowing some role to DG DEV in the negotiations with the ACP partners (Elgström 2008, 17–20). The final EPA institutional architecture has several drawbacks. Due to the lack of infrastructure and high transport costs, and given the high tariff and non-tariff barriers still existing in the region, the implementation of trade liberalization measures included in the IEPAs has been expected to produce trade diversion, from either third party sources or even local producers, with a transfer of tariff revenue away from poor African consumers to EU (comparatively less efficient) producers (Brenton et al. 2008).

In the opinion of the World Bank's trade experts, the EU should reduce ROOs' restrictiveness, support reform efforts by ACP partners through 'aid for trade' to tackle internal constraints to competitiveness and, finally, postpone the implementation of the envisaged reductions until countries have substantially liberalized to MFN levels across the Africa region. In several instances the agreements have already been signed, so that the practical recommendation to the African partners is to start to liberalize and reform as soon as possible, to minimize the impact of EPAs regressive effects on domestic economies (Andriamanajara et al. 2009). By advising the weakest partners to liberalize unilaterally, once preferential rules have already been agreed on, these World Bank studies have shown in full the economic downsides of the EU's EPAs with Sub-Saharan Africa.

Beyond the promotion of trade liberalization, the EU's role in the region, however, has gained political traction, particularly since the launch of Africa–EU Partnership. Donors' coordination in general, and EU–World Bank cooperation in particular, in conflict-torn African states have become priority goals. A mixed picture has emerged, however, about the quality and effectiveness of the EU–WB interaction, both at the high strategic level, through the Paris process, and in partner countries. Coordinating in highly unstable contexts has proven particularly challenging, unveiling profound differences in the accountability systems of the two organizations, as shown by the analysis of their interaction in Zimbabwe and Ethiopia, the subject of the next two sections.

9.4 The EU and the WB in Zimbabwe: coordinating under fragility

The tensions between the EU and the World Bank about continuing development assistance to Zimbabwe between the late 1990s and 2002 indicate how differences in the two organizations' respective mandates have at times hindered cooperation where it was most needed. The situation was further complicated by the lack of trust by the ZANU–PDF Government led by Robert Mugabe in the EU and World Bank assistance programs. Refusal by the Government to follow along financing procedures required by the Bank was behind its decision to leave the country in October 2000, stopping lending on most lines. Such withdrawal bore the criticism of the EU. The Union did not approve of the Bank suspending the implementation of Trust Funds to which it was a substantial contributor, on grounds that it did not share and that did not correspond to the EU own political mandate in Zimbabwe.[12] Additionally, Brussels was worried about continuing its own cooperation programs without the backing provided by the Bank's presence in the country.

The Union had long worked to establish an inclusive dialogue with Zimbabwe, to accommodate the country's preferences after independence from the UK, gained in 1980 at the end of decade-long civil war. The EU had also publicly claimed to pursue a course independent from that sponsored by the Washington-based IFIs. In the early 1990s, from the early start of its new support program for Zimbabwe under the revised Lomé Convention (IV Protocol), the Union officially distanced itself from the 'overly rigid approach to adjustment of the Washington institutions' (CEC-DG VIII, 1996 in Brown 1999, 76), claiming its 'ideological neutrality' with respect to development 'doctrines, be they neo-liberal or otherwise' (CEC-DG VIII, 1992, quoted in Brown, 1999, 76).[13] However, some EU MS successfully pressured to subject the implementation of the EU programs to the approval of Zimbabwe as eligible for continuation of support under World Bank and, particularly, IMF programs. Both official data on the amount devoted to structural adjustment within the overall EU package for Zimbabwe under Lomé IV between 1990 and 1995, approximately 50% of the total, as well as interviews with relevant officials, have questioned the EU ability to set and consistently follow an independent course in the country during those years (Brown 1999, 87). Apparently, Brussels had provided a 'fairly rigid and slow response' to the requests of the Zimbabwean Government about relaxing the strict criteria that were attached to the use of the Counterpart Funds (local currency equivalent of the foreign exchange provided by the Union), criteria that were deemed 'unnecessarily restrictive' even by World Bank's officials (Brown 1999, 87). All in all, limited political gains were reaped, in spite of the fact that the EC had been the third donor to the country between 1980 and 2002, providing almost 141 million USD, after Germany (337 million USD) and Japan (166 million USD) (Leo and Moss 2009, 21).

After the World Bank's withdrawal in the fall of 2000, the Union proceeded along the lines of political dialogue well beyond infringing the basic principles that it had set for itself. In spite of pressures from the UK to take a tougher stance on the violations of human rights and basic democratic principles perpetrated under the Mugabe regime, the Union decided to postpone the adoption of negative sanctions. Notwithstanding the failure of consultations ex article 96 of the Cotonou Agreement in the fall of 2001, Brussels declared its support to the efforts of the SADC (Southern African Development Community) and the Abuja process towards a normalization in Zimbabwe (Smith 2006, 10). Only upon a further aggravation of the situation, which included the expulsion from the country of the then head of the EU observer mission, Pierre Schori, did the EU resort to negative inducements, in the hope that the pressure would lead Mugabe and his entourage to end their oppressive ruling.[14] While critical of the early withdrawal of the Bank, therefore, the EU had its own problems in dealing with the deteriorating situation in Zimbabwe.

As noted above, the Government of Robert Mugabe had blatantly mistrusted external donors, so that even the slightest communication issues were to be handled very skillfully by the external actors in the country. The context also presented donors with a number of challenges, which, in addition to slow budgetary processes, included the effects of very severe droughts in 1992 and 1995 and, most importantly, the disastrous consequences of the land reform. Initiated in the late 1980s, and subsequently turned into the Land Acquisition Reform of 1992, the reform had deteriorated into what was called by the government in 2000 a 'Fast track resettlement program'. While the debate on its effects was highly polarized,[15] there seems little doubt that agricultural production and exports had drastically fallen since 2000 (with the exception of a rise in production in 2005/6 as a result of good rainfall), raising food and tenure insecurity to alarming levels. In 2009, and based on food assistance levels of the time, the IFRC estimated that 75% of Zimbabweans (9 over 12 millions) would face severe hunger (while mid-income, according to the World Bank classification, the country ranked third after Afghanistan and Ethiopia in food aid levels in that year) (IFRC 2009). In 2011 Zimbabwe still ranked 157 out of 183 countries in the World Bank 'Doing Business' database. An African Development Bank (AfDB) country brief explicitly linked such low achievement to 'the land policy reform and indigenization law' (AfDB 2011, 7).

The mistrust of Zimbabwe's Government about concessional loans was further exacerbated by the meager results of the reforms advised by the Bank and the Fund. Based on appraisals by an evaluation group set up ad hoc by the IMF

(1998), growth targets outlined in the 1991 Zimbabwe's ESAP (Economic Structural Adjustment Program) appeared largely unrealistic to achieve the expected reduction of budget deficit. The World Bank also prompted the Government to speed up liberalization and trade opening, upon which the disbursement of additional tranches was made conditional (Brown 1999). The timing of trade reform had a particularly adverse impact on Zimbabwe's economy, with goods from import-competing industries quickly replaced by more competitive imported products. The expected improvement in growth rates did not materialize, and neither did the planned cuts in budget deficit. Worse, the Government's cuts in social expenditures exacerbated the country's already precarious social balance. In contrast with such critical reading of the Bank's allegedly too rigid application of conditionality clauses, a subsequent Country Assistance Evaluation (CAE) from the World Bank Operations Evaluation Department (OED) indicated that in fact the Bank had relied too much 'on commitments from technocrats in the absence of political consensus for reforms' (OED 2004, vi). The OED CAE remarked how 'in the absence of will from the political leadership, the World Bank should have insisted that conditions be fulfilled and not proceed to lend on the basis of promises' (ibid.). While not uniformly negative, the evidence on the World Bank's role in supporting Zimbabwe out of its development deadlock was at best mixed.

Similar to other fragile African countries, development support by the EU and the Bank in Zimbabwe has been subject to several constraints. Multiple issues were lumped together with the task of promoting development, particularly supporting democratic transition in a post-colonial milieu, where people had been coerced for decades into one among the most racist regimes of that period (British Rhodesia). Serious regime fragility, and a virtually absent respect for the rule of law complicated the picture: the British system had generated severe inequalities among the white minority, which owned 70% of the land, and the then disenfranchised black majority. Deep-seated animosity by the black majority was skillfully manipulated by President Mugabe. After an apparently promising start, through the Land Acquisition Act of 1992, Mugabe had turned land redistribution into brutal confiscations and, in the end, mass looting. In spite of an initial good start in economic policy, and different from other former British colonies, where enabling conditions had helped the elites to contain centrifugal forces through a viable constitutional system, Zimbabwe was now facing the collapse of its institutional system.

Ranking eighth, over a total of 141 weakest states in the Brookings-CGD ranking (Rice and Patrick 2008), Zimbabwe was also considered one among the most fragile states by the World Bank. As discussed in Chapter 8 on the EU–World Bank cooperation in the oPt, supporting homegrown development in fragile contexts both magnifies and intensifies the challenges faced by external players, compared to contexts where institutional vulnerability is not a binding issue. The very absence of a reliable counterpart in the negotiations severely curtails the role that external actors can play in fragile environments. The OED remarks quoted above exemplify a more general sort of criticism raised against Bank programs that have entailed ongoing relations between the Washington-based institution and crooked elites in partner countries, to little development effect. Relative to the case of Zimbabwe, the 'fragile state' *problématique* has been further compounded with the differences in the official approaches that the World Bank and the Union officially stated that they would follow in their relations with the country. The wavering of the Union between the poles of economic-cum-political conditionality along the lines of the earlier IMF and WB structural adjustment programs in the 1980s and mid-1990s, and its own 'distinctive' approach to conditionality in the subsequent period, contributed to shape a context where the major donors were split along two different camps. The major cleavage was, at least until 2002, between positive and negative inducements to obtain a cooperative response from the Government of Robert Mugabe.

On the EU's side, the divisions between the group of Northern MS, asking for sanctions, and that of Southern states, which favoured a continuation of the dialogue, had greatly reduced the impact of the consultation procedure ex art. 96 of the Cotonou Agreement invoked by Brussels in 2002 (Smith 2006). Additionally, the two institutions wielded substantially different incentives, reflecting their respective missions and most immediate goals. The World Bank management was, in the end, bound to respect the Bank's operational criteria, without much flexibility to work around arrear payments beyond what the Board allowed. Under conditions of high country indebtedness and in times of extreme political duress, the only tool in the hands of the Bank is to suspend loans and resort to technical assistance and humanitarian aid, managing programs funded by other donors. No major positive incentives, short of technical and humanitarian-emergency assistance, are therefore available when a country moves to what is defined as 'non accrual' status (longer than six months arrears on debt repayments).

Differently, the Union has at its disposal a range of both positive and negative inducements. It can also diversify between political and economic conditionality, and try, through gradual steps, with different degrees of pressure. Brussels' preference has broadly gone to positive incentives and normative suasion, with the resorting to sanctions limited to conditions of severe human rights violations and deterioration of core democratic principles. Criticism and distance from other regional African partners was certainly a major reason behind the failure of the EU approach to help Zimbabweans (Smith 2006). In addition, the EU and the Bank were not on the same side between 2000 and 2002, as the former had to resort to negative pressure through withdrawal, while the latter continued through positive pressure for a longer time before shifting to negative inducements. To the broad critical evaluation of poor timing in supporting reforms, the OED CAS claims that 'Additionally the World Bank's willingness to lend sent the wrong message to the client and to the partners' (OED 2004, vi). The absence of a homogeneous, aligned pressure (either on the negative or the positive line) had doomed the prospect for effective joint action.

The extreme aversion of Robert Mugabe's government to external aid suggests particular caution in drawing general inferences on the EU–World Bank cooperation in Zimbabwe over that span of time. However, some of the elements discussed above also apply to other cases of cooperation between the two institutions in fragile contexts. From a development angle, the challenge is to identify which elements of coordination under fragility are crucial for the success of external assistance. From a policy analytic perspective, the issue is why and how the two organizations have followed those particular courses, and how their interactions have eventually impacted on their institutionally codified practices.

9.5 Trusting no more? Delays and disagreements over the implementation of the Productive Safety Nets Program in Ethiopia

Albeit formally bound to political neutrality, the World Bank has been often considered by the Union as a vehicle for channeling funds under difficult political conditions in partner countries, i.e. when the Union was not able (or willing) to engage because of outright violations of human rights or democratic principles. The case of EU channeling through WB managed Trust Funds in West Bank and Gaza, discussed in the previous chapter on the MENA region, and, in Sub-Saharan Africa, the case of Ethiopia, are two core examples of this sort.

On general counts, the choice of WB-managed Trust Funds over other channeling options in highly fragile countries has been motivated on multiple grounds. Among them, the political need to avoid enmeshing with suspect mass killers and serial violators of human rights. In Ethiopia, the EU participated to the WB-managed PSNP Trust Fund (Productive Safety Nets Program), aimed at addressing food insecurity, through the support of a reform program for meeting the Poverty and Hunger MDG. Established by the WB in 2005 upon request by the Ethiopian Government, the fund was managed by this latter.[16] In spite of the long-term engagement of the Commission in Ethiopia (1976), channeling through a WB-managed Trust Fund was seen in 2005 as the only alternative to pool a substantial amount of funds under the guidance of an agent of proven experience in coordinating large groups of donors (even if not necessarily specialized in providing food aid). The main reason was that 'donors were required to stop funding' – i.e. provide direct budget support, after the election of May 2005 (ADE 2008, Vol. IIa, Annex IV, 12, 22).[17] The World Bank appeared at the time as the best intermediary between the Ethiopian Government (which had requested that it took that role) and a group of donors (in addition to the WB and EC, DFID, Irish Aid, Sida, CIDA) that relied on its expertise on fund pooling and on harmonization among different national approaches. With expected significant cost benefits (charged administrative costs for the PSNP were about 0.5% to 2%, depending on phases), the World Bank's technical assistance also provided help to compensate the weaknesses of the Ethiopian Government in fund absorption. Above all, channeling through the World Bank's Trust Fund track enabled the Commission to continue spending from the EDF (which it would not be able to do in a context where budget support was not a viable option, as it was the case in Ethiopia then).

Indeed, regarding the EU (EC) contribution to World Bank-managed PBS (Protection of Basic Services) Trust Fund for Ethiopia since 2007, explicit reference has been made to its role as a substitute for direct budget support, after the shocking episodes of massive violence perpetrated by the Zenawi government following the elections of May 2005 (ADE 2008, Vol. IIa, Annex 4, 22). 'Continuity of aid delivery in a difficult context', along with 'maintaining a close control of the expenditure and providing additional accountability (trust) are quoted as the main reasons for the choice of the WB managed PBS as an alternative to global budget support by the Commission (ADE 2008, Vol. IIa, Annex 8, Country Mission to Ethiopia, slide 8).[18] In turn, the Commission's participation had apparently a catalytic effect in reassuring other bilateral donors about the importance of their continued presence. Complementarity of roles, the EU as a leader in political dialogue and generous donor, and the Bank as the conveyor of funds to unstable governments in difficult times, is, however, just a part of a broader picture. Transaction and implementation costs turned out to be higher than expected, and burdened the interaction between the EU and the World Bank, which was further troubled by the serious weaknesses on the side of the Ethiopian Government, particularly in reporting about the financial implementation of the program.

As discussed in Chapter 2, one of the most contested issues in the EU–WB relation has been the visibility of the Commission/EU channeled funds. Through its policy of unearmarking, the Bank has since long clarified that it could not restrict the use of funds mobilized through its trusts funds to specific activities or in specific regions or countries. Conversely, the Commission has been keen on having its channeled funds tied to the EU's own strategies and priorities. In addition to accountability issues, disagreement on visibility clauses has also spelled lengthy negotiations of Administrative Agreements between the EU and the Bank on specific Trust Funds. Furthermore, references to different interpretations of specific provisions in the overall Framework Agreement have caused delays in implementation, making the choice of World Bank-managed Trust Fund less effective than expected. PBS and PSNP (phase II) in Ethiopia appear as two prominent examples of how contrasting views on visibility have impaired EU–WB cooperation.[19] Albeit a very generous donor to the PSNP (Euros 79 million for the first two years, out of an annual budget of Euros 220 million, ADE 2008, Vol.IIa, Annex 3, 13), the Commission has been the only donor to complain about having been given lower than expected visibility. The Bank, on its side, 'considered visibility requirements ... fulfilled'. While other donors and the Ethiopian government were fully aware of the EU's contributions, the final recipients were not, as they perceived their Government as the source of those resources. The issue raised concerns in Brussels, while, in the eyes of the Bank, the occurrence appeared in line with the management procedures of World Bank RETFs (Recipient Executed Trust Funds), customarily administered by recipient governments.

Over time, the World Bank approach has gathered a higher consensus, particularly since the adoption of the Paris–Accra Agenda. Demand-driven policies, owned by partners, have been advocated to increase aid effectiveness, the rationale being that reducing the number of restrictions placed by donors and embedding aid policies in the partner country system limits aid fragmentation and improves outcomes on the ground. As in the EU–WB cooperation over managing the effects of the economic crisis in new members and candidate countries (see Chapter 7), communicative action has developed between the two actors through the development of the 'notional approach', according to which the Commission can specify its preference about the use of funding, but overall accepts that its channeled money is entirely fungible within a given World Bank managed Trust Fund. In turn, the Bank takes into account these preferences by devoting 'at least a proportion of the total TF budget equal to the Commission's preferred contribution' (ADE 2008, Vol. I, 38). Subsequently, further progress has occurred, as the two organizations have agreed to specifically support country ownership in dealing with EU visibility issues. At the level of official discourse, they also have successfully resorted to delegating to donors' 'discretion' the particular size and type of community outreach that is linked to visibility, displaying a notably higher level in reciprocal trust (EC–WBG 2009, 3). Also relevant is the fact that such increased trust does not appear to be a mere by-product of the Paris–Accra process on donor coordination, but is explicitly situated 'in the context of the special EC (now EU)–WB relationship' (EC–WBG 2009, 1). On the other side, in spite of clear inputs on the importance of strategic coordination with the Bank at high levels and stronger cooperation in the field (ADE 2008, Vol. I), continuous detailed reference to material elements of visibility (flags, banners, procedures for press releases) that should be followed by implementing agencies, including international organizations, has left the impression that the EU is more concerned with procedural rather than strategic issues regarding its role in WB Trust Funds.

Resorting to WB-managed Trust Funds for political reasons (to avoid engagement with regimes that violate human rights and basic governance requirements) may be the right move under emergency conditions, and in the absence of viable alternatives (which seemed to be the case for Ethiopia in 2006, before the creation of the DCI by the Union). However, that same choice has a built-in flip side: the World Bank cannot formally engage in political dialogue, so that objectives attached to its actions cannot logically be expected by the Union from shifting to the sole Bank's Trust Fund channels.[20] Moreover, as shown by the case of Zimbabwe between 2000 and 2002, the Bank's specific mandate requires it to withdraw funds on grounds of concerns about financial reliability, even in the absence of outright human rights violations, which could obviously hinder the attainment of EU broader (political) goals.

It clearly appears how 'the WB' [could] 'not be an unconstrained agent of the European Union': while the EU somehow 'has to engage in political dialogue, the World Bank's explicitly non-political mandate prevents it from engaging in political dialogue'.[21] True, the degree of discretion enjoyed by the leaders of each organization varies according to multiple factors. With increased discretion, however, tighter monitoring from the counterpart can also be expected. Relative to their activities in Zimbabwe, the Bank was criticized by the Union for having withdrawn too early, on matters of financial liability that, plausibly, were perceived as below the Commission's own alert thresholds at that time.[22] On the contrary, it was the Commission that suspended disbursement to the Ethiopia PSNP in 2006, lamenting the weak accountability 'coverage' provided by the Bank. The point made by World Bank sources was that the Washington-based IFI had not shirked on its mandate as a fiduciary intermediary, as it had stuck with its non-political mission and adhered to the contractual requirements of its routine lending, which asked for guarantees from the final recipients on how the loans were to be repaid and funds implemented. In 2006, lamenting poor timing and quality in the reporting about how funds were spent, the Commission suspended its disbursement, followed by other donors, causing delays in the scheduled implementation of the PSNP for that year. The matter re-opened the debate on the relative benefits that the EU could derive from channeling through the Bank's Trust Fund system. While the Bank offered comparatively lower management costs, providing 'fiduciary comfort' and a single interlocutor in highly unstable Ethiopia at that time, it had not been able – in the opinion of the Commission – to supply enough guarantees on how effectively funds would be spent and, ultimately, on who should be responsible for the achieved outcomes. The cost of obtaining (and interpreting) reliable financial reporting, as well as of monitoring the implementation of the program in the field (only one staff was deployed by the Commission) proved too high for the Union, that engaged lengthy discussions with the Bank's managers on the specifics of the Administrative Agreement that regulated the relation between the two organizations in Ethiopia.

A particularly contentious issue was the divergence between the EU and the WB respective definitions of 'final recipient' of allocated funds. While the World Bank holds the recipient country as liable for the repayment and use of funds under its managed programs-projects, the Union expects the proximate receiver of its channeled funds (i.e. the Bank, in this particular case) to reimburse them in cases of misuse, even when this stems from corruption or wrongdoing on the side of the partner country. Formally, each institution was backed in its own view by specific *interna corporis*. More precisely, the Bank makes a distinction between own-executed Trust Funds (BETF, Bank Executed Trust Funds), where it has a specific trustee role ('involving its responsibility for managing, investing and administering the funds on behalf of and for the benefit of others (including procurement, reporting on progress made and so forth'), and, respectively, RETF (Recipient Executed Trust Funds) and FIFs (Financial Intermediary Funds) (ADE 2008, Vol. I, 63), where its functions are closer to those customarily attributed to fiscal agents (which are 'responsible for ensuring the disbursement from one entity to another ... [but not for] monitoring the use of funds by the recipients, [while still providing] limited report on the holding, investment and transfer of funds', ADE 2008, Vol. I, 63). On the contrary, the EU, through the Commission, is retained accountable under the Financial Regulation on the use of funds from its general budget, and, as discussed in Chapter 2 with respect to WB channeled funds, has also been questioned on the matter by the Parliament.

In this respect, the EU relates itself to the World Bank exactly as a principal would to its contracted agent, and therefore expects it to provide reporting and hold liabilities for the funds channeled as in a regular delegation process from a hierarchically superior actor to an agent selected among many others. However, as shown by the quarrels over respective roles and responsibilities in Zimbabwe and Ethiopia, the role expectation that the EU retains on the Bank – as well as its own role conception in the matter – differs from the Bank's own role conception and its expectations of the EU's behavior. As discussed in Section 5 of Chapter 2, the accountability streams that are established upon the FA and related AAs do not technically fall into the vertical system of delegated authority from member states to an international organization, rather qualifying as horizontal ties between two equal international agents. Furthermore, and very different from what happens in the World Bank, the accountability system within the EU tends to shorten the distance between ultimate principals (EU citizens) and each subsequent agent in the delegation chain, so that legitimacy issues pertaining to the EU-own financing system are passed on straight to the Bank.

Both sides have taken steps to address the issue, but the avenues explored have been indicative of multiple strategies, not always pointing in the same direction (World Bank 2011b). On the one side, as discussed in Chapter 7 on the EU–WB cooperation in the ECA region, there is a high level will from both sides to overcome the technical difficulties stemming from clashes between respective accountabilities through a problem-solving approach, which marks a difference with past bargaining over diverging preferences.[23] A discussion of the full implications of the replication of a similar approach in Sub-Saharan Africa is beyond the scope of this chapter. Particularly, aside from social, economic and political differences, a comparison between the conditions in the new EU MS and in the African partners would reveal a number of structural differences. Nonetheless, the case-specific evidence discussed above on the difficulties of EU–WB joint financing in fragile countries that do not have the option of accession seems to show that a more pragmatic approach could greatly improve the situation on the ground.

Paradoxically, the lighter political approach that the EU has devised for Sub-Saharan Africa, compared to that adopted with neighbors, and more so with new members and candidate countries, put the EU both at a disadvantage and at an advantage with respect to the Bank. On the one side, the Union, and particularly the Commission, did not enjoy the leverage that it holds, with varying degrees, in the ECA candidates, potential candidates and neighbors. In comparative terms, this obviously weakens the influence that the EU can exert on the World Bank's sponsored solutions. On the other side, the absence of a comparably strong political mandate allows Brussels to engage in a more equal dialogue with the Bank, and to push harder to define its role in a region where member states still enjoy wide margins of independent action. The tensions about the implementation of the PSNP in Ethiopia seem to show that 'the use of a WB TF is not the only solution for pool funding' and that 'in the future other channels could now be envisaged' (ADE 2008, Vol. IIa, Annex 8, Country Mission to Ethiopia, Debriefing). Additionally, the high transaction costs experienced in Ethiopia worked against further pre-commitments between the two organizations, so that maintaining 'flexibility to allow a case by case approach' was the solution suggested to the Commission by an independent evaluation mission sent to Ethiopia in 2008. Other perplexities had arisen with respect to the field outcomes of the PSNP. The same evaluation suggested that the outcomes of the program had been rather uneven up to then. The PSNP had provided an opportunity to train contributing actors in donor harmonization, achieving several basic objectives (broad reduction of the number of food insecure citizens, shielding from the draught shock of 2008, building of new community infrastructures). However, no information was available on the main objective of the PSNP in terms of the exact number of beneficiaries graduating out of food insecurity.

Chosen in 2004 under the pressing need to reduce food insecurity towards the attainment of the MDGs, the World Bank channeling option was the response to the unavailability of other solutions from the EU side. Along with other, broader concerns, the mixed records of the PSNP experience contributed a further input into the gradual evolution of a new financing tool devised by Brussels towards Sub-Saharan partners. Upon successful efforts by the Commission, and particularly by DG DEV, the first EU-sponsored multidonor Trust Fund for the Africa region (Africa Infrastructure Trust Fund, AITF) was about to be launched.

9.6 EU–World Bank frictions over the EU–AITF: role change in the Commission and the blending approach to EU development finance in Africa

Since 2007, the Commission has set its own, independent course towards the establishment of EU-managed financing facilities. Through its starting grants, the aim is one of leveraging loans from different potential donors, public and private. As seen above, pursuant to the proactive impetus already provided through the Development Consensus of 2005, the Commission had also played a major role to strengthen the existing network of EU special relationships with African countries, via the launch of the Joint Africa–EU Strategy in 2007. While being pivotal in the endeavor, DG DEV also played a key role to support the political partnership with Africa with an EU own funding facility. Created with the joint energies of the Commission and the EIB, the EU Africa Infrastructure Trust Fund is aimed at supporting the building of infrastructure networks across Sub-Saharan Africa, with the objective of promoting regional integration, which is deemed key to spur Africa's development. Set up with a minimum capital requirement of as low as Euros 500 mn in 2007, the EU–AITF has increased its total amount in grant operations to Euros 110.6 mn in 2010, for a cumulated Euros 208.9 mn over the period 2007–2010. According to the 2010 EU–AITF Annual Report, prepared by the EIB, and verified by an external financial auditor, the multiplier effect of the grant portion amounted to 12.7 for the period between 2007 and 2010, suggesting that the grant operations financed by the Union had facilitated 12 new infrastructure projects. In turn the Project Financing Group (PFG) multiplier amounted to 7.2 over the same time span, indicating that for each Euro provided in grants by the Union, seven additional Euros had been raised in loans by eligible donors (EU–Africa Infrastructure Trust Fund Annual Report 2010).

The relevance of this innovation, indeed the first step on the EU side towards blending loans and grants, pooling and leveraging resources from different donors under the umbrella of EU institutions, rests more in the process that led to its creation, at more than ten years since its inception, than in its achievements on the ground. The EU–AITF has marked a clear success for the EU in political terms. According to high level DG DEV sources involved in the AITF launch at the time, the main goal of the Commission was not to antagonize the extensive work done by the Bank in the Africa region, but to widen the market where the Union offered its grants, as well as to expand the scope of its actions in a region where EU delegations had long been actively cultivating political relations. In fact, the decision to proceed with an own EU sponsored Trust Fund was also a way for the Commission to gradually rebalance the gap between the resources that it channeled through the World Bank Trust Fund track and the absence of EU shareholding right in Washington. While accounting for the relative majority of the contributions to the World Bank via the collective weight of EU-cum-MS financial efforts, the Commission could not exert a matching leverage when key decisions had to be made at the Board.

The debate that ensued with the Bank on the establishment of a new EU new blending facility for Africa at some point landed on particularly confrontational terms, involving patent criticism against the Commission, from both the World Bank Presidency and relevant VPs. The move was seen as a 'war declaration', an indication that the EU had chosen to 'go it alone' about a business that was perceived as being the special preserve of the World Bank.[24] Instead of backing up, DG DEV top levels read the World Bank opposition to the planned EU–AITF as a confirmation that their attempt to redefine the role of the Commission, and, more broadly, of the Union, as a strategic grant-provider, leverage agent and manager of pooled development funds was in fact to be matched by similar role expectation from the 'main role holder in town', i.e. the World Bank. External criticism from the actor who had been since then perceived as the major multilateral gatekeeper of funds to Africa gave an additional boost to DG DEV self-awareness. First, DG DEV management had succeeded in projecting its new role conception for the Commission in the eyes of the Bank, based on an agreement with the EIB and, subsequent support from traditionally critical member states such as the UK, which, in this case, sided markedly with the Commission's envisaged project. Second, the new EU projected role was mirrored back to the Commission through the critical remarks by the Bank, which had perceived the EU–AITF proposal as an undue invasion into what it thought constituted its elective domain (i.e. loan leveraging and management of development finance, particularly in the Africa region since the 'poverty turn' years). Far from feeling weakened in its planned course of action, the Commission was strengthened in its expectations about the possibility of successfully setting up the EU–AITF: the intense reaction by the Bank's management seemed to prove the soundness of the envisaged change. On the one side, the assertive stance of DG DEV in this issue is related to its achievements in triggering higher ODA volumes and donor alignment at Monterrey, via the 2005–2006 Consensus on Development, and through the Africa–EU Partnership. However, evidence from the interviews, complemented by World Bank overview papers, indicates that the critical stance of the Bank on the planned AITF also helped DG DEV in structuring a new role conception, and, presumably, it also pushed it to proceed more speedily along pragmatic lines.

The datum is relevant in the context of the EU–World Bank relations as an indicator of the quality of interaction between the two organizations in an area where the two pledged to cooperate further under the Paris–Accra Agenda. While it may be true that through the creation of the EU–AITF first (and the NIF shortly afterwards) the Union has ventured into a territory traditionally falling within the remit of the World Bank's range of activities (Orbie and Versluys 2009), the turf battle that ensued suggests a perception of 'supplementarity' on the side of the Bank, rather than the (publicly advocated) complementarity of action between the two multilateral partners in Africa.

Inputs from high level officers in the World Bank indicate that the main focus of the Union's strategic involvement in the Africa region has been perceived primarily in terms of the EU's ability to entertain political dialogue and promote development through trade liberalization. Otherwise, and particularly in the area of designing and implementing financial tools for development, the Union has appeared best placed to follow Washington's leading role. A paper sponsored by the World Bank Concessional Finance and Global Partnership VP (Kitt 2010), quotes the EU–AITF (along with the NIF, relative to neighboring partners) listing them as 'bilateral' initiatives (according to which 'the EC or member states would manage resources coming from member states bilateral policies', Kitt 2010, 11–12), therefore contrasting them with the aid flows channeled by the Commission to the World Bank. The paper adds how 'to date, EU member states have not committed large sums of funding and some have not even joined' (ibid.). Specific to the EU–AITF, the paper notes how 'The Trust Fund was given a new push by the decision of the UK, which traditionally is skeptic of ceding competences to the EU level, to join donors with a Euros 10mn contribution'. As seen above, the low amount of start-up funding has been, on the contrary, quoted by Commission sources as a mark of merit for what is retained as a pioneering initiative, started with a low budget and gradually expanding in terms of both committed resources and achieved goals.

In fact, seen from the EU side, the 'bilateral' nature reported in Kitt's paper, is a positive indication that the Commission is being increasingly – even though gradually – successful in enlisting member states, as well as other international financial partners – not excluding the World Bank – to take part in EU-managed multi-donor initiatives. Since 2007 the situation has further evolved. The World Bank has displayed a more positive stance with respect to cooperating under Union-sponsored multi-donor initiatives, and the Union has proceeded further in its attempt to give material substance to its endeavor towards the definition of a more coherent development policy. The creation of similar blending facilities to finance development in other areas of the world (Neighborhood, Balkans, Central Asia, Latin America) supports the hypothesis of a role change by the Commission and, more broadly, by the Union. With an interesting reversal of organizational roles, the Union is now among the group of main shareholders within these facilities, and coordinates the strategies and approaches to be followed on the ground, while the Bank contributes with its funds and expertise, when eligible, but does not have yet a formal voice in the Boards of those facilities, with the notable exception of the WBIF, discussed in Chapter 7.

These developments point to the potential that role change through adaptation and learning can have both with respect to actors' identities and their own social interaction. On the one side, the World Bank's critical receiving of the EU plans to launch its own blending facility for Africa indicate the constitutive influence that 'counter-roles and the recognition of others' (Coser 2003, 340 in Harnisch et al. 2011, 7) play with respect to role conceptions, as defined in this book (the 'I' part of a role (Mead 1934), the 'corporate role' (Wendt 1999)). On the other side, the EU replication of its blending approach in ECA and MENA regions, as well as the institutional evolutions of these facilities through time, unveils the potential that role change undergone by large multilaterals can have with respect to specific features of the context within which they interact. From a theoretical standpoint, these developments appear to confirm the constitutive nature that role change has with respect to the structure within which these actors operate.

In policy terms, and with the caveats indicated above about the evaluation on the effectiveness of the EU-created blending facilities, the indication seems to be that multidonor coordination must be flexible, and roles interchangeable when needs be. As evidenced in Chapter 7 (ECA), the replication of the EU–AITF template through the creation of the WBIF in the Balkans suggests that financial cooperation between the EU and the World Bank through trust-fund facilities that are outside the Framework Agreement can indeed occur along collaborative lines, even when this happens with the EU being in the driver's seat on both political and financial counts. The governance and outcome effectiveness of programs financed under these facilities will likely be revealed over time.[25] Certainly, and in spite of past frictions in the case of the EU–AITF, the learning process engaged by the EU and the Bank on the occasion of its launch has shown that plurality of schemes, and diversity of donors, have played a positive role in addressing the causes of poverty eradication and inequality reduction in the post-2008 new global context.

9.7 Conclusions

Analyzing evidence from a diversified set of sources, this chapter has argued that role theories, on the one side, as well as delegation and bargaining models, on the other, provide key inputs to reconstruct the EU–World Bank interaction, as well as to investigate their individual and contributed development performances in Sub-Saharan Africa. Relative to the Cotonou–EPA process, the hypothesis of an EU 'normatively entrapped' in the World Bank 'Washington Consensus' is not embodied in role perceptions from the Bank's groups of trade specialists, which had long since moved away from the liberalizing purism of the 1980s. Conversely, a trans-institutional cleavage has emerged, whereby several US, UK and Nordic officers on both the EU and WB sides have expressed concerns about the limited (policy) effects of the EU's role as a trade liberalizer-cum-development promoter, notwithstanding the Commission's efforts since the mid-2000s. Those role perceptions and expectations of the EU trade policy in Africa have been explicitly qualified by statements about the non-involvement of the World Bank in the EPA process, to mark the difference between research-based advice from the official stance in a joint effort. From a development perspective, however, the low degree of implementation effectiveness (low utilization rate, slow and contested negotiations on the new IEPAs with a number of reluctant African partners) indicate that the gap between the EU normative aspirations and achieved results may well reverberate back into the policy process. Low policy consistency has hampered the EU development outcomes: inconsistencies between MS and within EU institutions have coupled with weak pass-through of trade liberalization effects into poverty reducing impacts, as discussed in recent appraisals of the IEPAs.

The analysis of the EU–World Bank cooperation under fragility, in Zimbabwe and Ethiopia, respectively, has investigated the evolution of their inter-institutional relations there and their efforts to fine-tune their respective accountability systems. As shown with respect to the numerous EU–WB partnerships that have been set up particularly in the ECA region, the issue has relevant implications for the overall redefinition of the new architecture of development policymaking. On the one side, the tensions over who should be ultimately responsible for the implementation of projects financed with EU contributed funds has led to delays in disbursement. Lengthy discussions have also followed, over the specifics of the institutional umbrella provided by the Administrative Agreement and, more broadly the EU–WB Framework Agreement, that resulted in lower benefits for the Ethiopian recipients. On the other side, these frictions have been instrumental to stimulate a role change in the Commission, through the launch of its first blending facility to promote development, the Africa Infrastructure Trust Fund.

The analysis of the interaction between the EU and the Bank through the eyes of actors in both organizations, complemented with inputs from third parties, has revealed a peculiar type of role change by the Commission, which has been strengthened by the (early) frictions with the Bank about the two organizations' respective roles in development finance. Through a sensible realization that they had both the financial resources (increased relevantly since the Monterrey Consensus of 2002), and the political backing of the EU Consensus on Development in 2006 and the the Africa–EU Partnership, top officers in DG DEV proceeded to set up the EU first fiduciary facility to finance development through a blending of Commission grants and multi-donor loans. The Commission now sits in the driver's seat during most phases of the financed activities, which has minimized accountability problems experienced in other cases of joint EU–WB actions.

In the relatively less constrained framework for action that the EU enjoys in the Africa region (compared to the more 'EU regulated' ECA and MENA contexts), the Commission has been able to act as an innovator through the creation of the said EU Trust Fund facility to finance infrastructural projects in the region. The move has sent a pragmatic signal to the Bank about Brussels' resolve to take up a leading role in Sub-Saharan Africa. While the EU–AITF's financial volumes are still not comparable to the resources mobilized by the Bank in the region, the very process that led to its creation, and the replication of similar facilities in other regions of interest of the EU, indicates that coordination with the Bank will happen along increasingly infra-functional lines.

Notes

1 In the words of the two covenants 'The four main objectives of this long-term strategic partnership set the comprehensive framework within which specific strategies will have to be put in place in the following areas: (a) peace and security, (b) governance and human rights, (c) trade and regional integration and (d) key development issues' EU Council (2007b, 5).
2 Interviews with World Bank (Washington) and EU officers (Brussels) were conducted between 2008 and 2011. On the launch of the EU–AITF in the broader context of the EU–World Bank relations also see Baroncelli (2013b).
3 On the Paris Agenda see World Bank (2006a).
4 The collaboration between the EC and the Bank in the Africa region dates back to 1987, when the two informally joined their efforts in the framework of the Strategic Partnership for Africa (SPA), an association of donors aimed at improving development assistance to Sub Saharan Africa. Further collaboration on the PRSP (Poverty Reduction Strategy Papers) framework was set to tackle implementation problems at the country level. See World Bank Brussels Office (2007b).
5 Interviews with high level WB management and Commission officers (2008).
6 Interview with high level WB management, SSA Unit, 2008.
7 Interview with World Bank managerial officer, Washington 2008.
8 Interview with World Bank managerial officer, Washington 2008.
9 Under diagonal cumulation, inputs that originate from regional partners, and that are further processed in another country in the group, are treated as if the materials were originating in the country where the processing is undertaken. However, within the GSP, to which the EBA Scheme belongs, diagonal cumulation is available only to ASEAN, CACM, Andean Community and SAARC partners, to the effect that exports from poor ACP partners to the EU cannot enjoy the benefits of diagonal cumulation under the EBA scheme. Additionally, the special value-added requirements incorporated in the EBA Scheme (the value added generated 'in the final stage of production must exceed the highest customs value of any of the inputs used from countries in the regional grouping', Brenton 2003, 13) substantially reduce the advantages of diagonal cumulation. Differently, under full cumulation 'any working or processing (even if does not confer origin) undertaken in one country [can] . . . be carried forward to another country and counted as if it were undertaken in the country of final processing' (ibid.).
10 In August 2011, the DG Trade website listed IEPA (Interim EPAs) with six countries from the Eastern and Southern Africa Group (within ESA: Comoros, Madagascar, Mauritius, Seychelles, Zambia and Zimbabwe); a collective interim EPA with the East African Community (EAC, i.e. Kenya, Uganda, Tanzania, Burundi and Rwanda); an interim EPA with SADC (Botswana, Lesotho, Namibia, Swaziland and Mozambique, with Namibia still being pressured by the EU to sign the agreed text). Some African countries, such as Nigeria and Senegal, expressed their aversion to enter the agreements early on. EPAs with the Caribbean and Pacific Countries were signed in 2007 (with Cariforum) and in 2009 (with Papua and New Guinea). In October 2016, only

12 African countries had implemented their EPAs, while 12 others did not list EPAs in their trade agendas. In the Pacific only two out of the 14 countries had an EPA.

11 While this is the mainstream position among trade specialists in the World Bank Research Department and PREM Anchor unit, voices from top management in the Africa region have been keen to acknowledge that 'we are not involved in the negotiations' (Author's interview, Washington, January 2008).

12 Interview with high level World Bank's official, April 2011.

13 Quotes from Michael Laidler, then Head of the EU delegation in Harare, pointed to a clear intention not 'to subject its [EU] actions to decisions taken by them [IMF and WB] alone' (Brown 1999, 87, integrations in square bracket are mine).

14 A visa ban was imposed on most of the top government officials in the Mugabe Government and their assets frozen from February 2002. The EU sanctions were still in place as of August 2011. However, they have been selectively waived through the granting of (much contested) travel exemptions multiple times by France, Belgium (several times to allow participation of Zimbabwean officials to EU–ACP summits), Italy and the UK.

15 Earlier on, Mugabe's official statements located the main causes of the severe economic deterioration suffered by the country on harsh droughts. Evidence from econometric and descriptive studies however proved the direct effect of bad policies by the Zimbabwean Government (Moss and Patrick 2005; World Bank 2005b; Richardson 2005). Micro-evaluations pointing to positive evidence of the land reform are in Scoones et al. (2010).

16 The EU has signed an Administrative Agreement with the World Bank to regulate the management of its channeled funds through the Bank-managed PSNP, in accordance with the broader EU–WB Framework Agreement. An MoU has also been signed between all donors and the Ethiopian Government, and so have separate bilateral agreements between each donor and the Ethiopian Government.

17 Legalistic tone aside, the EU had condemned the massive human rights violations that were perpetrated against the oppositions by the incumbent government of Prime Minister Meles Zenawi, in which almost 200 people (193 civilians and six policemen) were killed, and, along with other donors, withdrew its direct budget support to channel funds to humanitarian emergencies through the WB PSNP and PBS Trust Funds (Oxfam 2008, 32; ADE 2008, Vol. IIa, Annex 8, Country Mission to Ethiopia, slide 8). The case is also important because Ethiopia has been a pilot country for the Commission's effort to improve aid effectiveness and donor coordination.

18 Subsequent evidence points however to inconsistencies between the EU's public condemnation of Zenawi's undemocratic rule (EU Election Observation Mission 2010, at https://eeas.europa.eu/headquarters/headquarters-homepage/24414/eu-election-observation-mission-ethiopia-2010_en) and classified information about its intent to support his regime towards overall stability goals in the Horn of Africa (particularly in the light of Eritrea's and Somalia's threats to regional and global security, see *Europeans track U.S. on East Africa but remain reluctant to sanction Eritrea*, from the US ambassador to Germany, Ref ID: 09BERLIN1467, 11/18/2009 9:20, available at http://ethiopia forums.com/wikileaks-european-meeting-on-meles-zenawi-eritrea-and-east-africa.

19 Other notable examples have been the frictions between the Commission and the Bank over the Commission/EU visibility in CGIAR MDTF and AHIF (Avian and Human Influenzas Facility) (see ADE 2008, Vol. I, 38, 60).

20 By resorting to Bank managed Trust Funds, the EU frees its hands from negative political responsibilities (both internal and external). In normative terms, withdrawing its direct grant contributions certainly increases the Union's credibility in the subsequent adoption of negative incentives towards the restoration of viable political conditions in the partner country. However, as shown in the case of Ethiopia, inconsistencies

between official statements and the Union's covert support to the Menawi regime have plagued the moral credibility of the EU as a coherent defender of human rights.

21 Author's interview with high level WB official, 2011.

22 Author's interview with WB official, 2011.

23 Often the process has relied on tacit – but widely shared – consensus on the need to implement programs more effectively. Reimbursable technical assistance provided by the Bank to Romania and Bulgaria to mobilize domestic capacities to absorb EU structural funds is a case in point. High and mid-level officials have clearly indicated that, while an institutional structure to manage such an approach is not present yet, they are willing to work cooperatively to make sure that the pledges made at the high political level are given substance through practical solutions. The evidence suggests that an evolution has taken place, from a situation where the Bank learnt from experience that doing business with candidate and prospective candidates required it to redefine its role in the region, to one where an EU–WB consensus has been forged on specific needs of ECA partners, opening the way to mechanisms of closer communicative action and normative persuasion (Harnisch et al. 2011, 13).

24 Author's interview with top EU management source (2011).

25 See the different feedbacks provided in European Think Tanks Group (2011), and a (more EU-friendly) Ferrer and Behrens CEPS paper (2011).

10 Cooperation among developers

Hybrid delegation, role change and the accountability–effectiveness trade off revisited

10.1 The EU and the World Bank: hybrid delegation, policy change and effective performance

The EU and the World Bank mobilize resources and influence development policies worldwide as no other global governor. Notwithstanding their joint endeavors, their cooperation has been mostly neglected by the policy literature. Academic research has also gone by the anomaly of these two multilaterals, which delegate to one another, but do not have either formal shareholding or full voice rights in their respective decision-making bodies. This book has provided analytical and empirical ground to start filling that gap. It has also shown how the relation between the two governors has significantly influenced their policies, programs and development performance, at headquarters and in the field. This chapter answers the questions advanced in the Introduction (Chapter 1), based on the three major findings of the book: the conceptualization of the EU–World Bank relations as hybrid delegation; the dynamics of policy changes undergone by the two organizations across the turn of the millennium and, last, the impact of their cooperation, through an analysis of their development performance. A case is made to support analytic eclecticism as a promising approach to study the relations, policies and performance of global governors. Finally, the chapter advances selected policy inputs to strengthen the EU–WB cooperation to end extreme poverty and reduce inequality in the global context of the third millennium.

10.2 The anatomy of hybrid delegation

The partial overlapping between the EU and WB memberships, coupled with the dual channeling track, pursued individually by the EU MS through the Board, on the one side, and by the Union-cum-MS through the Trust Fund system, on the other, points to the EU–World Bank reciprocal accountabilities as a hybrid set, built around multiple strands of delegation and corresponding principality rights. All the 28 EU MS are World Bank members, collectively the IBRD majority shareholder (accounting for approximately 27% of its shares). Since the consolidation of informal coordination among EU EDs through the Eurogroup, the Union partakes in its MS' vertical delegation to the organization. Via the EU EDs, the EU is a potential principal to the Bank, which is in turn 'internally' accountable to Brussels. Yet, such accountability is mediated by the EU EDs' propensities to coordinate around EU agendas in Board discussions. Usual delegation pathologies, particularly those related to collective principality, are further complicated by the fact that EU EDs sit in different constituencies at the Board (eight at the time of this writing), and have to coordinate with non-EU EDs, along lines that may not correspond to Brussels' desiderata.

In spite of the Commission's support, Brussels' principality rights through the Board track have an essentially informal nature, their strength varying across issue, country and constituency-specific interests. The EU EDs' informal tie to Brussels is inherently complex, as the former have collective principality rights as Directors of the World Bank (which pays their salaries), but are ultimately accountable to their respective national governments (which appoint them). The internal dimension of their 'performance as EU agents', investigated in Chapter 5, has revealed self-identification processes with the Union, as well as successful coordination dynamics, most notably in advancing the EU agenda in environmental matters through the Bank, in further engendering World Bank's projects, as well as on EU priority areas in candidate, potential candidate and neighborhood countries. The high number of joint positions, and the regular consultation practice further indicate a trend towards increased cohesion. Yet, the trajectory of the Eurogroup's consultations on compacting an EU single voice during the IBRD 'voice and participation' reform of 2008–2010, suggests that such informal principality is virtually non-existent when changes to constituent politics are on the agenda. When key transformations of the 'rules of the game' are debated, as is the case under potential major redefinition of shareholding rights, consultation via the Eurogroup most likely plays as a hindrance, rather than an opportunity to share views on EU matters. As reconstructed in Chapter 5, months-long consultations postponed a frank expression of true preferences by several EU EDs. As a result, the Eurogroup was weakened in the eyes of the Bank's management, compared to other IBRD shareholders, on the redefinition of the quota framework. In consultations over IBRD institutional reform and under time pressure, collective EU principality is most difficult to materialize, and the eventual maximization of (member-specific) relative gains seems the preferred strategy by EU MS.

Trust-funded projects follow a separate path, which does not earn the Union formal shareholding rights at the Board. Officially, the EU and WB respective rights and responsibilities are laid out in the FA, regulating their relations on non-core ODA allocations. Having provided grants worth USD 2.2 bn to the WB TFs between 2007 and 2012, the EU is one of its major contributors. Relative to such flows, the EU covers both authorizing and funding roles, thus being a formal principal to the Bank. Different from the Board channel, accountability through the FA is direct (non mediated by MS) and external to the Board, as the EU and the Bank are two separate organizations. It is also horizontal, as the two organizations are contracting parties to an agreement between pre-delegation equals (not one through which an existing principal creates its agent). Compared to the hierarchical delegation between an IO and MS, the horizontal nature of the EU delegation to the WB in the TF business has left substantial margins of discretion to both parties. Furthermore, the EU shares these roles with other donors to each different multi-donor Trust Fund, thus facing collective principality problems in variable degrees, according to the governance rules of each specific TF board. Negotiated and agreed on an ad hoc basis, these latter are incorporated in a multitude of different AAs. While regrouped under the FA umbrella, AAs are in fact discrete contracts, whereby the EU can only claim limited principality rights over the World Bank's agency, rights that are circumscribed by the specific nature of each TF. Additionally, while in the parallel financing mode (RETF) the EU grants are channeled directly to the recipients in partner countries, in the joint financing schemes (BETF) funds from Brussels are merged with resources provided by other donors, with allocations decided by the World Bank on the basis of its own criteria. The unearmarking of such pooled resources further parcels the EU's principality rights, fragmenting them across different TFs.

The two sets of relations described above between the Union and the Bank yield a hybrid mix of hierarchical and horizontal, internal and external, formal and informal accountability flows. As argued in the book, on a number of respects, their origin and evolution can be explained through the lenses of rational choice PA, signaling and bargaining approaches. In spite of its (treaty-based) vocation to promote increased prosperity (also) in the outside world, the EU has for a long time lacked in-house expertise to go about that mission. Brussels' resolve has also been marred by principality problems, so that, until the late 1990s, the development agenda of the Commission has been largely shaped by the heterogeneous preferences of EU MS. Before the new millennium, the EU (Commission's) delegation to the World Bank via the Trust Fund System has therefore largely responded to informational, expertise, pooling and neutrality needs. Brussels has relied on the World Bank's prior knowledge of country systems and/or economic sectors, as well as on its experience in development project financing. The Union has also consciously counted on the Bank's ability to leverage Brussels' grants with additional funds from other donors, and through its activity in financial markets.

Classic PA models can also explain some aspects of the recontracting that has occurred between the Union and the Bank after 2001, particularly the revision of the FA through the two re-formulations of 2003 and 2009.[1] The pressure exerted by Brussels on the World Bank to enhance the EU's visibility, and to grant the EU more substantial control rights, particularly after the Cocobu interrogation of 2006, supports the case of a dissatisfied principal that partially succeeds in reining in its (supposedly slacking) agent. As discussed on the EU–WB cooperation-cum-coordination in Ethiopia (Chapter 9), and in the occupied Palestinian territories (Chapter 8), channeling through the World Bank Trust Funds has provided the EU with a commitment-signaling device, plausibly employed to overcome time-consistency problems. The WB managed Trust Funds have offered the EU a – formally – a-political tool to keep providing budget support in highly fragile and/or poorest countries under emergency conditions, where direct EU financing would have clashed against the principles of Brussels' development policy.

Classic PA-based explanations also have a superior explanatory value when employed to investigate outcomes of formal Board negotiations over constituent politics. EU MS are not yet ready to move formally towards a more compact representation at the Bank because they do not consider themselves as a collective principal (and indeed have reaffirmed, post-Lisbon, that development is a shared competence). As detailed in Chapter 5, the main reasons behind the absence of a stronger push towards unified representation are the different political preferences of EU MS in their respective development programs, the low salience of development policy and consequent weak traction towards a change in EU representation at the Bank, and, last, a seemingly shared uneasiness about 'rocking the boat' against the US dominance at the Board.

10.3 Studying hybrid delegation in motion: the promise (and limits) of institutional approaches

As dynamic elements are included in the analysis, to understand the evolution of hybrid delegation between the EU and the World Bank, however, classic PA hypotheses show their limits. The process leading to Brussels' launch of its own facility to finance trust-funded development in Sub-Saharan Africa – the AITF – Africa Infrastructure Trust Fund (and the replication of that template through similar EU-led facilities in other regions), cannot be accounted for solely through a classic PA setting. As emerged from the analysis of the quarrels between the EU and the World Bank over the redefinition of respective rights and duties across the multiple amended versions of the FA, a policy-failure-based explanation may account for the EU's willingness to renegotiate cooperation with the Bank in the Trust Fund track. However, the shirking hypothesis is not verified, as shown by Washington's behavior in the EU–World Bank negotiations over Trust Fund financed projects in Palestine, Ethiopia and Zimbabwe analyzed in Chapters 8 and 9, respectively. As confirmed by interviews with high ranking officers from both sides, the ambiguity over each organization's specific roles played a major part in shaping the evolution of hybrid delegation. It was precisely the horizontal nature of the FA which allowed such ambiguity to be incorporated in the EU–World Bank Trust Fund compact from the start.

As a result, the World Bank enjoyed a substantially higher leverage on contract redefinition compared to a 'normal' type of agent. As a matter of fact, the context where trust-funded projects were negotiated and managed by the two organizations cannot be equated to a 'pure' PA delegation space. Thanks to its professional reputation and experience on development finance in fragile countries – an 'incumbency bonus' not available to the EU – the Bank has enjoyed higher independence, wider autonomy and stronger discretional leverage than any other agent in development financing. The Bank's activity pre-dates EU delegation (and the very creation of the EEC, for what matters): Brussels' channeling is therefore non-constitutive, technically referring only to the World Bank's agency as defined in the FA and in each specific AA.

At times, the relatively high independence of the Bank in managing Trust Fund projects has allowed its officers to operate as fiduciary agents acting on behalf of that Trust Fund board's members, making it harder to identify behavior outside of a principal's expectation as an abuse of power (Grant and Keohane 2005). The close ties between the Bank's staff and constituencies in the field have also enhanced its authority, irrespective of threatened recontracting by (TF) principals, thus likening its role to that of a trustee (Alter 2008; Hawkins and Jacoby 2006; Carpenter 2001). Yet, in the eyes of the World Bank's management, the 'deviations' from the agreed mandate blamed by the EU, were instances of regular discretion by authorities in borrowing countries, managing funds that the Bank was supposed to supervise only as a fiscal agent. Disproving the expectation of PA models about an agent's opportunistic expansion of its mandate (slacking and shirking), the World Bank creatively succeeded in claiming for itself the role of 'fiscal agent', which circumscribed its functions to supervising project financing, as opposed to performing a wider task of trusteeship, which would have entailed responsibilities to ensure both financial soundness and field performance at once.

Thus, the World Bank too relied on the channeling relation that it had with the EU to signal its commitment to neutral financing, and its enduring support to the poor, particularly under extreme distress in politically fragile partner countries. However, the World Bank 'commitment to neutrality' had at least two built-in flip sides from the EU's standpoint. First, Brussels could not plausibly rely on the Bank as its main intermediary to pursue political dialogue, which is excluded from the latter's mandate. Second, the World Bank's mandate requires it to withdraw funds under low financial reliability of final recipients, even in the absence of outright human rights violations, which could obviously hinder the attainment of EU broader (political) goals, as shown by the EU–WB quarrels over aid financing in Zimbabwe, between 2000 and 2002.

Greater-than-usual uncertainty about true agent's type (Murshed 2004) has punctuated the relation between the two organizations, as shown by the quarrels about the exact role of financial intermediation provided by the Bank (fiscal agent vs trustee). Washington was able to bargain with the Commission on an equal footing about respective rights and duties, depending on what was at stake at the moment. While it is quite possible that the World Bank's management at some point consciously manipulated such uncertainty to its advantage, retrenching to a more circumscribed role (fiscal agent) compared to what it had previously signalled, a similar hypothesis can be advanced about the European Union too, which found it costlier to tolerate politically inefficient allocations under post-9/11 tightened security concerns.

The hybrid nature of the EU–World Bank relation reduces the scope for the occurrence of the *typical* delegation pathologies, but leaves the door open to other potentially unwanted behaviors and policy outcomes. To make sense of the hybrid stream of accountabilities that flows from that relation, and account for the autonomy of the World Bank's agency, PA frameworks must be appropriately 'augmented' with inputs specific to the political economy literatures on signaling and bargaining. More broadly, particularly relative to their use in the current IR literature on the relations between States and IOs, PA frameworks should be further re-calibrated if they are to provide a meaningful contribution to the research on the relations *between* IOs.

Combining with sector-specific elements (diffuse costs and concentrated benefits of aid allocation, security concerns in fragile contexts), the role of third parties, such as other major donors and relevant CSOs in partner countries, must be incorporated in the equation. Allowing for longer delegation chains, including governments and contractors in the field, returns a more complex picture on how the relations between the EU and the World Bank have evolved in the new millennium. Escaping from the straitjackets of the assumption of delegation under hierarchy (the usual hypothesis in the PA–neoinstitutionalist research),[2] the hybrid accountability that exists between the EU and the World Bank cannot be equated to the world of contractual ties that is typical of market-based dynamics either, as it ultimately takes place in the shadow of an (admittedly fluid) anarchic context at the international level. The two organizations, and their respective constituencies, have operated in a plurality of venues (the EU space, the World Bank system, their 'interaction space' in the field(s), within the international system), where different 'ordering principles' (Waltz 1979), each endowed with varying degrees of institutional strength, have been at play at different points in time. The EU–World Bank relations, and hybrid delegation in particular, possess features that are typical of heterarchic systems (McCulloch 1945; Jessop 2002), whereby mutually interdependent (hybrid) hierarchies interact, and coordinate horizontally with one another, according to logics that cut across both command- and exchange-based mechanisms. The self-motivated, collaborative nature of horizontal relations between these two distinct hierarchies, and its weight with respect to competitive and authoritative modes, are, ostensibly, a matter of degrees. While in some cases the World Bank has adjusted to EU interests, receding from incumbency as in most Central and Eastern European countries after enlargement, other examples, also analyzed in this book, point to more competitive dynamics, such as in Sub-Saharan Africa. Yet, the case of the EU–WB collaboration in the WBIF – and the intermixing of roles between the two organizations – shows that repeated interaction even with (according to some, thanks to) friction can lead to innovation and development-effective outcomes.

10.4 External triggers, ideas and role change: the EU–WB relation and the evolution of the EU development policy

Across the turn of the new millennium the rising prominence of development challenges put the EU–World Bank relations under the spot light. Questioning EU's channeling through the World Bank TF system, the EU Parliament tightened verification on several accountabilities from the Commission. After a massive internal reorganization in 1999, and the resignation of the Santer Commission, the new Prodi Commission pursued a major effort to enhance Brussels' development mandate. The new course fostered better coordination among EU EDs at the World Bank's Board and the institutionalization of the EU–World Bank compact in the Trust Fund business through a formal agreement. Thus, a multiplicity of EU internal stimuli supported the drive towards increased coordination.

Yet, the effort of the Prodi Commission at forging a more assertive development role also responded to factors that were external to the EU, material and ideational, which operated through rational and non-rational logics. First, after the terrorist attacks of 9/11, an (almost) global rally around the flag of antiterrorism took place. Securitization of aid policies ensued, with a higher premium put on targeting aid to stabilization needs in sensitive spots (most notably the Mediterranean, Middle Eastern, South-Asian regions and selected areas in Sub-Saharan Africa). The EU channeling through the WB TF system came under tightened scrutiny, with the Parliament and the Commission playing watchdogs with the WB bureaucrats almost on a daily basis. The analysis of the ongoing negotiations on the FA revisions, and of the EU–WB frictions on the management of budget support to the oPt between 2006 and 2007, bear witness of such evolution: a disturbance in the structure of the international system that politicized aid, was percolating through the EU–World Bank relations. Brussels responded by renegotiating the terms of its delegation to the Bank, and pushed for increased verification powers, monitoring rights, and interpretive letters to clarify each step of the re-contracting. A shock in the broad context of delegation had triggered a change in the preferences of the EU principal, exposing the ambiguities inherent in its earlier choice to channel through the WB TF system to pursue neutrality needs (both from possible capture by particular EU MS preferences and from enmeshing with non-democratic regimes in the field).

Secondly, however, in the new millennium the EU–World Bank relation has evolved as a result of the change in the ideational context surrounding the discourses and practices of multilateral development. After more than a decade of criticism, the dismal performance of the World Bank's SAPs, and, subsequently the difficulties to help client countries out of the Asian crisis, indicated that the Washington Consensus had reached a point of no return. Ideational inputs – including those external to the Bank and to the Union – exerted a crucial influence on the World Bank's shift to the post-Washington Consensus, as well as on the evolution of the EU development policy. Ideas on what constituted appropriate strategies to promote development (particularly the MDGs' emphasis on poverty eradication) played a major role in the changes undergone from both sides, with the epistemological pressure exerted by the World Bank's new paradigm having a visible influence on the EU's reshaping its development policy.

The book has deepened the focus on how the EU perceived – and reacted to – the mission and policy changes that the World Bank, up to then its most 'significant other' in the business of trust-funded development, was undertaking during those critical turns. Imitation dynamics have occurred in the uncertain times of redefining the Washington Consensus, with the Bank playing the role of a socializing agent for the EU, through the immaterial power of its (newly restored) anti-poverty and pro-governance envelopes. While different under several respects, the post-Washington Consensus and the Brussels' Consensus of 2006 have been both premised on the fundamental belief that development policies only succeed if they are embedded in a broader context of – supposedly – synergic links, a 'comprehensive' approach to poverty reduction for the Bank, 'policy coherence for development', for the EU Commission. The two blueprints have been broadly aligned, to use a term dear to the Paris–Accra jargon, also on the need to manage development aid by results, focusing on achieved outcomes, rather than on the technicalities of delivery processes. Very much in line with the emphasis put by the School of New Public Management on result-based management (RBM), the two organizations have incorporated and refined a variety of methods and tools to assess their own performance.

Those changes were mediated by conscious processes of role take-ups by the management apexes in the two organizations. At the Bank, a crucial influence was played by President James Wolfensohn, on the side of policy redefinition, and by Joseph Stiglitz, who provided top-level analytical layout to the new role that the Bank would play to address market and institutional fallacies. In turn, the Commission – through particularly pro-active officers in DG-DEV – had been working on a new approach to development, to respond to criticisms voiced by the Bank and the OECD, about the excessive bureaucratization and politicization of EU aid. The post-Santer DG DEV and the newly created EuropeAid Agency agreed on carving a more autonomous role for the Commission in the making of EU development policy, in both agenda setting and implementation phases. Overall, while it was prompting the Commission to strengthen its role as a strategic goal setter, the post-Washington Consensus search for enhanced effectiveness also opened the avenue to increasingly sophisticated roles in knowledge provision for the Bank.

Roles were however being increasingly intermixed. Within the broader 'poverty turn', the Bank also pushed the 'good governance agenda' through: coupled with the 'comprehensiveness' of its new approach to development, the net result was one of increased potential for political leverage through its – supposedly neutral – lending. On the other side, the Commission worked to improve the quality of its policies: the criticism against the excesses of Washington-sponsored neo-liberal SAPs was clearly perceived as a window of opportunity to reposition the EU (then Commission) in the market for development policies, in an attempt to match economic leverage with improved technical supervision and better targeted political direction. As shown in the previous chapters, there was an underlying consensus in both Brussels and EU capitals about the need to start pushing through the Board a common approach to development, alternative to the ways of neo-liberal SAPs, and strong enough to exert an independent influence on the new World Bank's agenda. Setting up the practice of Eurogroup Friday meetings among EU EDs at the Board, the EU signaled that it could create new instruments – if yet informal – to project its ambitions in the relation with the Bank beyond the boundaries of the FA and of ad hoc Trust Fund boards. Furthermore, the Commission went beyond imitative socialization of the Bank's post-Washington Consensus, redefining strategies and goals according to its own aims and methods. Learning from the World Bank's past mistakes (particularly its top-down approach and at times limited dialogue with partners in the field) it launched its own first Trust Fund facility, the EU–AITF, in SSA (followed by other blending instruments, and dedicated investment platforms). Complex learning in financing trust-funded development has occurred on the side of the EU, which has used the relation with the World Bank (particularly the frictions generated by the news that Brussels intended to set up its own fiduciary facility to support infrastructural projects in SSA) as a springboard to redefine itself by difference from the Washington-based IFIs. Instead of delaying the creation of the new facility, Washington's dissatisfaction with what was read as an instance of Brussels' non-conformity with current role expectation, prompted a process of altercasting, whereby DG Dev officers ended up in being further confirmed that their plan of an independent EU Trust Fund facility was worth pursuing.

Thus, PA 'augmented' models help to explain the EU multiple attempts at recontracting its relations with the World Bank (restricting mandate, tightening control, emphasizing visibility, in the cases of Zimbabwe, Ethiopia and the oPt), but do not tell us much about the ways in which the 'Brussels' consensus' of 2006 came about, or why the AITF was created. While EU studies have mostly targeted the Commission's entrepreneurial leadership as the main determinant for these changes, the evidence discussed in the book suggests that other variables, material and ideational, situated at the international-systemic and EU–WB relational levels have played an equally relevant role, through both strategic and appropriateness logics. These factors have crucially interacted with the evolution of the EU–World Bank hybrid delegation across the turn of the millennium. In some respects (institutional changes within the EU, systemic shocks), they can be accounted for within a rationalist paradigm, through hypotheses advanced by either the public policy or the IR–IPE literatures. In other cases (mission and policy changes within both the EU and the World Bank), socialization and learning dynamics at play are best understood through approaches from the constructivist camp. Overall, analytical eclecticism appears a promising approach to study the effects of hybrid delegation, and to appreciate the impact of its evolving features on the development performance of the two global governors. In the next section, EU and World Bank dynamics of role change through inter-organizational cooperation are summarized, for the three regional cases analyzed in the previous chapters, and preliminary remarks on role performance advanced.

10.5 The EU–World Bank relations in the ECA, MENA and SSA regions: inter-organizational cooperation and role redefinition

The EU–WB cooperation in MENA has unfolded mostly in Ricardian terms, with the Union working towards poverty reduction and political dialogue through economic incentives, and the World Bank mostly engaged in sector work and support to macroeconomic stabilization. During the Arab Springs, the red flag to seriously reconsider the EU and WB approaches to the MENA countries was raised by oppressed populations in the countries themselves, however, not by either organization, as it had happened instead on numerous occasions in the ECA and SSA regions. There, role changes and innovative solutions emerged from the interaction between the two multilaterals. Conversely, while both organizations kept negotiating with elites in MENA partners, the EU's lack of courage in putting more pressure on MENA governments to implement the political conditionalities included in the Association Agreements, and even the decision to increase support to brutal regimes, such as Gaddafi's Libya, nullified the synergies expected from economic support-cum-political dialogue.

A similar permanence in roles has characterized the cooperation between the EU and the World Bank in the occupied Palestinian territories. The EU has remained a generous donor, and the World Bank a lender and knowledge provider. The analysis conducted in Chapter 8 shows that the strategy of resorting to the Bank by political actors when they need a 'neutral' coverage only works if the leash is long enough to allow some negotiating room with players on the ground. James Wolfensohn, former World Bank President appointed as a special envoy in 2005, could play 'honest broker' only as long as that role served the interests of the (major) delegating powers. Neither the EU, nor the UK (which stepped in with Blair, when Wolfensohn was removed a year later), wanted to antagonize the Bush Administration. The expected synergies between budget support, country ownership and stabilization efforts assumed by World Bank managers since the early days of the first Trust Fund for the Territories, fell through the security priorities of the United States, with the Commission caught up in disagreement with the Bank about their respective roles in fund management. The different interpretation of mutual accountability ties on either side, and the different role conceptions and expectations about what should be done under maximum security alerts, spelled quarrels about respective roles and little achievements on the ground. On the one side, the Bank was retained as the guarantor of last resort by the Commission, under pressure by EU NGOs concerned about the funding of terrorist factions by the Palestinian Authority. On the other side, the Bank claimed for itself the role of a financial intermediary, leaving the ultimate liability on how funds had been implemented to the Palestinian Authority. Eventually though, and under extreme pressure, the EU and the Bank managed to coordinate successfully to provide humanitarian and emergency aid, finding practical solutions to problems on the ground, to the point of merging two previously separate programs (the World

Bank SSNRP and the EU SHC to support reforms of the Palestinian social safety embodied in the Palestinian National Cash Transfer Program (PNCTP). While praiseworthy, these achievements have much to do with the exceptionally serious local conditions, and may not be easily replicable in other cases of EU–WB cooperation in regular (non emergency) budget support programs for fragile countries.

Similar frictions over respective role conceptions and expectations, notably their different receiving of mutual accountabilities, have emerged on the occasion of the EU–WB coordination in Zimbabwe, and of their cooperation through the WB-managed PSNP Trust Fund in Ethiopia, investigated in Chapter 9. In both cases the Bank reaffirmed its role as a (pure) financial intermediary, against the EU's claim that the Bank should be fully liable, beyond intermediation, for the complete implementation of programs funded with transferred resources. Those tensions have also originated from the difference in each organization's relations with partner countries. While the Bank bases its 70-plus years long experience on the knowledge of – and increasing reliance on – the partner countries' systems, the EU has been repeatedly restrained by its own, internal accountability ties, to do so to advance its goals. Budget support entails potentially higher gains for partner countries, under ownership and reputation respects. In fragile contexts, however, it also carries substantially higher risks for donors (particularly multiple principals, as is the case for MS in EU development policy), relative to the implementation of contributed funds by often contested local elites operating in poorly institutionalized settings.

Cooperation between the EU and the Bank in Sub-Saharan Africa, the least EU-regulated context, compared to the MENA-Neighborhood countries and ECA – Balkans and Neighborhood – regions, played a relevant impact on a most innovative shift, and role change, on the side of the Union, through the creation of the EU–Africa Infrastructure Trust Fund, in 2007.[3] The first loan-leveraging facility of this kind to be autonomously initiated by the Commission, the EU–AITF has been the template for other similar blending facilities, launched by the Union in the Balkans (WBIF), the Neighborhood (NIF), Asia (AIF – Asia Invesment Facility, IFCA – Investment Facility for Central Asia and IFP – Investment Facility for the Pacific) and Latin America (LAIF – Latin America Investment Facility and CIF – Caribbean Investment Facility). By endorsing the creation of regional blending funds under its aegis, the EU has developed 'in house' technical expertise to forge a more autonomous role across the different phases of its development programs. Time will tell if such role change spells a major detour from the EU's past reliance on the World Bank's Trust Fund System. The analysis of the EU–WB interaction on the occasion of the AITF creation indicates, however, that role clashes have in fact reinforced in the Commission's officers the belief that the EU could and should support its political leverage in Sub-Saharan Africa by funding development through its own blending facilities.

In turn, the launch of the Western Balkans Investment Framework at the end of 2009, and the inclusion of the World Bank as an associate partner (different from the initial exclusion of non-EU financial institutions), indicates that a growing interpenetration between the fiduciary facilities, as well as between the parallel sets of accountabilities of the two organizations is taking place, along such role change on the side of the EU. As discussed in Chapter 7, in the broader ECA region, Balkans and Neighborhood, the EU–WB cooperation has been most structured, and most influenced by the priorities of accession and approximation to the EU *acquis*, respectively. Through their cooperation in the Stability Pact, and the establishment of a Joint EU–World Bank office for South-East Europe, the EU and the Bank have redefined their roles. While Brussels has taken the lead on developing synergies between economic incentives and political stabilization, through its SAPs, the Bank has reduced its engagement as countries progressed along the accession process. The downsizing of the Bank's own lending in the region, as new EU member states were graduating out of their borrowing status, has been reflected in a conscious redefinition of its role in candidate countries, and its specialization as a strategic 'knowledge provider'. The difficulties faced by Romania and Bulgaria in the absorption of EU structural funds led their governments to request the WB technical advice on how to best spend them by 2013 in a context of controlled fiscal deficit. The Union actually welcomed the Bank's comeback, returning an expectation that matched the Washington-based IFI role conception. On that occasion, however, the Union has indirectly conveyed the idea that its role is still primarily that of a political-economic player with little technical expertise: Brussels provides resources but does not have the know-how, or is still not able to transfer such know-how, to its MS on how to best spend those resources. This leads us to the last of the three major themes addressed in the book, that of performance-as-effectiveness.

10.6 Beyond normative influence and sheer size: a thick conceptualization of the EU abilities in development policymaking

As discussed at the beginning of this chapter, the EU policy performance at the Board has been heavily impacted by EU MS preferences and by the post-Lisbon permanence of development as a shared competence. Similarly, in all the three IBRD regional units where the EU's contributed effectiveness has been investigated, ECA, MENA and SSA, the Union's action has been hampered by internal divergences, either horizontal within its institutions or between MS, or vertical between institutions and MS (even if, given the shared nature of development competence the degree of such 'verticality' much depended on the matters at stake). Inconsistent EU behavior emerged from divides between DG DEV and DG Trade, as well as from the group of more development-conscious Northern MS, to which the UK also added a particularly strong support, on the one side, and the group of Southern MS, along with France, on the other, during the negotiations of the EPAs. A similar divide came about during the debate on sanctions against Zimbabwe in 2002, with the UK pressing for sanctions against the Mugabe regime, and the Commission waiting until new bloodshed had occurred before imposing them against the dictator and his entourage. The piecemeal enforcement of those very sanctions, in the following years, with several MS suspending their application based on – questionable – domestic needs, has further exposed the EU's inconsistent application of Article 96 of the Cotonou Agreement. Similarly, institutional inconsistencies in the MENA region have spelled concessions to brutal regimes, such as Gaddafi's Libya, offered a DCFTA in spite of blatant violations of human rights and basic EU requirements to obtain assistance. Opposition from Northern, pro-development EU MS against the continued support to authoritarian regimes in the region has been reconciled by the Union with the preference for a softer approach, supported by Southern Members, particularly Italy, France and Spain at the cost of reduced consistency in pursuing the goals of the Association Agreements. Substantial EIB investments in Syria were lost in the quarrels between France and the UK about how to best negotiate with the Assad regime in the second half of the 2000s. In the ECA region, Germany has shown its propensity to negotiate on its own an energy deal with Russia, while new members have barely concealed their aversion to the EU's plans towards renewing the Union's Partnership with Moscow. After 2007, official declarations by France, Germany and the Netherlands, pushed an unwilling Commission to revise the Thessaloniki commitments on the accession of Balkan partners, initiating a controversial debate on absorption fatigue, very much disguised as enlargement fatigue.

A further gap has emerged relative to Brussels' wavering resolve to stick to its commitment on developing inter-sectoral synergies across EU programs and policies. A major evidence of such incongruence between blueprints and results on the ground refers to the patent EU weakness to generate benefits for its developing partners from – supposed – increased market access and trade liberalization. Multiple studies have proven how the EU's trade policies in the MENA and SSA regions have in fact reduced the opportunities for most of those countries to further integrate into world markets, discouraging efficient sourcing from third parties and burdening their economies with prohibitive red tape costs. The debates on the effects of the pan-Euromed System of Rules of Origin, and on the EPAs, respectively, seem to indicate that development outcomes may not come about as hoped from the EU's preferential schemes with MENA and SSA countries. A second, major, case of inter-sectoral consistency gap is related to the difficulties of the Union in realizing the promised synergies between development promotion and the support to democratic transition. The EU's incongruent enforcement of previously set political conditionalities on human rights and the rule of law, particularly, has rendered the implementation of the Association Agreements in most MENA neighbors a mutual exercise in diplomatic denial.

More serious, and often intermixed with the previous type of inconsistency, a third type has emerged, relative to the EU's apparent lack of uniformity in assessing progress achieved by some Balkan countries in the SAP process, discussed in Chapter 7. Low horizontal-geographical consistency has appeared particularly serious in the case of the EU's inability to start accession negotiations with Macedonia, in spite of three consecutive progress reports by the Commission and repeated calls from the Parliament to that effect. The opposition of Greece on the name issue has proven an obstacle greater than that of implementing the EU's

– constantly – upward revised benchmarks. Less-than-consistent EU performance has also plagued progress along the association path by Bosnia and Herzegovina. Even discounting the country's many institutional fragilities, the EU's handling of stabilization and association issues through the Special EU Representative has appeared questionable. In the context of higher-bar-raising engaged by the EU since 2007, the datum has gained further prominence in light of Brussels' reward of progress by Serbia, which, in spite of the country's multiple problems, earned the country a green light to start accession negotiations. While voiced by Macedonia and Bosnia and Herzegovina representatives, these concerns appeared largely shared by some World Bank's top managers, who confirmed the existence of multiple political hindrances on the EU's side to the eventual accession of the two countries, suggesting that a genuine and concerned feeling of discouragement in the governmental elites of the Balkan laggards added unnecessary burdens to those countries' overwhelmingly challenging transitions.

Those very same sources, however, praised Brussels' ability to start the SAP process, and expressed their admiration for the political courage behind the broader EU's effort in the Balkans. They noted the positive achievements in the promotion of trade integration, development and political transition simultaneously, and commended the normative potential of exporting the EU model – peace and prosperity through sectoral economic integration – in the troubled Balkan area. Compared to synergies in the Balkans, the low consistency between stated and achieved goals in promoting development through trade liberalization, along with fostering horizontal integration, in the MENA and SSA regions has appeared even more serious. Parallels were drawn between how good the EU had been in supporting trade liberalization in the Balkans, and how inconsistent it had been, on the contrary, with neighbors in the MENA region. While perhaps justified under EU political standards (the differentiation between neighbors and candidates), Brussels' selective granting of country-specific cumulation rules to the different Maghreb and Mashrek partners indicates that discrimination has ended in less than effective development outcomes. Complaints about other geographical EU's inconsistencies, particularly relative to CIS vs non-CIS countries in the ECA region are being gradually overcome since the launch of the ENP, with tangible progress in some Eastern Neighbors. However, other cases (Ukraine being an example) indicate that a major role in growth performance may be played by autonomous take-up of the EU acquis, not by the (absent) incentive to accession.

An additional, fourth type of discrepancy between stated and achieved goals, has become apparent with respect to the consistency between what the EU does internally on social inclusion and what it pursues externally, particularly vis à vis its North-African partners. Since the late 2000s, concerned voices from the World Bank had pointed to the detrimental effect of the EU's poor handling of migration flows from the Southern basin of the Mediterranean, an evidence unfortunately confirmed by the numbers of human lives lost in the ongoing attempts to flee from Northern Africa to Maltese, Greek and Italian coasts, as well as by the violations perpetrated in migrants' camps in the enclaves of Ceuta and Melilla, and in Southern Italy. While not investigated in depth in this book, such an inconsistency between internally pursued goals and externally projected values has already struck a serious blow to the EU's credibility as a normative promoter of social inclusion through its development policy.

Finally, the regional case studies presented in Chapters 7, 8 and 9 have pointed to the existence of an across-the-board deficit between the EU's official aims and the Union's technical competence available to put them into being. Often such inconsistency has interacted with one or more of the other types described above, so that political hindrances and technical unpreparedness have conflated towards poor development results, as in the case of the weak enforcement of previously set conditionalities with MENA associate countries, or in the continuous redefinition of accession criteria for the Balkan laggards. EU technical deficits have also emerged as problematic for the achievement of outcomes on the ground in their own respect, as in the case of the PSNP in Ethiopia, discussed in Chapter 9, where the Commission's poor expertise and staffing problems put support to implementation and monitoring functions at risk. World Bank inputs from the field have lamented the weak expertise, and virtually non-existent independence, of the EU (then Commission) delegations in SSA, quoting their constant need to refer to Brussels for advice on even minor issues, as well as the need for the EU personnel on the ground to rely on external expertise to contribute comments and inputs on proposed solutions to the day-to-day issues that arose on development matters. More worrisomely, third parties commenting on the EU's ability to monitor and evaluate its own performance have hinted at a rooted preference for poorly prepared external personnel, re-hired even under proven inability to produce impartial results.

While some of these inconsistencies are still there, others have been superseded through the post-Lisbon reorganization of the EU's EEAS system. The Commission has also produced more sophisticated tools to monitor partner countries and MS' progress in reaching the MDGs first, and SGDs subsequently. Along the multi-stakeholder governance principles, the Commission has pushed for the inclusion of a reference to 'verifiable annual action plans' on how bilateral ODA is spent annually by MS, to be peer reviewed and reported to the European Council. Strengthening mutual accountability in donor and partner countries, it is believed, should ideally trigger self-standing cycles to improve aid effectiveness. As a matter of fact, however, the Council has opted for a more general reference to verifiable annual actions, with no time deadline, with some MS quoting the supposed loss in needed flexibility that would result from such an additional requirement. To what extent is it possible for the Union to capitalize on these enhanced efforts by the Commission, particularly in the absence of a shared will by MS to align their aid policies under EU-monitored criteria? What are the implications of these development challenges for the future of the cooperation between the Union and the World Bank? The next section summarizes the main results achieved by the two organizations to improve their cooperation, and provides policy inputs based on the analysis conducted in the previous chapters.

10.7 Between coordination and competition?

Over time, the EU and the World Bank have developed increasingly denser ties, to advance their respective missions in development, improve effectiveness and donor harmonization, to eradicate poverty and reduce inequality worldwide. Impressive results have been reached compared to the past, when the two IOs appeared to act in a 'totally uncoordinated fashion'. Their relations have been further improved since the mid-2000s, also thanks to the establishment of good high level direct contact between the then President Zoellick and former EU Commissioner for Development Louis Michel. Regular meetings between the WB President and the High Representative-VP of the Commission now occur twice a year on the occasion of the Spring Meetings. The yearly Brussels trip by EU EDs complements missions from the Commission's DGs to Washington. Multiple staff exchange programs have further strengthened contacts at intermediate and lower levels.

Factual evidence, as well as role perceptions from both EU (notably Commission) and World Bank's views (notably management) confirm the trend. Fragmentation of entry points has been reduced on both sides. Cooperation in the WB ECA region has triggered organizational developments, through the establishment of the EU–World Bank Joint Office for South-Eastern Europe, active between 1999 and 2008. In 2008 a position of Special World Bank representative to the EU was established, for the different Commission DGs to interact with a single interlocutor, prior to engaging with World Bank counterparts in regional and thematic units. An ECA Brussels Unit was also created, in charge of coordinating with EU institutions on cooperation in the ECA region. On the EU side, the creation of a Task Force for an enhanced cooperation with the IFIs marked the Commission's effort to upgrade the EU–World Bank relations to a strategic partnership for Brussels.

In 2007 the Bank launched the WB Center in Vienna to provide support to SMEs in candidate countries in approximating the Union's system of financial reporting, and to support the DG Regio-World Bank Regional Future Initiative. These templates, particularly the organization of forward looking knowledge initiatives, sponsored by the two institutions and involving networks of experts regularly consulting with partner countries, could be fruitfully adopted by other regional and functional units in the Bank. An input from the top WB management suggested that a single VP should also be in charge of managing the relations with the EU, to facilitate the cooperation between respective personnel at different organizational levels. Through time, progress has been made and, since 2016, a VP for the 2030 Development Agenda, United Nations Relations, and Partnerships has been created. Priority is given to the UN, to support the implementation of the 2030 Agenda and achieve the SDGs. Such evolution however also indicates that the World Bank attaches enhanced relevance to inter-organizational cooperation. The possibility of better targeted EU–WB relations is very much an interactive matter. Ultimately, however, the primary trigger depends on whether Brussels is able to achieve the collective EU-cum-MS objectives that it has set in the 2017 Consensus on development, namely, whether the pendulum swings more towards the unitary rather than the 'coordinated' extreme.

From a development perspective, strengthened cooperation between the two multilaterals is of paramount importance for many a reason. As discussed in this book, the Union, MS-cum-institutions, plays multiple roles at the Bank, at vertical and horizontal levels. Relative majority in shareholding (EU MS), and absolute majority in non-core funding (EU cum MS) have put Europe in a potentially very influential position vis à vis the Bank's management. EU–WB interaction in the ECA region bears witness to the trend, which has also emerged with innovative potential in the SSA region. In turn, the Bank has over time played a multiplicity of roles, in addition to that of managing agency of EU-channeled resources. The example of regional joint forward looking knowledge initiatives premised on the cooperation between the World Bank ECA Unit and the Commission (ENL and REGIO) show how mutual learning from both sides has led to welfare-improving outcomes. Frictions have been overcome when the EU has openly asked the World Bank for support in maximizing the effectiveness impact of Structural and Cohesion Funds beyond the area and deadlines of accession countries, within the wider framework of the post-2013, post-enlargement phase. Similarly, with the support of DG Internal Market, the Bank has engaged in a learning process on the *acquis communautaire*, tailoring its programs to help candidates and neighbors to comply with EU regulations.

Evidence on the EU's effectiveness in specific policies and regions, however, has shown how 'politics can get in the way' and create 'substantial obstacles in client countries'. EU aid delivery has at times appeared 'cumbersome', 'bureaucratic' and 'slow'. As noted in Chapters 5 and 6, while these effects have surfaced more seriously during implementation, independent external evaluations, and inputs from top level Bank officials suggest that both policy and role definitional issues may be at stake for the Union. While regarded as a key partner in development, in the eyes of the World Bank the EU has at times appeared as 'lacking expertise', prey to 'old fashioned politics', questionable in its recruiting policies of hiring 'young EU professionals instead of building capacity at the local level'.

While progress has been achieved, particularly through the multiple revisions of the Framework Agreement, less weight on immediate 'general visibility' targets, and a renewed emphasis on redefinition of goals and methods is advisable. Complex political and economic priorities should be better harmonized in the EU's own strategies, to ensure consistency both in the eyes of partner countries and at the Bank. If development support is linked to the attainment of governance standards, the EU should be clearer in the definition of these benchmarks, as well as more consistent in evaluating the countries' achievements towards the allocation of funds.

Second, the EU could further capitalize on the trusting relation that it enjoys with the Bank. Enhanced dialogue could be further pursued by all the DGs involved in development policies, and DG DEVCO could positively entertain more regular exchanges of information with relevant counterparts at the Bank. Disturbing perceptions over competition between the EIB and the World Bank, or the EBRD and the IFC, could be overcome altogether: into the 2010s voices from both ECA and MENA WB units have spoken of largely positive interactions with the Commission, welcoming greater EU–WB cooperation. Trust could also be enhanced by the EU on the commitment that the Bank appears to have with respect to a generally neutral pursuit of development goals. Closeness to the EU approach, especially in social and environmental issues, proves that a substantial overlap exists for the two institutions to strengthen cooperation also in these policy areas. Fears of undue influence of the US, and of the Bank's reliance on past strict conditionality approaches in privatization programs may not reflect in full the approach that the Bank had envisaged in the 2000s on investment climate improvement and private sector development. Particularly relevant since the post-2008 'Great recession', and in light of the US turn to a more mercantilist approach to its foreign economic policies under the Trump presidency, the EU development-minded components and the Bank should join in promoting a more equitable, coordinated approach to development finance. In light of the strengthened role of emerging donors, and particularly China, now the third largest shareholder country to the IBRD, the EU and its MS should make it a priority to maximize the development impact of the resources that they allocate to the World Bank Group.

Third, closely linked to the two previous points, the Union should define more clearly its goals according to its mission and policy roles, relying on the Bank to complement its efforts. This would provide a means to tackle the perceived lack of expertise, and the ensuing reputational effect, while allowing some time for the EU to upgrade its know-how where it deems necessary. Alternatively, the EU could focus on prioritizing its strategic goals and coordinating them with those of the Bank in areas of mutual interest. The political nature of the Union, its ideological drive and the 'emulation capital' that it enjoys before the Bank and partner countries provide an exceptional basis to develop more ambitious foreign policy goals. In the eyes of the World Bank, Brussels has both the honors and responsibility of a major trade power, and a pivotal actor in development. Its role in security and military affairs has appeared at times negligible, remarkably less assertive than the US, and often unable to get attention, yet some say that it may have a high potential in these fields as well. While migration and cohesion issues dictate the current EU agenda, a forward looking approach to development should not forget past positive achievements. Extending the EU concept to the Balkans, for example, incorporating the coordination of police forces in addition to the military, or carrying further on the development of a new overall concept of security, including gender and environmental issues are steps in that direction. Incorporating those innovations also in the EU partnerships with African countries could improve the chances of a wider and more coherent foreign policy role for the EU worldwide.

Finally, to develop synergies building on existing comparative advantages, the EU could positively rely on the extensive knowledge that the Bank has not just of technical management in development financing, but also of institutions in partner countries, which are key players in the making of development policies. Poor results and low effectiveness in the past have often depended on the unsatisfactory levels of participation by developing partners to the overall policy process.

Seen from the EU side, the 'competition issue' takes on a different nuance. As shown in Chapters 7 through 9, although its roles as a norm setter, political sponsor and grant-provider are by far prominent, and prevail over the provision of technical assistance and mission coordination on the ground, the Commission has substantially upgraded its expertise, and has started to develop sector-specific comparative advantages (notably in infrastructural, environmental and social policies, also building on the relevant progress achieved internally in these areas). The creation of grant-leveraging tools such as the the different investment and infrastructural funding facilities to blend EU grants with other donors' loans goes into that direction, even if utilization rates and result assessments vary.

The EU undeniable preeminence in advancing political dialogue in sensitive matters (human rights, democratic transition in former Soviet and post-conflict countries) constitutes a learning stock accumulated through past decades that places it in a unique position to provide its leadership to development programs and policies in areas where these issues are particularly at stake. Its achievements in the new and prospective members have been remarkable, particularly considering starting conditions on the ground in the early 2000s. Almost 20 years into the third millennium, migration and security challenges in the MENA and SSA regions have brought about new, daunting tests for Brussels. They have not, however, diminished the need to search for synergies to address the development roots and implications of the crises in those two areas. It is therefore imperative for the Union to develop a more coherent approach towards both closer and less proximate neighbors.

The key element to unlock these dynamics is, no less, the quest for an EU internal consensus on the Union's external priorities. Absent enhanced effectiveness, through an improvement on all the five 'consistency dimensions' identified in Chapter 5, it is difficult to expect a sound EU effort to promote balanced political and economic development, particularly in third countries outside the neighbor circle. While the renewal of the Strategic Partnership with Central Asia has been a welcome move, voices from Asian Governments and World Bank officers have suggested that through a more modest approach to value promotion, and higher consideration of the political traction exerted in the area by Russia and China, respectively, the Union could be more successful in preserving its credibility. In the eyes of its Asian partners, however, Brussels would still lead by example in the areas where challenging tradeoffs between energy and security issues on the one side, and human rights and democracy on the other, are at stake.

A balanced assessment of results must necessarily acknowledge that the Bank's action has not been immune from inconsistencies across time either. Harsh criticism was levied against Washington's managerialist consensus on measuring progress solely by the implementation of conditionality clauses by client countries, often irrespective of outcomes on the ground. In 2003, on the occasion of the 67th semi-annual meeting of EuropeAid, DG Koos Richelle poignantly reflected before the Development Committee on the need to shorten the gap between tools and achievements: 'the methodological link between policies and agreed development objectives. . .needs to be clarified' (Richelle 2003). A long way has been travelled since the launch of the World Bank's PRSPs-within-CDF broad strategies and objectives against the specific targets set by the MDGs in 2000. Different from stasis in its internal governance, changes in the Bank policies, products and organizational structure indicate a high responsiveness to evolutions in the external environment. Effectively navigating multiple challenges across decades, the organization has reshaped its mission from a 'poverty bank', since the 1990s and into the 2000s, to a 'knowledge bank', to the post-2008 'crisis bank' and 'solutions bank', coming full circle with the IBRD original mission as a 'reconstruction bank' (a systemic war requiring rebuilding then; systemic economic, health, environmental, security and migratory shocks into the 2010s). Through the WBG 2013 Strategy, President Jim Yong Kim has designed a sweeping group-wide reorganization ('One World Bank Group'), with radical resizing and organizational transformations.[4] Aiming at ending extreme poverty (of people living with less than USD 1.25 per day) and boosting shared prosperity (for the bottom 40% in developing countries) by 2030, the Group has shown the usual alignment with the UN-mandated development goals. While the results of the 2013 internal reorganization have been questioned on multiple grounds,[5] much remains to be done, to balance new equilibria between major shareholders since notable graduations (China in particular), and to redefine the Group's mission in light of more frequent, diverse and intense system-wide shocks.

Brussels' blueprints for aid harmonization and their streamlining into an EU-wide coherent set of policies have suffered, nonetheless, from similar deficiencies. Ten years after the launch of the MDGs, World Bank's sources who have been working for decades on EU–World Bank cooperation noted how even the EU inputs on policy coherence for development, as well as the calls for an improved coordination between the Commission and MS, had to a non-trivial extent remained shelved in high level policy documents, such as the Code of Conduct on Complementarity and Division of Labour of 2007, with highly variable impact on policy practice, and, more seriously, still too few tangible results.[6] The launch of a New Development Consensus in 2017 indicates that EU institutions and member states have converged around shared priorities to implement the SDGs and bring the Agenda 2030 forward. Time will tell the extent to which that consensus can be turned into impactful efforts on the ground.

10.8 The accountability-effectiveness trade off revisited: cooperation among developers

Fine-tuning respective accountability systems has been a challenging, yet promising endeavor to improve the EU–WB cooperation. The dilemmas faced by either side to find the 'right' balance between input and output legitimacy have combined, causing strains and stalemates. Through the EP, the Union has sought to replicate at the supra-national level domestic chains of democratic accountability. In turn, the World Bank has become the most relevant among non-traditional development banks: global in scope, formally accountable to shareholders that are sovereign states, but largely able to raise a good part of its resources independently in the market. Along with a wider mission, and a mandate with wide policy implications, have also come new stakeholders, to whom the Bank has been increasingly held accountable, whether rightly or not being a contested matter. As discussed in Chapters 3 and 5, reforming its internal governance along development-oriented criteria would require introducing principles of (general) democratic accountability, a fairer distribution of votes/shares and a change in voting rules to increase the voice of least developed shareholders. Compacting the EU representation into either one or two seats would also be a step in the direction of a more equitable representation. The shift may secure the Union with a higher influence on Board decisions only if multiple principality problems are resolved at the EU level first, which does not seem the case in the post-Lisbon scenario of an enduring shared nature of development competence. Additionally, fewer EU-homogeneous seats would increase the EU's influence at the Board only if the US veto power is overcome through a revised framework, where shares and votes reflect more closely each country's actual subscriptions as weighted by appropriate parameters. Added to the demands for accountability that each organization faces, these changes may put a higher burden on their efforts to enhance bilateral cooperation.

Relevant for our purpose, even though highly desirable, EU and WB institutional changes may not solve the problems that have stemmed from accountability gaps on the ground. To a large extent the entrenchment of political and economic dynamics in development policymaking is somehow the norm, rather than the exception. Such a norm becomes particularly problematic under conditions of institutional fragility, high political violence and extreme poverty. In the cases analyzed in Chapter 8 and 9, the Bank either chose to withdraw support from client countries on grounds of their deteriorating political situations, or was criticized, on the contrary, for failing to appreciate how the continuation of its programs and loans in authoritarian contexts had diminished the chances of democratization. In some of these instances (Zimbabwe, Ethiopia) criticism came directly from the EU, on both political and humanitarian grounds. The increased politicization of the Bank's governance agenda, on the one side, and the growing technical content of Brussels' role in development, through its strengthened evaluation systems and the EU blending facilities may be signs of a future EU–WB competition along increasingly infra-sectoral dimensions.

No ultimate answer is provided here to the question whether the World Bank should circumscribe its mission to avoid the pitfalls of democracy promotion under the coverage of associating good governance targets to its loans. Its remarkable sector-specific and field experience, as well as its global convening power, extensive knowledge and substantial financial resources suggest a continued engagement, and certainly an enhancement of its role as provider of global public goods. Perhaps, in countries where the EU has a significant presence, the Bank could redefine its action along lines that profit from a better fine-tuning with the policy dialogue pursued by Brussels. This book has documented how some World Bank top management officers would have welcomed a more active EU approach to good governance promotion, particularly in some countries in the Western Balkans and MENA. The room to develop synergies based on complementary roles seem to be particularly ample there.

Learning from past cooperation has prompted changes to address both visibility and accountability issues. A more pragmatic approach to the issue has been developed by the Commission since the end of the 2000s, resulting in tangible improvements by both DG DEVCO–EuropeAid and the EEAS. Thanks to its empowering role on matters of external representation, the Lisbon turn has produced a shift in mindsets, particularly at mid-levels in the Commission staff, making it somewhat obvious that stickers and flags with EU logos on facilities provided under joint missions would not achieve much, in the absence of a common EU voice at the Board. The shift has been received with general enthusiasm by the Bank's management. It remains to be seen how the EU MS will support those efforts, within the current WB constituency system, in the post-crisis, post-Brexit context.

In turn, the Bank has targeted the acquisition of a 'culture on EU institutions' to help its staff in dealing with both Commission staff and EU MPs. Putting aside past instances of questioning the EU *acquis* on development grounds, the Bank has wholly endorsed the EU objectives in potential candidate and neighbor countries. Additionally, it has welcomed other financing partners and new frameworks set up by the Union, as opportunities for a broader and more effective development action, rather than as a source of competition and undue hindrance. EU blending facilities still have a long way to go, on ensuring transparent governance, harmonizing accountabilities and monitoring effectiveness (European Think Tanks Group 2011). However, they indicate that the Commission is putting substance to a new role as development leader in areas of EU's privileged action (Ferrer and Behrens 2011). The recent accession of the IBRD as an associate partner to the WBIF, upon request by DG Enlargement and DG Transport, and the potential for similar developments for the other blending facilities in the Neighborhood, Asia and Latin America along the same template, show that cooperative practices can evolve even in areas of past friction.

The interaction between the EU and the Bank on the Accra–Paris agenda has opened up further opportunities to identify overlaps between the two respective accountability systems. The Commission and the Bank share a clearly joint stake in financing projects, programs and policies in ways that are both effective for citizens in borrowing member states and transparent for citizens in lending countries. To this effect, a good dose of flexibility has been required from both sides, but obstacles are being overcome, as shown at multiple junctures in this book, either within the existing Trust Fund system, through the use of 'verification procedures' in lieu of formal auditing, or outside that framework, through the creation of alternative financing mechanisms, as shown by WB service contracts with new EU MS, based on simpler accountability mechanisms.

The theoretical and practical considerations advanced in the book have offered alternative solutions to counterbalance the tradeoffs variously advanced by either accountability paladins or insulation technocrats. 'In a development-ideal world there should be a single system working according to commonly agreed rules, to solve accountability problems of interaction between international organizations sharing at least some of their goals', a World Bank officer told me over the course of an interview. To that remark he added sarcastically that, by then, his grandchildren would be retired. In spite of the cosmopolitan resonance, that comment brought to my mind the worrisome echo of a perfect hierarchical order with bureaucrats faultlessly implementing the mandates of their political principals. As he went on however, his point got clearer. The harmonization agenda, a topic in that conversation, was important but would always reach limits, given the differences between the EU and World Bank's respective missions, governance structures and memberships. 'That' he concluded 'is the limit we have and we have to find practical, pragmatic solutions to these insurmountable differences'. There it was, I thought, the essence of the daily duties of EU and WB development practitioners: searching for practical ways to develop the synergies between their organizations. There lay, perhaps, an alternative to the strictures of the trade off between accountability and effectiveness. When applied to the expanded space of the interaction between two – imperfectly – intersecting multilaterals, the higher complexity of such trade off had triggered a quest for limited, yet innovative, solutions that had not been found within the closed space of their respective formal boundaries. Coordinating the work of the EU and the World Bank has raised problems and mobilized energies from both sides. Yet, and particularly in light of the financial, security and migration challenges of the new global context, the benefits of their cooperation seem to have by far outweighed their costs.

In sectors and countries of joint interest, accountability and effectiveness could be augmented through an improved division of labor. Sticking to non-interference in the political systems of borrowing partners could be easier for the Bank if the burden of managing governance standards (setting, evaluating, enforcing) were shared with Brussels, which can in turn rely on an explicitly political mandate. Such moves would require the Union to capitalize on an enhanced action of its wide diplomatic network. It would also require that cooperation between the EEAS and functional DGs be based on solid foundations and clear political inputs from the HR and relevant Commissioners. Finally, but most importantly, it would need a substantial agreement by the EU MS, both in Brussels and Washington. These steps will take time and effort from both sides, during which the many pragmatic, ad hoc solutions developed across decades of daily practice will come to aid. It will however be time and effort well spent to improve the EU and the World Bank's performances in their joint endeavor to promote global development.

Notes

1 Further revisions have occurred in 2014 and 2016.
2 Valid for most organizational and public policy literatures on domestic delegation, the claim broadly applies to a large portion of the early IR literature on states' delegation to IOs as well.
3 In November 2015, and for the 2014–2020 Multiannual Financial Framework the EU–AITF was replaced by the broader Africa Investment Facility (AfIF). Since September 2017, the AfIF has been integrated in the European Fund for Sustainable Development (EFSD), as the Africa Investment Platform (AIP). In turn, the AIP is part of the broader effort by the Commission to maximize the EU's role in the market for blending, via the launch of a European External Investment Plan (EIP).
4 Implementation of the 2013 New Strategy started in 2014. Previous reorganizations had occurred in 1987 and 1996.
5 In the opinion of the evaluators those changes did not produce 'a significant change in learning in lending because they touched neither the culture nor the incentives' of the institution and its staff (World Bank 2014, vii).
6 Author's interview with high level World Bank official (May 2011).

Bibliography

Abdelal, R. (2007) *Capital Rules: The Construction of Global Finance*, Harvard, MA, Harvard University Press.

Açemoglu, D., Johnson, S., Robinson, J. and Yared, P. (2005) 'Income and Democracy', NBER Working Paper No. W11205.

ADE – Aide à la Décision Economique (2008) 'Evaluation of Commission's Aid Delivery through Development Banks and EIB', Final Report, Vol. I, Vol. IIa Annexes 1 to 10, Vol. IIb Annexes 11 and 12, Inventory Note, commissioned by the EU Joint Evaluation Unit, EuropeAid Co-operation Office, DG Development, DG External Relations, Brussels, November 2008.

Adler, E. (1987) *The Power of Ideology: The Quest for Technological Autonomy in Argentina and Brazil*, Berkeley, CA, University of California Press.

Adler, E. and Haas, P. (1992) 'Conclusion: Epistemic Communities, World Order, and the Creation of a Reflective Research Program', *International Organization*, 46, 1, 367–390.

ADS–Eurodad (2006) 'European Coordination at the World Bank and International Monetary Fund: A Question of Harmony?', *European Network on Debt and Development*, Brussels, January 2006.

African Development Bank and African Development Fund (2011) 'Zimbabwe Country Brief, 2011–2013', 1–22, available at https://www.afdb.org/fileadmin/uploads/afdb/Documents/Project-and-Operations/Zimbabwe%20Country%20Brief%20June%202011.pdf

Aggestam, L. (2006) 'Role Theory and European Foreign Policy: A Framework for Analysis', in O. Elgström and M. Smith, *The European Union's Roles in International Politics*, London, Routledge, 11–29.

Ahearne, A. and Eichengreen, B. (2007) 'Europe's External Monetary and Financial Relations: A Review and a Proposal', paper prepared for the Bruegel Project Europe and the Global Economy, Brussels, available at http://www.econ.berkeley.edu/~eichengr/ahearne_eichengreen.pdf

Aid Flows (2017) Web Portal – Data Sets, *OECD, the World Bank, the Asian Development Bank and the Inter-American Development Bank*, available at http://www.aidflows.org/

Alchian, A. and Demsetz, H. (1972) 'Production, Information Costs and Economic Organization', *American Economic Review*, 62, 777–795.

Alesina A. and Dollar, D. (2000) 'Who Gives Foreign Aid to Whom and Why?', *Journal of Economic Growth*, 5, 1, 33–63.

Alter, K. (2008) 'Agents or Trustees? International Courts in their Political Context', *European Journal of International Relations*, 14, 1, 33–63.

Anderson, J. (1990) 'Skeptical Reflections on a Europe of Regions: Britain, Germany, and the ERDF', *Journal of Public Policy*, 10, 4, 417–447.

Andreopoulos G., Andreopoulos, C.G. and Panayides, A. (2011) 'Multilateral vs Bilateral Aid: Addressing Some Puzzles', *European Journal of Management*, 11, 4, 73–78.

Andriamananjara, S., Brenton, P., von Uexküll, J.E. and Walkenhorst, P. (2009) 'Assessing the Economic Impacts of an Economic Partnership Agreement on Nigeria', Policy Research Working Paper 4920. April 2009, Washington, DC, The World Bank.

Andronova Vincelette, G. and Vassileva, I. (2006) 'Untangling the Maze of European Union Funds to Bulgaria', World Bank Policy Research Working Paper WPS3962, Washington, DC, The World Bank

Archibugi, D. (2004) 'Cosmopolitan Democracy and its Critics: A Review', *European Journal of International Relations*, September, 10, 3, 437–473.

Archibugi, D. (2008) *The Global Commonwealth of Citizens: Toward Cosmopolitan Democracy*, Princeton, NJ, Princeton University Press.

Archibugi, D. and Held, D. (1995) *Cosmopolitan Democracy: An Agenda for a New World Order*, Cambridge, Polity Press.

Archibugi, D. and Held, D. (2011) 'Cosmopolitan Democracy: Paths and Agents', paper presented at ISA 2011 Annual Convention, Montreal, Quebec.

Archibugi, D., Held, D. and Kohler, M. (1998) *Re-imagining Political Community*, Cambridge, Polity Press.

Argyris, G. and Schön, D. (1978) *Organizational Learning: A Theory of Action Perspective*, Reading, MA, Addison Wesley.

Arndt, H. (1987) *Economic Development: The History of an Idea*, Chicago and London, University of Chicago Press.

Ascher, W. (1992) 'The World Bank and US Control', in M. Karns and K. Mingst (eds.) *The United States and Multilateral Institutions*, London, Routledge, 78–94.

Åslund, A. and Jenish, N. (2007) 'The Eurasian Growth Paradox', in F. Bourguignon and B. Pleskovic, *Beyond Transition*, ABCDE Annual World Bank Conference on Development Economics Regional, Washington, DC, The World Bank, 25–40.

Åslund, A. and Warner, A. (2004). 'The EU Enlargement: Consequences for the CIS Countries', in M. Dabrowski, J. Neneman and B. Slay (eds.) *Beyond Transition: Development Perspectives and Dilemmas*, Aldershot, Ashgate Publishing.

Augier, P., Gasiorek, M. and Lai-Tong, C. (2009) 'Relaxing Rules of Origin: Or Can those PECS be Flexed', refereed conference paper, in P. Low and R. Baldwin (eds.), *Multilateralising Regionalism*, Cambridge, Cambridge University Press.

Avant, D., Finnemore, M. and Sell, S. (eds.) (2010) *Who Governs the Globe?*, Cambridge, Cambridge University Press.

Avant, D., Finnemore, M. and Sell, S. (2010) 'Who Governs the Globe?', in *Who Governs the Globe?*, Cambridge, Cambridge University Press, 1–32.

Azam, J.-P. and Laffont, J.J. (2003) 'Contracting for Aid', *Journal of Development Economics*, 70, 25–58.

Backé, P. (2002) 'Fiscal Effects of EU Membership for Central European and Baltic EU Accession Countries', in Oesterreichische Nationalbank (ed.) *Focus on Transition 2/2002*, Vienna.

Balfour, R. (2008) 'The Balkans in Europe: Containment or Transformation? Twelve Ideas for Action', European Policy Centre Working Paper 31, June 2008, accessed at http://www.epc.eu/documents/uploads/337249309_EPC%20Working%20Paper%2031%20The%20Balkans%20in%20Europe.pdf

Balkanalysis (2012) 'The Future of the EU Enlargement in the Western Balkans: Interview with Edward Kukan', by Maria-Antoaneta Neag, 11 March 2012, accessed at http://www.balkanalysis.com/macedonia/2012/04/11/the-future-of-eu-enlargement-in-the-western-balkans-interview-with-eduard-kukan/

Balogh T. (1967) 'Multilateral versus Bilateral Aid', *Oxford Economic Papers*, 19, 3, 332–344.

Banerjee, A. and Duflo, E. (2011) *Poor Economics*, New York, Public Affairs.

Bărbulescu, I. and Troncotă, M. (2012) 'The Ambivalent Role of the EU in the Western Balkans – "Limited Europeanisation" between Formal Promises and Practical Constraints. The Case of Bosnia-Herzegovina', *Romanian Journal of European Affairs*, 12, 1, March 2012.

Barkan, J.D., Simba Kayunga, S., Ng'ethe, N. and Titsworth, J. (2004) 'The Political Economy of Uganda: The Art of Managing a Donor-financed Neo-patrimonial State', 6 July 2004, World Bank Commissioned Report.

Barkowski, S. and Wiatr, K. (2012) 'External Representation of the European Union and Shared Competences –an Unsolved Puzzle', *Yearbook of Polish European Studies*, 15, Warsaw, 155–175.

Barnett, M. and Finnemore, M. (2004) *Rules for the World: International Organizations in Global Politics*, Ithaca and London, Cornell University Press.

Baroncelli, E. (2008a) 'Preferenze, istituzioni e idee: il "policy making" economico esterno dell'Unione europea', in M. Ferrera e M. Giuliani (eds.), *Governance e politiche nell'Unione Europea*, Bologna, Il Mulino, 341–375.

Baroncelli, E. (2008b) 'On the EU Foreign Economic Policy Role in Multilateral Contexts: Perceptual Dynamics and Policy Responses in the World Bank', Paper presented at The IES-GARNET Conference 'The EU in International Affairs?', Brussels, 24–26 April 2008. Mimeo.

Baroncelli, E. (2009) 'The External Image of the EU in Multilateral Settings: A View from the World Bank', Report from the Survey II on The External Image of the European Union, The Italian Ministry of Foreign Affairs and GARNET-EU Network of Research Excellence, 1–44; now in Sonia Lucarelli and Lorenzo Fioramonti (eds.), *Research Report: The External Image of the European Union–Phase Two*; Garnet Working Papers Series, 2009.

Baroncelli, E. (2010) 'Aid, Trade and Development: World Bank's Views on the EU's Role in the Global Political Economy', in S. Lucarelli and L. Fioramonti (eds.), *External Perceptions of the European Union as a Global Actor*, London, Routledge.

Baroncelli, E. (2011) 'The EU at the World Bank: Institutional and Policy Performance', *Journal of European Integration*, 33, 6, 637–650.

Baroncelli, E. (2013a) 'The World Bank', in K.E. Jørgensen and K. Verlin Laatikainen (eds.), *Routledge Handbook on the European Union and International Institutions: Performance, Policy, Power*, London, Routledge, 2013, pp. 205–220.

Baroncelli, E. (2013b) 'Eclecticism and the Study of Delegation between Global Governors: The EU, the World Bank, and Trust-Funded Development in Sub-Saharan Africa', *Rivista Italiana di Politiche Pubbliche*, 1/2013, 131–158.

Baroncelli, E. (2018) 'The World Bank in the Post-Crisis Landscape: Stasis and Change after the Post-Washington Consensus', in A. Poletti and S. Raudino (eds.) *World Economic Governance and the Challenge of Human Development, Theoretical Perspectives and Experiences from the Ground*, London, Routledge.

Barrett, S. (1981) 'Local Authorities and the Community Land Scheme', in S. Barrett and C. Fudge (eds.), *Policy and Action*, London, Methuen.

Barrett, S. (2004) 'Implementation Studies: Time for a Revival?', *Public Administration*, 82, 2, 249–262.

Barrett, S. and Fudge, M. (eds.) (1981) *Policy and Action: Essays on the Implementation of Public Policy*, London, Methuen.

Barro, R. (1997) *Determinants of Economic Growth: A Cross-Country Empirical Study*, Cambridge, MA, MIT Press.

Batt, L. (2009) 'Bosnia and Herzegovina: The International Mission at a Turning Point', FRIDE Policy Brief, 5, February, available at http://www.fride.org/descarga/PB5_Bosnia_Herzegovina_ENG_feb09.pdf

Bechev, D. (2006) 'Carrots, Sticks and Norms: The EU and Regional Cooperation in Southeast Europe', *Journal of Southern Europe and the Balkans*, 8, 1, 27–43.

Bengtsson, R. and Elgström, O. (2011) 'Reconsidering the EU's Role in International Relations – Do Role Performances Fit to Role Conceptions?', in S. Harnisch, C. Frank, and H. Maull (eds.), *Role Theory in International Relations*, London, Routledge, 113–130.

Bercio, A. and Böttger, K. (2012) 'A Wake-Up Call from Enlargement Fatigue: The Cases of Bosnia-Herzegovina and Serbia', *IEP Policy Briefs on Enlargement and the Neighbourhood*, No.1 2012, 1–8.

Berle, A. and Means, G. (1932) *The Modern Corporation and Private Property*, New York, The Macmillan Co., 1932; new edition 1991, Brunswick and London, Transaction Publishers.

Berman, S. (2007) 'The Vain Hope for "Correct" Timing', *Journal of Democracy*, XVIII, 14–17.

Bhagwati, J. (2002) 'Coping with Antiglobalization: A Trilogy of Discontents', *Foreign Affairs*, January–February, 2–7.

Bierman, R. (2008) 'Toward a Theory of Inter-organizational Networking, the Euro-Atlantic Security Institutions Interacting', *Review of International Organizations*, 3, 151–177.

Bierman, R. and Koops, J. (eds.) (2017) *Palgrave Handbook of Inter-Organizational Relations in World Politics*, Palgrave Macmillan.

Bilal, S. and Stevens, C. (2009) 'The Interim Economic Partnership Agreements between the EU and African States', *Policy Management Report 17*, ODI and Ecdpm, 1–320.

Bini Smaghi, L. (2004) 'A Single Seat in the IMF?', *Journal of Common Market Studies*, 42, 2, 229–248.

Bini Smaghi L. (2006) 'Powerless Europe: Why is the Euro-Area Still a Political Dwarf?' *International Finance*, 9, 2, 261–279.

Bini Smaghi, L. (2009) 'Going Forward: Regulation and Supervision after the Financial Turmoil', Paolo Baffi Centre Research Paper, 2009–47, June 2009.

Birdsall, N. (2009) 'Double Majorities at the World Bank and IMF: For Legitimacy and Effectiveness', Bretton Woods Non-Commission, Centre for Global Development, available at https://www.cgdev.org/doc/Non-Commission/CGD-NC-Birdsall3-18.pdf

Biscop, S. (2004) 'Effective Multilateralism: Bringing the European Way into Practice', in S. Biscop (ed.) *Audit of European Strategy*, Egmont Paper No. 3, Brussels, Royal Institute for International Relations.

Boix, C. and Stokes, S. (2003) 'Endogenous Democratization', *World Politics*, 55, 4, 2003, 815–849.

Bonaglia, F., Goldstein, A. and Petito, F. (2006) 'Values in European Union Development Cooperation Policy', in S. Lucarelli and I. Manners (eds.), *Values, Images and Principles in EU Foreign Policy*, London, Routledge, 164–184.

Boone, P. (1996) 'Politics and the Effectiveness of Foreign Aid', *European Economic Review*, 40, 2, 289–329.

Bradlow, D. and Hunter, D. (eds.) (2010) *International Financial Institutions and International Law*, Alphen aan den Rijn, Kluwer Law International.

Brett, E. (2003) 'Participation and Accountability in Development Management', *Journal of Development Studies,* 40, 2, 1–29.

Brenton, P. (2003) 'Integrating the Least Developed Countries into the World Trading System: The Current Impact of EU Preferences under Everything But Arms', Policy Research Paper 3018, April 2003, Washington, DC, The World Bank.

Brenton, P. and Ikezuki, T. (2005) 'The Value of Trade Preferences for Africa', in R. Newfarmer (ed.) *Trade, Doha and Development: A Window on the Issues*, Washington, DC, The World Bank.

Brenton, P., Baroncelli, E. and Malouche, M. (2006) 'Trade and Investment Integration of the Maghreb', Middle East and North Africa Working Paper Series, No. 44. Washington, DC, The World Bank. http://documents.worldbank.org/curated/en/997471468278036144/Trade-and-investment-integration-of-the-Maghreb

Brenton, P., Newfarmer, R. and Hoppe, M. (2008) 'Economic Partnership Agreements and the Export Competitiveness of Africa', Policy Research Working Paper 4627, PREM Unit, Washington, DC, The World Bank.

Bretherton, C. and Vogler, J. (1999) *The European Union as a Global Actor*, London, Routledge.

Bretherton, C. and Vogler, J. (2006) *The European Union as a Global Actor*, London, Routledge, second edition.

Bretton Woods Project (2010) 'Analysis of World Bank Voting Reforms', 30 April, available at: http://www.brettonwoodsproject.org/doc/wbimfgov/wbgovreforms2010.pdf

Brown, B. (1992) *The United States and the Politicization of the World Bank: Issues of International Law and Policy*, London and New York, Kegan Paul International.

Brown, W. (1999) 'The EU Structural Adjustment Support: The case of Lomé IV and Zimbabwe', *Review of African Political Economy*, 26, 79, 75–91.

Brown, W. (2004) 'From Uniqueness to Uniformity? An Assessment of EU Development Aid Policies', in K. Arts, and A. Dickson (eds.), *EU Development Cooperation: From Model to Symbol*, Manchester and New York, Manchester University Press, 17–41.

Buira, A. (2005) *Reforming the Governance of the IMF and the World Bank*, London, Anthem Press.

Bulmer, S. (1994) 'Institutions, Governance Regimes and the Single European Market: Analyzing the Governance of the European Union', paper prepared for panel on 'Contending Approaches to EC Governance', Conference of Europeanists, 31 March to 2 April 1994, Chicago.

Bunce, V. (1999) *Subversive Institutions: the Design and the Destruction of Socialism and the State*, Cambridge, Cambridge University Press.

Bunse, S. and Klein, Ch. (2013) 'What's Left of the Rotating Presidency? The Future of "National" Presidencies', in F. Foret and Y.-S. Rittelmeyer (eds.), *The European Council and European Governance The Commanding Heights of the EU*, London Routledge.

Burnside, C. and Dollar, D. (2000) 'Aid, Policies, and Growth', *American Economic Review*, 90, 4, 847–868.

Burnside, C. and Dollar, D. (2004) 'Aid, Policies, and Growth: Reply', *American Economic Review*, 94, 3, 781–784.

Carbone, M. (2007) *The European Union and International Development*, London and New York, Routledge.

Carbone, M. (2008) 'Mission Impossible: the European Union and Policy Coherence for Development', *Journal of European Integration*, 30, 3, 323–342.

Carbone, M. (2009) 'Desperately Seeking Policy Coherence: Aid and Security in the Development Policy of the European Union', Paper prepared for the Workshop on Transforming Political Structures: Security, Institutions and Regional Integration Mechanisms, organized by the European Report on Development, Florence, 16–17 April 2009.

Carbone, M. (ed.) (2013a) 'Special Issue: Development Policy and the EU's External Action', *Cambridge Review of International Affairs*, 26, 3.

Carbone, M. (ed.) (2013b) *The European Union in Africa*, Manchester, Manchester University Press.

Carlsnaes, W. and Smith, S. (eds.) (1994) *European Foreign Policy: The EC and Changing Perspectives in Europe*, London, Sage.

Carlsnaes, W. (1987) *Ideology and Foreign Policy: Problems of Comparative Conceptualization*, Oxford, Basil Blackwell Ltd.

Carothers, T. (2007) 'Misunderstanding Gradualism', *Journal of Democracy*, XVIII, 18–22.

Carothers, T. and De Gramont, D. (2013) *Development Aid Confronts Politics: The Almost Revolution*, Washington, DC, Carnegie Endowment for International Peace.

Carpenter D. (2001) *The Forging of Bureaucratic Autonomy*, Princeton, NJ, Princeton University Press.

Casier, T. (2011) 'The EU's Two-Track Approach to Democracy Promotion. The Case of Ukraine', *Democratization*, 18, 4, 956–977.

Chaban, N., Elgström, O. and Holland, M. (2006) 'The European Union as Others See It', *European Foreign Affairs Review*, 11, 245–262.

Chwieroth, J. (2009) *Capital Ideas: The IMF and the Rise of Financial Liberalization*, Princeton, NJ, Princeton University Press.

Clemens, M., Bhavnani, R., Radelet, S. and Bazzi, S. (2011) 'Counting Chickens when they Hatch: Timing and the Effects of Aid on Growth', *The Economic Journal*, 122, 561, 590–617.

Coase, R. (1937) 'The Nature of the Firm', *Economica*, 4, 386–405.

Coase, R. (1960) 'The Problem of Social Cost', *Journal of Law and Economics*, 3, 1–44.

Coeuré, B. and Pisani-Ferry, J. (2007) 'How Many Voices? The Governance of the European Union's International Economic Relations', Bruegel Paper, Mimeo, Final Version, April 2007.

Cohen, B. J. (1993) 'The Triad and the Unholy Trinity: Lessons for the Pacific Region', in R. Higgott, R. Leaver and J. Ravenhill (eds.), *Pacific Economic Relations in the 1990s: Conflict or Cooperation?* Boulder, CO, Lynne Rienner, 133–158.

Collinson, S. (1999) '"Issue-systems", "Multi-level games" and the Analysis of the EU's External Commercial and Associated Policies: A Research Agenda', *Journal of European Public Policy*, 6, 2, 206–224.

Cooley, A. (2010) 'Contracting Global Governors: How Project Contracts Transform Global Governance Networks', in D. Avant, M. Finnemore and S. Sell (eds.) *Who Governs the Globe?*, Cambridge, Cambridge University Press, 238–264.

Cornia, G., Jolly, R. and Stewart, F. (eds.) (1987) *Adjustment with a Human Face*, Oxford, Clarendon Press.

Coser, L.A. (2003) *Masters of Sociological Thought: Ideas in Historical and Social Contexts*, Long Grove, IL, Waveland Press.

Costa, O. and Jørgensen, K.E. (2012) *The Influence of International Institutions on the EU*, Houndmills, Palgrave Macmillan.

Council of the European Communities (1988) 'Council Resolution of 31 May 1988 on the Economic Situation and Adjustment Process in Sub-Saharan Africa', in Compilation of Texts Adopted by the Council (Ministers for Development Cooperation), 1 January 1981 to 31 December 1988, Council of the EU. Luxembourg, Office for Official Publications of the European Communities, 1989.

Dahl, R. (1994) 'A Democratic Dilemma: System Effectiveness versus Citizens Participation', *Political Science Quarterly*, 109, 1, 23–34.

Dahl, R. (1999) 'Can International Organizations be Democratic? A Skeptic's View', in I. Shapiro and C. Hacker-Cordón (eds.), *Democracy's Edges,* Cambridge, Cambridge University Press, 19–36.

Dai, X. (2005) 'Why Comply? The Domestic Constituency Mechanism', *International Organization*, 59, 2, 363–398.

Damro, C. (2006) 'The New Trade Politics and EU Competition Policy: Shopping for Convergence and Cooperation', *Journal of European Public Policy* 13, 6, 867–886.

Dawson, T. (2002) 'Letter to the Editor: The IMF Responds', *The Wall Street Journal*, 17 June 2002.

Dearden, S. (2003) 'The Future Role of the European Union in Europe's Development Assistance', *Cambridge Review of International Affairs*, 16, 1, 105–117.

Deaton, A. (2013) *The Great Escape: Health, Wealth and the Origins of Inequality*, Princeton, NJ, Princeton University Press.

De La Rocha (2003) 'The Cotonou Agreement and its Implications for the Regional Trade Agenda in Eastern and Southern Africa', Policy Research Working Paper 3090, The World Bank, Africa Region, Washington DC, June 2003.

Del Sarto, R. and Schumacher, T. (2005) 'From EMP to ENP: What's at Stake with the European Neighborhood Policy towards the Southern Mediterranean?', *European Foreign Affairs Review*, 10, 17–38.

De Melo, J. and Panagaryia, A. (1992) *New Dimensions on Regional Integration*, Cambridge, Cambridge University Press.

Devrim, D. and Maršić, T. (2009) 'Croatia, Macedonia and the EU: Setting the Bar Too High?' Notes Internacionals CIDOB No.8, December 2009, 1–6.

De Wulf, L. and Maliszewska, M. (eds.) (2009) 'Economic Integration in the Euro-Mediterranean Region', Final report, Center for Social and Economic Research, September 2009.

Diamond, L. and Plattner, M. (1995) (eds.), *Economic Reform and Democracy*, Baltimore, Johns Hopkins University Press.

Doidge, M. and Holland, M. (2012) *Development Policy of the European Union*, London, Palgrave Macmillan.

Dollar, D. and Kraay, A. (2002) 'Spreading the Wealth', *Foreign Affairs*, January–February, 120–133.

Doran, C.F. (1989) 'Systemic Disequilibrium, Foreign Policy Role, and the Power Cycle: Challenges for Research Design', *Journal of Conflict Resolution*, 33, 3, 371–401.

Driscoll, D. (1996) 'The IMF and the World Bank: How Do They Differ?', IMF paper, available at http://www.imf.org/external/pubs/ft/exrp/differ/differ.htm

DRN–ECDPM–ECORYS–PARTICIP (2014) 'Evaluation of the European Union's Cooperation with the Occupied Palestinian Territory and Support to the Palestinian People', Final Report, Volume 1, June 2014, Evaluation carried out on behalf of the European Commission, DEVCO-EuropeAid, 1–256.

Ducasse-Rogiers, (2012) 'EU Enlargement, EU Conditionality and EU State Building: Could Less EU Create More EU?', in J. Lagendijk, and J.M. Wiersma, (2012) *Beyond*

the Deadlock? Perspectives on Future EU Enlargement, E-publication, Clingedael Insitute, The Hague, 31–33.
Dür, A. and Zimmermann, H. (2007) 'Introduction: The EU in International Trade Negotiations', *Journal of Common Market Studies*, 45, 4, 771–787.
Easterly, W. (2007) *The White Man's Burden*, Oxford and New York, Oxford University Press.
Easterly, W., Levine, R. and Roodman, D. (2004) 'New Data, New Doubts: Comment on *Aid, Policies and Growth* (2000) by Burnside and Dollar', *American Economic Review*, 94, 3, 774–780.
Easton, D. (1965) *A Systems Analysis of Political Life*, New York, Wiley.
Economist, The (2002) 'Facing Responsibility', Special Report on Europe in the World, 23 November, US Edition.
Economist, The (2006) 'Europe: Third Time Lucky?'; Charlemagne, London Vol. 378, Fasc. 8460, (14 January 2006): 44.
EEC (1957) EEC Treaty (Rome Treaty), accessed at https://eur-lex.europa.eu/legal-content/EN/TXT/?uri=CELEX:11957E/TXT
Ehrenfeld, R. (2003) *Funding Evil, How is Terrorism Financed and How to Stop It, The Palestinians*, ACD (American Center for Democracy), mimeo, 1–45.
Eichengreen, B. (1999) *Towards a New International Financial Architecture: A Practical Post-Asia Agenda*, Washington, DC, Institute for International Economics.
Eide, E.B. (2004) 'Global Europe, Report I: "Effective Multilateralism": Europe, Regional Security and a Revitalised UN', London, The Foreign Policy Centre.
Elbasani, A. (2008) 'EU Enlargement in the Western Balkans: Strategies of Borrowing and Inventing', *Journal of Balkan and Near Eastern Studies*, 10, 3, 293–307.
Elgström, O. (2006) 'Leader or Foot-Dragger? Perceptions of the European Union in Multilateral International Negotiations', SIEPS Report 1, March 2006.
Elgström, O. (2007) 'The European Union as a Leader in International Multilateral Negotiations — a Problematic Aspiration?', *International Relations*, 21, 4, 445–458.
Elgström, O. (2008) 'Trade. . .and Aid? EU Policy and Economic Partnership Agreements', UCD Dublin European Institute Working Paper 08–10, July 2008.
Elgström, O. and Frennhoff Larsén, M. (2010): 'Free to Trade? Commission Autonomy in the Economic Partnership Agreement Negotiations', *Journal of European Public Policy*, 17, 2, 205–223.
Elgström, O. and Smith, M. (2006a) *The European Union's Roles in International Politics*, London, Routledge.
Elgström, O. and Smith, M. (2006b) 'Introduction', in O. Elgström and M. Smith (eds.), *The European Union's Roles in International Politics*, Routledge, London, 1–10.
Emerson, M., Balfour, R., Corthaut, T., Wouters, J., Maciej Kaczynski, P. and Renard, T. (2011) *Upgrading the EU's Role as a Global Actor*, Brussels, CEPS.
Epstein D. and O'Halloran, S. (1999) *Delegating Powers: A Transaction Cost Politics Approach to Policy Making Under Separate Powers*, Cambridge, UK, Cambridge University Press.
Etzioni, A. (1964) *Modern Organizations*, Englewood Cliffs, NJ, Prentice-Hall.
EU (2008) 'The EU at a glance', accessed at http://europa.eu/abc/panorama/index_en.htm
EU–Africa Infrastructure Trust Fund (2010) *Annual Report 2010*, 1–84.
European Commission (1996) 'Green Paper on Relations between the European Union and the ACP countries on the Eve of the 21st Century: Challenges and Options for a New Partnership', COM (96) 570 final, 20 November 1996.
European Commission (2000a) 'White Paper on Reforming the Commission', COM (2000) 200, Brussels, March.

European Commission (2000b) 'The European Community's Development Policy', COM (2000) 212 final, Brussels, April.

European Commission (2000c) 'On the Implementation of Measures Intended to Promote Observance of Human Rights and Democratic Principles in External Relations for 1996–1999', COM (2000) 726 final, Brussels, 14 November.

European Commission (2002) 'Communication from the Commission to the Council and the European Parliament Integrating Migration Issues in the European Union's Relations with Third Countries', COM (2002) 703 final, Brussels, 3 December.

European Commission (2003a) 'Communication from the Commission to the Council and the European Parliament - The Western Balkans and European Integration', COM (2003) 285 final, Brussels, 21 May.

European Commission (2003b) 'The European Union and the United Nations: The Choice of Multilateralism, Communication from the Commission to the Council and the European Parliament', COM (2003) 526 final, Brussels, 10 September.

European Commission (2004) 'European Neighborhood Policy – Strategy Paper', COM(2004) 373.

European Commission (2005) 'Communication from the Commission to the Council, the European Parliament and the European Economic and Social Committee, EU Strategy for Africa: Towards a Euro-African Pact to Accelerate Africa's Development', SEC(2005)1255.

European Commission (2006) 'Enlargement Strategy and Main Challenges 2006–2007, including Annexed Special Report on the EU's Capacity to Integrate New Members', COM(2006) 649, 8 November 2006.

European Commission (2007) 'Keeping Europe's Promises on Financing for Development, Annual Report to the European Parliament, the Council, the European Economic and Social Committee and the Committee of the Regions', COM (2007) 164.

European Commission (2008) 'Minutes of the Seminar on the Commission's Aid Delivery through Development Banks and EIB', 9/12/08.

European Commission (2009a) 'Supporting Developing Countries in Coping with the Crisis, Communication from the Commission to the European Parliament, the Council, the European Economic and Social Committee and the Committee of the Regions', COM(2009) 160 final.

European Commission (2009b) 'EU Toolkit for the Implementation of Complementarity and Division of Labour in Development Policy', DG.DEV.C1, January 2009.

European Commission (2009c) 'Aid Effectiveness Agenda: Benefits of a European Approach, Brussels, Project 2008/170204' conducted by HTSPE.

European Commission (2010a) 'Financing for Development: Annual Progress Report 2010, Getting Back on Track to Reach the EU 2015 Target on ODA Spending?' SEC (2010) 420 final, Brussels, 21 April.

European Commission (2010b) 'Green Paper on The Future of the EU Budget Support to Third Countries', COM(2010) 586 final, Brussels, 19 October.

European Commission (2011) 'Communication from the Commission to the European Parliament and the Council: Enlargement Strategy and Main Challenges', COM(2011) 666 Final, 12 October.

EU Commission–DG Development and Cooperation–EuropeAid (2012) 'The Cotonou Agreement', http://ec.europa.eu/europeaid/where/acp/overview/cotonou-agreement/

EU Commission–DG DEVCO–EuropeAid (2016) 'Information Note on Multidonor Trust Funds Supported by the European Union', available at https://ec.europa.eu/europeaid/multidonor-trust-funds-supported-european-union-2003-dec-2016_en

EU Commission–DG DEVCO (2017a) 'EU External Investment Plan', at https://ec.europa.eu/europeaid/sites/devco/files/factsheet-eu-external-investment-plan-20170710_en.pdf

EU Commission–DG DEVCO (2017b) 'Blending Operations', at https://ec.europa.eu/europeaid/policies/innovative-financial-instruments-blending/blending-operations_en.

European Commission–DG RELEX and The World Bank Group (2006) 'Interpretative Letter on the Visibility Clause of the EC–WB Framework Agreement', accessed at https://ec.europa.eu/europeaid/sites/devco/files/framework-agreement-ec-wb-visibility-interpretative-letter-20060602_en.pdf

European Commission–DG Development and The World Bank Group (2007) 'European Commission–World Bank Meeting with Civil Society on EC–World Bank Collaboration on Africa', Note, Brussels, 17 September.

European Commission (EC)–World Bank Group (WBG) (2009) 'Annual Consultation-Operational Conclusions', Paris WBG Office, (27–28 May), 1–7.

European Commission (EC)–World Bank Group (WBG) (2009) 'Joint Visibility Guidelines Relating to EC-funded WB-administered Trust Funds and Co-financings', 1–16.

European Commission (EC)–World Bank Group (WBG) (2010) 'Annual Consultation-Operational Conclusions', Paris WBG Office, (20–21 May), 1–13.

European Commission, Directorate General for Enlargement (2007) 'Infrastructure Project Facility (IPF) for Western Balkans – Concept Paper', Brussels, DG ELARG D3/NB/DB – REP. D (2007).

European Commission, EIB, EBRD, IBRD, IFC and other relevant IFIs (2006) 'Amended MoU between the EC, in liaison with the EIB, and other relevant IFIs on cooperation in (i) economic development in the new member states of Central and Eastern Europe, Cyprus, Malta and (ii) accession preparation in the EU candidate and potential candidate countries', Headquarters of different IFIs, mimeo, 1–8.

EU Council (2007a) 'The EU and Central Asia: Strategy for a New Partnership', European Communities, Brussels, October 2007.

EU Council (2007b) 'The Africa–EU Strategic Partnership: A Joint Africa–EU Strategy', Lisbon, December 2007, 16344/07 (Presse 291).

European Council (2001a) 'Council Regulation (EC) No. 416/2001 of 28 February 2001 amending Regulation (EC) No. 2820/98 applying a multiannual scheme of generalised tariff preferences for the period 1 July 1999 to 31 December 2001 so as to extend duty-free access without any quantitative restrictions to products originating in the least developed countries', *Official Journal of the European Communities* L 60/43, 1 March.

European Council (2001b) 'Council Regulation (EC) No. 2501/2001 of 10 December 2001 applying a scheme of generalised tariff preferences for the period from 1 January 2002 to 31 December 2004', *Official Journal of the European Communities* L 346/1, 31 December.

European Council (2003a) 'A Secure Europe in a Better World: European Security Strategy', Brussels, 12 December.

European Council (2003b) Press Release, 6941/03 Presse 63, 18 March.

European Council (2010a) 'Council Conclusions on the Millennium Development Goals for the United Nations High-Level Plenary Meeting in New York and Beyond', 3023rd Foreign Affairs Council meeting Luxembourg, 14 June 2010, 11080/10 available at http://register.consilium.europa.eu/doc/srv?l=EN&f=ST%2011080%202010%20INIT

European Council (2010b) 'Council Conclusions on the Western Balkans', 3023rd Foreign Affairs Council meeting, Luxembourg, 14 June 2010, Press Release, 1–3.

European Council (2011) 'Council Regulation (EC) No 747/2001 of 9 April 2001 providing for the management of Community tariff quotas and of reference quantities for products eligible for preferences by virtue of agreements with certain Mediterranean countries and repealing Regulations (EC) No. 1981/94 and (EC) No. 934/95'.

European Council (2012) 'Conclusions 1–2 March 2012', EUCO 4/2/12 REV 2, 1–16.

EU Delegation to the United States of America, DELUSW (2011) 'WB EU Plus Group Coordination Meeting', E-note, 15 June 2011.

EU Rapid Press Release (2010) 'The EU Contribution to the Global Fund to Fight AIDS, Tuberculosis and Malaria', MEMO/10/470, 4 October, available at http://europa.eu/rapid/pressReleasesAction.do?reference=MEMO/10/470&format=HTML&aged=0&language=EN&guiLanguage=en

Eurodad (2006) 'European Coordination at the World Bank and International Monetary Fund: A Question of Harmony?', European Network on Debt and Development, Brussels, January.

Eurodad (2007) 'How to Fit 27 Elephants in a Single Chair', Eurodad Briefing, May, 1–8.

Eurodad (2009) Eurodad Briefing on the European Commission's April 2009 Development Finance Communication: 'Supporting Developing Countries in Coping with the Crisis', available at: http://eurodad.org/uploadedfiles/whats_new/news/eurodad_analysis_ec_development_finance_communication_april2008.pdf.

EuropeAid (2008a) 'Temporary International Mechanism (TIM) Key Facts', 18 January 2008, available at http://ec.europa.eu/europeaid/where/neighbourhood/country-cooperation/occupied_palestinian_territory/tim/index_en.htm

EuropeAid (2008b) 'Commission Participation in the HIPC Initiative, 2008 Status Report', AIDCO C4/AT D(2009) available at http://ec.europa.eu/development/icenter/repository/HIPC_status_report_2008_en.pdf

EuropeAid (2010) 'Financial Contribution of EuropeAid to the World Bank Group 2000–2009', now updated at: https://ec.europa.eu/europeaid/sites/devco/files/wbg_2012_en.pdf.

EC Press Rapid Release (2012) 'European Commission launches accelerated infringement proceedings against Hungary over the independence of its central bank and data protection authorities as well as over measures affecting the judiciary', IP/12/24, 17 January, accessed at http://europa.eu/rapid/pressReleasesAction.do?reference=IP/12/24

European Parliament (2003) Working Group on Budgetary Assistance to the Palestinian Authority, 'Draft conclusions endorsed by Mr. Wynn and Mrs. Theato', available at http://www.eufunding.org/accountability/WGPA-DRA.pdf

European Parliament (2011a) 'Draft Report on the Future of EU Budget Support to Developing Countries' (2010/2300 INI, 4.3.2011).

European Parliament (2011b) Directorate-General for External Policies of the European Union, 'The EU as a Global Actor: Its Evolving Role in Multilateral Organizations', EXPO/B/AFET/FWC/2009–01/LOT2/06, prepared by Palacio, V. and De La Rocha, M. et al., Fundacion Alternativas, March.

European Parliament (2011c) Committee on Budgetary Control, 'Questions to Commissioner Piebalgs', available at http://www.europarl.europa.eu/document/activities/cont/201101/20110126ATT12573/20110126ATT12573EN.pdf

European Parliament (2012) 'Resolution of 14 March 2012 on the 2011 progress report on the former Yugoslav Republic of Macedonia' (2011/2887(RSP)).

European Parliament, Council, Commission (2006) 'Joint statement by the Council and the representatives of the governments of the Member States meeting within the Council, the European Parliament and the Commission on European Union Development Policy: "The European Consensus"' (2006/C 46/01).

European Union (2017) Joint statement by the Parliament, the Council and the representatives of the governments of the Member States meeting within the Council, and the Commission on 'The new European Consensus on Development – Our World, Our Dignity, Our Future', available at: https://ec.europa.eu/europeaid/sites/devco/files/european-consensus-on-development-final-20170626_en.pdf

European Union Election Observation Mission (2010) Final Report, House of People's Representatives and State Council Elections, Ethiopia, May 2010, 1–41, available at https://eeas.europa.eu/headquarters/headquarters-homepage/24414/eu-election-observation-mission-ethiopia-2010_en

European Think Tanks Group (2011) 'EU Blending Facilities: Implications for Future Governance Options', 1–91, January 2011. Available at https://www.odi.org/sites/odi.org.uk/files/odi-assets/publications-opinion-files/6658.pdf

Eurostat (2017a) 'Share of EU in the World Trade', accessed July 2017 at http://appsso.eurostat.ec.europa.eu/nui/setupDownloads.do

Eurostat (2017b) 'Foreign Direct Investment Statistics', last updated on 10 April 2017, at http://ec.europa.eu/eurostat/statistics-explained/index.php/Foreign_direct_investment_statistics

Faini, R. and Grilli, E. (2004) 'Who Runs the IFIs?', Development Working Papers 191, Centro Studi Luca d'Agliano, 1–32, available at http://www.dagliano.unimi.it/media/WP2004_191.pdf

Fama, E. (1980) 'Agency Problems and the Theory of the Firm', *Journal of Political Economy*, 88, 2, 288–307.

Farrell, M. (2008) 'Internationalizing EU Development Policy', *Perspectives on European Politics and Society*, 9, 2, 225–240.

Faure, R. and Maxwell, S. (2017) 'The Proposed New European Consensus on Development: Has the Commission Got It Right?', *ODI Policy Brief*, February 2017, 1–8.

Feldstein, F. (1998) 'Refocusing the IMF', *Foreign Affairs*, March–April, 20–33.

Ferrer, J. and Behrens, A. (2011) 'Approaches to EU Blending Mechanisms for Development Finance', CEPS Special Report, May 2011.

Fioramonti, L. (2007) 'Different Facets of a Strategic Partnership: How the EU is Viewed by Political and Business Elites, Civil Society and the Press in India', *European Foreign Affairs Review*, 12, 349–362.

Financial Times (2010) 'Europe's Hidden Billions; Cohesion for a Reason', by Stanley Pignal, 2 December 2010.

Finger, M. and Schuler, F. (2002) 'Implementation of WTO Commitments: The Development Challenge', in B. Hoekman, A. Mattoo and P. English (eds.), *Development, Trade and the WTO: A Handbook*, Washington, DC, The World Bank.

Finnemore, M. and Sikkink, K. (1998) 'International Norm Dynamics and Political Change', *International Organization*, 52, 4, 887–917.

Fischer, S. (1998) 'The IMF and the Asian Crisis', 1–17, 1998, available at www.imf.org/external/np/speeches/1998/032098.htm

Fleck, R. and Kilby, C. (2006) 'World Bank Independence: A Model and Statistical Analysis of US Influence', *Review of Development Economics*, 10, 2, 224–240.

Florini, A. (1996) 'The Evolution of International Norms', *International Studies Quarterly*, 40, 363–389.

Folz, R. (2011) 'Does Membership Matter? Convergence of Sweden's and Norway's Role Conceptions by Interaction with the European Union', in S. Harnisch, C. Frank and H. Maull (eds.), *Role Theory in International Relations*, London, Routledge, 147–164.

Fraser, C. (2007) *An Introduction to European Foreign Policy*, London, Routledge.

Freedom House (2011 to 2017) 'Freedom in the World Country Index', available at https://freedomhouse.org/report/freedom-world/2012/bosnia-and-herzegovina, various years.

Freyburg, T. and Richter, S. (2010) 'National Identity Matters: The Limited Impact of EU Political Conditionality in the Western Balkans', *Journal of European Public Policy*, 17, 2, 263–281.

Frieden, J. (2004) 'One Europe, One Vote? The Political Economy of European Union Representation in International Organizations', *European Union Politics*, 5, 2, 261–276.

Friedson, F. (2009) 'Wolfensohn: "Fayad's Two-year Plan is a Very Smart Move" ', *The Jerusalem Post*, 1 November 2009.

Friends of Europe and Konrad Adenauer Stiftung (2010) 'Beating the Balkan Blues', Report of the European Policy Summit, December 2010, Brussels, 1–56.

Füle, S. (2010) 'EU Enlargement Commissioner, on "Accession Fatigue" ', in Friends of Europe and Konrad Adenauer Stiftung, 'Beating the Balkan Blues', Report of the European Policy Summit, 6–7.

Galtung, J. (1973) *The European Community: A Superpower in the Making*?, London, Allen and Unwin.

Gavin, F.J. (2004) *Gold, Dollars, and Power: The Politics of International Monetary Relations, 1958–1971*, Chapel Hill, The University of North Carolina Press.

Gawrich, A., Melnykovska, I. and Schweickert, R. (2010) 'Neighbourhood Europeanization Through ENP: The Case of Ukraine', *Journal of Common Market Studies*, 48, 5, 1209–1235.

GAP–Government Accountability Project (2010) 'Bar Complaint Charges Former World Bank Official with Ethics Violations', available at https://www.whistleblower.org/press/bar-complaint-charges-former-world-bank-official-ethics-violations

Gerring, J., Bond, P., Barndt, W. and Moreno, C. (2005) 'Democracy and Economic Growth: A Historical Perspective', *World Politics*, 57, 3, 323–364.

Ghoneim, A. and Kheir-El-Din, H. (2006) 'The Economic and Regulatory Policy Implications of Overlapping Preferential Trade Agreements in the Arab Countries: The Case of Egypt', in *The Economic and Regulatory Policy Implications of Overlapping Preferential Trade Agreements in the Arab Countries*, ERF Special Report, Research Report Series No. 0425 (2005).

Giddens, A. (1984) *The Constitution of Society: Outline of the Theory of Structuration,* Basingstoke, Macmillan.

Gilbert, C., Powell, A. and Vines, D. (2000) 'The World Bank's Structure: The Bank as an Institution', in C. Gilbert and D. Vines, *The World Bank: Structure and Policies*, Cambridge, Cambridge University Press.

Gill, I. and Raiser, M. (2012) (eds.) *Golden Growth: Restoring the Lustre of the European Economic Model*, Washington, DC, The World Bank.

Gilpin, R. (1981) *War and Change in World Politics*, MA, Mass. Cambridge, Cambridge University Press.

Gligorov, V. (2001) 'Bosnia and Herzegovina', *Journal of Southeastern Europe and Black Sea Studies*, 1, 1, 132–139.

Goldstein, J. (1993) *Ideas, Interests, and American Trade Policy*, Ithaca, NY, Cornell University Press.

Goldstein, J. and Keohane, R. (1993) *Ideas and Foreign Policy: Beliefs, Institutions, and Political Change*, Ithaca, NY, Cornell University Press.

Gourevitch, P. (1978) 'The Second Image Reversed: The International Sources of Domestic Politics', *International Organization*, 32, 4, 881–912.

Grant, Ch. (2011) 'A New Neighborhood Policy for the EU', Policy Brief, Centre for European Policy Reform, London.

Grant, R., and Keohane, R. (2005) 'Accountability and Abuses of Power in World Politics', *American Political Science Review*, 99, 1, 29–43.

Greig, A., Hulme, D. and Turner, M. (2007) *Challenging Global Inequality: Development Theory and Practice in the 21st Century*, Houndmills, Basingstoke, Palgrave Macmillan.

Grilli, E. (1993) *The European Community and the Developing Countries*, World Bank and Johns Hopkins University Press.

Grimm, S. and Phillips, L. (2006) 'European Policy Coordination in the Bretton Woods Institutions and ways to increase its coherence with European development goals', ODI, London, study commissioned by the DEV Committee of the European Parliament, released on 1 March 2006 under DGExPo/B/PolDep/Study/2005/16.

Grossman, G. and Helpman, E. (1994) 'Protection for Sale', *American Economic Review*, 84, 4, 833–850.

Gsthöl, S. (2007) 'EU External Action: European Neighborhood Policy', in M. Chang, E. de Souza, S. Gstöhl and D. Hanf, 'Working for Europe: Perspectives on the EU 50 Years after the Treaties of Rome'. Bruges Political Research Papers, April, Bruges, College of Europe, 19–31.

Gustavsson, J. (1999) 'How Should we Study Foreign Policy Change?', *Cooperation and Conflict*, 34, 1, 73–95.

Gutner, T.L. (2005) 'Explaining the Gaps between Mandate and Performance: Agency Theory and World Bank Environmental Reform', *Global Environmental Politics*, 5, 2, 10–37.

Gutner, T. and Thompson, A. (2010) 'The Politics of IO Performance: A Framework', *Review of International Organizations*, 5, 3, 227–248.

Hall, P. (2003) 'Adapting Methodology to Ontology in Comparative Politics', in J. Mahoney and D. Rueschmeyer (eds.), *Comparative Historical Analysis in the Social Sciences*, New York, Cambridge University Press, 373–404.

Harnisch, S., Frank, C. and Maull, H. (eds.) (2011) *Role Theory in International Relations*, London, Routledge.

Hawkins D. and Jacoby W. (2006) 'How Agents Matter', in D. Hawkins et al. (eds.), *Delegation and Agency in International Organizations*, Cambridge, Cambridge University Press, 199–228.

Hawkins, D., Lake, D., Nielson, D. and Tierney, M. (eds.) (2006) *Delegation and Agency in International Organizations*, Cambridge, UK, Cambridge University Press.

Held, D. (1999) 'The Transformation of Political Community: Rethinking Democracy in the Context of Globalization', in I. Shapiro and C. Hacker-Cordón (eds.), *Democracy's Edges*, Cambridge, Cambridge University Press, 91–102.

Held, D. (2002) 'Law of States, Law of Peoples: Three Models of Sovereignty', *Legal Theory*, 8, 1, 1–44.

Helm, C. and Sprinz, D. (2000) 'Measuring the Effectiveness of International Environmental Regimes', *Journal of Conflict Resolution*, 45, 5, 630–652.

Henökl, T. (2013) 'Inside the External Action Service: Institutional Change and Its Impact on the European Political Order', UACES Working Paper, presented at Passau UACES Conference, 2012.

Hermann, Ch. (1990) 'Changing Course: When Governments Choose to Redirect Foreign Policy', *International Studies Quarterly*, 34, 1, 3–21.

High Level Commission on Modernization of World Bank Group Governance (2009) 'Repowering the World Bank for the 21st Century', sponsored by The World Bank President Robert Zoellick, Washington, DC.

Hill, C. (1990) 'European Foreign Policy: Power Bloc, Civilian Model – or Flop?', in R. Rummel (ed.), *The Evolution of an International Actor*, Boulder, CO, and London, Westview Press.

Hill, C. (1993) 'The Capability–Expectations Gap, or Conceptualising Europe's International Role', *Journal of Common Market Studies*, 31, 3, 305–328.

Hill, C. (1996) *The Actors in Europe's Foreign Policy*, London, Routledge.

Hill, C. (1998) 'Closing the Capabilities-Expectations Gap?' in J. Peterson and H. Sjursen (eds.), *A Common Foreign Policy for Europe? Competing Visions of the CFSP*, London, Routledge.

Hill, C. and Smith M. (eds.) (2005) *International Relations and the European Union*, Oxford and New York, Oxford University Press.

Hjern, B. and Porter, D.O. (1981) 'Implementation Structures: A New Unit of Administrative Analysis', *Organisation Studies*, 2, 211–227.

Hoebink, P. (ed.) (2004) *The Treaty of Maastricht and Europe's Development Cooperation*, Amsterdam, Aksant.

Hoffmann, K. (2010) 'The EU in Central Asia: Successful Governance Promotion?', *Third World Quarterly*, 31, 1, 87–103.

Holland, M. (2002) *The European Union and the Third World*, New York, Palgrave.

Holland, M. (2004) 'Development Policy: Paradigm Shifts and the "Normalization" of a Privileged Partnership?', in M.G. Cowles and D. Dinan (eds.) *Developments in the European Union 2*, Houndmills, Palgrave.

Holland, M. and Doidge, H. (2012) *Development Policy of the European Union*, Basingstoke and New York, Palgrave Macmillan.

Holmstrom, B. and Milgrom, P. (1991) 'Multitask Principal-Agent Analyses: Incentive Contracts, Asset Ownership and Job Design', *Journal of Law, Economics, and Organization*, 7, 24–52.

Holsti, K. (1970) 'National Role Conceptions in the Study of Foreign Policy', *International Studies Quarterly*, 14, 233–309.

Holsti, K. (1972) 'Foreign Policy Decision Makers Viewed Psychologically: "Cognitive Process" Approaches', in J. Rosenau (ed.) *In Search of Global Patterns*, New York, Free Press, 120–144.

Holsti, K. (1970/1987) 'National Role Conceptions in the Study of Foreign Policy', in S. Walker (ed.) *Role Theory and Foreign Policy Analysis*, Durham, NC, Duke University Press.

Hombach, B. (2000) 'A Stability Pact for South-Eastern Europe: A New Perspective for the Region', *Perceptions*, 3, 5–21, accessed at http://sam.gov.tr/wp-content/uploads/2012/01/Bodo-Hombach.pdf, in April 2012.

Hoppe, M. (2007) 'Economic Partnership Agreements: Does Preferential Access of Non-LDC African Countries Increase?', World Bank Trade Note No. 32, 12 July.

House of Commons International Development Committee (2002) *The Effectiveness of the Reforms of European Development Assistance*, Second Report of Session 2001–02, HC 417. Quoted in: S. Dearden, *Does the European Union Development Policy Have any Future?*, Discussion paper, p. 23, Department of Economics, Manchester Metropolitan University, Manchester.

Howard, L.M. (2008) *UN Peacekeeping in Civil Wars*. New York, Cambridge University Press.

Huber, J. and Shipan, Ch. (2002) *Deliberate Discretion? The Institutional Foundations of Bureaucratic Control*, New York, Cambridge University Press.

Hull, C. (1948) *The Memoirs of Cordell Hull*, New York, The Macmillan Co.

Hungarian Presidency at the World Bank (2011a) 'EU-coordination Principles', mimeo.

Hungarian Presidency at the World Bank (2011b) 'Mid-term Performance Review', mimeo.

Huntington, S. (1991) *The Third Wave: Democratization in the Late Twentieth Century*, Norman, OK, University of Oklahoma Press.

IBRD (1944) *Articles of Agreement*, as amended effective 16 February 1989, available at http://siteresources.worldbank.org/EXTABOUTUS/Resources/ibrd-articlesofagreement.pdf

IEG (Independent Evaluation Group) (2011) 'Trust Fund Support for Development: An Evaluation of the World Bank's Trust Fund Portfolio', Independent Evaluation Group, Washington, DC, The World Bank Group.

Ikenberry, J. (1992) 'A World Economy Restored: Expert Consensus and the Anglo-American Postwar Settlement', *International Organization*, 46, 1, 289–321.

IMF (1998) 'External Evaluation of the ESAF. Report by a Group of Independent Experts', Washington, DC, IMF, June 1998, available at https://www.imf.org/external/pubs/ft/extev/index.HTM

IMF WB Development Committee (2011) 'World Bank Corporate Scorecard 2011'. Integrated Results and Performance Framework, 2011–0014, Washington, DC, 29 August 2011.

Independent Evaluation Group (IEG) (2014) 'ICR Review Tunisia: Governance and Opportunity Development', ICRR 14156, Washington, DC, The World Bank Group.

International Court of Justice (2011) 'Press Release No. 2011/37', 5 December 2011, 1–3.

International Federation of the Red Cross and the Red Crescent Societies (IFRC) (2009) 'Zimbabwe: Food Insecurity', Operations Update No. 6, Emergency Appeal No. MDRZW003, last accessed July 2018 at http://www.ifrc.org/docs/appeals/08/mdrzw00306.pdf

Jakobeit, C. (2005) 'Enhancing the Voice of Developing Countries in the World Bank: Selective Double Majority Voting and a Pilot Phase Approach', in A. Buira, *Reforming the Governance of the IMF and the World Bank*, London, Anthem Press, 213–234.

Jensen, M. and Meckling, W. (1976) 'Theory of the Firm: Managerial Behavior, Agency Costs and Ownership Structure', *Journal of Financial Economics*, 3, 4, 305–360.

Jessop, B. (2002) *The Future of the Capitalist State*, Cambridge, Polity.

Jørgensen, K.E. (2006a) 'Intersecting Multilateralisms: The European Union and Multilateral Institutions', in K.V. Laatikainen and K. Smith, *The European Union and the United Nations*, Houndmills, Basingstoke, Macmillan, 195–211.

Jørgensen, K.E. (2006b) 'A Multilateralist Role for the EU?', in O. Elgström and M. Smith, *The European Union's Roles in International Politics*, London, Routledge, 30–46.

Jørgensen, K.E. (2007) 'Overview: The European Union and the World', in K.E. Jørgensen, M. Pollack and B. Rosamond (eds.), *Handbook of European Union Politics*, London, Sage, 507–525.

Jørgensen, K.E. (ed.) (2009) *The European Union and International Organizations*, London, Routledge.

Jørgensen K.E., Oberthür, S. and Shahin, J. (eds.) (2011a) 'The Performance of the EU in International Institutions', *Journal of European Integration*, Special Issue, 33, 6, now also in K.E. Jørgensen, S. Oberthür and J. Shahin (eds.) (2013) *The Performance of the EU in International Institutions*, Abingdon, Routledge.

Jørgensen K.E., Oberthür, S. and Shahin, J. (2011b) 'Introduction: Assessing the EU's Performance in International Institutions – Conceptual Framework and Core Findings', *Journal of European Integration*, 33, 6, 599–620.

Kahler, M. (2004) 'Defining Accountability Up: The Global Economic Multilaterals', *Government and Opposition*, 39, 2, 132–158.

Kaldor, M. (2003) *Global Civil Society: An Answer to War*, Cambridge, Polity Press.

Kapur, D., Lewis, J.P. and Webb, R. (1997) *The World Bank: Its First Half Century*, Vols I and II, Washington, DC, Brookings Institution Press.

Kaufmann, D., Kraay, A. and Mastruzzi, M. (2009) 'Governance Matters VIII: Aggregate and Individual Governance Indicators, 1996–2008', World Bank Policy Research Working Paper, 4978, Washington DC, The World Bank.

Kausch, K. and Youngs, R. (2009) 'The End of the "Euro-Mediterranean Vision"', *International Affairs*, 85, 5, 963–975.

Keohane, R. (1984) *After Hegemony: Cooperation and Discord in the World Political Economy*, Princeton, NJ, Princeton University Press.

Keohane, R. (2003) 'Global Governance and Democratic Accountability', in D. Held and M. Koenig-Archibugi, *Taming Globalization: Frontiers of Governance*, Cambridge, Polity Press, 130–159.

Keohane, R. and Martin, L. (2003) 'Institutional Theory as a Research Program', in C. Elman and M. Elman (eds.) *Progress in International Relations Theory*, Cambridge, MIT Press, 71–108.

Keynes, J.M. (1971–1989) *The Collected Writings of John Maynard Keynes*, D.E. Moggridge, E.S. Johnson, London, Macmillan for the London Royal Society.

Khasson, V., Vasilyan, S. and Vos, H. (2009) '"Everybody Needs Good Neighbours": The EU and its Neighbourhood', in J. Orbie (ed.) *Europe's Global Role, External Policies of the European Union*, Farnham, Ashgate.

Kiewiet, D.R. and McCubbins, M. (1991) *The Logic of Delegation: Congressional Parties and the Appropriation Process*, Chicago, University of Chicago Press.

Kim, J.Y. (2013) 'The World Bank Group Strategy: A Path to End Poverty'; World Bank Group President Jim Yong Kim Pre-Annual Meetings Speech, Washington, DC; as prepared for delivery; 1 October 2013; Speeches & Transcripts, available at http://www.worldbank.org/en/news/speech/2013/10/01/world-bank-group-president-jim-yong-kim-speech-at-george-washington-university.

Kindleberger, Ch. E. (1977) *America in the World Economy*, New York, Foreign Policy Association.

King, G., Keohane, R. and Verba, S. (1994) *Designing Social Inquiry*, Princeton NJ, Princeton University Press.

Kingdon, J.W. (1995) *Agendas, Alternatives and Public Policies*, 2nd ed, New York, Harper Collins.

Kitt, F. (2010) 'EU Aid Architecture: Recent Trends and Policy Directions', The World Bank Group Concessional Finance and Global Partnerships Vice-Presidency, Washington, DC, The World Bank, Mimeo.

Kleistra, Y. and Mayer, I. (2001) 'Stability and Flux in Foreign Affairs: Modelling Policy and Organizational Change', *Cooperation and Conflict*, 36, 4, 381–414.

Knodt, M. (2004) 'International Embeddedness of European Multi-level Governance', *Journal of European Public Policy*, 11, 4, 701–719.

Knodt, M. and Princen, S. (2003) *Understanding the European Union's External Relations*, London, Routledge/ECPR.

Koeberle, S., Bedoya, A., Silarsky, P. and G. Verheyen (eds.) (2005) *Conditionality Revisited: Concepts, Experiences and Lessons*, Washington, DC, The World Bank.

Koenig-Archibugi, M. (2011) 'Is Global Democracy Possible?', *European Journal of International Relations*, 17, 3, 519–542.

Kopits, G. and Székely, I. (2002) 'Fiscal Policy Challenges of EU Accession for the Baltics and Central Europe', presented at a conference organized by the Oesterreichische Nationalbank in Vienna, 3–5 November 2002.

Kramer, H. (2000) 'The European Union in the Balkans: Another Step towards European Integration', *Perceptions,* 5, 3, 22–38.

Krasner, S. (1982) 'Structural Causes and Regime Consequences: Regimes as Intervening Variables', *International Organization*, 36, 2, 185–205.

Krueger, A.O. (1997) 'Trade Policy and Economic Development: How We Learn', *American Economic Review*, 87, 1, 1–22.

Laatikainen, K.V. and Smith, K. (eds.) (2006a) *The European Union at the United Nations*, Houndmills, Basingstoke, Palgrave Macmillan.

Laatikainen, K.V. and Smith, K. (2006b) 'Introduction: The European Union at the United Nations: Leader, Partner or Failure?', in K.V. Laatikainen and K. Smith (eds.), *The European Union at the United Nations*, Houndmills, Basingstoke, Palgrave Macmillan, 1–23.

Labaki, M. (2011) 'Steven Vanackere critique Catherine Ashton', *Le Soir*, 4 May 2011.

Lagendijk, J. and Wiersma, J.M. (2012) 'Beyond the Deadlock? Perspectives on Future EU Enlargement', E-publication, Clingcdael Insitute, The Hague, http://www.europeanforum net/uploads/news/clingendael_publication_enlargement.pdf

Lake, D. and McCubbins, M. (2006) 'The Logic of Delegation to International Organizations', in D. Hawkins et al. (eds.) (2006) *Delegation and Agency in International Organizations*, Cambridge, UK, Cambridge University Press, 341–368.

Latif, A. (2005) 'Developing Country Coordination in International Intellectual Property Standard-Setting', Trade-Related Agenda, Development, and Equity (TRADE) Working Paper 24, South Centre (June 2005) available at http://www.southcentre.org

Laudan, L. (1996) *Beyond Positivism and Relativism: Theory, Method and Evidence*, Boulder, CO, Westview.

Lavenex, S. (2007) 'EU External Governance in "Wider Europe" ', *Journal of European Public Policy*, 11, 4, 680–700.

Le Monde (2011) 'Catherine Ashton sous le feu des critiques au Parlement européen', *Le Monde*, 3 February 2011, accessed at http://www.lemonde.fr/europe/article/2011/02/03/catherine-ashton-sous-le-feu-des-critiques-au-parlement-europeen_1474927_3214.html?xtmc=catherine_ashton_joseph_daul&xtcr=2

Legro, J. (1995) *Cooperation under Fire: Anglo-German Restraint during World War II,* Ithaca, NY, Cornell University Press.

Legro, J. (2005) *Rethinking the World: Great Power Strategies and International Order*, Ithaca, NY, Cornell University Press.

Leo, B. and Moss, T. (2009) 'Moving Mugabe's Mountain: Zimbabwe's Path to Arrears Clearance and Debt', CGD Working Papers, 190, November, 1–28, available at: https://www.cgdev.org/sites/default/files/1423217_file_Moss_Leo_Zimbabwe_Debt_Dynamics.pdf.

Levy, J. (2004) 'Learning and Foreign Policy: Sweeping a Conceptual Minefield', *International Organization*, 48, 2, 279–312.

Lijphart, A. (2008) *Thinking about Democracy: Power Sharing and Majority Rule in Theory and Practice*, Abingdon and New York, Routledge.

Linz, J. and Stepan, A. (1996) *Problems of Democratic Transition and Consolidation*, Baltimore, MD, Johns Hopkins University Press.

Lipsky, M. (1980) *Street Level Bureaucracy*, New York, Russell Sage.

Löwi, T. (1972) 'Four Systems of Policy, Politics, and Choice', *Public Administration Review*, 32, 4, 298–310.

Lucarelli, S. (2006) 'The External Image of the European Union', in *GARNET Report on 'Global Governance, Regionalisation and Regulation: the Role of the EU'* (EU 6th Framework Programme 2005–2010; call identifier: FP6–2002-Citizens-3).

Lucarelli, S. (2007) 'The European Union in the Eyes of Others: Towards Filling a Gap in the Literature', in *European Foreign Affairs Review*, 12, 249–270.

Lucarelli, S. and L. Fioramonti (eds.) (2010) *External Perceptions of the European Union as a Global Actor*, London, Routledge.

Lucarelli, S. and Manners, I. (2006) *Values, Images and Principles in EU Foreign Policy*, London, Routledge.

Lucarelli, S. et al (2007) *European Foreign Affairs Review*, 12, 3, 'Special Issue on the External Image of the European Union'.

Lyne, M., Nielson, D. and Tierney, M. (2006) 'Who Delegates? Alternative Models of Principals in Development Aid', in D. Hawkins et al. (eds.) (2006) *Delegation and Agency in International Organizations*, Cambridge, UK, Cambridge University Press, 41–76.

Lyne, M., Nielson, D. and Tierney, M. (2009) 'Controlling Coalitions: Social Lending at the Multilateral Development Banks', *Review of International Organizations*, 4, 4, 407–433.

Macdonald, K. (2012) 'Global Democracy for a Partially Joined-up World: Toward a Multi-level System of Public Power and Democratic Governance?', in D. Archibugi, M. Koenig-Archibugi and R. Marchetti (eds.), *Global Democracy Normative and Empirical Perspectives*, Cambridge and New York, Cambridge University Press.

Magen, A. and Morlino, L. (eds.) (2008) *International Actors, Democratization and the Rule of Law: Anchoring Democracy*, London, Routledge.

Maizels, A. and Nissanke, M. (1984) 'Motivations for Aid to Developing Countries', *World Development*, 12, 9, 879–900.

Majone, G. (2001) 'Two Logics of Delegation: Agency and Fiduciary Relations in EU Governance', in *European Union Politics*, 2, 1, 103–122.

Mallaby, S. (2004) *The World's Banker: A Story of Failed States, Financial Crises, and the Wealth and Poverty of Nations*, New York, Penguin Books.

Manners, I. (2002) 'Normative Power Europe: a Contradiction in Terms?', *Journal of Common Market Studies*, 40, 2, 235–258.

Marini, A. and Kovacheva, R. (2010) 'The World Bank is Taking Control over its Money', Euinside Brief, at http://www.euinside.eu/en/news/world-bank-takes-control-over-its-own-money, accessed in May 2012.

Marks, G. (1993) 'Structural Policy and Multilevel Governance in the EC', in A. Cafruny and G. Rosenthal (eds.) *The State of the European Community*, Boulder, Lynne Rienner.

Maršić, T. and Marko, J. (2007) 'The Constitutional Reform Process in Bosnia and Herzegovina', European Parliament, Directorate General External Policies of the Union, Briefing Paper, Brussels, December 2007, 1–30.

Martens, J. (2007) 'Multistakeholder Partnerships: Future Models of Multilateralism?', Dialogue on Globalization, Occasional Papers No. 29, Berlin, Friederich Ebert Stiftung, 1–78.

Martin, L. (2006) 'Distribution, Information and Delegation to International Organizations: The Case of the IMF Conditionality', in D. Hawkins et al. (eds.), *Delegation and Agency in International Organizations*, Cambridge, UK, Cambridge University Press, 140–164.

Martin, L. and Woods, N. (2005) 'Multiple-state Constituencies in the IMF: An Agency Approach', paper presented at the Sixth Jaques Polak Annual Research Conference, 4 November, Washington, DC, available at http://www.imf.org/external/np/res/seminars/2005/arc/pdf/mart.pdf

Marzinotto, B. (2011) 'A European Fund for Economic Revival in Crisis Countries', Bruegel Policy Contribution, Issue 2011/01.

Mason, E. and Asher, R. (1973) *The World Bank since Bretton Woods*, Washington, DC, Brookings Institution.

Maxwell, S. and Gavas, M. (2010) 'The Spring Package is a Promising Start', European Development Cooperation Support Program (EDCSP) Opinion 2, ODI and DFID, April 2010, available at http://internationaldevelopmenteu.files.wordpress.com/2010/05/edcsp-opinion-2-electronic-version.pdf

Mayntz, R. (1978) *Soziologie der öffentlichen Verwaltung*, trans. *Sociologia delle organizzazioni pubbliche*, Bologna, Il Mulino, 1996.

McCubbins, M. and Schwartz, T. (1984) 'Congressional Oversight Overlooked: Police Patrols versus Fire Alarms', *American Journal of Political Science*, 28, 1, 165–179.

McCulloch, W.S. (1945) 'A Heterarchy of Values Determined by the Topology of Nervous Nets', *Bulletin of Mathematical Biology*, 7, 89–93.

McFaul, M. (2002) 'The Fourth Wave of Democracy and Dictatorship: Noncooperative Transitions in the Postcommunist World', *World Politics*, 54, 212–244.

McKinley, R. and Little, R.D. (1979) 'The U.S. Aid Relationships: A Test of the Recipient Need and Donor Interest Models', *Political Studies*, 27, 2, 236–250.

McNamara, K. and Meunier, S. (2002) 'Between National Sovereignty and International Power: What External Voice for the Euro?', *International Affairs*, 78, 4, 849–868.

Mead, G.H. (1934) *Mind, Self and Society: From the Standpoint of a Social Behaviorist*, Chicago, University of Chicago Press, reprinted 1970.

Meth-Cohn, D. and Shields, K. (2005) 'Accessing EU Funds in the New Member States: Best Practice from Around Europe', Economist Corporate Network briefing paper.

Meunier, S. (2000) 'What Single Voice? European Institutions and EU-US Trade Negotiations', *International Organization*, 54, 1, 103–135.

Meunier, S. and Nicolaïdis, K. (1999) 'Who Speaks for Europe? The Delegation of Trade Authority in the EU', *Journal of Common Market Studies*, 37, 3, 477–501.

Miller, V. (2011) 'The European Union at the United Nations', SN 5975 prepared for the International Affairs and Defence Section of the UK House of Commons, available at https://researchbriefings.parliament.uk/ResearchBriefing/Summary/SN05975#fullreport

Milner, H. (2006) 'Why Multilateralism? Foreign Aid and Domestic Principal-Agent Problems', in D. Hawkins et al. (eds.), *Delegation and Agency in International Organizations*, Cambridge, Cambridge University Press, 107–139.

Missiroli, A. (2011) 'The New EU "Foreign Policy" System after Lisbon: A Work in Progress', *European Foreign Affairs Review*, 15, 427–452.

Mitchell, R. (2009) 'The Influence of International Institutions: Institutional Design, Compliance, Effectiveness, and Endogeneity', in H. Milner and A. Moravcsik (eds.) *Power, Interdependence and Nonstate Actors in World Politics*, Princeton and Oxford, Princeton University Press, 66–83.

Molina, N. (2008) 'Europe Questions IFI's on Conditionality: Whose Outcome?', Bretton Woods Project News, April.

Moravcsik, A. (1998) *The Choice for Europe: Social Purpose and State Power from Messina to Maastricht*, Ithaca, NY, Cornell University Press.

Mosley, P. (1980) 'Aid, Savings and Growth Revisited', *Oxford Bulletin of Economics and Statistics*, 42, 2, 79–95.

Mosley, P., Harrigan, J. and Toye, J. (1991) *Aid and Power*, London, Routledge, Vols I and II.

Moss, T. and Patrick, S. (2005) 'The Day after Comrade Bob: Applying Post-Conflict Reconstruction Lessons to Zimbabwe', Center for Global Development Working Paper No. 72, December 8, available at: https://www.cgdev.org/publication/day-after-comrade-bob-applying-post-conflict-reconstruction-lessons-zimbabwe-working.

Montjoy, R.S. and O'Toole, R.J. (1979) 'Towards a Theory of Policy Implementation: An Organizational Perspective', *Public Administration Review*, 39, 5, 465–76.

Moyo, D. (2009) *Dead Aid, Why Aid Is Not Working and How There Is a Better Way for Africa*, New York, Farrar, Straus and Giroux.

Murphy, J. (2008) *The World Bank and Global Managerialism*, Routledge Studies in International Business and the World Economy, Abingdon and New York, Routledge.

Murshed, S.M. (2004) 'Strategic Interaction and Donor Policy Determination', *International Review of Economics and Finance*, 13, 3, 311–323.

Murshed, S.M. (2009) 'On the Non-Contractual Nature of Donor–Recipient Interaction in Development Assistance', *Review of Development Economics*, 13, 3, 416–428.

Murshed, S.M. and Sen, S. (1995) 'Aid Conditionality and Military Expenditure Reduction in Developing Countries: Models of Asymmetric Information', *Economic Journal*, 105, 429, 498–509.

Myrdal, G. (1968) *Asian Drama: An Inquiry into the Poverty of Nations*, New York, Pantheon Books.

Neumayer, E. (2003) 'The Determinants of Aid Allocation by Regional Multilateral Development Banks and United Nations Agencies', *International Studies Quarterly*, 47, 1, 101–122.

Nielson, B. (2007) 'The EU's Temporary International Mechanism: a lesson in how to break World Bank guidelines', June 24, 2007 in eu.Funding.org.uk, electronic resource, last accessed August 2011 at http://eufunding.org.uk/accountability/EUsTemporary InternationalMechanism.html

Nielson, D. and Tierney, M.J. (2003) 'Delegation to International Organizations: Agency Theory and World Bank Environmental Reform', *International Organization*, 57, 2, 241–276.

Nielson, D. and Tierney, M.J. (2005) 'Theory, Data and Hypothesis Testing: World Bank Environmental Reform Redux', *International Organization*, 59, 3, 785–800.

Nielson, D. and Tierney, M.J. (2009) 'Principals and Interests: Common Agency and Multilateral Development Bank Lending', Prepared for the 2010 Political Economy of International Organizations Meeting, Washington, DC, 28–29 January 2010.

Nielson, D., Tierney, M.J. and Weaver, Ch. (2006) 'Bridging the Rationalist-Constructivist Divide: Re-engineering the Culture of the World Bank', *The Journal of International Relations and Development* 9, 2, 1–33.

Nielson, P. (2001) 'Fighting Poverty and Promoting Development: the EU Strategy', speech delivered at the Japan National Press Club, Tokyo, 23 January 2001.

Nixon, J. (1980) 'The Importance of Communication in the Implementation of Government Policy at the Local Level', *Policy and Politics*, 8, 2, pp. 127–146.

Norad (2007) 'Review of Post-Crisis Multi-Donor Trust Funds', Country Study Annexes. Prepared by Scanteam/Norway Commissioned by the World Bank, Norwegian Ministry of Foreign Affairs and Norwegian Agency for Development Cooperation (Norad) in cooperation with Canadian International Development Agency (CIDA), Netherlands Ministry of Foreign Affairs and UK Department for International Development (DFID).

Nordic–Baltic Constituency Office to the Board of the World Bank Group (2010) 'Annual Report 2010: Highlights from the Financial Year July 1, 2009 – June 30, 2010', September 2010, 1–23.

North, D. (1990) *Institutions, Institutional Change, and Economic Performance*, Cambridge, MA, Cambridge University Press.

Nuttall, S. (2005) 'Coherence and Consistency', in C. Hill and M. Smith (eds.), *International Relations and the European Union*, Oxford, Oxford University Press.

Nye, J.S. and Donahue, J.D. (eds.) (2000) *Governance in a Globalizing World*, Washington, DC, Brookings Institutions.

O'Brien, M. (2009) 'Pan-Euro-Med Diagonal Cumulation: Can it Make a Difference to the Achievement of the Goals of the European Neighbourhood Policy in the Mediterranean Region?', *Current Politics and Economics of Europe*, Vol. 20, Issue 2-3, 1-29, New York, Nova Publishers.

ODI (2007) 'The Costs to the ACP of Exporting to the EU under the GSP', Final Report, March 2007, London.

ODI (2009) 'The Evolution of European Development Cooperation: Taking the change agenda forward, Simon Maxwell discusses the future of European development cooperation', 29 April 2009, National Liberal Club, London.

OECD (1998) *Peer Review of the European Community*, OECD Development Co-operation Review Series, No. 30.

OECD (2010) *DAC Report on Multilateral Aid*, DCD/DAC(2010)32/FINAL.

OECD (2016) 'FDI in Figures', 1–8, last accessed July 2017 at http://www.oecd.org/corporate/FDI-in-Figures-April-2016.pdf

OECD (2017) 'International Development Statistics Online Databases', accessed at http://stats.oecd.org/qwids/

OECD DAC (2007) 'Final ODA Flows in 2006', Room Document 2, DAC Senior Level Meeting, 11–12 December 2007, DCD/DAC/RD(2007)15/RD2.

OED (2004) 'Country Assistance Evaluation', Report No. 29058, Washington, DC, The World Bank, 21 May 2004, 1–74.

Oestreich, J. (ed.) (2012) *International Organizations as Self-directed Actors: A Framework for Analysis*, London, Routldege.

Olsen, G. (2000) 'Promotion of Democracy as a Foreign Policy Instrument of "Europe": Limits to International Idealism', *Democratization*, 7, 142–167.

Olsen, J. (2002) 'The Many Faces of Europeanization', *Journal of Common Market Studies*, 40, 5, 921–952.

Open Europe (2008) 'Trade and Development', *Parliamentary Briefing*, 6.

Open Europe (2011) 'The EU and the Mediterranean: Good Neighbours?', May 2011, London, accessed at http://www.openeurope.org.uk/research/enp2011.pdf

Orbie, J. (ed.) (2009) *Europe's Global Role, External Policies of the European Union*, Farnham, Ashgate.

Orbie, J. and Faber, G. (2011) 'The struggle for EPAs: A conflict between old and new regionalism', Paper for the EUSA Twelfth Biennial International Conference, Boston, MA, 3–5 March 2011.

Orbie, J. and Versluys, E. (2009) 'The European Union International Development Policy: Lending and Benevolent?', in J. Orbie (ed.) *Europe's Global Role, External Policies of the European Union*, Farnham, Ashgate, 67–90.

Oxfam (2002) *Rigged Rules and Double Standards: Trade, Globalization and the Fight Against Poverty*, Report accessed at http://en.oxfam.ru/upload/iblock/1ca/1ca3150c5e7d8c64ba45287978f0d4df.pdf

Oxfam (2005) 'Making Trade Work for Development in 2005. What the EU should do', Oxfam Briefing Paper 75, May.

Oxfam (2006a) 'Unequal Partners: How EU–ACP Economic Partnership Agreements (EPAs) could harm the development prospects of many of the world's poorest countries', Oxfam International Briefing Note, September.

Oxfam (2006b) 'Slamming the Door on Development: Analysis of the EU's response to the Pacific's EPA negotiating proposals', Oxfam Background Paper, December.

Oxfam (2007a) 'A Matter of Political Will: How the European Union can maintain market access for African, Caribbean and Pacific countries in the absence of Economic Partnership Agreements', Oxfam Briefing Note, April.

Oxfam (2007b) 'Poverty in Palestine: The Human Cost of the Financial Boycott', Oxfam Briefing Note, April.

Oxfam (2008) 'Fast Forward: How the European Commission can take the lead in providing high-quality budget support for education and health', Oxfam Briefing Paper 111, May 2008.

Oxfam (2010) 'Oxfam Contribution to the EC Green paper on the Future of Budget Support: Ensuring EC Budget-Support is Long-Term, Predictable and Accountable', The Hague, available at http://ec.europa.eu/development/icenter/files/green_paper_contributions_future_eu_budget/Organisations/gp_org_Oxfam_en.pdf

Oxfam and WWF (2005) 'Critique of the EC's Action Plan for ACP Countries Affected by EU Sugar Reform', WWF and Oxfam Briefing Paper, June.

Panagariya A. (2002) 'Developing Countries at Doha: A Political Economy Analysis', *World Economy*, 25, 9, 1205–1233.

Papanek, G (1973) 'Aid, Foreign Private Investment, Savings, and Growth in Less Developed Countries', *Journal of Political Economy*, 81, 1, 120–130.

Pape, R. (1997) 'Why Economic Sanctions do not Work', *International Security*, 22, 2, 90–136.

Park, S. and Vetterlein, A. (2010) *Owning Development: Creating Policy Norms in the IMF and the World Bank*, Cambridge, UK, Cambridge University Press.

Patterson, L.A. (1997) 'Agricultural Policy Reform in the European Community: A Three-Level Game Analysis', *International Organization*, 51, 1, 135–165.

Petrov, R. and Serdyuk, O. (2008) 'Ukraine: The Quest for Democratization between Europe and Russia', in A. Magen, and L. Morlino (eds.) *International Actors, Democratization and the Rule of Law*, Abingdon, Routledge, 189–223.

Phillips, N. (2006) 'Global Governance and the World Bank', in G.D. Hook and H. Dobson (eds.) *Global Governance and Japan: The Institutional Architecture*, Abingdon and New York, Routledge, 92–109.

Phinnemore, D. and Siani-Davies, P. (2003) 'Beyond Intervention? The Balkans, the Stability Pact and the European Union', in P. Siani-Davies (ed.) *International Intervention in the Balkans since 1995*, London and New York, Routledge.

Piening, C. (1997) *Global Europe: The European Union in World Affairs*, Boulder, CO, Lynne Rienner.

Pisani-Ferry, J. (2005) 'The Accidental Player: The EU and the Global Economy', Lecture delivered at the Indian Council for Research on International Economic Relations, Delhi (25 November), now in K.E Jørgensen (ed.) (2009) *The European Union and International Organizations*, London, Routledge, 21–36.

Poggi, P. (2017) 'Europe 2020 Programmatic Trust Funds', The World Bank–ECCBX, Brussels.

Poletti, A. (2007) 'The EU for Brazil: A Partner Towards a "Fairer" Globalization?', *European Foreign Affairs Review*, 12, 3, 271–297.

Poletti, A. (2012) *The European Union and Multilateral Trade Governance: The Politics of the Doha Round*, London and New York, Routledge.

Pollack, M. (1994) 'Creeping Competence: The Expanding Agenda of the European Community', *Journal of Public Policy*, 14, 2, 95–145.

Pollack, M. (1995) 'Regional Actors in an Intergovernmental Play: The Making and Implementation of EC Structural Policy', in M. Rhodes and S. Mazey (eds.) *The State of the European Union*, Vol. 3, Harlow, Longman.

Pollack, M. (1997) 'Delegation, Agency and Agenda Setting in the European Community', *International Organization*, 51, 1, 99–134.

Pollack, M. (2006) 'Delegation and Discretion in the European Union', in D. Hawkins et al. (eds.), *Delegation and Agency in International Organizations*, Cambridge, Cambridge University Press, 165–196.

Prodi, R. (2002) 'Europe in Transition: Hopes and Fears', speech at the V Europa Forum Europe Facing the Decision: EU Enlargement and Global Challenges, Brussels, December 3.

Pressman, J.L. and Wildavsky A. (1973) *Implementation: How Great Expectations in Washington are Dashed in Oakland; Or, Why It's Amazing that Federal Programs Work at All*, Berkeley, CA, University of California Press.

Putnam, D. (1988) 'Diplomacy and Domestic Politics: The Logic of Two Level Games', *International Organization*, 42, 3, 427–460.

Quinn, R.E. and Rohrbaugh, J. (1983) 'A Spatial Model of Effectiveness Criteria: Towards a Competing Values Approach to Organizational Analysis', *Management Science*, 29, 3, 363–377.

Rajan, R.G. and Subramanian, A. (2008) 'Aid and Growth: What Does the Cross-Country Evidence Really Show?', *The Review of Economics and Statistics*, 90, 4, 643–665.

Rice, S. and Patrick, S. (2008) *Index of State Weakness in the Developing World*, Washington, DC, The Brookings Institution, 1–47.

Richardson, C. (2005) 'How the Loss of Property Rights Caused Zimbabwe's Collapse', Cato Institute Economic Development Bulletin, No. 4, 14 November.

Richelle, K. (2003) 'Statement by Mr. Koos Richelle Director General European Commission DG Development, to the Development Committee of the World Bank', DC/S/2003–0015, 13 April 2003.

Risse-Kappen, T. (1994) 'Ideas do not Float Freely: Transnational Coalitions, Domestic Structures, and the End of the Cold War', *International Organization*, 48, 2, 185–214.

Risse-Kappen, T. (1995) *Bringing Transnational Relations Back In*, Cambridge, Cambridge University Press.

Rodrik D. (1996) 'Why is there Multilateral Lending?', in M. Bruno and B. Pleskovic (eds.), *Annual World Bank Conference on Development Economics 1995*, The World Bank, Washington, DC, also in NBER Working Papers 5160.

Rodrik, D. (1997) *Has Globalization Gone Too Far?*, Institute for International Economics, Washington, DC.

Rosecrance, R. (2008) 'The Failure of Static and the Need for Dynamic Approaches to International Relations', in *The Oxford Handbook of International Relations*, Oxford, UK, Oxford University Press, 716–724.

Rosenau, J.N. and Czempiel, E.O. (1992) *Governance without Government: Order and Change in World Politics*, Cambridge Studies in International Relations, Cambridge, UK, Cambridge University Press.

Rostow, W.W. (1960) *The Stages of Economic Growth: A Non-Communist Manifesto*, Cambridge, Cambridge University Press.

Ruggie, J. (1982) 'International Regimes, Transactions, and Change: Embedded Liberalism in the Postwar Economic System', *International Organization*, 36, 2, 379–415.

Santiso, C. (2002) 'The Reform of EU Development Policy: Improving Strategies for Conflict Prevention, Democracy Promotion & Governance Conditionality', CEPS, Working Paper No. 182, available at http://aei.pitt.edu/1826/

Santiso, C. (2003) 'Sisyphus in the Castle: Improving European Union Strategies for Democracy Promotion and Governance Conditionality', *The European Journal of Development Research*, 15, 1–28.

Scharpf, F. (1999) *Governing Europe: Effective and Democratic?*, Oxford, Oxford University Press.

Schiff, M. (2002) '*Regional Integration and Development in Small States*', Working Paper No. 2797, The World Bank, Washington, DC, March 2002.

Schimmelfennig, F., Engert, S. and Knobel, H. (2005) 'The Impact of EU Political Conditionality', in F. Schimmelfennig and U. Sedelmeier (eds.), *The Europeanization of Central and Eastern Europe*, Ithaca, NY, Cornell University Press, 29–49.

Schmitter, P. (2000) *How to Democratize the European Union ... and Why Bother?*, Lanham, MD, Rowman & Littlefield Publishers.

Scoones, I., Marongwe, N., Mavedzenge, B., Murimbarimba, F., Mahenehene, J. and Sukume, C. (2010) *Zimbabwe's Land Reform: Myths and Realities*, London, Currey.

Searing, D. (1991) 'Roles, Rules and Rationality in the New Institutionalism', *American Political Science Review*, 85, 4, 1239–1260.

Sherman, M. (2010) 'Palestinians Have Built the Institutions but Sustainable Growth is Frustrated', West Bank and Gaza Country Webpage, Washington, DC, The World Bank, http://web.worldbank.org/WBSITE/EXTERNAL/COUNTRIES/MENAEXT/WESTBANKGAZAEXTN/0,,contentMDK:22878709~pagePK:1497618~piPK:217854~theSitePK:294365,00.html

Sil, R. and Katzenstein, P. (2010) *Beyond Paradigms. Analytic Eclecticism in the Study of World Politics*, Basingstoke, UK, Palgrave Macmillan.

Singer, P.W. (2003) *Corporate Warriors: The Rise of the Privatized Military Industry*, Ithaca, NY, Cornell University Press.

Sjöstedt, G. (1977) *The External Role of the European Community*, Farnborough, Saxon House.

Slaughter, A.M. (2005) *A New World Order*, Princeton NJ, Princeton University Press.

Smith, K. (2004) 'The ACP in the European Union's Network of Regional Relationships: Still unique or just one in the crowd?', in K. Arts and A. Dickson (eds.), *EU Development Cooperation: From Model to Symbol*, Manchester, Manchester University Press, 60–79.

Smith, K. (2006) 'The Limits of Proactive Cosmopolitanism, The EU and Burma, Cuba and Zimbabwe', in O. Elgström and M. Smith, (eds.) *The European Union's Roles in International Politics: Concepts and Analysis*, London, Routledge.

Smith, M. (2003) 'The Framing of European Foreign and Security Policy: Towards a Post-Modern Policy Framework?', *Journal of European Public Policy*, 10, 4, 556–573.

Smith, M. (2013) 'The European External Action Service and the Security–Development Nexus: Organizing for Effectiveness or Incoherence?', *Journal of European Public Policy*, 20, 9, 1299–1315.

Söderbaum, F. and Stålgren, P. (eds.) (2010) *The European Union and the Global South*, Boulder, CO, Lynne Rienner.

Sørensen, G. (1996) 'Development as a Hobbesian Dilemma', *Third World Quarterly*, 17, 5, 903–916.

Stetter, S. (2013) 'The EU as a Structured Power, Organizing EU Foreign Affairs within the Institutional Environment of World Politics', *Journal of International Organizations Studies*, 4, 2, 54–71.

Stiglitz, J. (2002a) *Globalization and its Discontents*, New York, W.W. Norton.

Stiglitz, J. (2002b) 'Joseph E. Stiglitz: Biographical', in *The Nobel Prizes 2011*, Tore Frängsmyr, Stockholm. Accessed at http://www.nobelprize.org/nobel_prizes/economic-sciences/laureates/2001/stiglitz-bio.html

Stokke, O. and Hoebink, P. (eds.) (2005) *Perspectives on European Development Cooperation: Policy and Performance of Individual Donor Countries and the EU*, London, Routledge.

Stone, R. (2009) 'Institutions, Power and Interdependence', in H. Milner and A. Moravcsik (eds.), *Power, Interdependence and Nonstate Actors in World Politics*, Princeton, NJ, Princeton University Press, 31–49.

Stone, R. (2011) *Controlling Institutions: International Organizations and the Global Economy*, Cambridge and New York, Cambridge University Press.

Strand, J. and Rapkin, D. (2005) 'Voting Power Implications of a Double Majority Voting Procedure in the IMF's Executive Board', in A. Buira (ed.) *Reforming the Governance of the IMF and World Bank*, London, Anthem Press, 235–250.

Strange, S. (1988) *States and Markets*, London, Pinter. Second Edition (1998) London and New York, Bloomsbury.

Strauss, A. (1978) *Negotiations: Varieties, Contexts, and Social Order*, San Francisco, CA, Jossey-Bass.

Stumm, M. (2011) 'World Bank: More Responsibility for Developing Countries', *Development and Cooperation*, Online edition 4 March 2011, accessed at http://www.dandc.eu/articles/193054/index.en.shtml

Szewczyc, B. (2010) 'The EU in Bosnia Herzegovina: Power, Decisions and Legitimacy', European Institute for Security Studies, Occasional Paper, March 2010, 83, 1–60.

Tan, C. (2010) 'Regulation and Resource Dependency: The Legal and Political Aspects of Structural Adjustment Programmes', in D. Bradlow and D. Hunter (eds.) *International Financial Institutions and International Law*, Alphen aan den Rijn, Kluwer Law International, 167–197.

Tannock, C. (2004) 'Reports of the E.P. on the Direct Budgetary Assistance to the Palestinian Authority', last accessed December 2017 at http://www.charlestannock.com/pressrel.asp?id=130

Taylor, P. (2006) 'The EU in Geneva: Coordinating Policy in the Economic and Social Arrangements of the United Nations System', in K.V. Laatikainen and K. Smith (eds.), *The European Union at the United Nations*, Houndmills, Basingstoke, Palgrave Macmillan, 133–153.

Tirole, J. (2001) 'Corporate Governance', *Econometrica*, 69, 1, 1–35.

Tonra, B. (2003) 'The European Union's Global Role', FORNET Working Group 1: Theories and Approaches to the CFSP, London School of Economics, London, 7/8 November 2003.

Torsvik, G. (2005) 'Foreign Economic Aid: Should Donors Cooperate?', *Journal of Development Economics*, 77, 2, 503–515.

Truman, E. (2006) *Reforming the IMF for the 21st Century*, Washington, DC, Peterson Institute.

Trumbull, W. and Wall, H. (1994) 'Estimating Aid Allocation Criteria with Panel Data', *Economic Journal*, 104, 425, 876–882.

Tsebelis, G. (1990) *Nested Games: Rational Choice in Comparative Politics*, Berkeley, CA, University of California Press.

Türkes, M. and Gökgöz, G. (2006) 'The European Union's Strategy towards the Western Balkans: Exclusion or Integration?', *East European Politics & Societies*, 20, 4, 659–690.

Underdal, A. (2002) 'One Question, Two Answers', in E.L. Miles, A. Underdal, S. Andresen, J. Wettestad, J.B. Skjaerseth and E.M. Carlin (eds.), *Environmental Regime Effectiveness: Confronting Theory with Evidence*. Cambridge, MIT Press.

United Nations (2000) 'United Nations Millennium Declaration', Resolution adopted by the General Assembly, A\Res\55\2, 18 September 2000.

United Nations General Assembly (1974) 'Status of the European Economic Community in the General Assembly', Resolution 3208 (XXIX) adopted by the General Assembly on 11 October 1974, available at http://www.worldlii.org/int/other/UNGA/1974/6.pdf

United Nations General Assembly (2011) 65/276 on 'Participation of the European Union in the Work of the United Nations', Resolution adopted by the General Assembly on 3 May 2011, A/Res765/276, http://repository.un.org/handle/11176/288270?show=full

Vahl, M. (2006) 'International Agreements in EU Neighborhood Policy', *SIEPS Report* 10, November.

Van Meter, D. and Van Horn, C.E. (1975) 'The Policy Implementation Process: A Conceptual Framework', *Administration and Society*, 6, 4, 445–488.

Vanheukelom, J., Colin, S. and van Seters, J. (2011) 'The Future of EU Budget Support to Third Countries?', Report of the consultation with experts from Civil Society Organisations on the EU Green Paper on Budget Support, Brussels, 13 December 2010, European Centre for Development Policy Management (Ecdpm) Briefing Note 22, March 2011.

Vanhoonacker, S. and Pomorska, K. (2013) 'The European External Action Service and Agenda-setting in European Foreign Policy', *Journal of European Public Policy*, 20, 9, 1316–1331.

Vanhoonacker, S., Pomorska, K. and Maurer, H. (2010) 'The Council Presidency in CFSP: Challenges for Poland in 2011', Report of the Centre for International Relations (CSM), Warsaw (www.csm.org.pl)

Vestergaard, J. (2011) 'The World Bank and the Emerging World Order', DIIS Report, Copenhagen, 2011, 05, available at https://www.diis.dk/files/media/publications/import/extra/rp2011-05-world-bank-voice-reform_web_0.pdf

von Burgsdorff, S. (2010) 'The EU's Spring Package: The Radical Agenda the EU Needs?', ODI Footage, 17 June 2010, ODI, London. Accessed at https://www.youtube.com/watch?v=KEvOBkZxkUA

Vreeland, J. (2006) 'Self-Reform: The IMF Strategy', mimeo, Paper prepared for the Reinventing Bretton Woods Committee and World Economic Forum Conference, 'The International Monetary fund in Transition: Rediscovering its Monetary Role?' Cape Town, 29–30 May 2006.

Wade, R. (1997) 'Greening the Bank: The Struggle over the Environment, 1970–1995', in D. Kapur, J.P. Lewis and R. Webb, *The World Bank: Its First Half Century*, Vol. 2, Washington, DC, Brookings Institution Press, 611–734.

Wade, R. (2000) 'A Defeat for Development and Multilateralism: The World Bank has been Unfairly Criticised over the Qinghai Resettlement Project', *Financial Times*, 4 July 2000.

Wæver, O. (1990) 'Review essay: The Language of Foreign Policy', *Journal of Peace Research*, 27, 3, 335–343.

Waltz, K. (1959) *Man, the State and War*, New York, Columbia University Press.

Waltz, K. (1979) *Theory of International Politics*, Reading, MA, Addison-Wesley.

Weaver, K. (2008) *Hypocrisy Trap: The World Bank and the Poverty of Reform*, Princeton, NJ, Princeton University Press.

Weaver, K. and Park, S. (2012) 'The Anatomy of Autonomy: The Case of the World Bank', in J. Oestreich (ed.) *International Organizations as Self-directed Actors: A Framework for Analysis*, London, Routledge,

Welfens, P. (2001) *Stabilizing and Integrating the Balkans: Economic Analysis of the Stability Pact, EU Reforms and International Organizations*, Berlin, Heidelberg and New York, Springer-Verlag.

Wendt, A. (1992) 'Anarchy is What States Make of it: The Social Construction of Power Politics', *International Organization*, 46, 2, 391–425.

Wendt, A. (1994) 'Collective Identity Formation and the International State', *American Political Science Review*, 88, 2, 384–396.

Wendt, A. (1999) *Social Theory of International Politics*, Cambridge, Cambridge University Press.

Wessel, R.A. (2011) 'The Legal Framework for the Participation of the European Union in International Institutions', *Journal of European Integration*, 33, 6, 621–635.

Western Balkans Investment Framework (WBIF) (2011) 'WBIF 2011 Annual Report', 1–19.

Williams, W. (1971) *Social Policy Research and Analysis*, New York, Elsevier.

Williamson, J. (ed.) (1990) *Latin American adjustment: How much has happened?*, Washington, Institute for International Economics.

Williamson, O. (1975) *Markets and Hierarchies: Analysis and Anti-trust Implications*, New York, Free Press.

Williamson, O. (1985) *The Economic Institutions of Capitalism: Firms, Markets, Relational Contracting*, New York, The Free Press.

Winters, A. (2002) 'Doha and the World Poverty Targets', Paper presented at the Annual Bank Conference on Development Economics. The World Bank, Washington, April 2002.

Wish, N. (1987) 'National Attributes as Source of National Role Conceptions: A Capability-Motivation Model', in S. Walker (ed.) *Role Theory and Foreign Policy Analysis*, Durham, NC, Duke University Press.

Wolfensohn, J. (1999) 'A Proposal for a Comprehensive Development Framework, Memorandum to the Board, Management and Staff of the World Bank Group', Washington, DC, World Bank, 21 January, available at http://web.worldbank.org/archive/website01013/WEB/0__CO-87.HTM

Wolfensohn, J. (2011) 'HBO History Maker Series with James D. Wolfensohn', Council on Foreign Relations, 31 January 2011, https://www.cfr.org/event/hbo-history-makers-series-james-d-wolfensohn-0

Woods, N. (2001) 'Making the IMF and the World Bank More Accountable', *International Affairs* (Royal Institute of International Affairs 1944–), 77, 1, January, 83–100.

Woods, N. (2003) 'The United States and the International Financial Institutions', in R. Foot, N. MacFarlane and M. Mastanduno (eds.), *US Hegemony and International Organizations*, Oxford, Oxford University Press.

Woods, N. (2006) *The Globalizers: The IMF, the World Bank and Their Borrowers*, Ithaca, NY, Cornell University Press.

Woods, N. (2007) 'Power Shift: Do We Need Better Global Economic Institutions?', London, Institute for Public Policy Research.

Woods, N. (2008a) 'From Intervention to Cooperation: Reforming the IMF and the World Bank', London, Progressive Governance, April.

Woods, N. (2008b) 'Governing the Global Economy: Strengthening Multilateral Institutions', New York, International Peace Institute.

Woods, N. and Lombardi, D. (2006). 'Uneven Patterns of Governance: How Developing Countries Are Represented in the IMF', *Review of International Political Economy* 13, 3, 480–515.

World Bank (1980) *Structural Adjustment Lending*, R80–122, IDA/R80–83, Washington, DC.

World Bank (1993) *Developing the Occupied Territories: An Investment in Peace*, 6-Volume Report, Washington, DC.

World Bank (1999) *Assessing Aid: What Works, What Doesn't and Why*, Oxford, Oxford University Press.

World Bank (2000) 'China Western Poverty Reduction Inspection Panel Report', Washington, DC, The World Bank.

World Bank (2002–2009) *Global Monitoring Report*, various years.

World Bank (2004) 'From Adjustment Lending to Development Policy Lending: Update of World Bank Policy' (R2004–0135) 25 June 2004.

World Bank (2005a) 'Meeting the Challenge of Africa's Development: A World Bank Group Action Plan', Washington, DC, The World Bank, September.

World Bank (2005b) 'Interim Strategy Note for Zimbabwe', Country Department 3, Africa Region, The World Bank, 31 August 2005.

World Bank (2006a) 'Paris Declaration at a Glance', prepared by The World Bank OPCS, available at http://siteresources.worldbank.org/INTDIASPORA/General/21512731/ParisDeclaration.pdf

World Bank (2006b) 'Morocco, Tunisia, Egypt and Jordan after the End of the Multi-Fiber Agreement: Impact, Challenges and Prospects', Report No. 35376, MNSED Washington, DC, The World Bank, 1–70.

World Bank (2007a) 'Aid Architecture: An Overview of the Main Trends in Official Development Assistance Flows', Background Report, Washington, DC.

World Bank (2007b) 'Country-Based Scaling Up: Assessment of Progress and Agenda For Action', Background Report for the 21 October Development Committee Meeting.

World Bank (2007c) 'Movement and Access and Restrictions in the West Bank, Uncertainty and Inefficiency in the Palestinian Economy', World Bank Technical Team, 9 May 2007, available at http://siteresources.worldbank.org/INTWESTBANKGAZA/Resources/WestBankrestrictions9Mayfinal.pdf

World Bank (2007d) 'Background Note: The World Bank's Role in EU10, EU Candidate, and Potential Candidate Countries', June.

World Bank (2008a) 'International Bank for Reconstruction and Development', external website at http://www.worldbank.org/en/who-we-are/ibrd

World Bank (2008b) 'Strengthening Mena's Trade and Investment's Links with China and India', MNSED Mena Social and Economic Development group, 2 September.

World Bank (2009) 'Fund-Channeling Options for Early Recovery and Beyond: The World Bank Perspective', International Conference in Support of the Palestinian Economy for the Reconstruction of Gaza, World Bank, March 2009, available at http://siteresources.worldbank.org/INTWESTBANKGAZAINARABIC/Resources/GazaConferenceFeb2709final.pdf

World Bank (2010a) 'World Bank Group Reform: Enhancing Voice and Participation of Developing and Transitioning Countries in 2010 and Beyond', DC2010–0006, http://siteresources.worldbank.org/DEVCOMMINT/Documentation/22553921/DC2010-006(E)Voice.pdf

World Bank (2010b) 'Development Committee Communiqué', 25 March 2010.

World Bank (2010c) 'Project Information Document (PID) on Palestinian National Cash Transfer Program (PNCTP)', Report No. AB5849, 1 August 2010.

World Bank (2010d) 'Palestinian Reform and Development Plan – Trust Fund (PRDP-TF): third quarterly review update' (July–September 2010), Working Paper 63581, available at http://www-wds.worldbank.org/external/default/main?pagePK=64193027&piPK=64187937&theSitePK=523679&menuPK=64187510&searchMenuPK=64187511&entityID=000333037_20110808004154&cid=3001_6

World Bank (2010e) 'Annual Report 2010: Financial Information', IBRD and IDA Cumulative Lending, Online resource, available at http://web.worldbank.org/WBSITE/EXTERNAL/EXTABOUTUS/EXTANNREP/EXTANNREP2010/0,,contentMDK:22626599~menuPK:7115719~pagePK:64168445~piPK:64168309~theSitePK:7074179,00.html#lending.

World Bank (2010f) 'World Bank: Concessional Finance and Global Partnership Directory of Programs Supported by Trust Funds', Washington, DC, The World Bank Group, 31 March 2010, last accessed December 2017 at http://siteresources.worldbank.org/CFPEXT/Resources/299947–1274110249410/Directory_Programs-2010_03_31.pdf

World Bank (2011a) 'World Development Report 2011: Conflict, Security, and Development', *World Development Report*, Washington, DC.

World Bank (2011b) World Bank Staff Comments on the European Commission's Green Paper on 'The Future of the EU Budget Support to Third Countries', 17 February, mimeo.

World Bank (2011c) 'Harmonized List of Fragile States Situations', Washington, DC, The World Bank, available at http://pubdocs.worldbank.org/en/963681410886171483/FY10toFY13Harmonized-list-Fragile-Situations.pdf

World Bank (2012) 'Knowledge is the Currency', World Bank Press Release on Bulgaria-World Bank Agreement to Accelerate EU Funds Absorption, 22 January 2012, accessed at http://www.worldbank.org/en/news/press-release/2012/01/22/knowledge-currency

World Bank (2013) 'Ending Extreme Poverty and Promoting Shared Prosperity', Feature Story, World Bank Website, 19 April, 2013, http://www.worldbank.org/en/news/feature/2013/04/17/ending_extreme_poverty_and_promoting_shared_prosperity

World Bank (2016) 'European Commission and World Bank sign agreement to boost development cooperation', Press Release, accessed at http://www.worldbank.org/en/news/press-release/2016/04/15/european-commission-and-world-bank-sign-agreement-to-boost-development-cooperation

World Bank (2017a) 'How IBRD is Financed' in 'International Bank for Reconstruction and Development', at http://www.worldbank.org/en/who-we-are/ibrd

World Bank (2017b) 'Sustainable Development Goals and the 2030 Agenda', World Bank Website, accessed July 2017 at http://www.worldbank.org/en/programs/sdgs-2030-agenda#1

World Bank, 'Global Monitoring Report', various years (2002–2007) available at http://www.worldbank.org/en/publication/global-monitoring-report/archives

World Bank Brussels Office (2007a) 'The World Bank in Brussels', June 2007, prepared by the World Bank Office in Brussels, http://www.worldbank.org/eu, last accessed on February 2008.

World Bank Brussels Office (2007b) 'European Commission-World Bank Group "Limelette" Partnership', Background Note for meeting with Civil Society Organization, 26 April, Brussels.

World Bank ECA (2011) 'Regional Strategy Update, Europe and Central Asia Region', Washington, DC, The World Bank, accessed April 2012 at http://siteresources.worldbank.org/ECAEXT/Resources/ECA_Strategy_2011.pdf

World Bank ECA Brussels (2011a) 'Note to the SC4, Non-paper on closer association of the World Bank Group to the WBIF', June. (Personal Correspondence).

World Bank ECA Brussels (2011b) 'Step-EU Consultation Draft', Brussels, The World Bank, 15 June.

World Bank, Operations Policy and Country Services (2009) 'Investment Lending Reform: Concept Note', Washington, DC, The World Bank, 26 January.

World Bank, Operations Policy and Country Services (2011) 'A New Instrument to Advance Development Effectiveness: Program-for-Results Financing', Board Report 66193, The World Bank, 29 December, Washington, DC.

World Bank, Operations Policy and Country Services (2012a) '2012 Development Policy Lending Retrospective: Results, Risks, and Reforms', Board Report 73488, Washington, DC, The World Bank, 31 October.

World Bank, Operations Policy and Country Services (2012b) 'Investment Lending Reform: Modernizing and Consolidating Operational Policies and Procedures,' Board Paper, Washington, DC, The World Bank, 1 November, accessed at http://pubdocs.worldbank.org/en/526341480525754718/ILPolicyReform-11-1-12-FinalPostBoard.pdf

Young, A. (2000) 'The Adaptation of European Foreign Economic Policy: From Rome to Seattle', *Journal of Common Market Studies*, 38, 1, 93–116.

Young, A. (2006) 'Punching its Weight? The EU's Use of WTO Dispute Resolution', in O. Elgström and M. Smith (eds.), *The European Union's Roles in International Politics*, London and New York, Routledge, 189–207.

Young, A. (2007) 'Trade Politics Ain't What it Used to Be: The EU in the Doha Round', *Journal of Common Market Studies*, 45, 4, 789–811.

Youngs, R. (2001) *The European Union and the Promotion of Democracy: Europe's Mediterranean and Asian Policies*, Oxford, Oxford University Press.

Zedillo, E. (2009) 'Repowering the World Bank for the 21st Century', Report of the High Level Commission for the World Bank Group Governance, available at http://siteresources.worldbank.org/NEWS/Resources/WBGovernanceCOMMISSIONREPORT.pdf

Zoellick, R. (2007) 'An Inclusive & Sustainable Globalization', World Bank Press Release, 10 October 2007, available at http://web.worldbank.org/WBSITE/EXTERNAL/NEWS/0,,contentMDK:21504730~pagePK:34370~piPK:42770~theSitePK:4607,00.html

Zürn, M. (2000) 'Democratic Governance Beyond the Nation-State: The EU and Other International Institutions', *European Journal of International Relations*, 6, 2, 183–221.

Zürn, M. (2002) 'From Interdependence to Globalization', in W. Carlsnaes, T. Risse and B. Simmons (eds.) *Handbook of International Relations*, London, Sage, 235–254.

Index

Note: page numbers in italic type refer to Figures; those in bold type refer to Tables.

For Product Safety Concerns and Information please contact our EU representative GPSR@taylorandfrancis.com
Taylor & Francis Verlag GmbH, Kaufingerstraße 24, 80331 München, Germany

www.ingramcontent.com/pod-product-compliance
Ingram Content Group UK Ltd.
Pitfield, Milton Keynes, MK11 3LW, UK
UKHW022015180926
475701UK00003B/369

* 9 7 8 1 0 3 2 0 9 3 9 2 5 *